17

Hiro Mashima

Translated and adapted by William Flanagan
Lettered by AndWorld Design

KC
KODANSHA
COMICS

Contents

FAIRY TAIL

フェアリーテイル

17

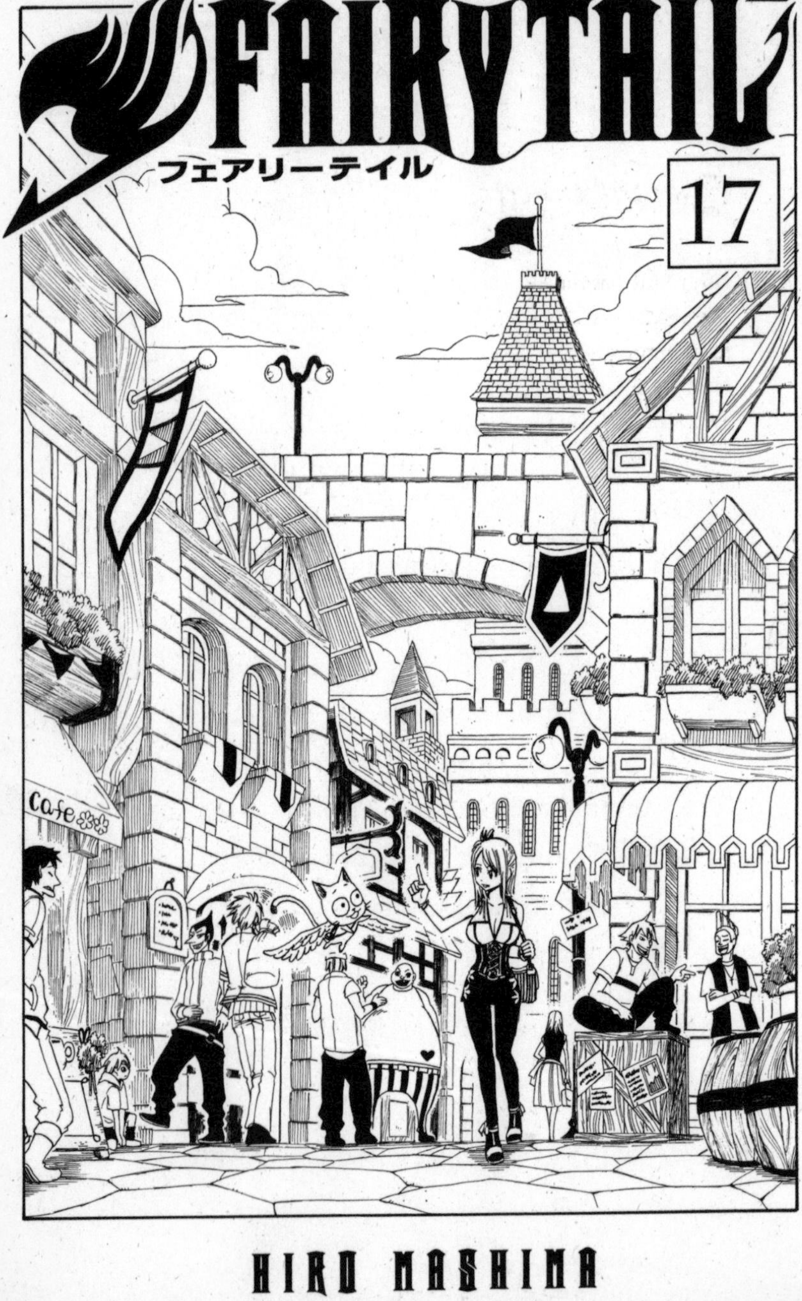
cafe

HIRO MASHIMA

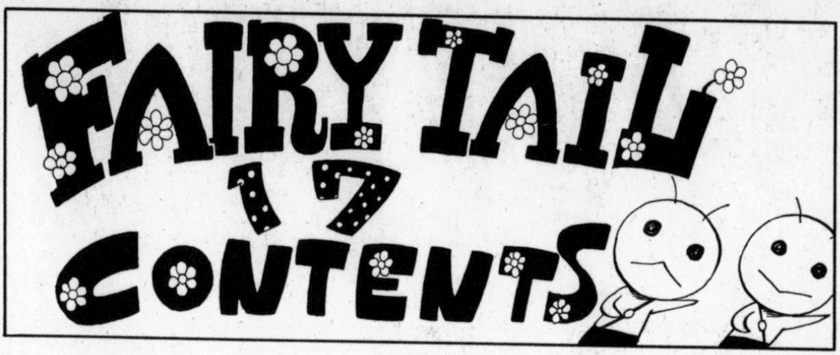
FAIRY TAIL
17
CONTENTS

Published in serial form by Weekly Shônen Magazine 2009 Volumes 25 - 33.

FAIRY TAIL
フェアリーテイル

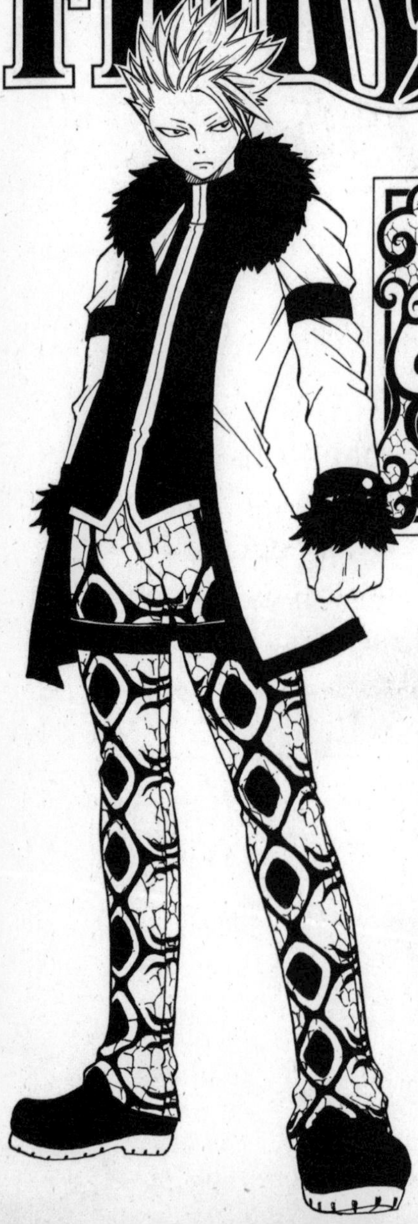

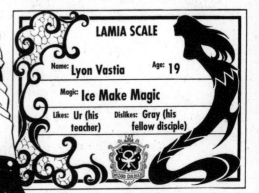

LAMIA SCALE

Name: Lyon Vastia **Age:** 19

Magic: Ice Make Magic

Likes: Ur (his teacher) **Dislikes:** Gray (his fellow disciple)

WIZARD GUILD X633

Chapter 127, Priestess of the Sky

Remarks

In his youth he learned Ice Make Magic with Gray under the tutelage of Ur. He entered the guild Lamia Scale after losing to Gray in a battle to determine the fate of Ur's mortal enemy, Deliora. While Gray uses his Ice Make to create inanimate objects like weapons, Lyon's specialty lies in making ice creatures. Although he used to ignore Ur's teaching and practice one-handed Ice Make, he later returned to two-handed Ice Make and progressed rapidly. He's risen to the level of guild ace and now takes high-level jobs.

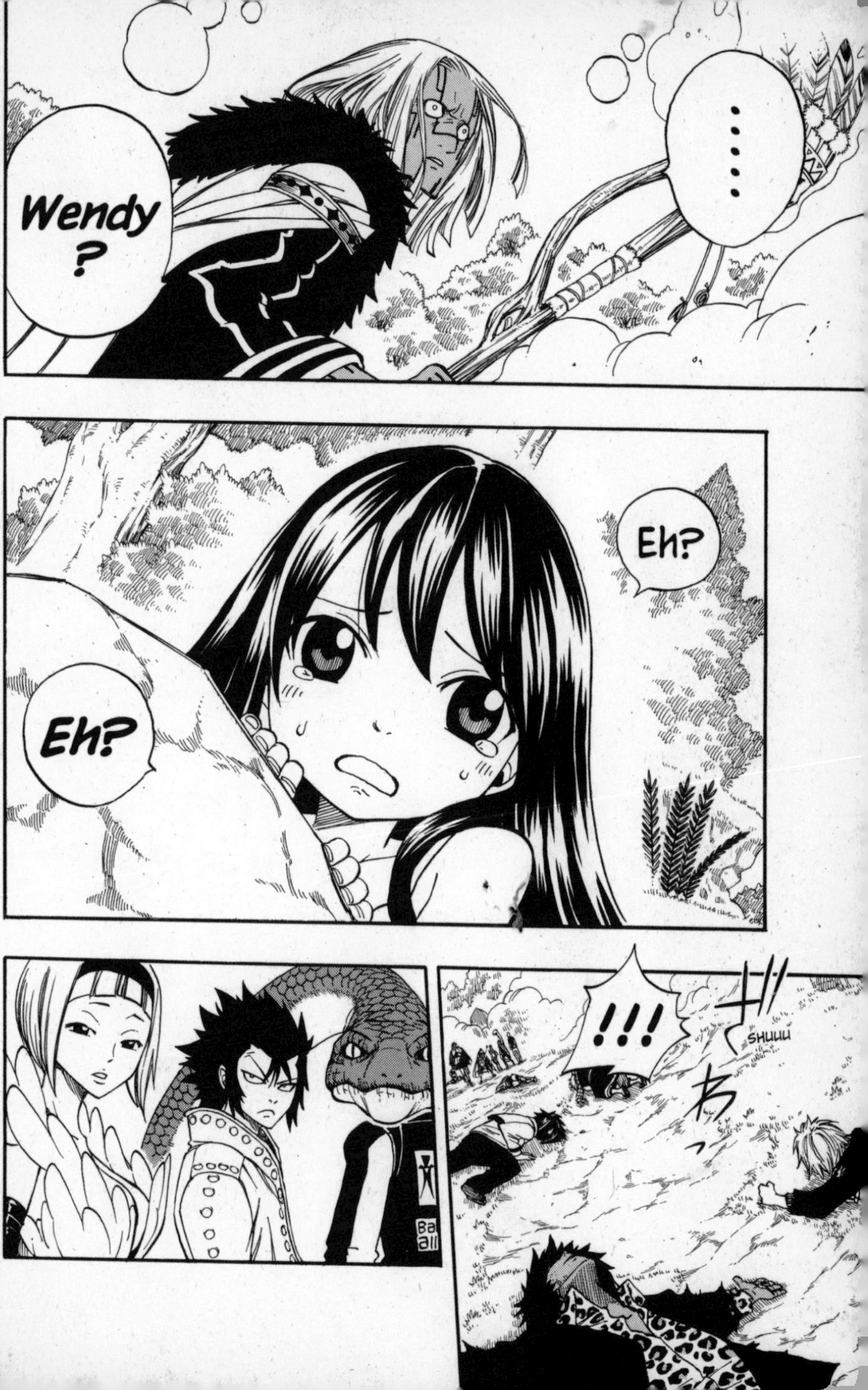
.....
Wendy ?
Eh?
Eh?
!!!
SHUUU

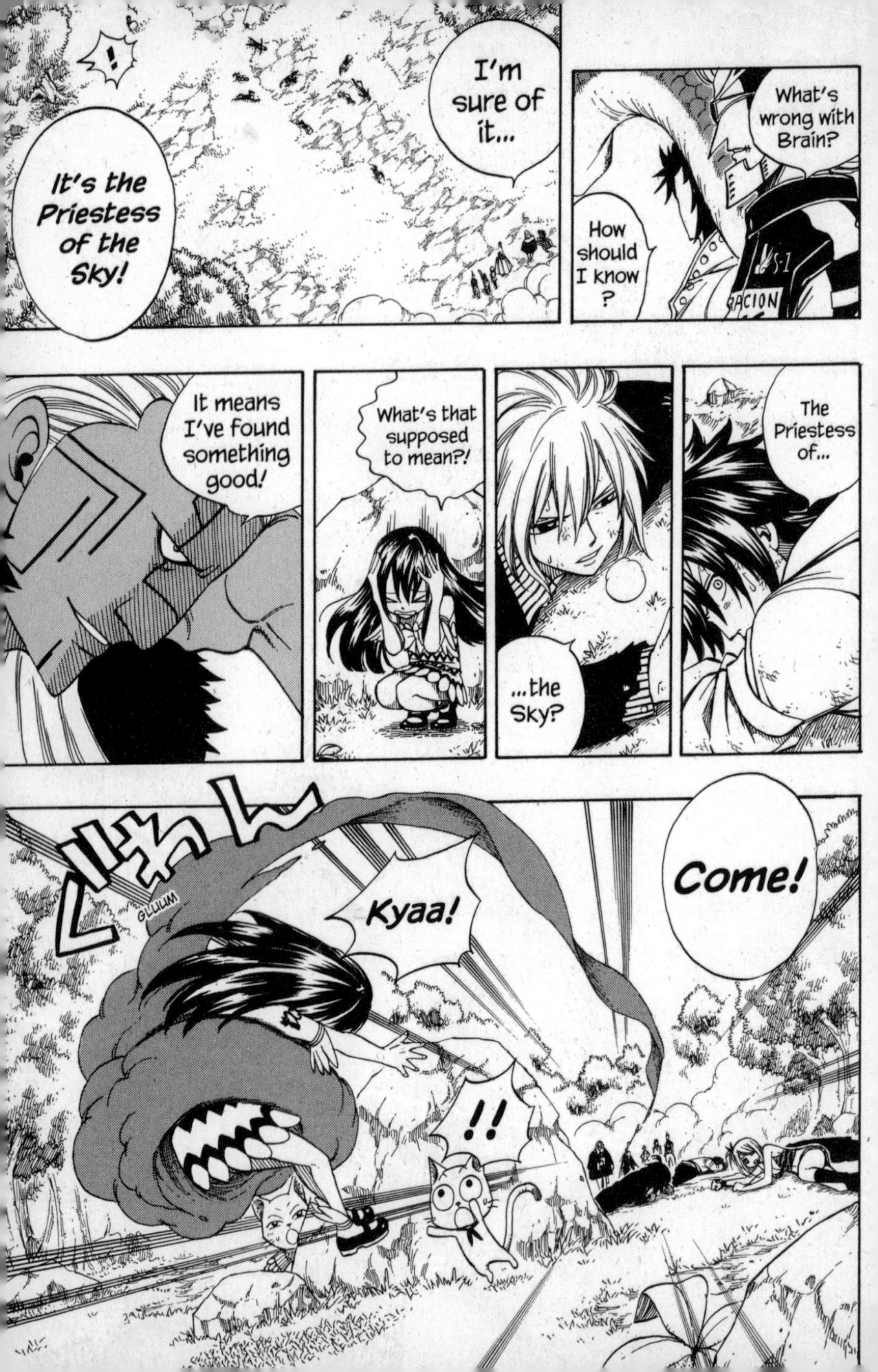
What's wrong with Brain?
How should I know?
I'm sure of it...
!
It's the Priestess of the Sky!
The Priestess of...
...the Sky?
What's that supposed to mean?!
It means I've found something good!
Come!
Kyaa!
GLUUM
!!

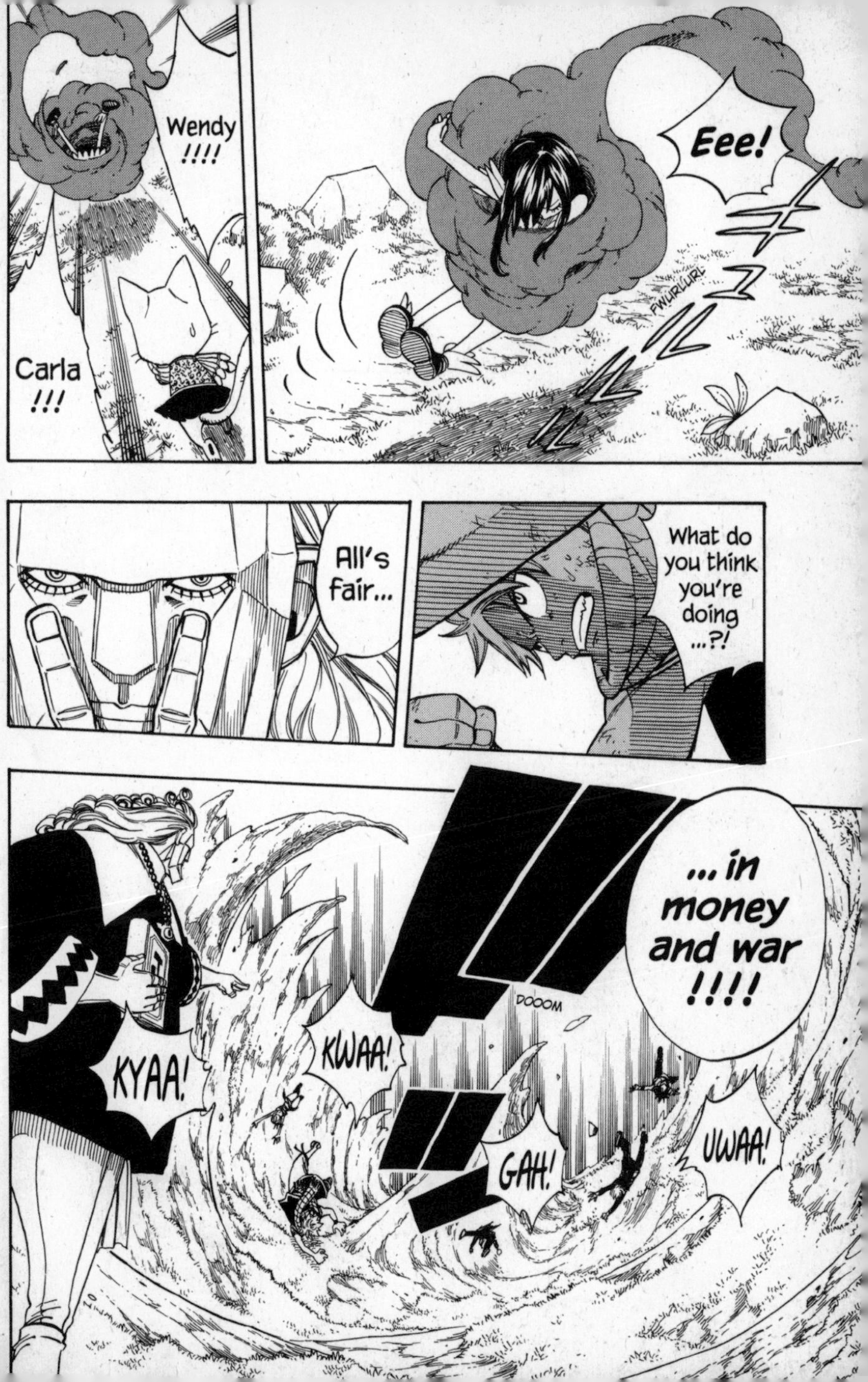

Eee!
FWURLURL
Wendy !!!!
Carla !!!
What do you think you're doing ...?!
All's fair...
... in money and war !!!!
DOOOM
UWAA!
GAH!
KWAA!
KYAA!

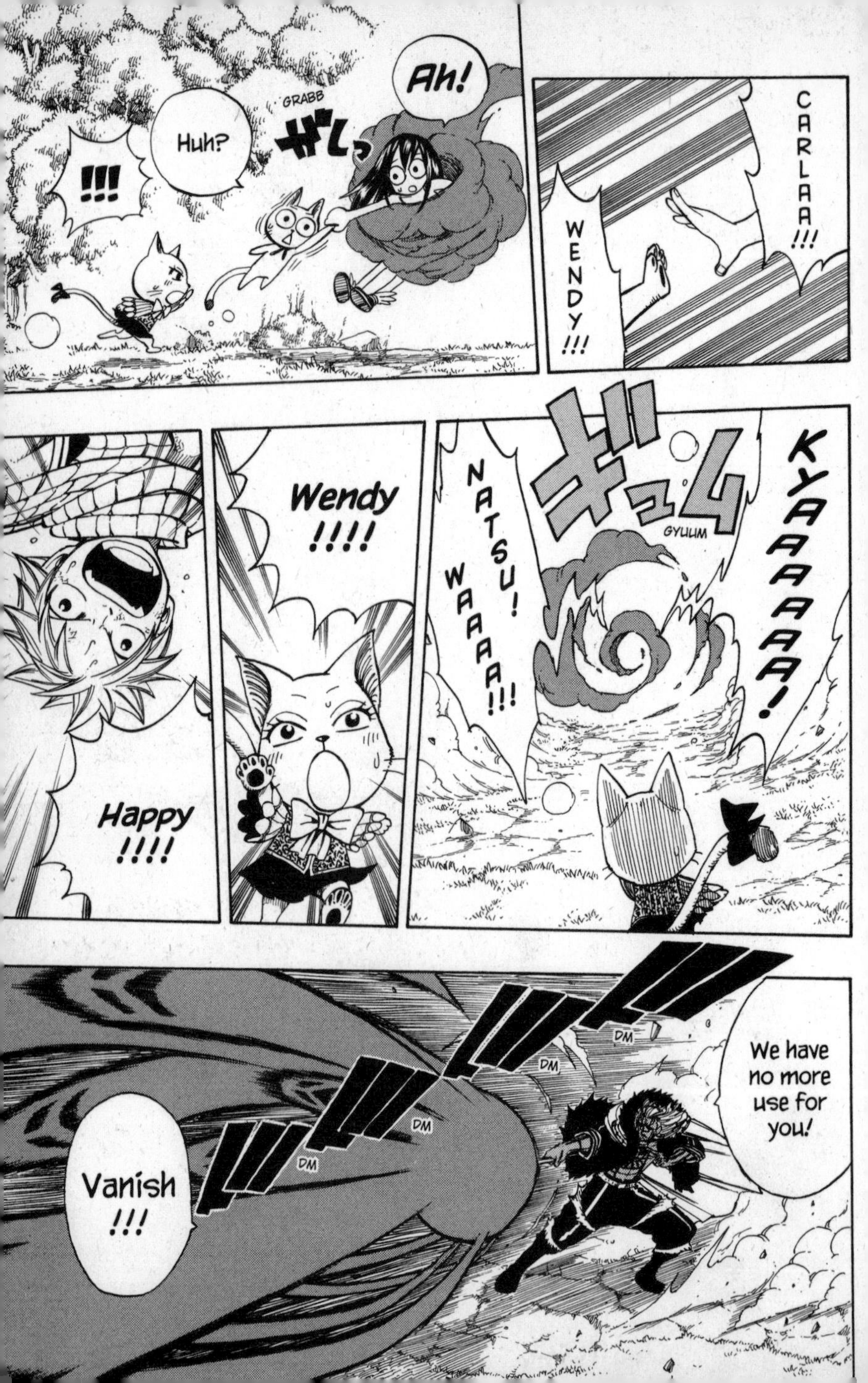
CARLAA!!!
WENDY!!!
Ah!
GRABB
Huh?
!!!
KYAAAAAAA!
GYUUM
NATSU! WAAAAA!!!
Wendy!!!!
Happy!!!!
We have no more use for you!
DM
DM
DM
DM
Vanish!!!

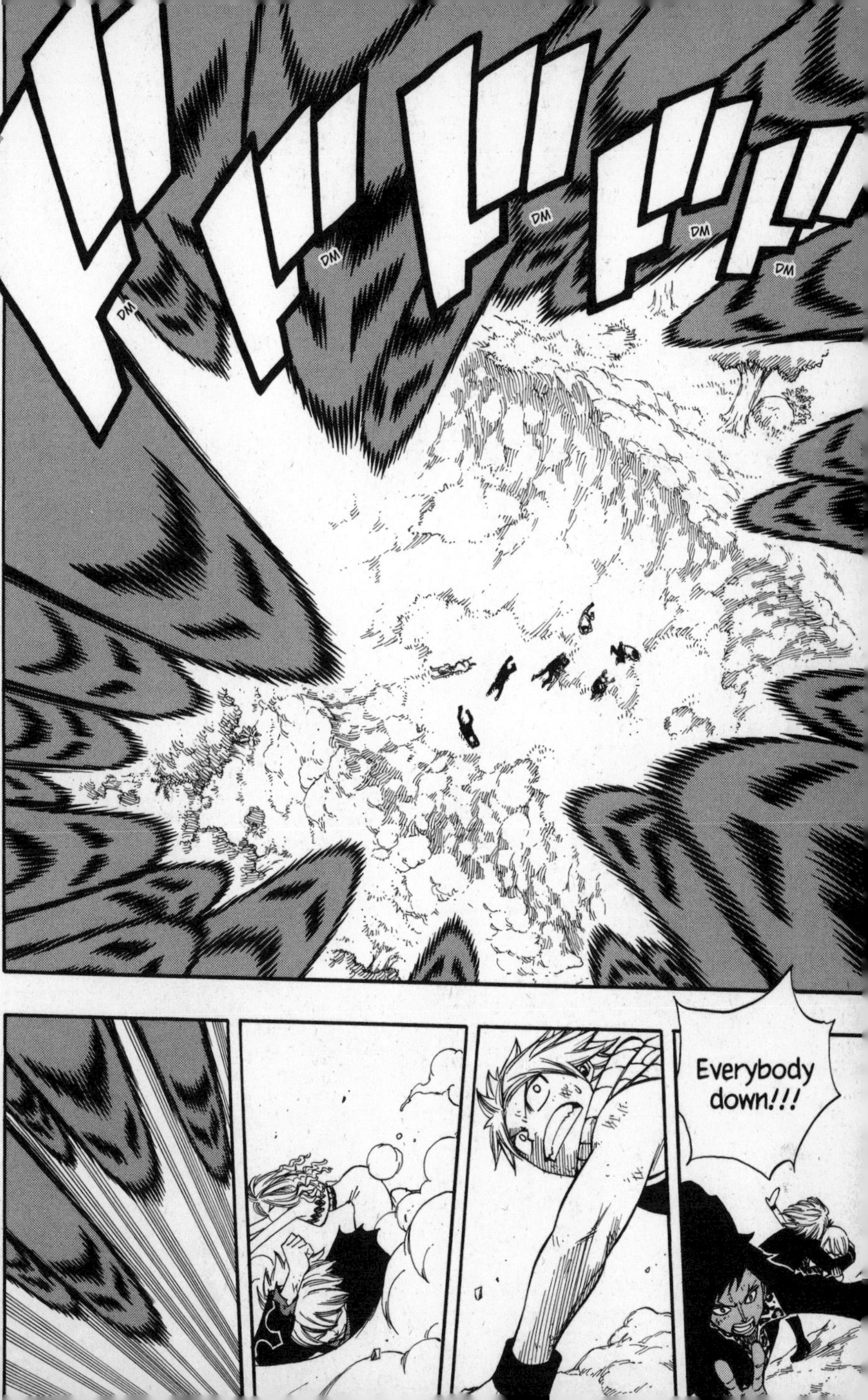
DM
DM
DM
DM
DM
Everybody down!!!

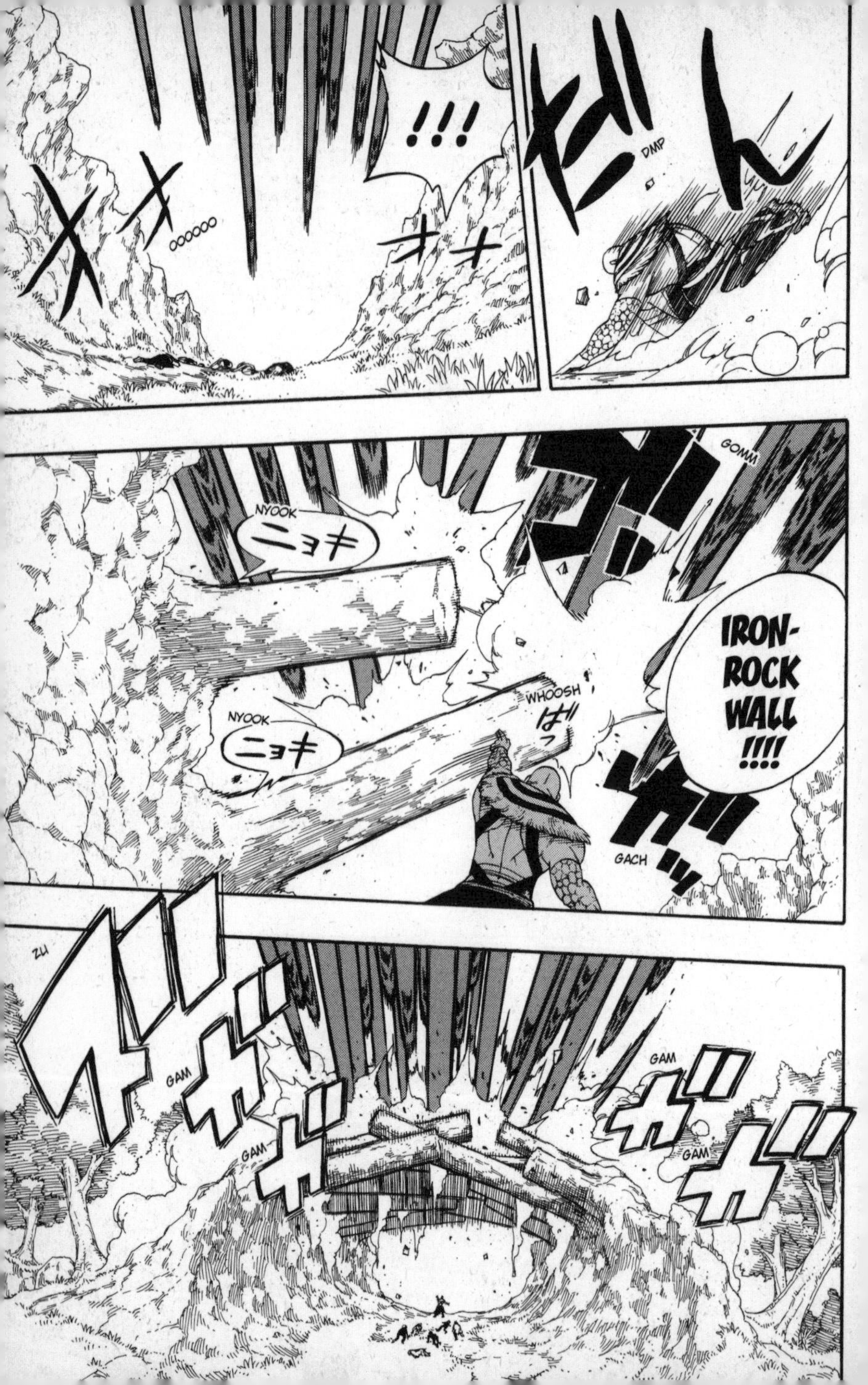
DMP
!!!
OOOOOO
GOMM
IRON-ROCK WALL!!!!
NYOOK
ニョキ
WHOOSH
ばっ
GACH
NYOOK
ニョキ
GAM
GAM
GAM
GAM
ZU

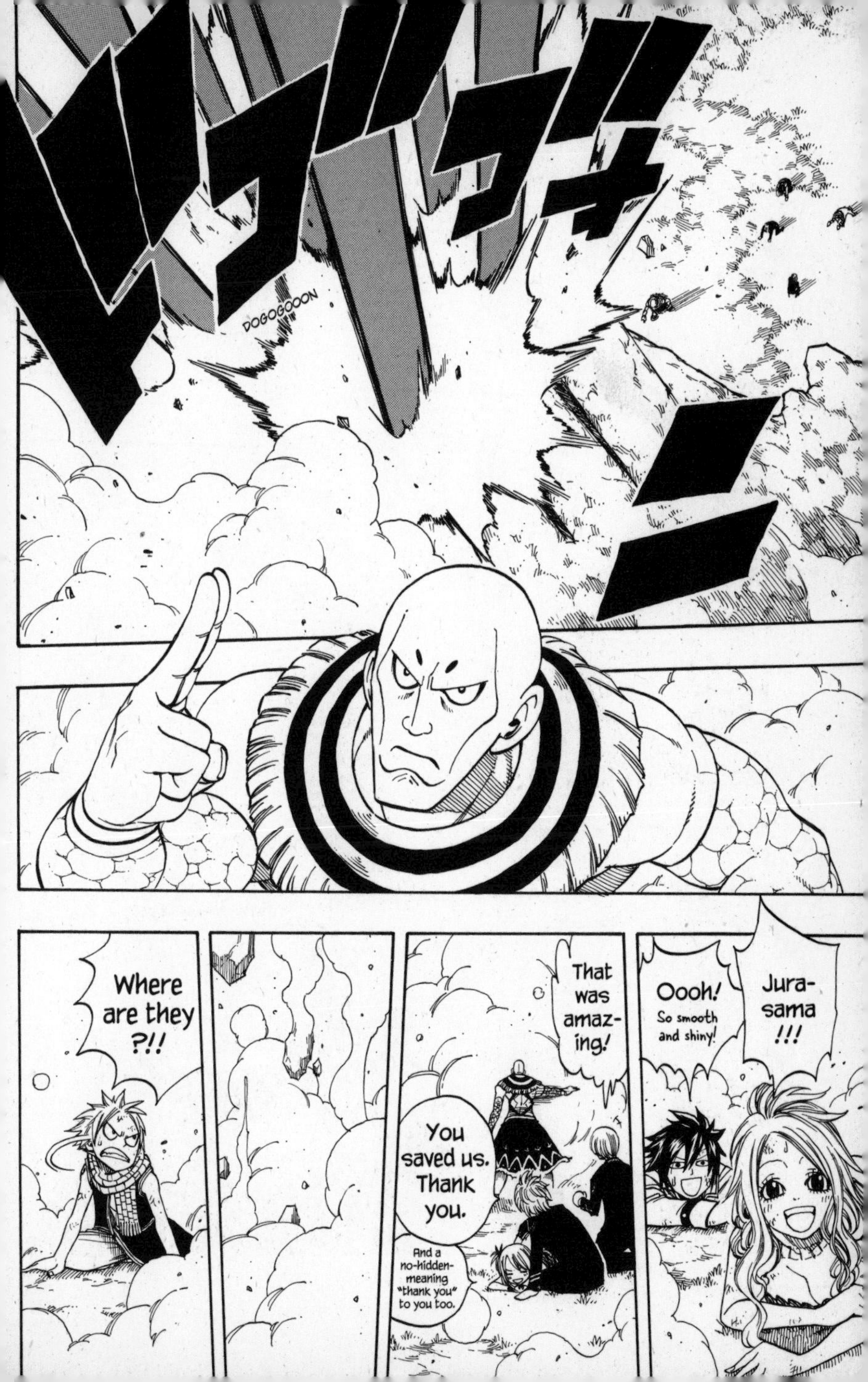
DOGOGOOON
Jura-sama!!!
Oooh! So smooth and shiny!
That was amazing!
You saved us. Thank you.
And a no-hidden-meaning "thank you" to you too.
Where are they?!!

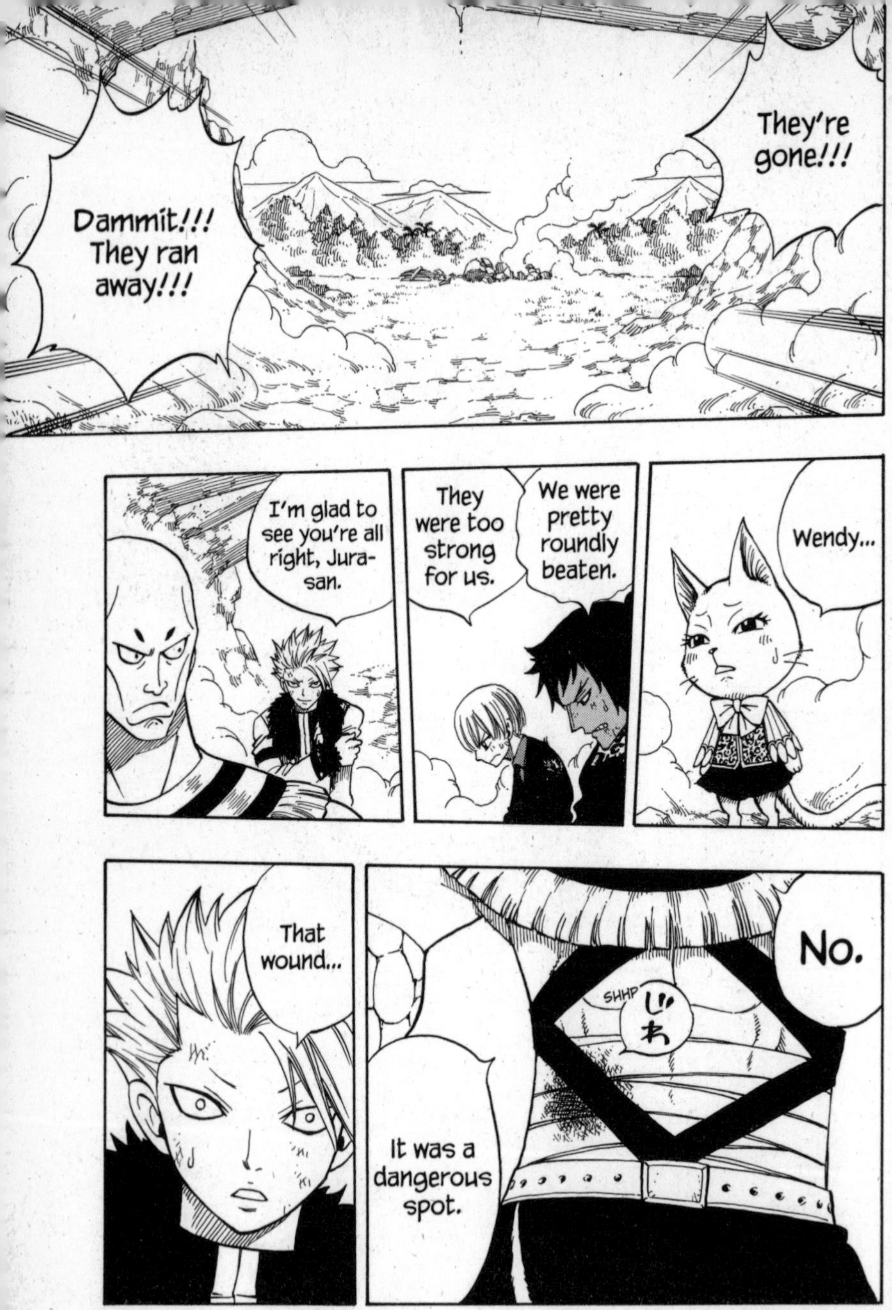
They're gone!!!
Dammit!!! They ran away!!!
Wendy...
We were pretty roundly beaten.
They were too strong for us.
I'm glad to see you're all right, Jura-san.
No.
SHHP
じわ
It was a dangerous spot.
That wound...

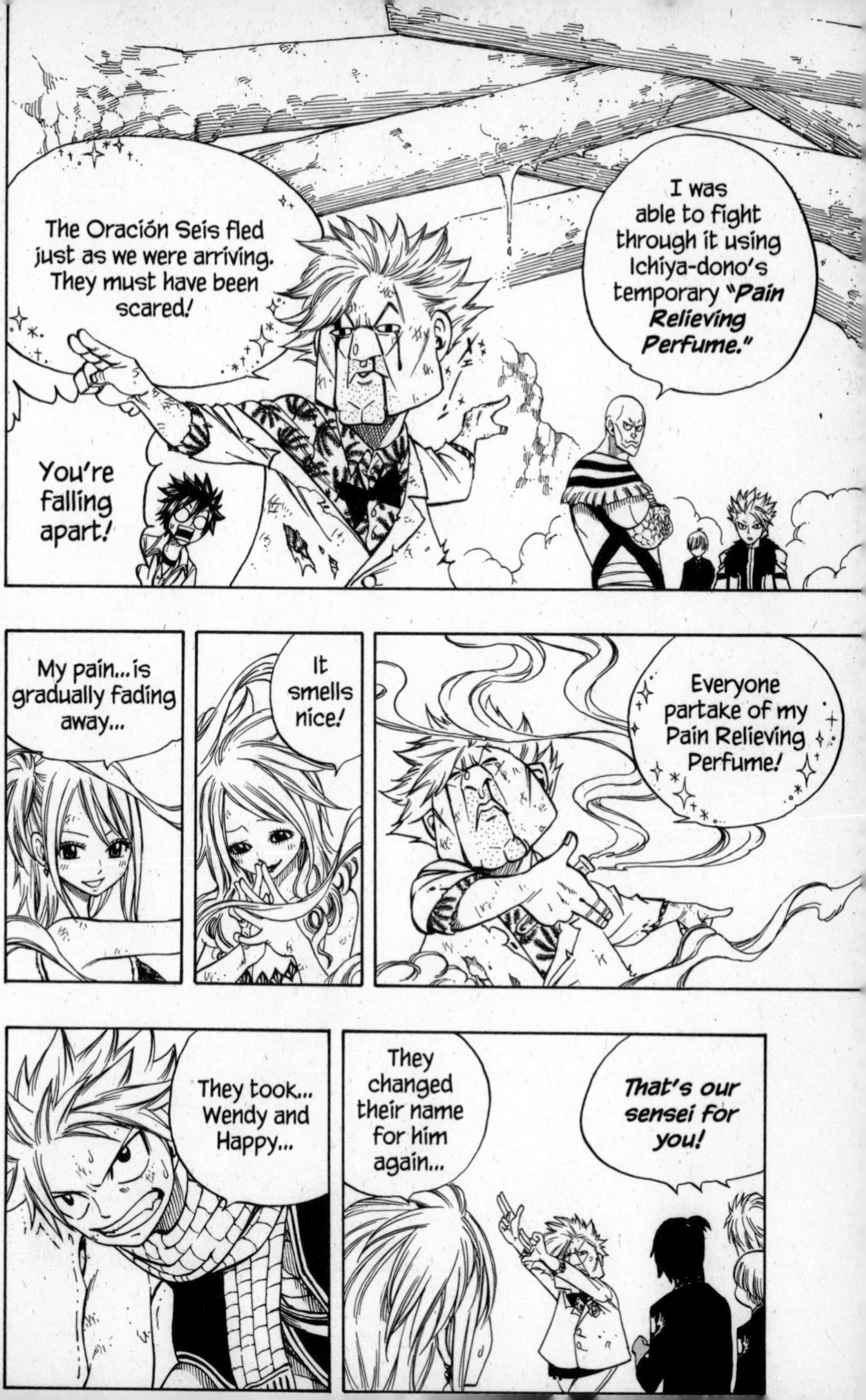
I was able to fight through it using Ichiya-dono's temporary *"Pain Relieving Perfume."*
The Oración Seis fled just as we were arriving. They must have been scared!
You're falling apart!
Everyone partake of my Pain Relieving Perfume!
It smells nice!
My pain...is gradually fading away...
That's our sensei for you!
They changed their name for him again...
They took... Wendy and Happy...

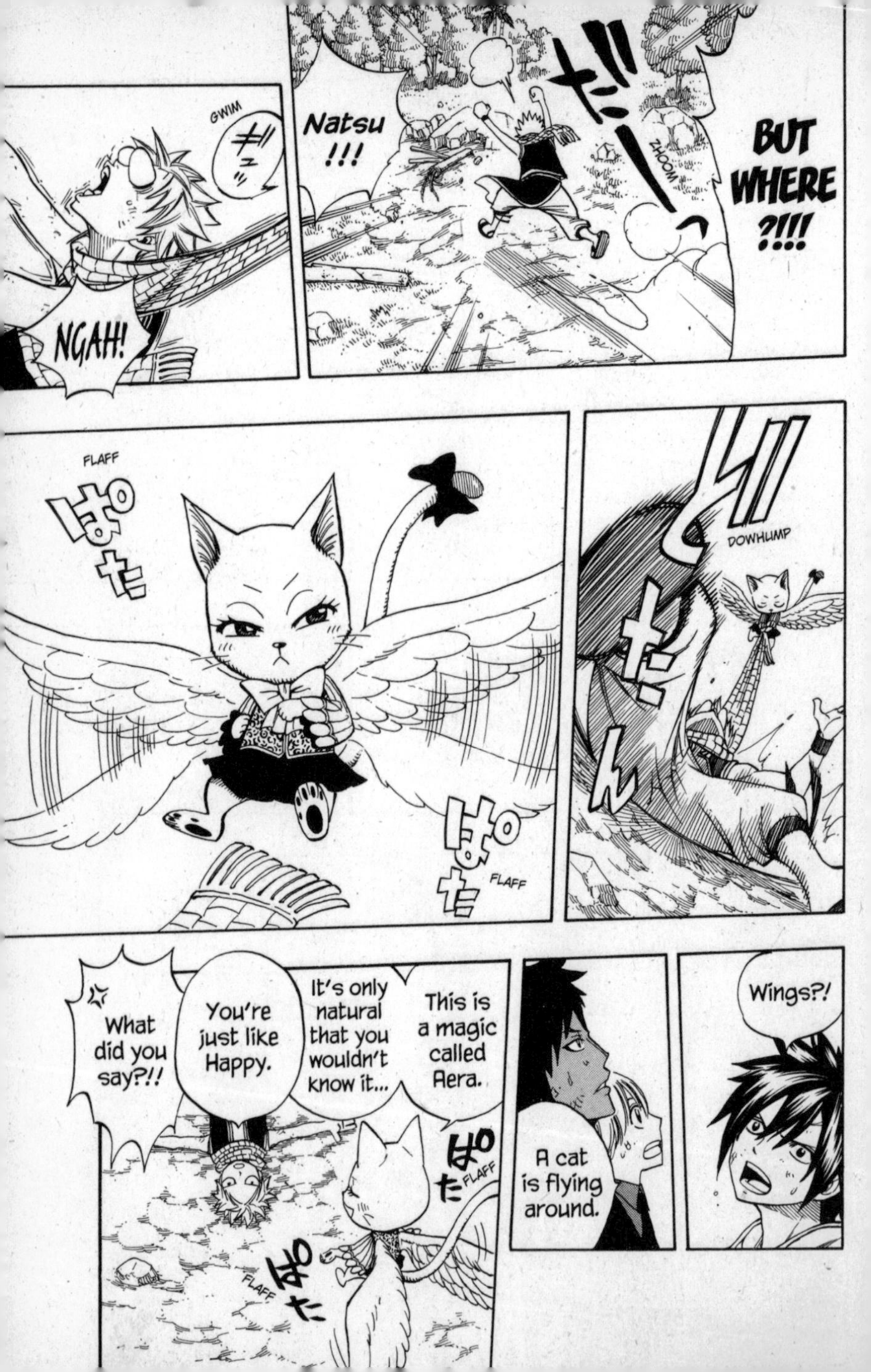

BUT WHERE ?!!!
ZHOOM
Natsu !!!
GWIM
NGAH!
DOWHUMP
FLAFF
FLAFF
Wings?!
A cat is flying around.
This is a magic called Aera.
It's only natural that you wouldn't know it...
You're just like Happy.
What did you say?!!
FLAFF
FLAFF

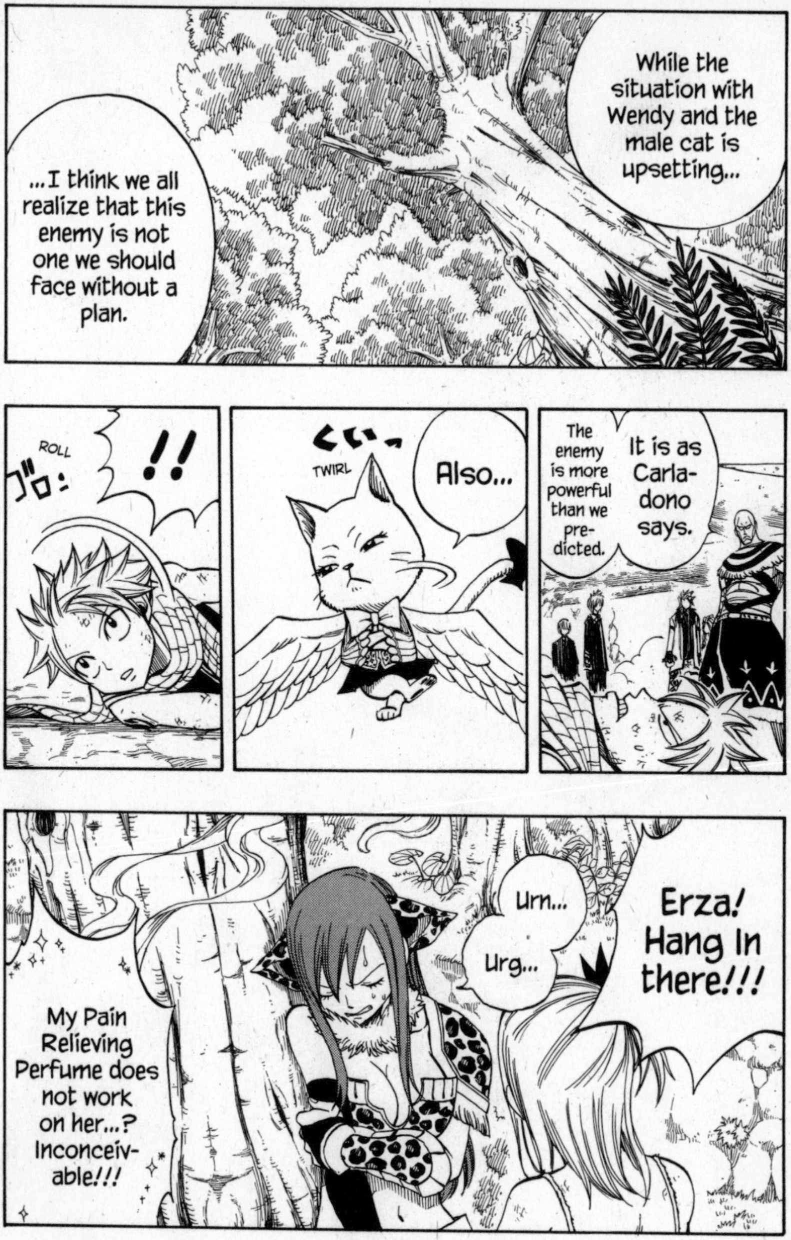
While the situation with Wendy and the male cat is upsetting...
...I think we all realize that this enemy is not one we should face without a plan.
It is as Carla-dono says.
The enemy is more powerful than we pre-dicted.
Also...
TWIRL
ROLL
!!
Erza! Hang In there!!!
Urn...
Urg...
My Pain Relieving Perfume does not work on her...? Inconceiv-able!!!

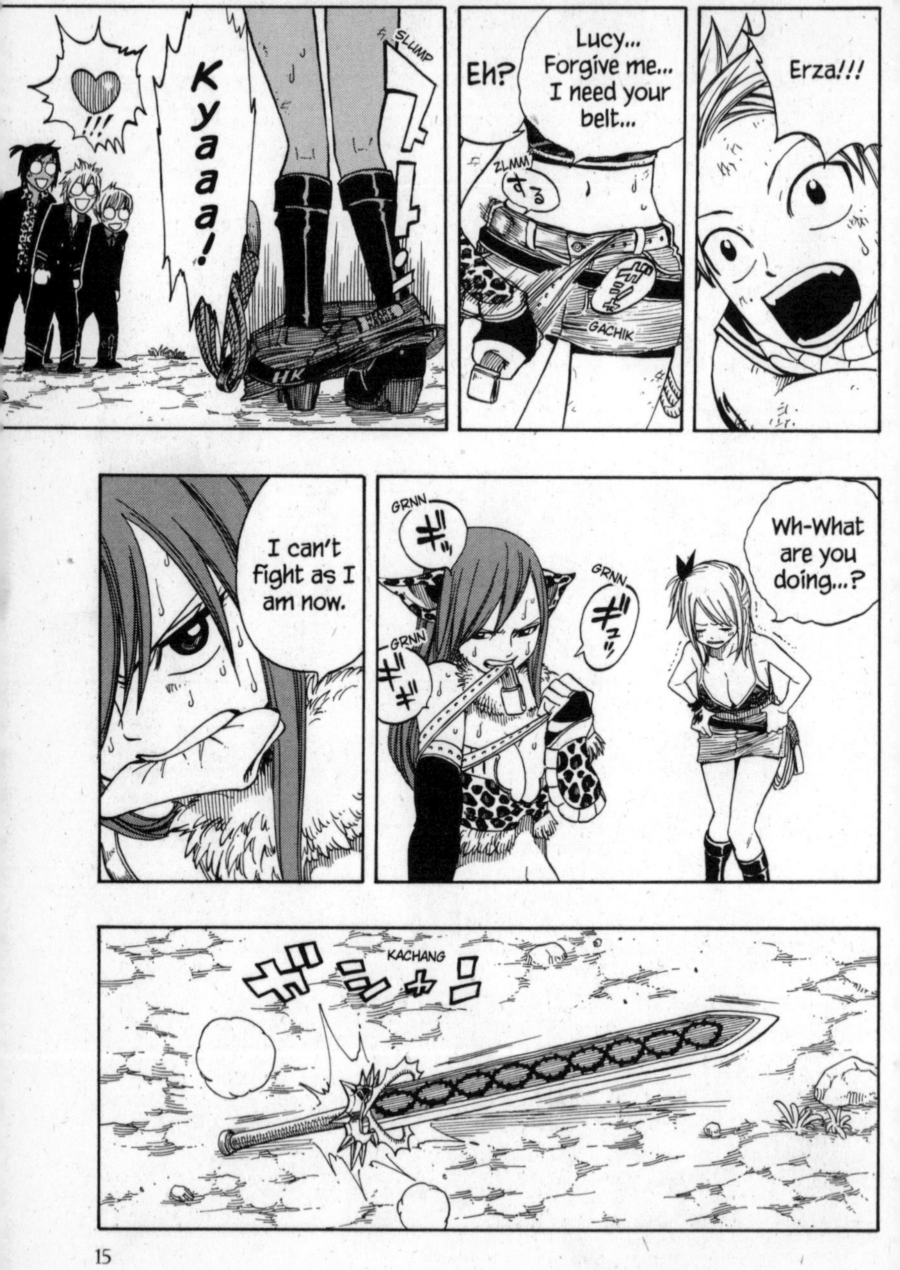
Erza!!!
Lucy... Forgive me... I need your belt...
Eh?
ZLMM
する
GACHIK
SLUMP
Kyaaa!
!!!
Wh-What are you doing...?
GRNN
GRNN
GRNN
I can't fight as I am now.
KACHANG

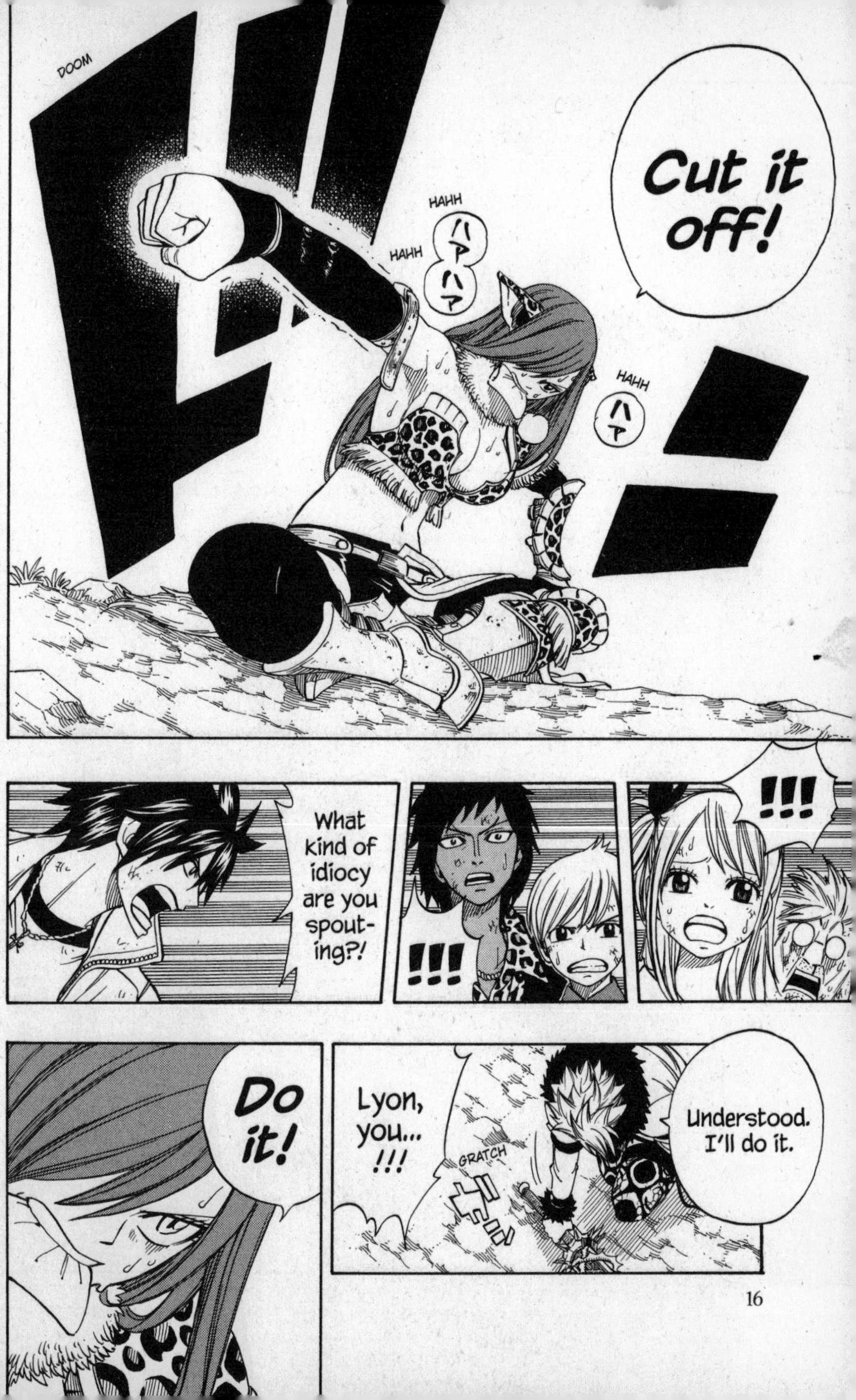
Cut it off!
HAHH
ハァ
HAHH
HAHH
ハァハァ
DOOM
!!!
!!!
What kind of idiocy are you spouting?!
Understood. I'll do it.
GRATCH
Lyon, you... !!!
Do it!

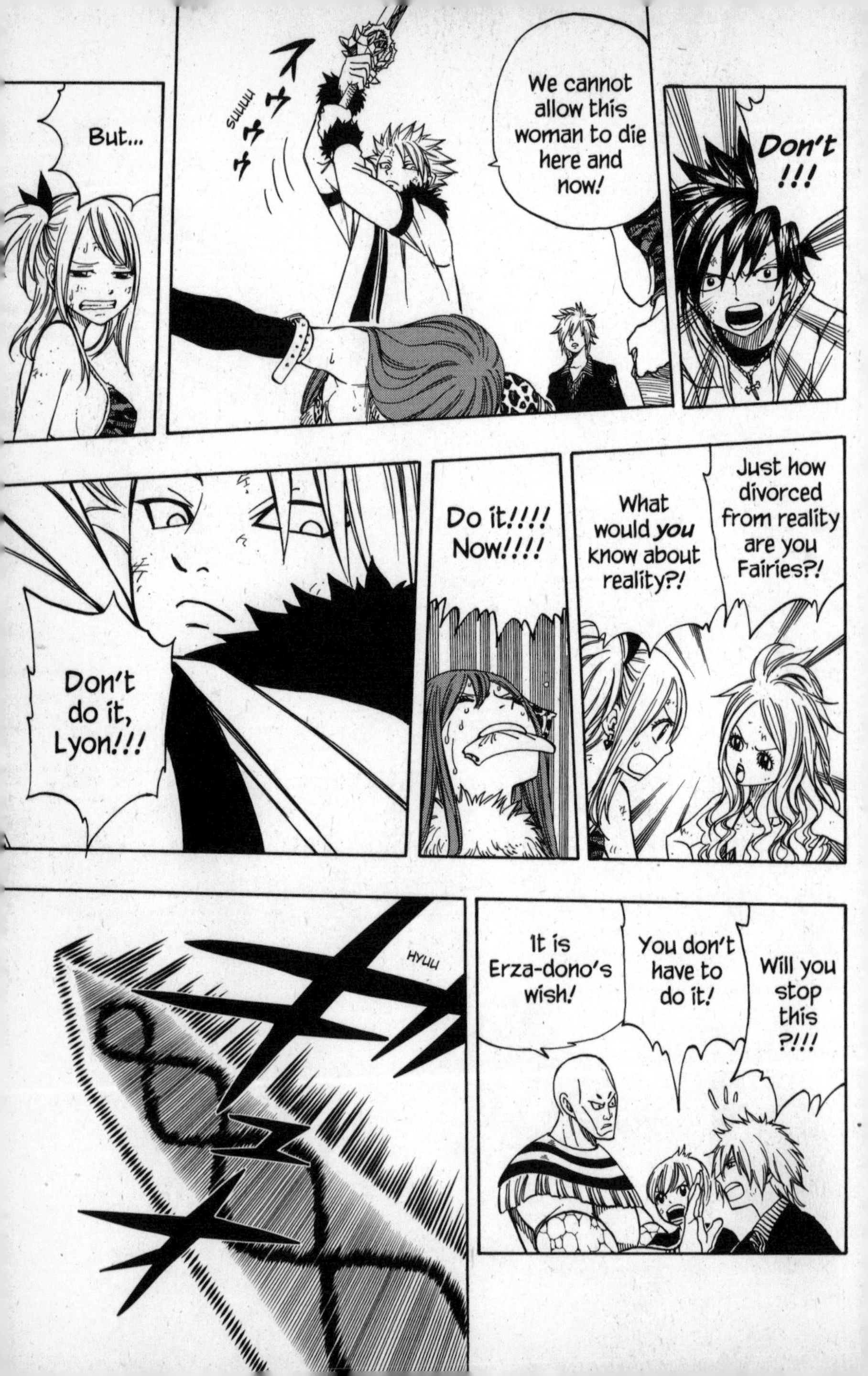
Don't !!!
We cannot allow this woman to die here and now!
スゥゥゥ
SUUUU
But...
Just how divorced from reality are you Fairies?!
What would *you* know about reality?!
Do it!!!! Now!!!!
Don't do it, Lyon!!!
Will you stop this ?!!!
You don't have to do it!
It is Erza-dono's wish!
HYUU

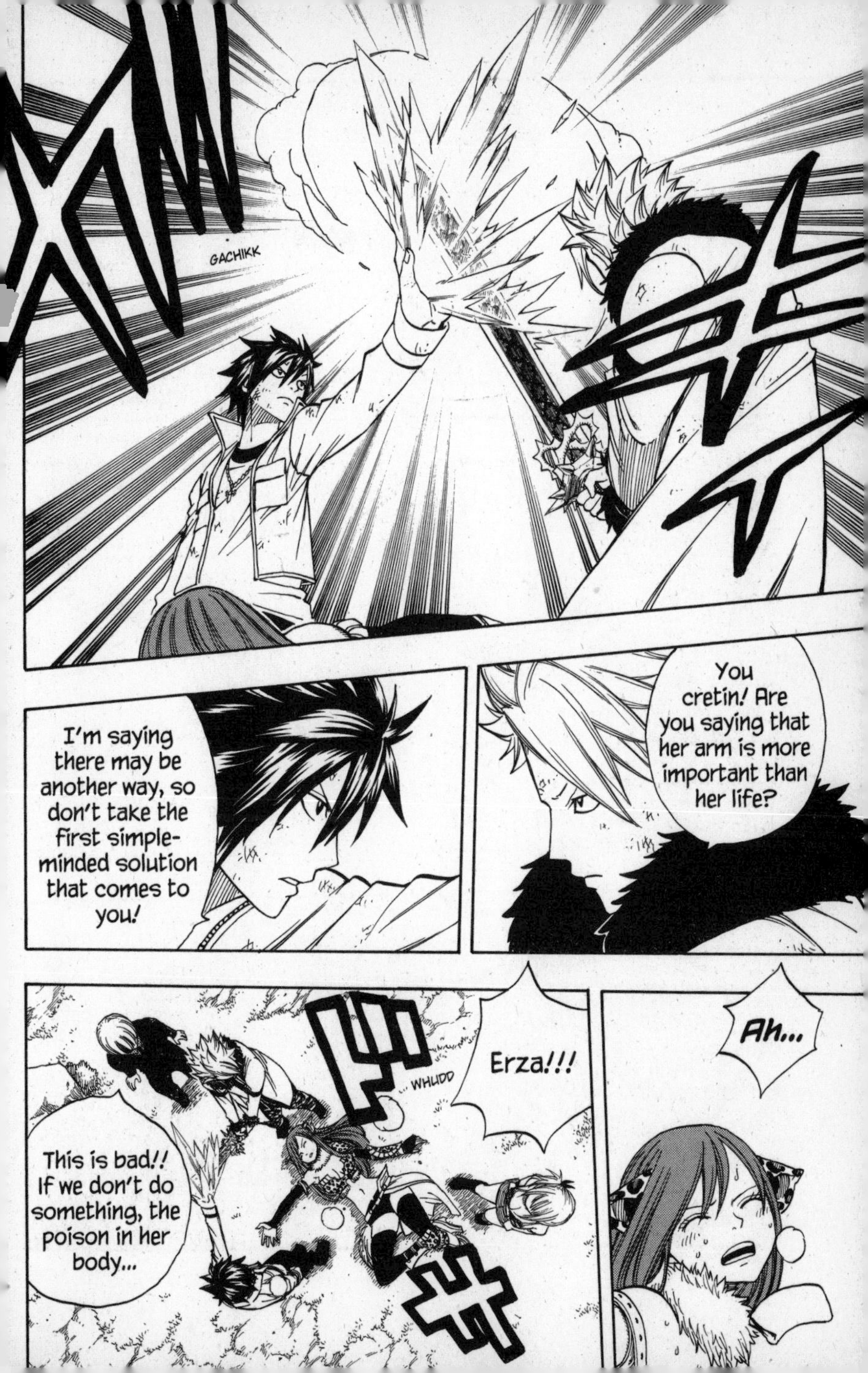
GACHIKK
You cretin! Are you saying that her arm is more important than her life?
I'm saying there may be another way, so don't take the first simple-minded solution that comes to you!
Ah...
Erza!!!
WHUDD
This is bad!! If we don't do something, the poison in her body...

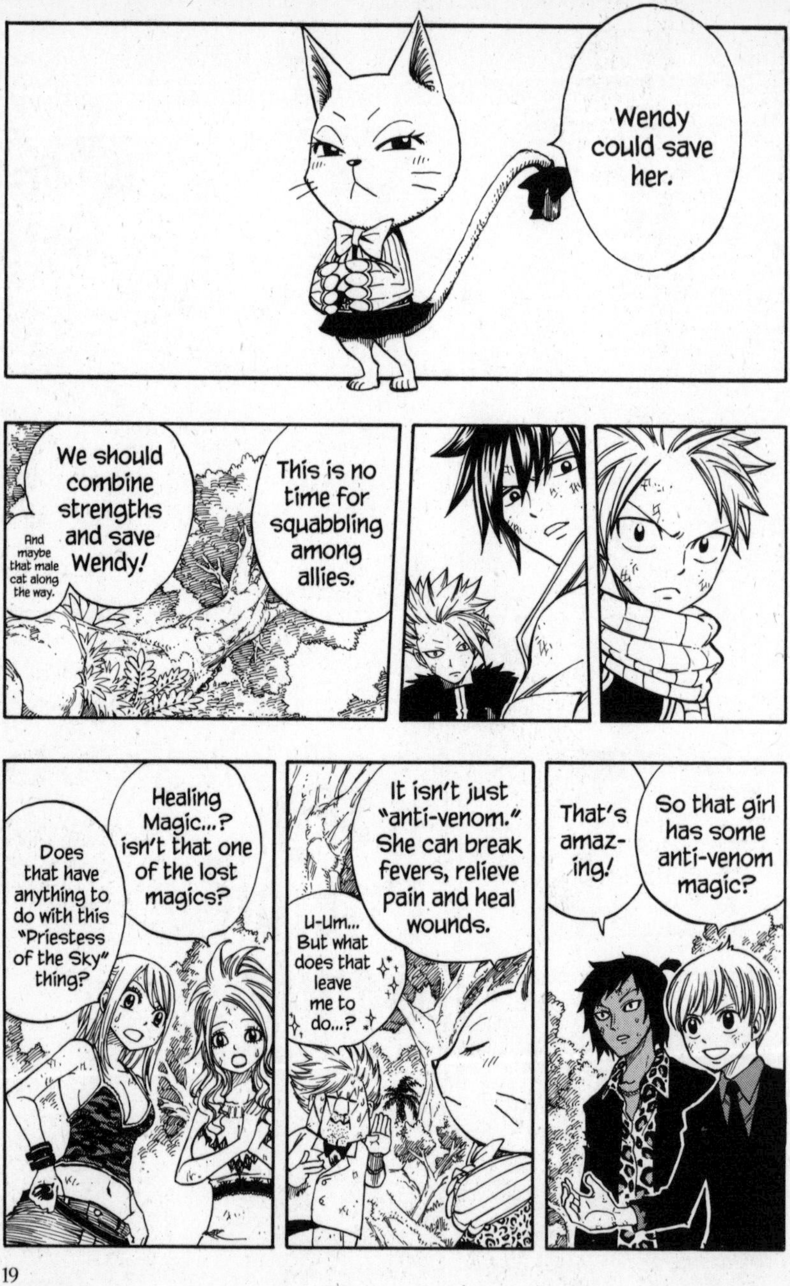
Wendy could save her.
This is no time for squabbling among allies.
We should combine strengths and save Wendy!
And maybe that male cat along the way.
So that girl has some anti-venom magic?
That's amaz-ing!
It isn't just "anti-venom." She can break fevers, relieve pain and heal wounds.
U-Um... But what does that leave me to do...?
Healing Magic...? isn't that one of the lost magics?
Does that have anything to do with this "Priestess of the Sky" thing?

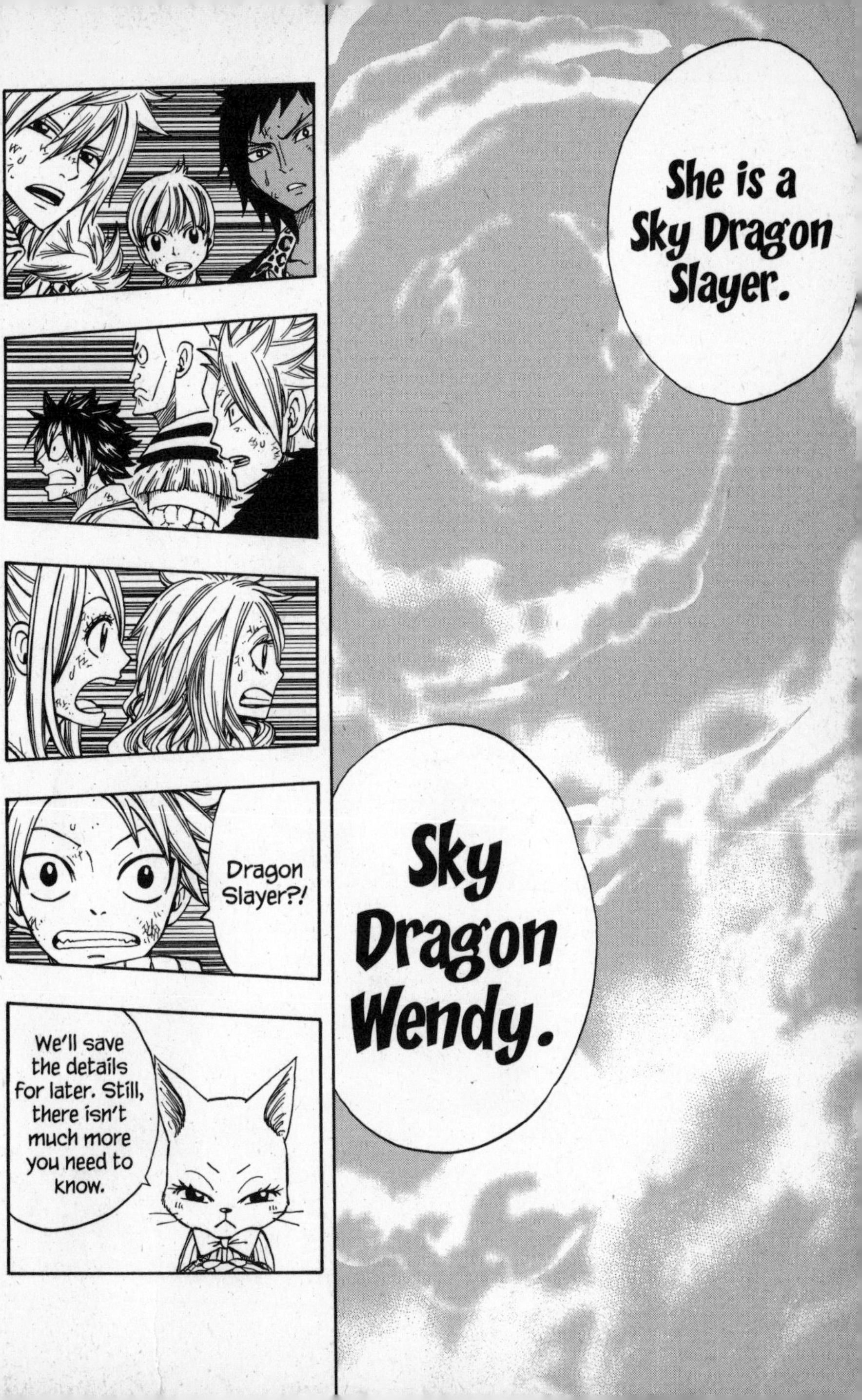
She is a Sky Dragon Slayer.
Sky Dragon Wendy.
Dragon Slayer?!
We'll save the details for later. Still, there isn't much more you need to know.

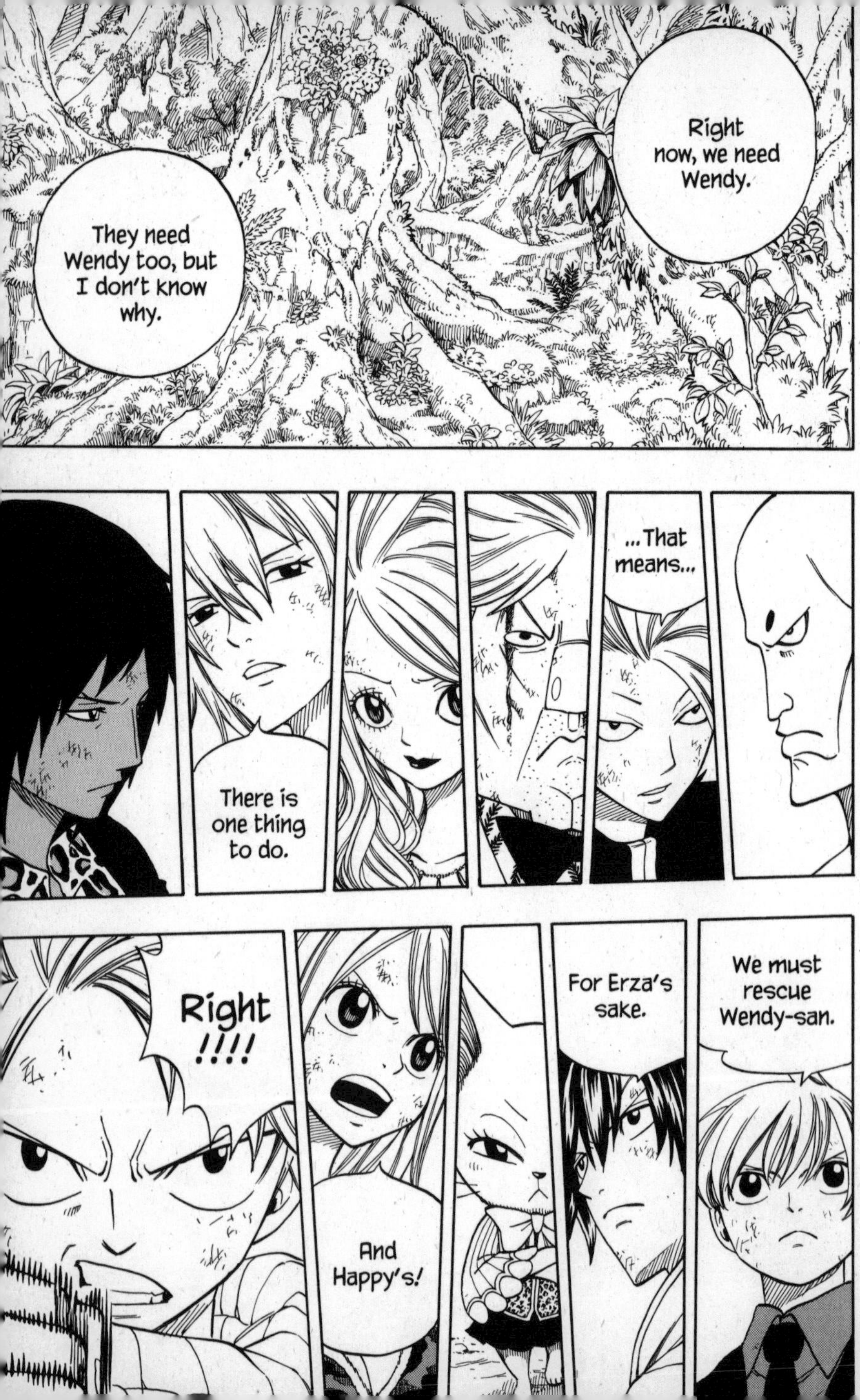
Right now, we need Wendy.
They need Wendy too, but I don't know why.
...That means...
There is one thing to do.
We must rescue Wendy-san.
For Erza's sake.
And Happy's!
Right !!!!

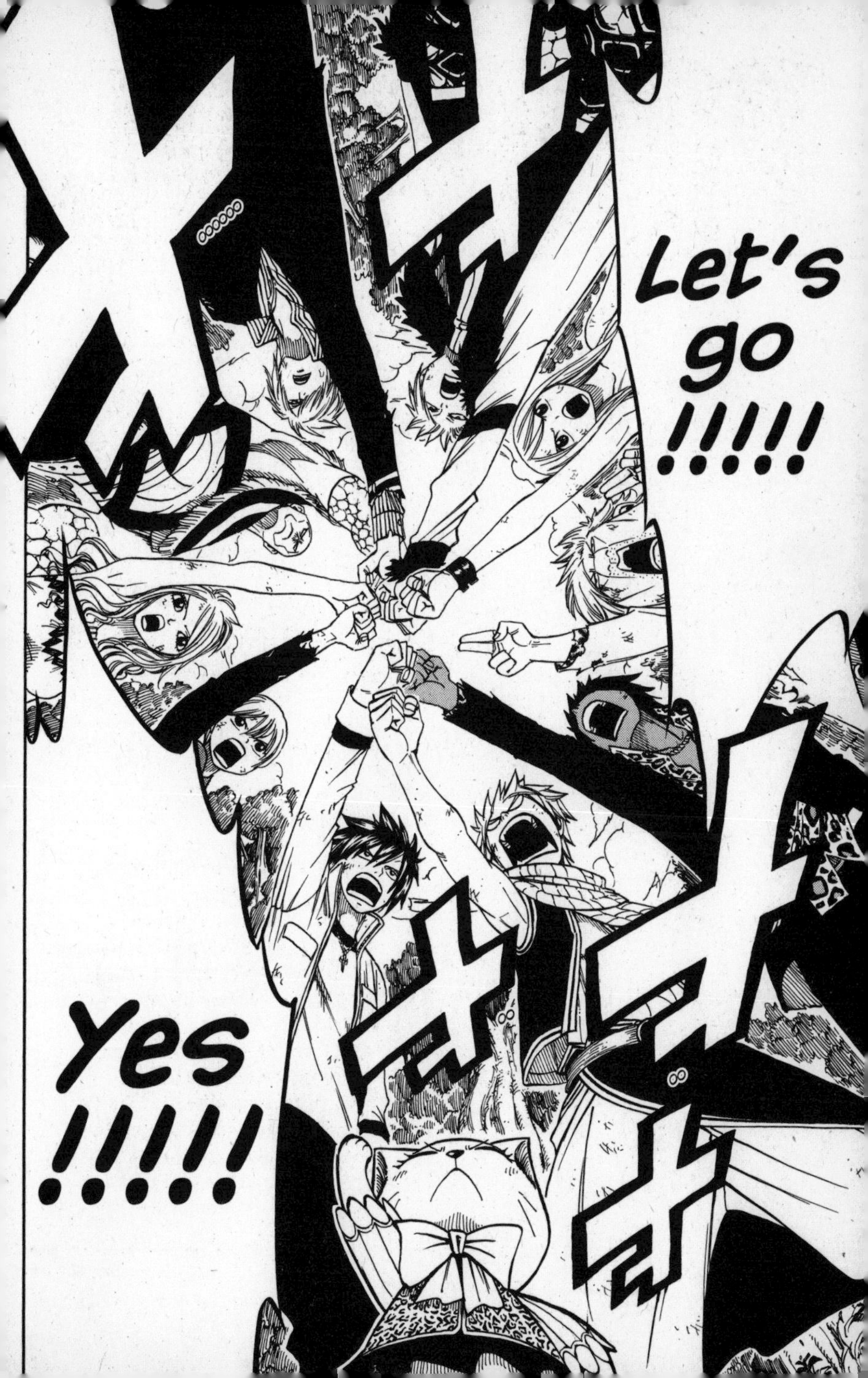
Let's go!!!!!
Yes!!!!!

FAIRY TAIL

フェアリーテイル

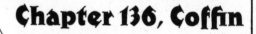

LAMIA SCALE

Name: Sherry Blendy   **Age:** 17

Magic: Doll Attack Magic

Likes: Love (her teacher)   **Dislikes:** Water

Chapter 136, Coffin

Remarks

She holds a grudge against the demon Deliora, who murdered both her parents when she was very young. She left Lamia Scale to follow Lyon in an attempt to take down Deloria, rejoining later to take on jobs in earnest. Her magic is Doll Attack Magic, with which she can manipulate anything non-human: trees, rocks, even Celestial Spirits. She claims that when she turned seventeen, she gave herself something of an attitude makeover.

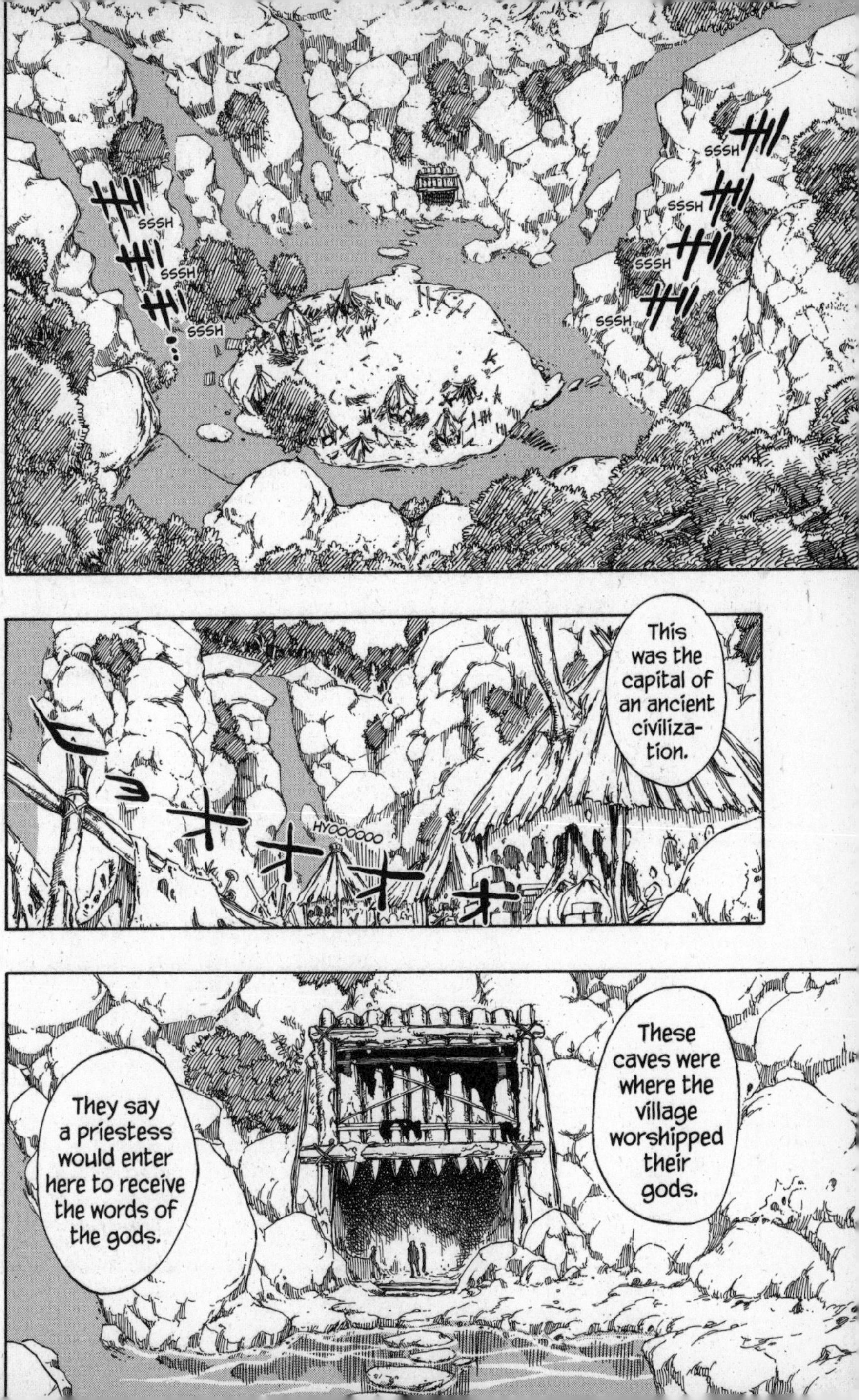
SSSH
SSSH
SSSH
SSSH
SSSH
SSSH
SSSH
This was the capital of an ancient civiliza-tion.
HYOOOOOO
These caves were where the village worshipped their gods.
They say a priestess would enter here to receive the words of the gods.

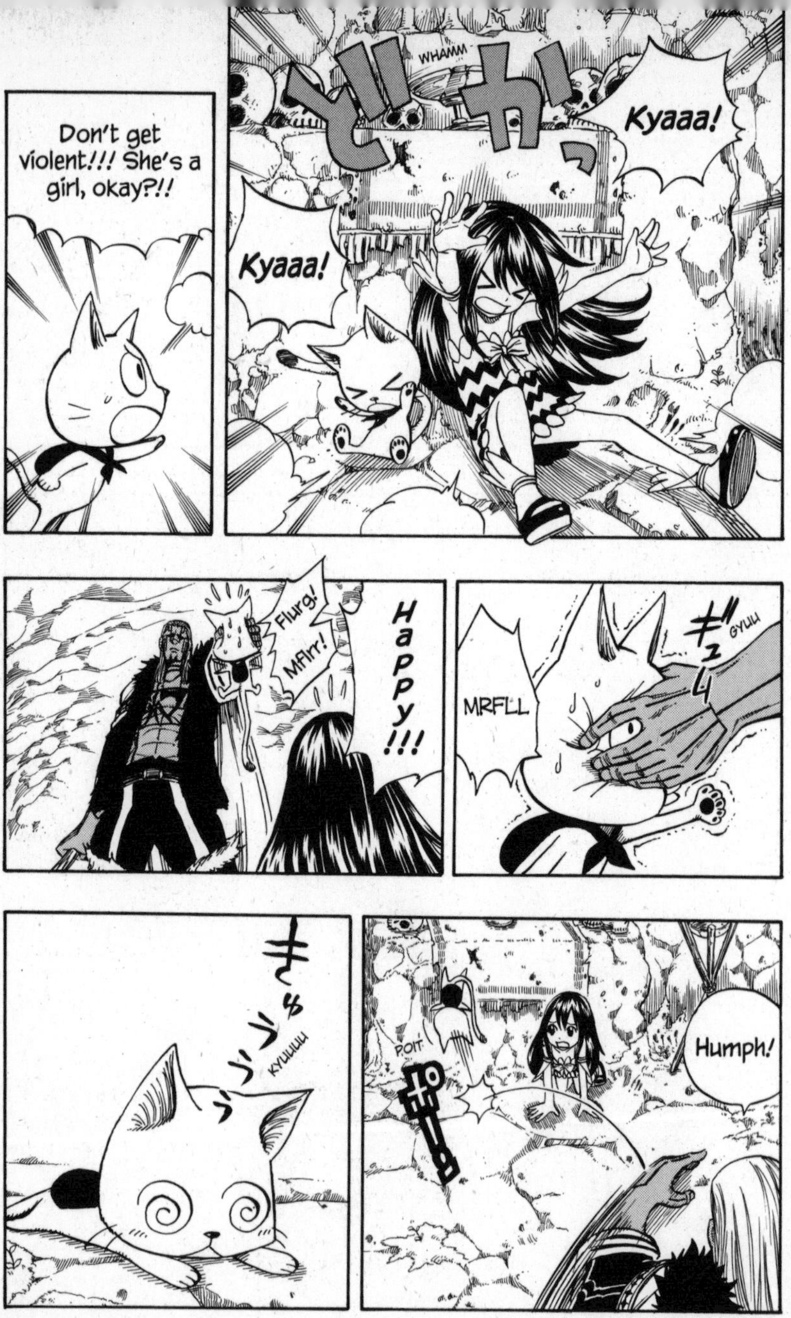
WHAMM
Kyaaa!
Kyaaa!
Don't get violent!!! She's a girl, okay?!!
GYUU
MRFLL
Happy!!!
Flurg!
Mflrr!
Humph!
POIT
KYUUUU

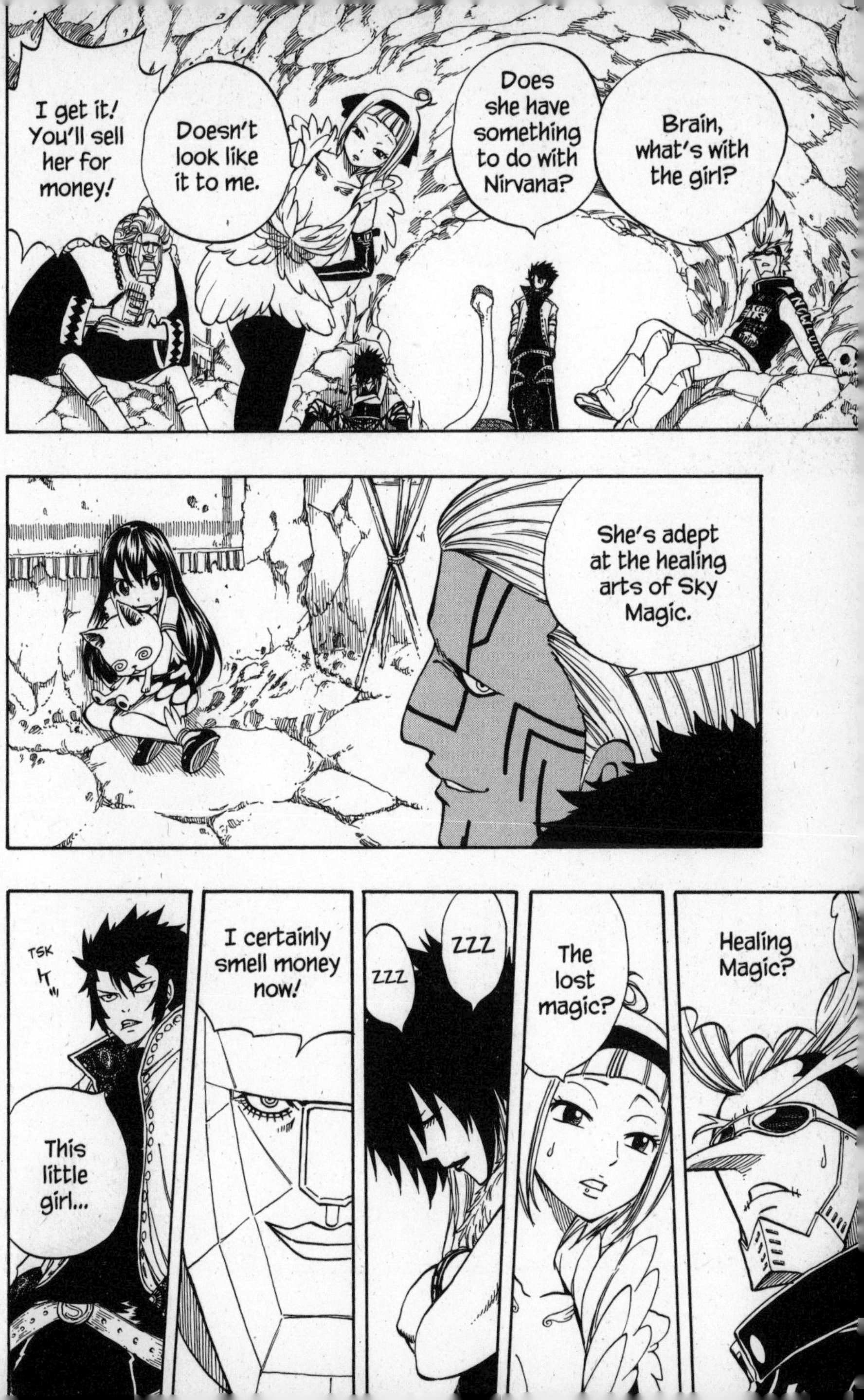
Brain, what's with the girl?
Does she have something to do with Nirvana?
Doesn't look like it to me.
I get it! You'll sell her for money!
She's adept at the healing arts of Sky Magic.
Healing Magic?
The lost magic?
ZZZ
ZZZ
I certainly smell money now!
TSK
This little girl...

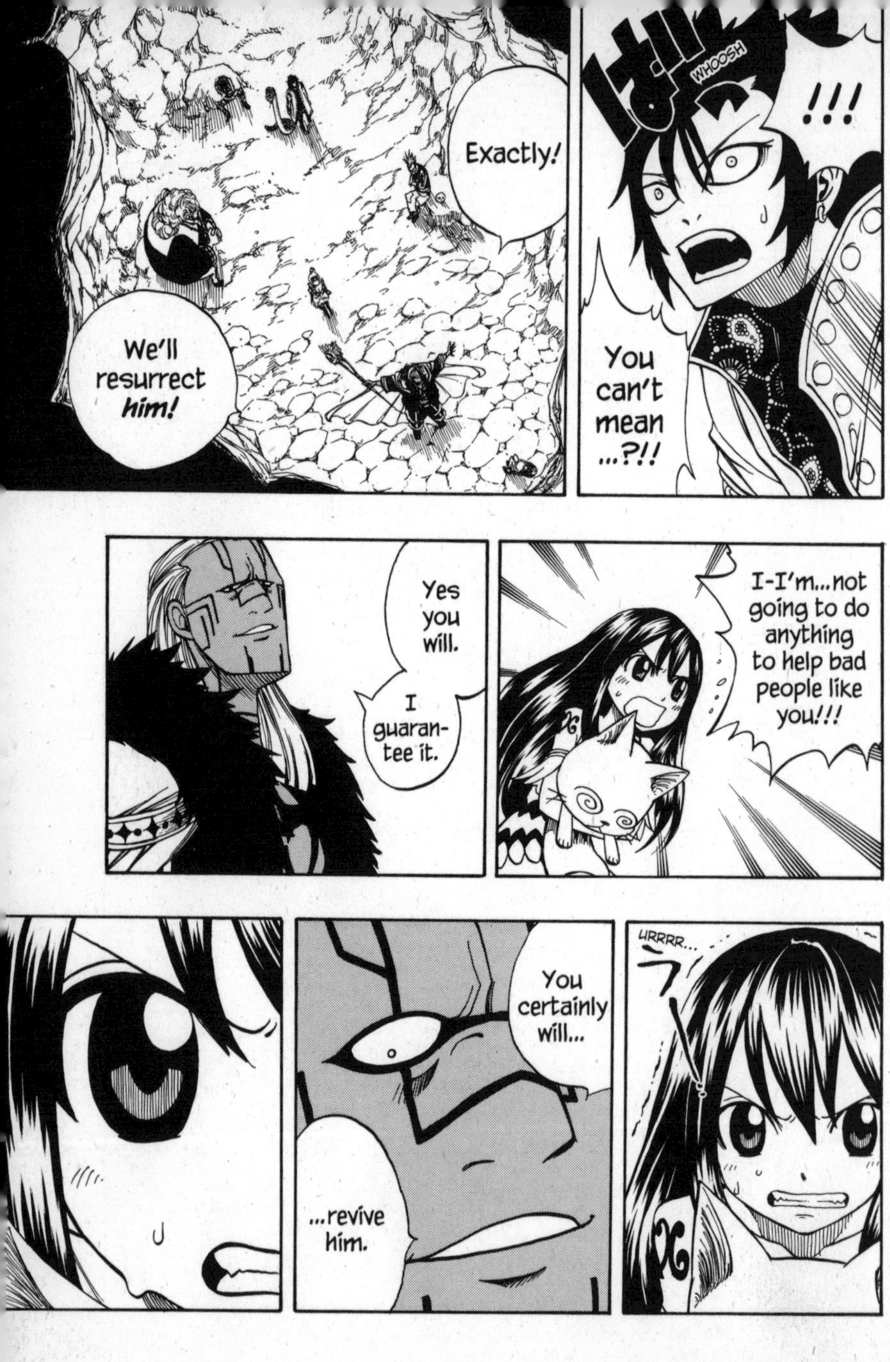
WHOOSH
!!!
You can't mean ...?!!
Exactly!
We'll resurrect him!
I-I'm...not going to do anything to help bad people like you!!!
Yes you will.
I guaran-tee it.
URRRR...
You certainly will...
...revive him.

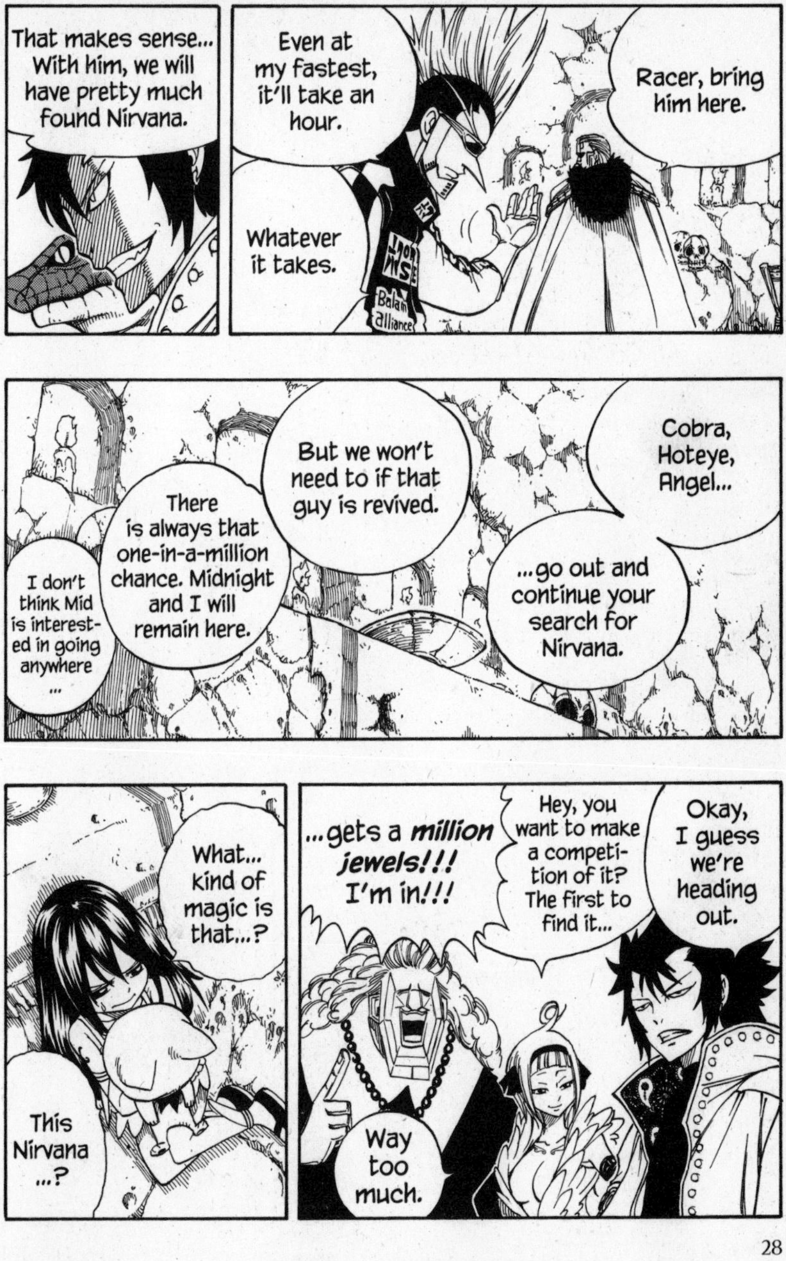
Racer, bring him here.
Even at my fastest, it'll take an hour.
Whatever it takes.
Balam alliance
That makes sense... With him, we will have pretty much found Nirvana.
Cobra, Hoteye, Angel...
...go out and continue your search for Nirvana.
But we won't need to if that guy is revived.
There is always that one-in-a-million chance. Midnight and I will remain here.
I don't think Mid is interest-ed in going anywhere ...
Okay, I guess we're heading out.
Hey, you want to make a competi-tion of it? The first to find it...
...gets a ***million jewels!!!*** I'm in!!!
Way too much.
What... kind of magic is that...?
This Nirvana ...?

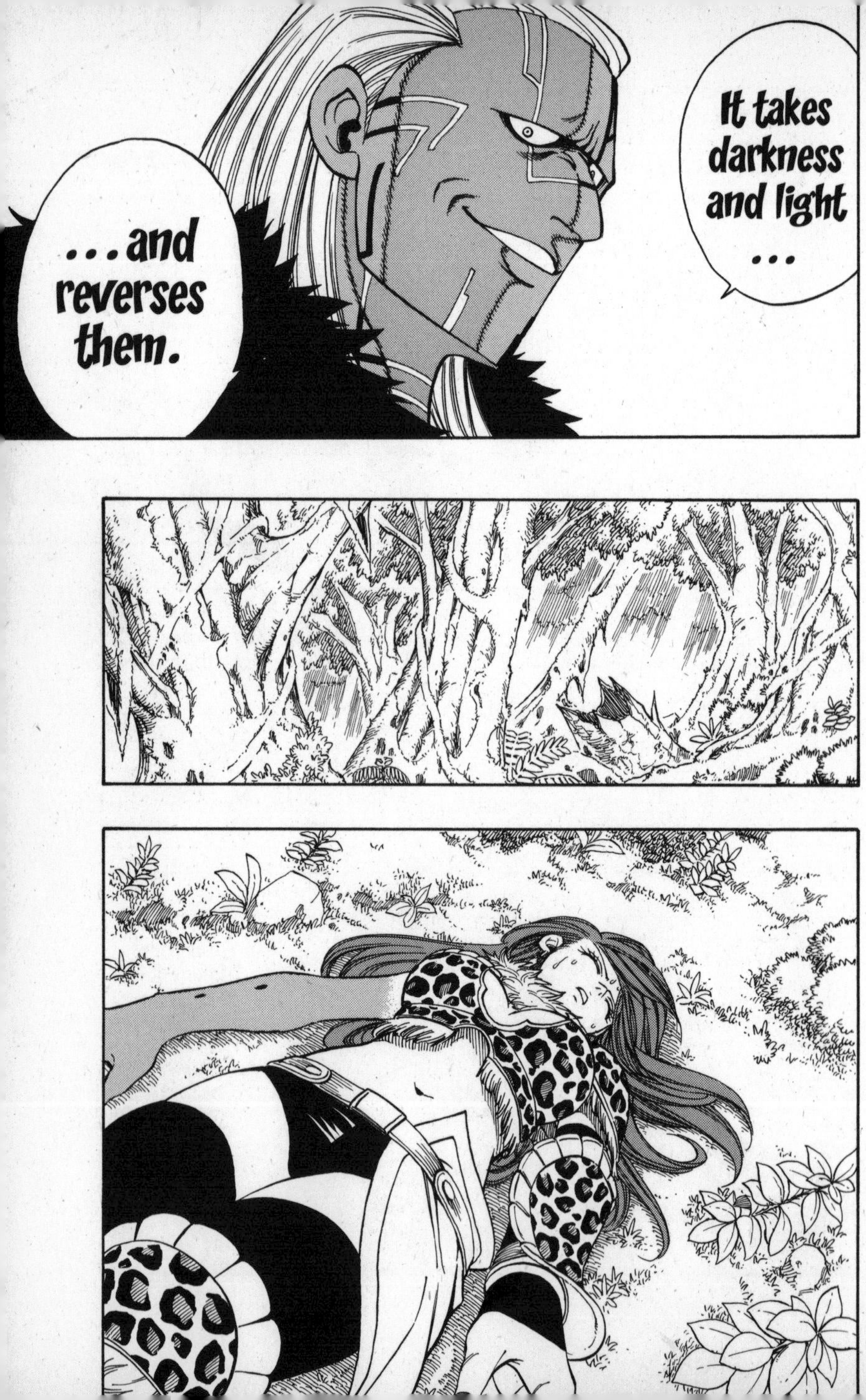
It takes darkness and light ...
...and reverses them.

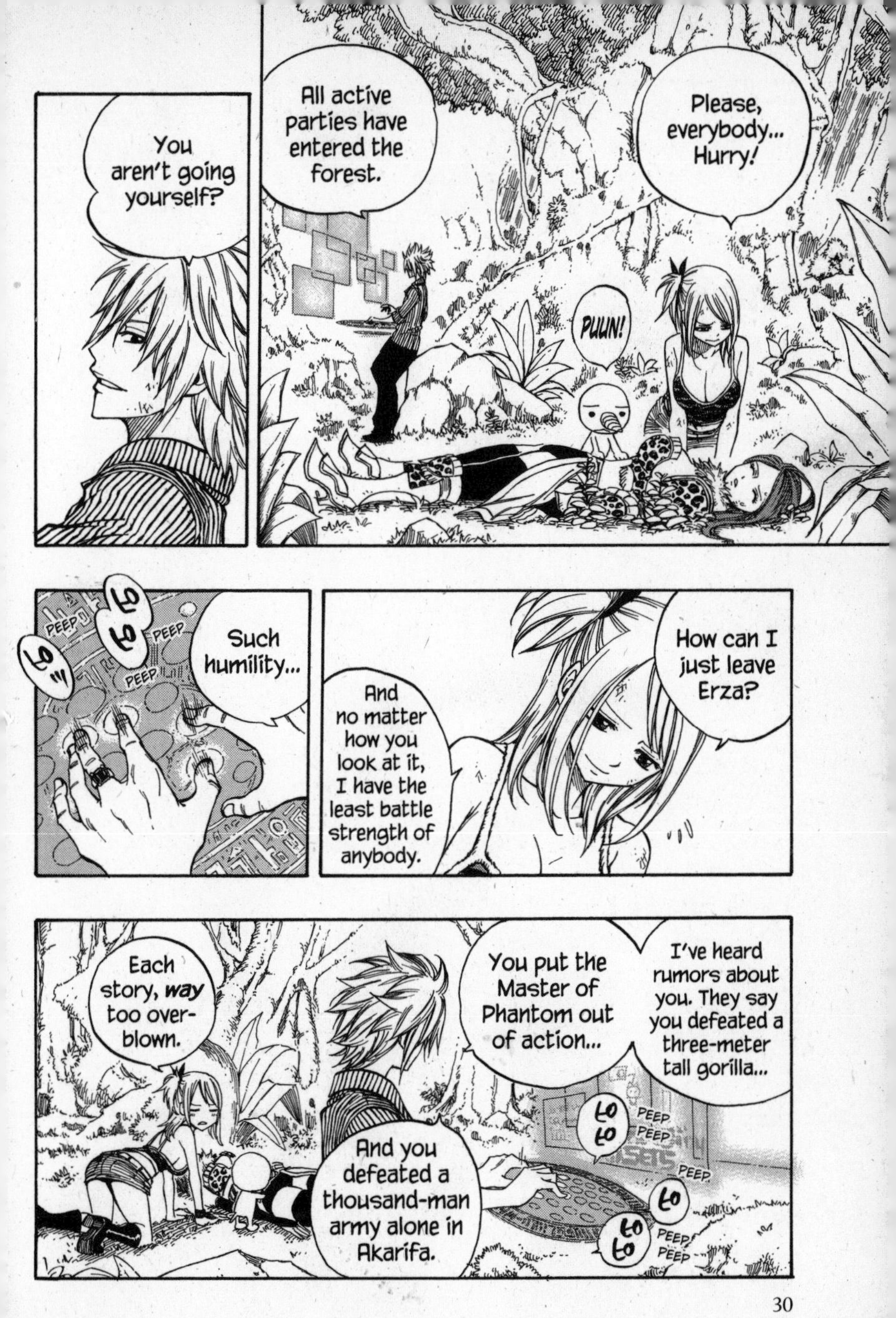

Please, everybody... Hurry!
All active parties have entered the forest.
PUUN!
You aren't going yourself?
How can I just leave Erza?
And no matter how you look at it, I have the least battle strength of anybody.
Such humility...
PEEP PEEP PEEP
I've heard rumors about you. They say you defeated a three-meter tall gorilla...
You put the Master of Phantom out of action...
And you defeated a thousand-man army alone in Akarifa.
Each story, *way* too over-blown.
PEEP PEEP PEEP PEEP PEEP

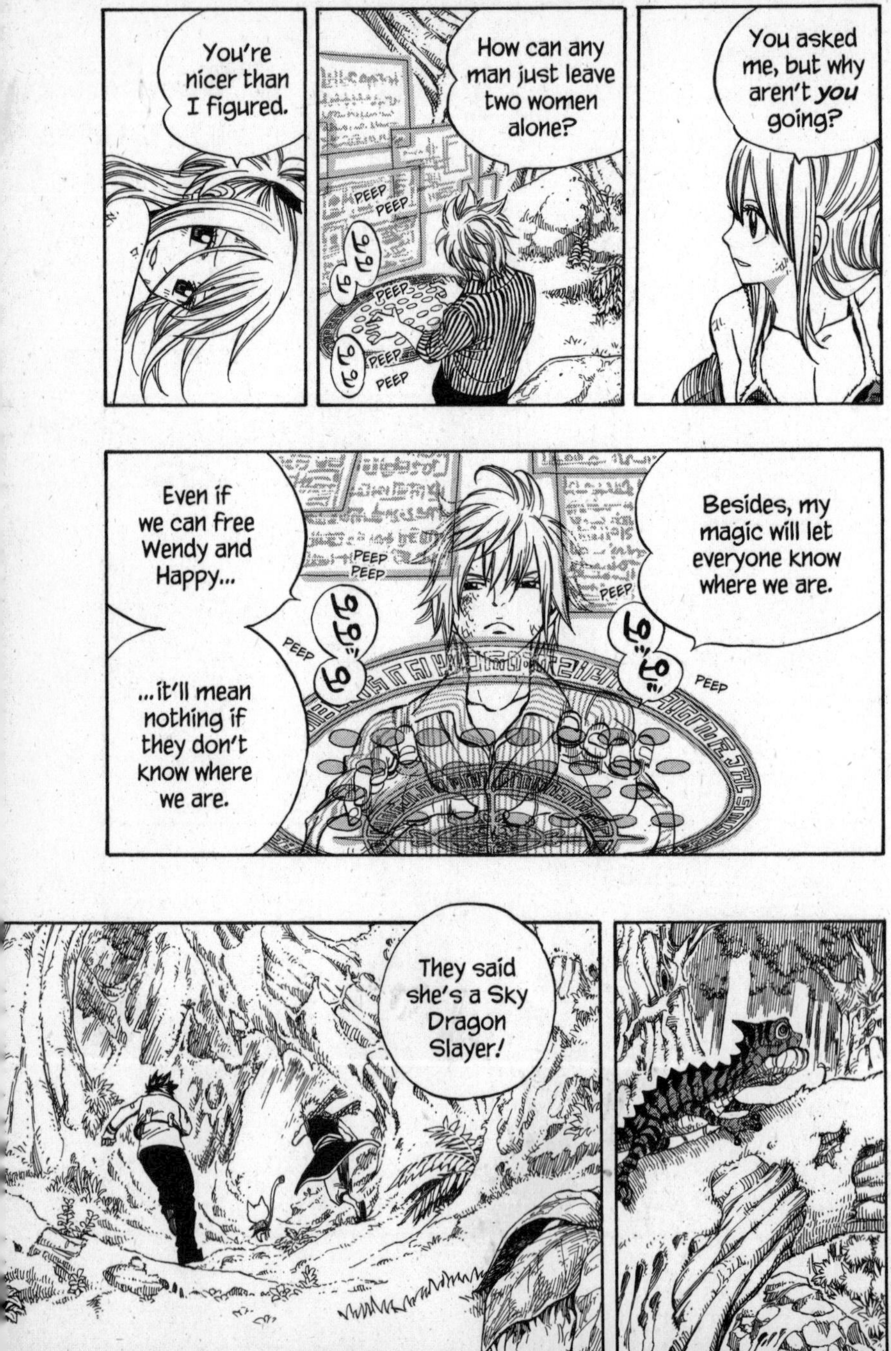
You asked me, but why aren't *you* going?
How can any man just leave two women alone?
PEEP PEEP
PEEP
PEEP
PEEP
You're nicer than I figured.
Even if we can free Wendy and Happy...
...it'll mean nothing if they don't know where we are.
Besides, my magic will let everyone know where we are.
PEEP PEEP
PEEP
PEEP
PEEP
They said she's a Sky Dragon Slayer!

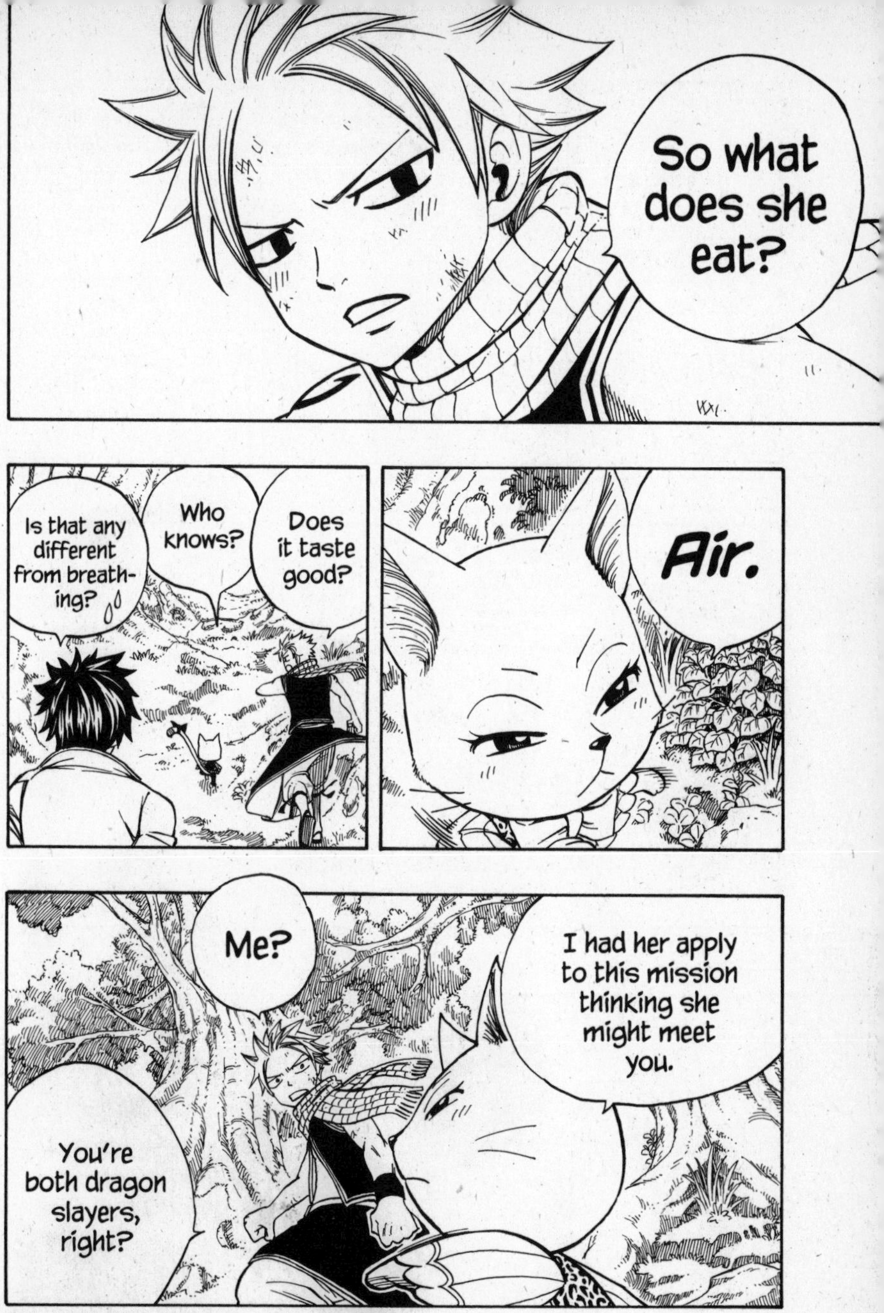
So what does she eat?
Air.
Does it taste good?
Who knows?
Is that any different from breathing?
I had her apply to this mission thinking she might meet you.
Me?
You're both dragon slayers, right?

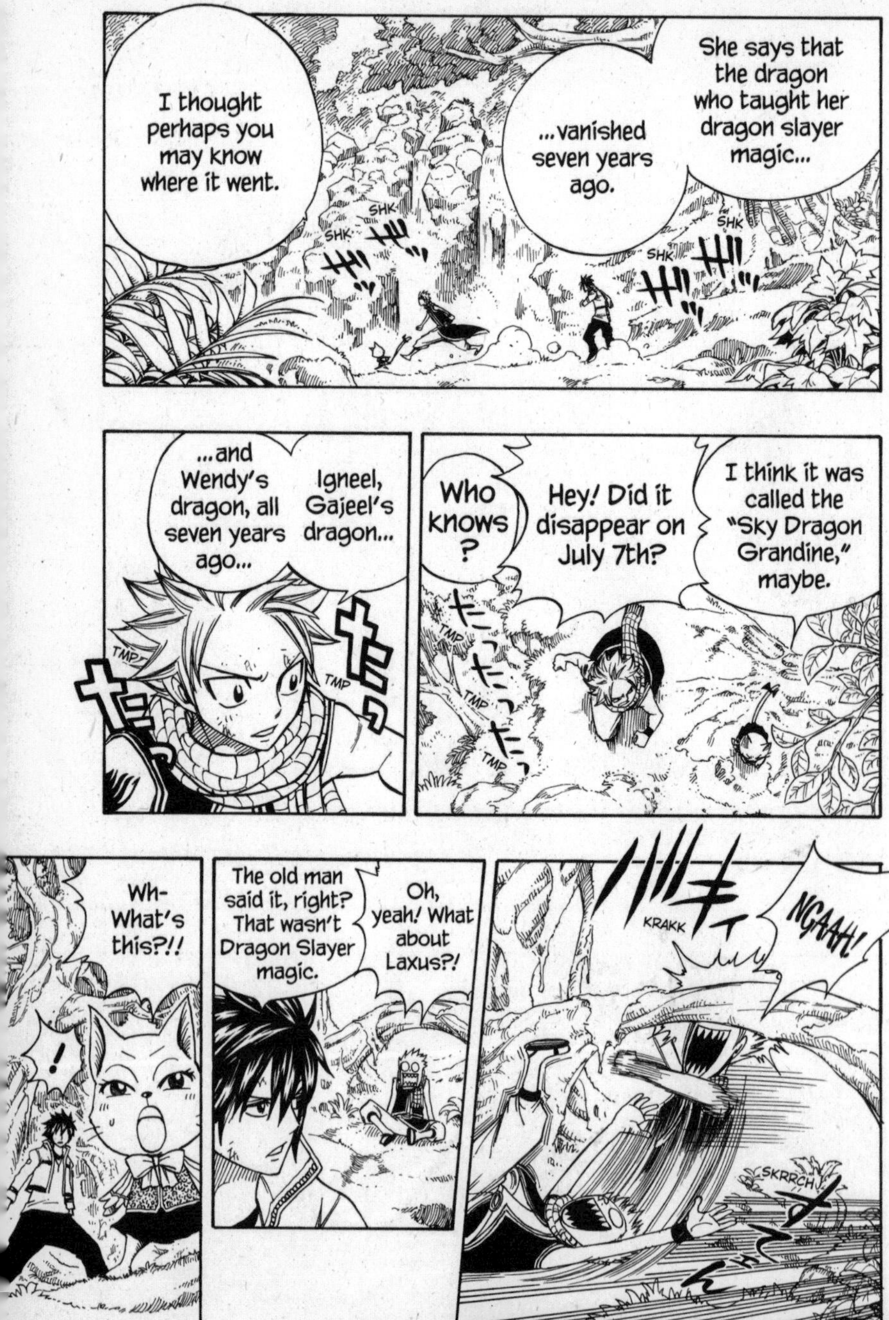
She says that the dragon who taught her dragon slayer magic...
...vanished seven years ago.
I thought perhaps you may know where it went.
SHK
SHK
SHK
SHK
I think it was called the "Sky Dragon Grandine," maybe.
Hey! Did it disappear on July 7th?
Who knows?
TMP
TMP
TMP
Igneel, Gajeel's dragon...
...and Wendy's dragon, all seven years ago...
TMP
TMP
NGAAH!
KRAKK
SKRRCH
Oh, yeah! What about Laxus?!
The old man said it, right? That wasn't Dragon Slayer magic.
Wh-What's this?!!
!

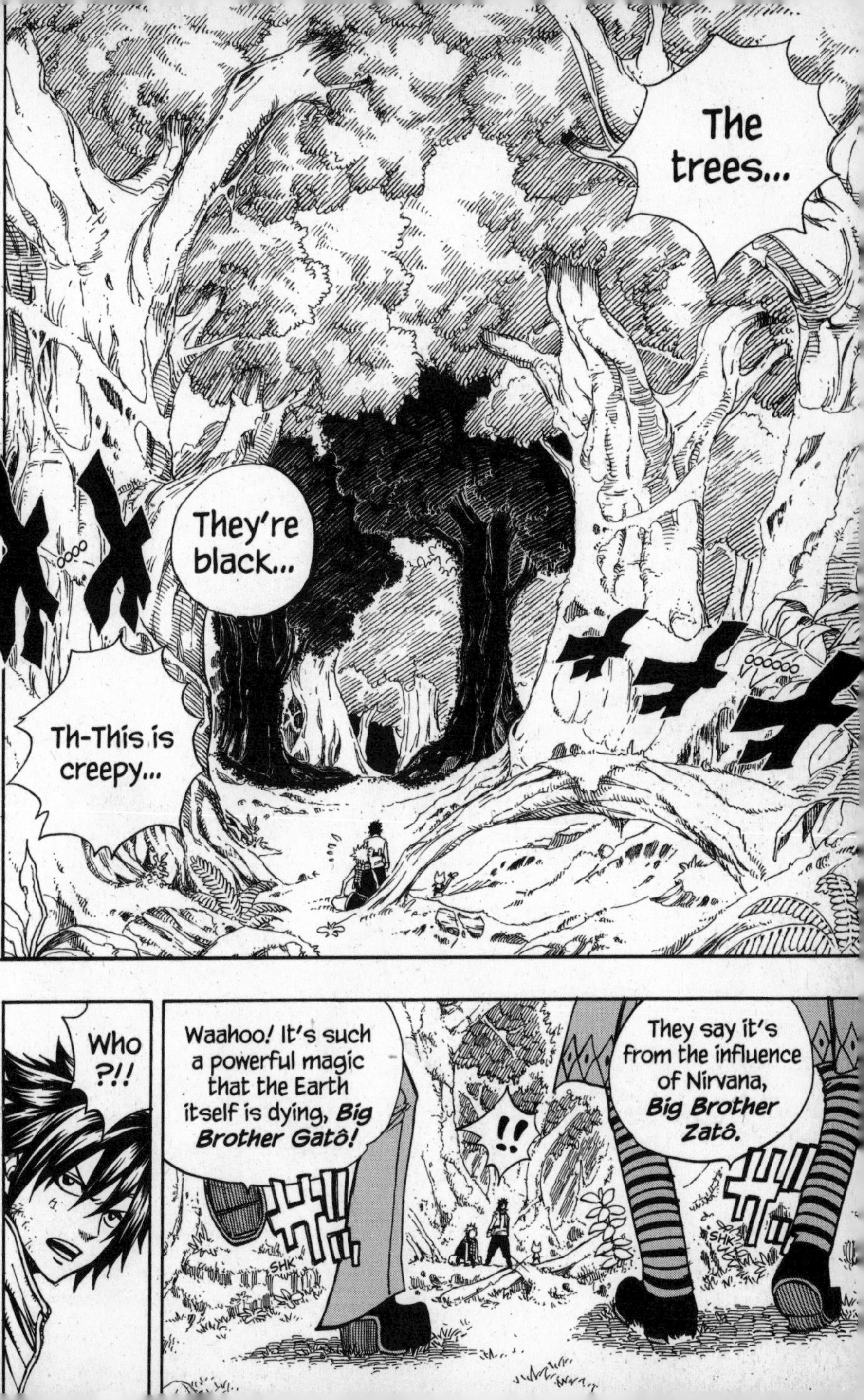
The trees...
They're black...
Th-This is creepy...
They say it's from the influence of Nirvana, *Big Brother Zatô.*
Waahoo! It's such a powerful magic that the Earth itself is dying, *Big Brother Gatô!*
!!
SHK
SHK
Who ?!!

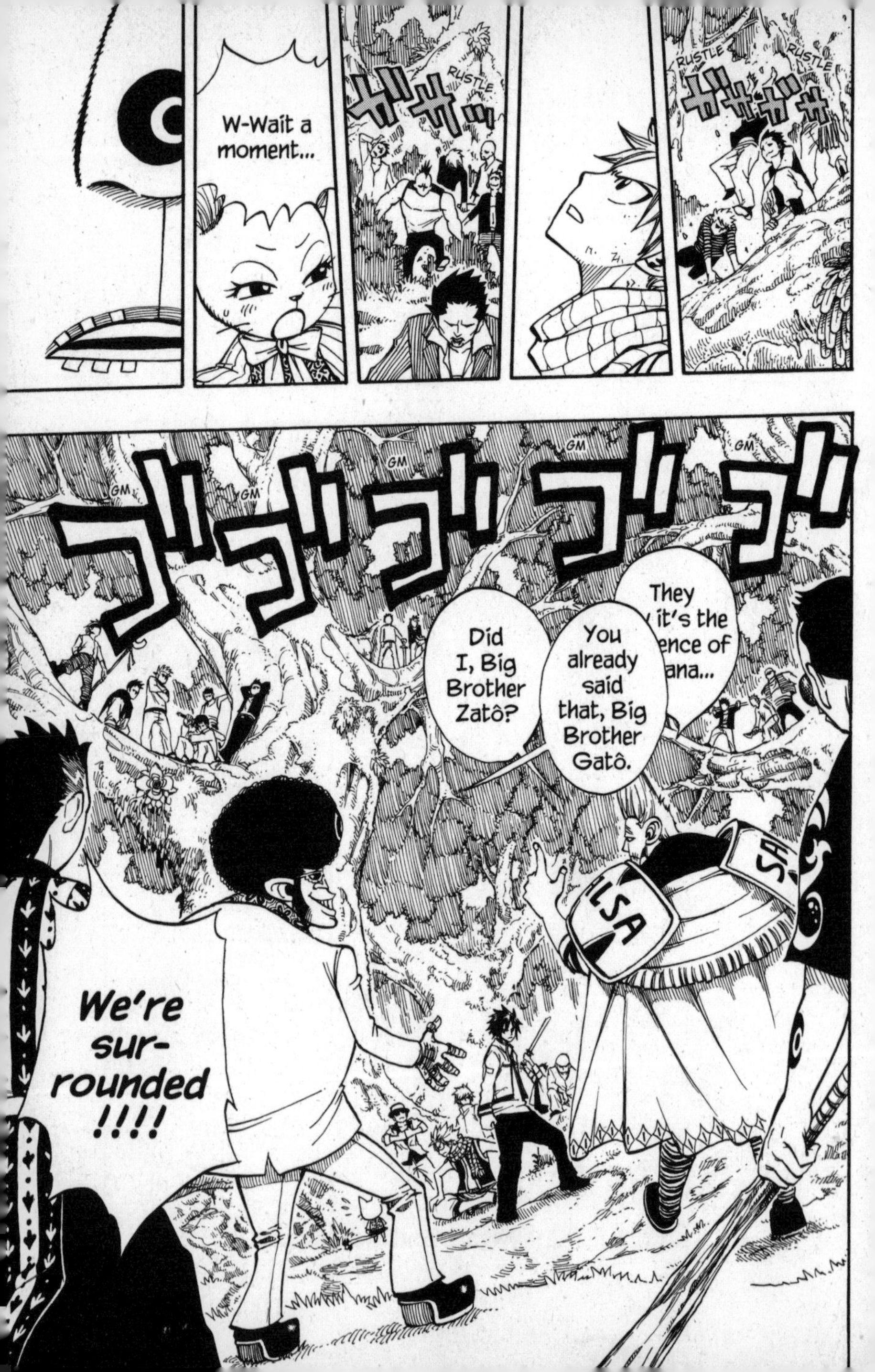
RUSTLE RUSTLE
ガサガサ
RUSTLE
ガサッ
W-Wait a moment...
GM GM GM GM GM
ゴゴゴゴ
They
y it's the
ence of
ana...
You already said that, Big Brother Gatô.
Did I, Big Brother Zatô?
We're sur-rounded!!!!

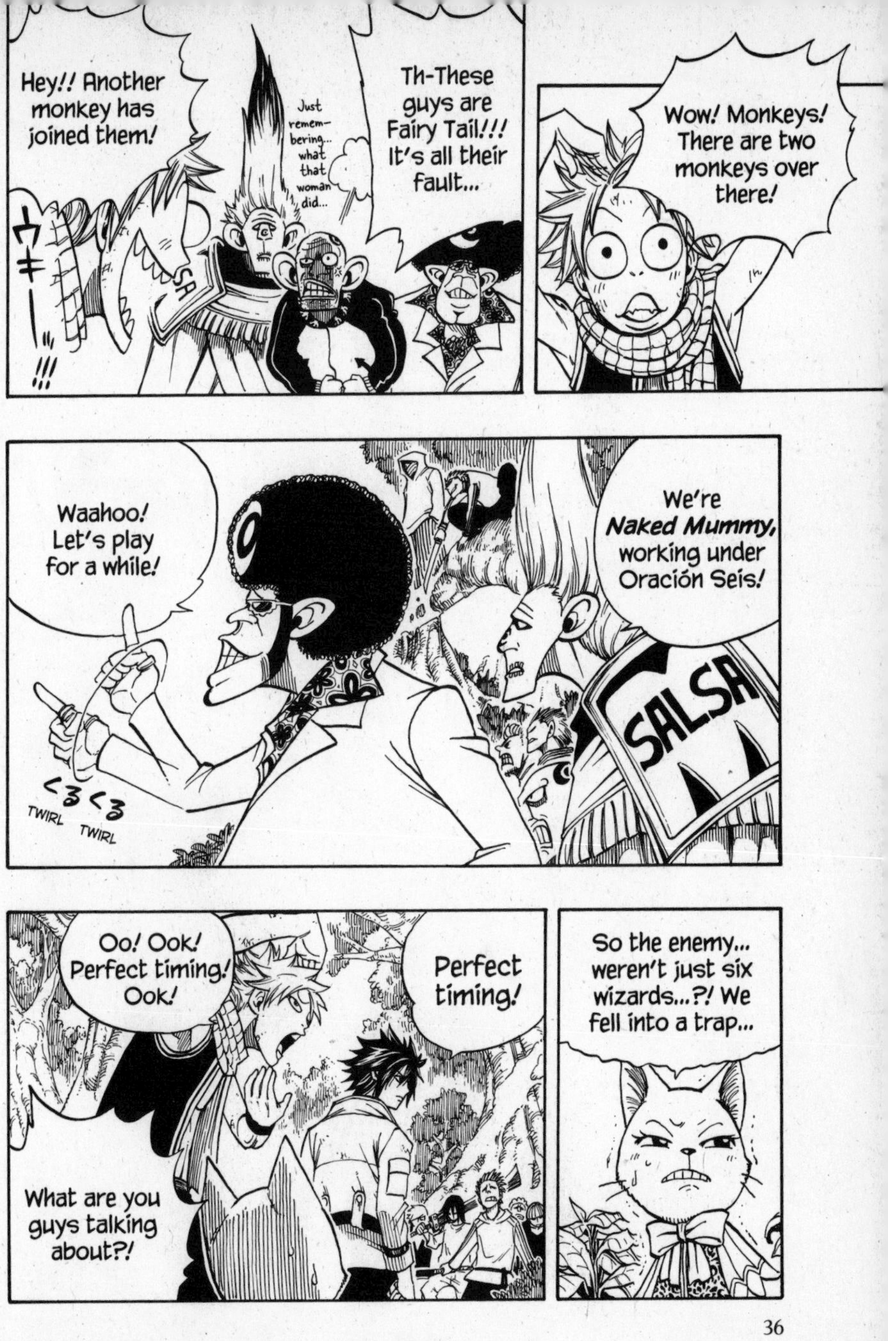
Wow! Monkeys! There are two monkeys over there!
Th-These guys are Fairy Tail!!! It's all their fault...
Just remembering... what that woman did...
Hey!! Another monkey has joined them!
ウキー!!!
SA
We're *Naked Mummy,* working under Oración Seis!
SALSA
Waahoo! Let's play for a while!
くるくる
TWIRL TWIRL
So the enemy... weren't just six wizards...?! We fell into a trap...
Perfect timing!
Oo! Ook! Perfect timing! Ook!
What are you guys talking about?!

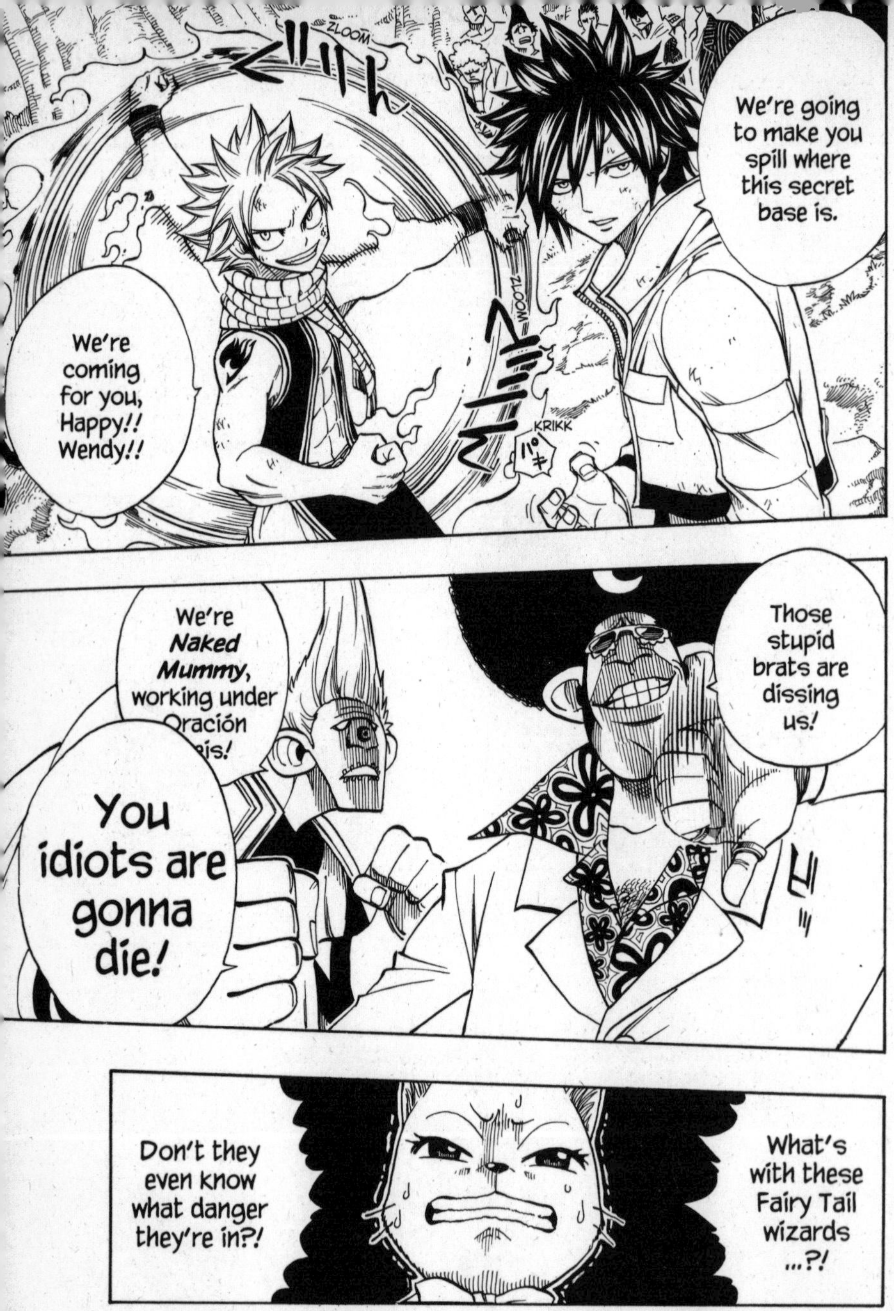
ZLOOM
We're going to make you spill where this secret base is.
ZLOOM
KRIKK
We're coming for you, Happy!! Wendy!!
Those stupid brats are dissing us!
We're *Naked Mummy*, working under Oración
You idiots are gonna die!
What's with these Fairy Tail wizards ...?!
Don't they even know what danger they're in?!

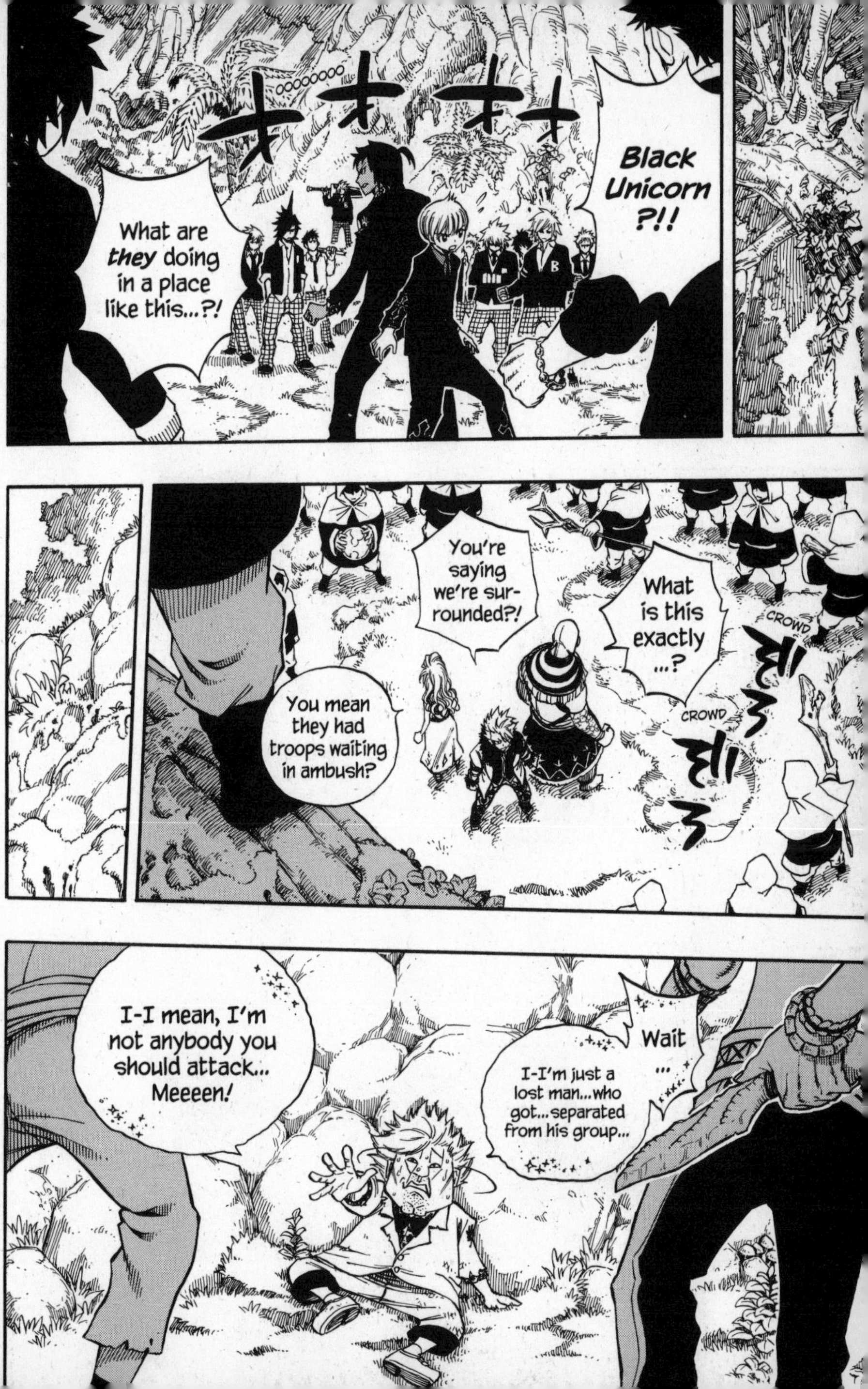
OOOOOOOOO
Black Unicorn ?!!
What are *they* doing in a place like this...?!
What is this exactly ...?
CROWD
CROWD
You're saying we're surrounded?!
You mean they had troops waiting in ambush?
Wait ...
I-I'm just a lost man...who got...separated from his group...
I-I mean, I'm not anybody you should attack... Meeeen!

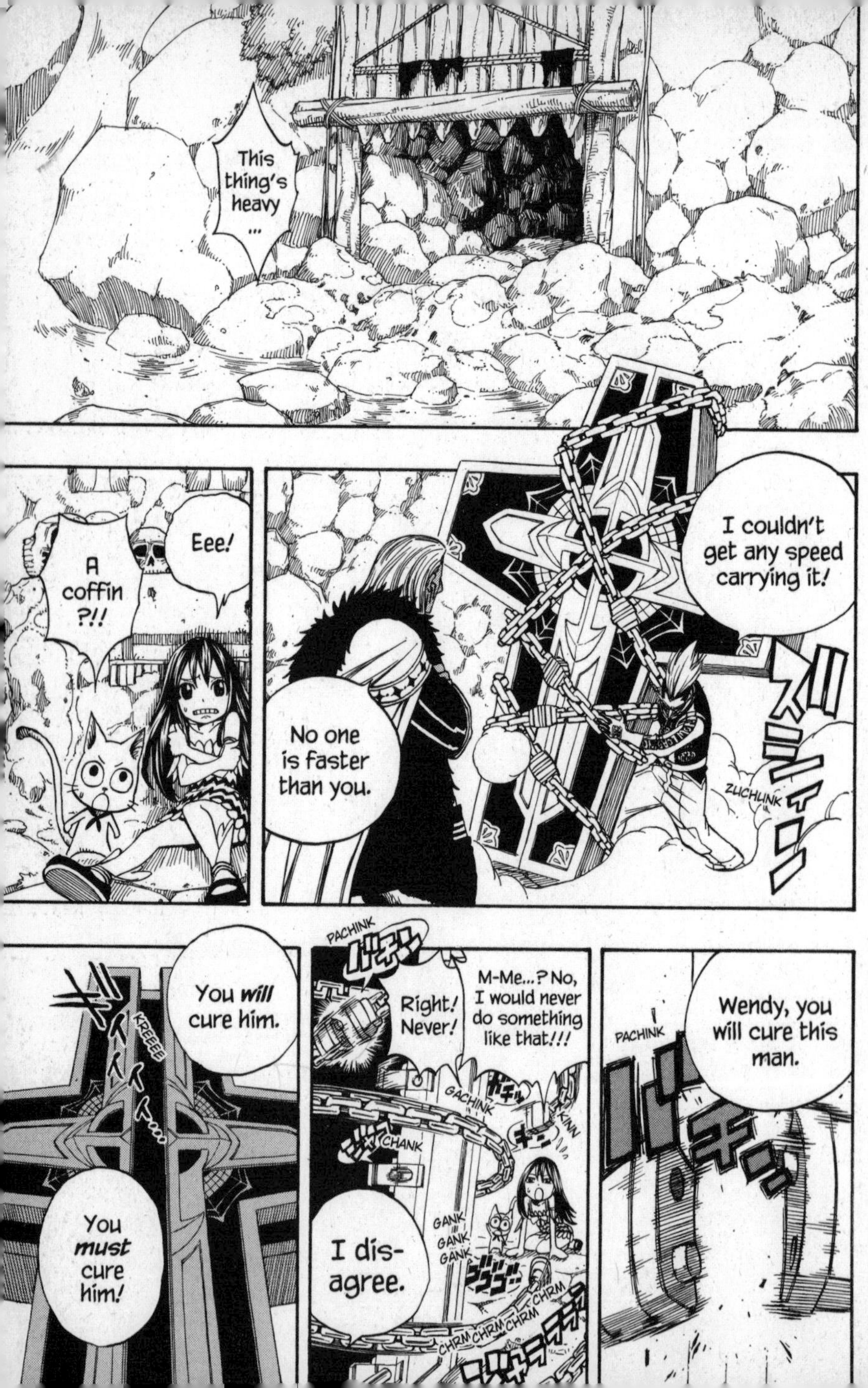
This thing's heavy ...
I couldn't get any speed carrying it!
ZUCHLINK
No one is faster than you.
Eee!
A coffin ?!!
Wendy, you will cure this man.
PACHINK
M-Me...? No, I would never do something like that!!!
Right! Never!
PACHINK
GACHINK
KINN
CHANK
GANK GANK GANK
CHRM CHRM CHRM CHRM
I dis- agree.
You *will* cure him.
KREEEEE
You **must** cure him!

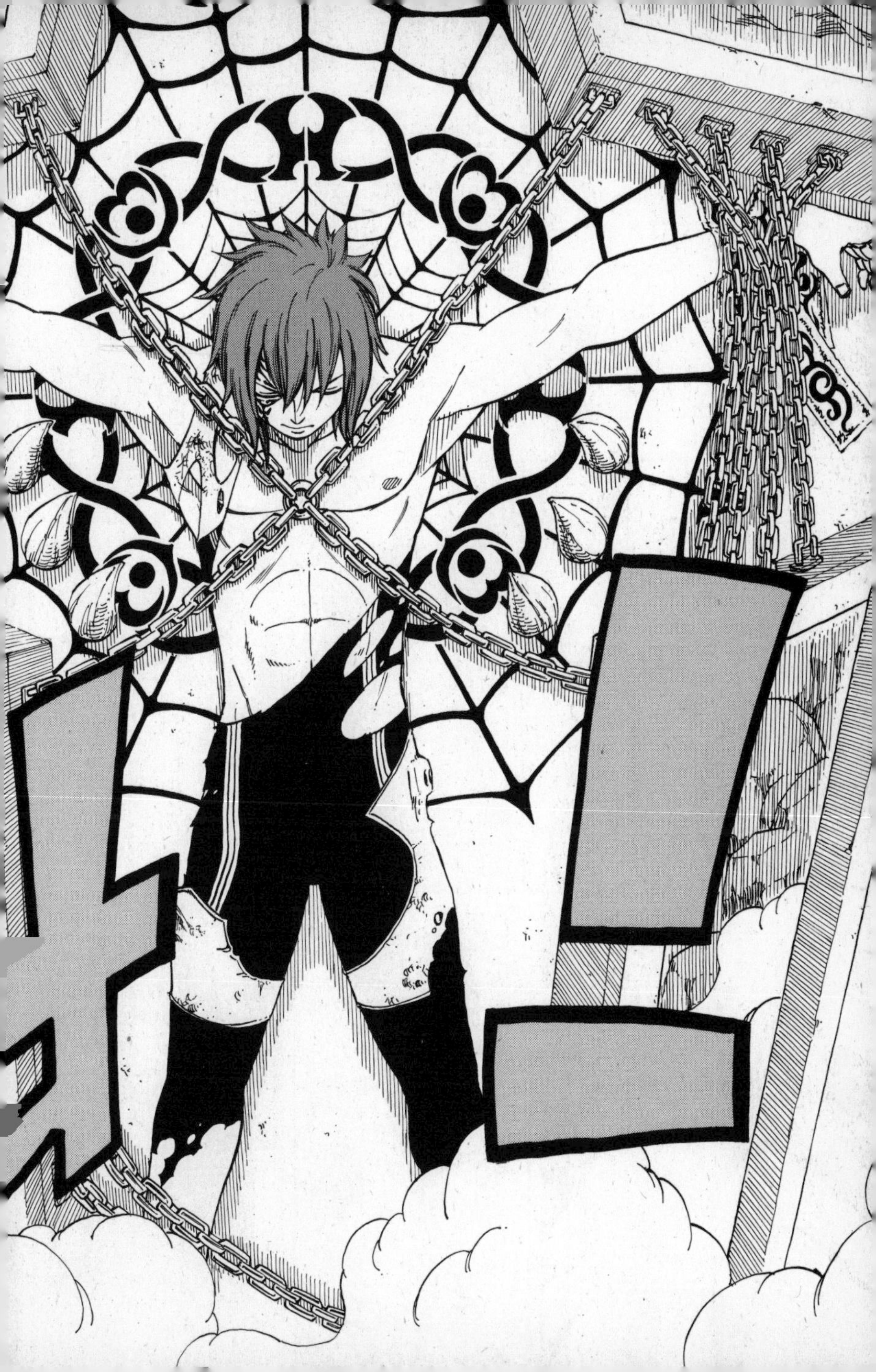

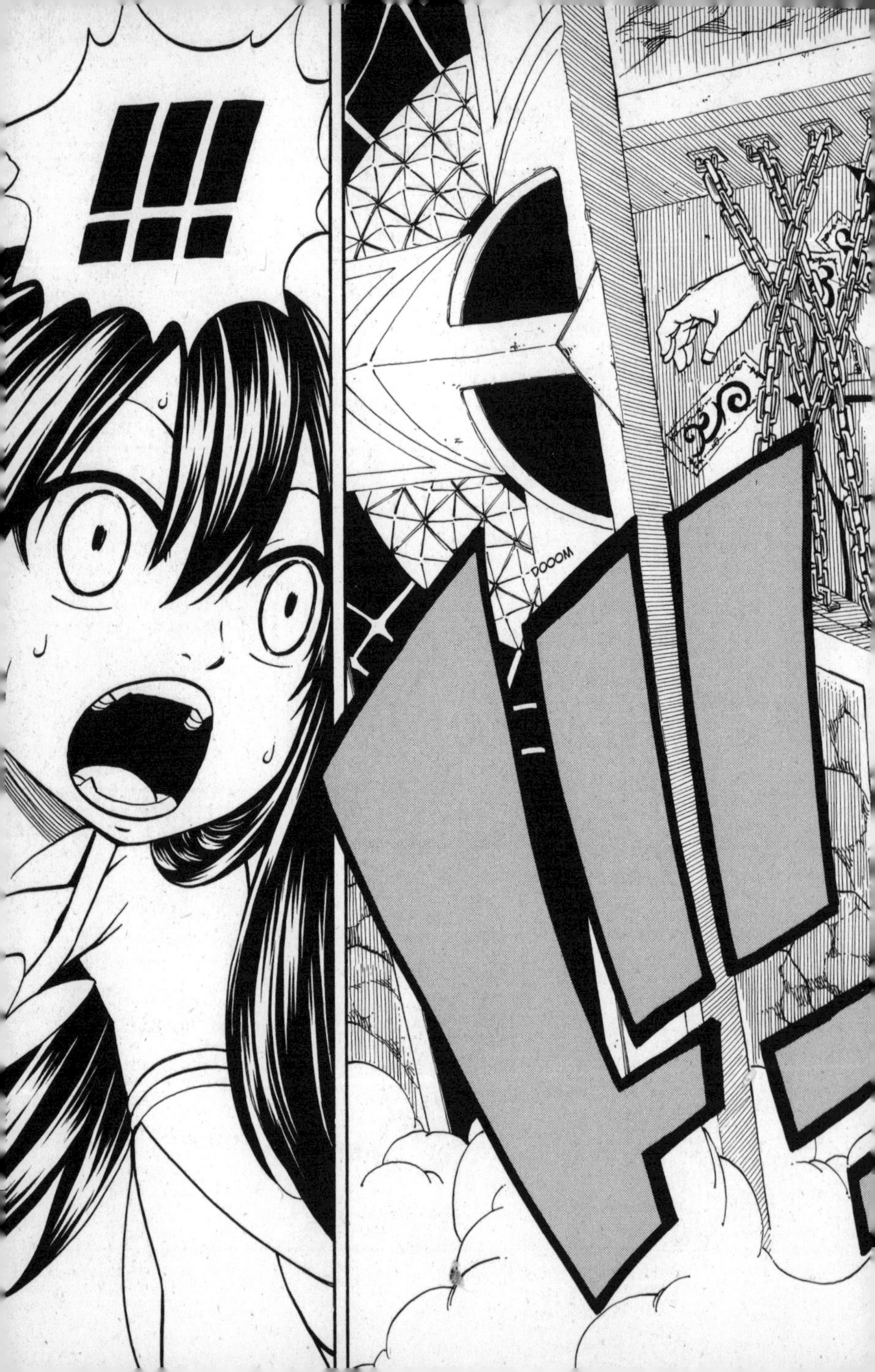
DOOOM
!!!

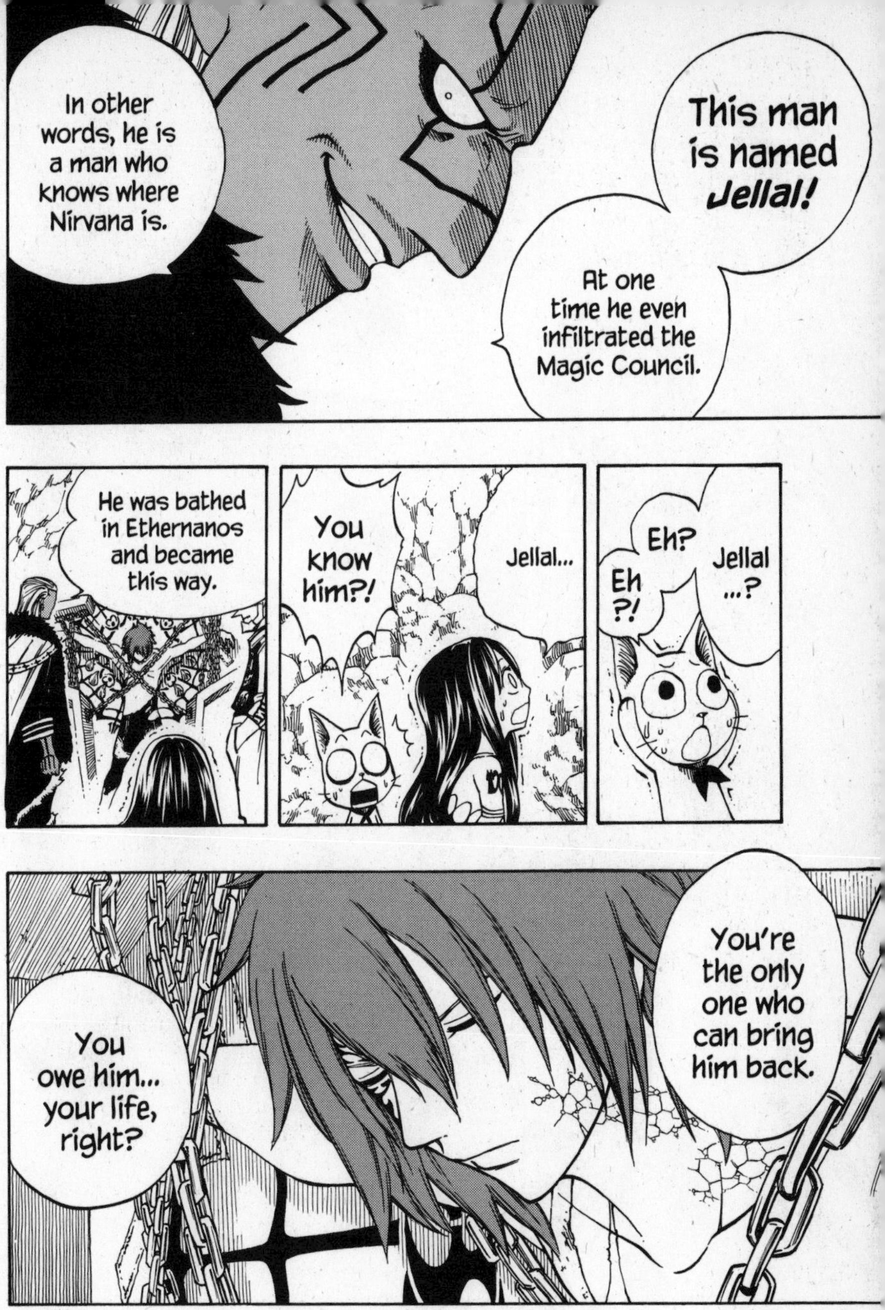
This man is named *Jellal!*
At one time he even infiltrated the Magic Council.
In other words, he is a man who knows where Nirvana is.
Jellal ...?
Eh?
Eh ?!
Jellal...
You know him?!
He was bathed in Ethernanos and became this way.
You're the only one who can bring him back.
You owe him... your life, right?

FAIRY TAIL

フェアリーテイル

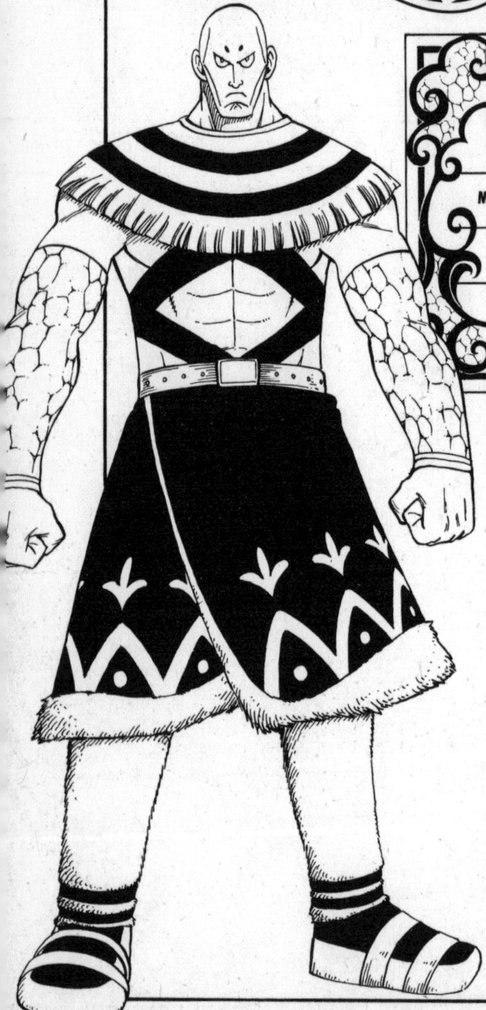

LAMIA SCALE

Name: Jura Neekis **Age:** 27

Magic: Master of All Earth Magics

Likes: His guild

Dislikes: Green peas

WIZARD GUILD X633

Remarks

Jura is considered the ace of the Lamia Scale guild and one of the Ten Wizard Saints, the ten best wizards on the continent. He is extremely powerful in Earth-type Magics–because he can take the softest sand and change it into iron-hard rock, he has been given the name Iron Rock Jura. He loves his guild and looks after its members, including Lyon and Sherry. Once while snacking on green peas as a child, he accidentally popped a green caterpillar into his mouth and can no longer stomach green peas.

Chapter 137, The Girl and the Ghost

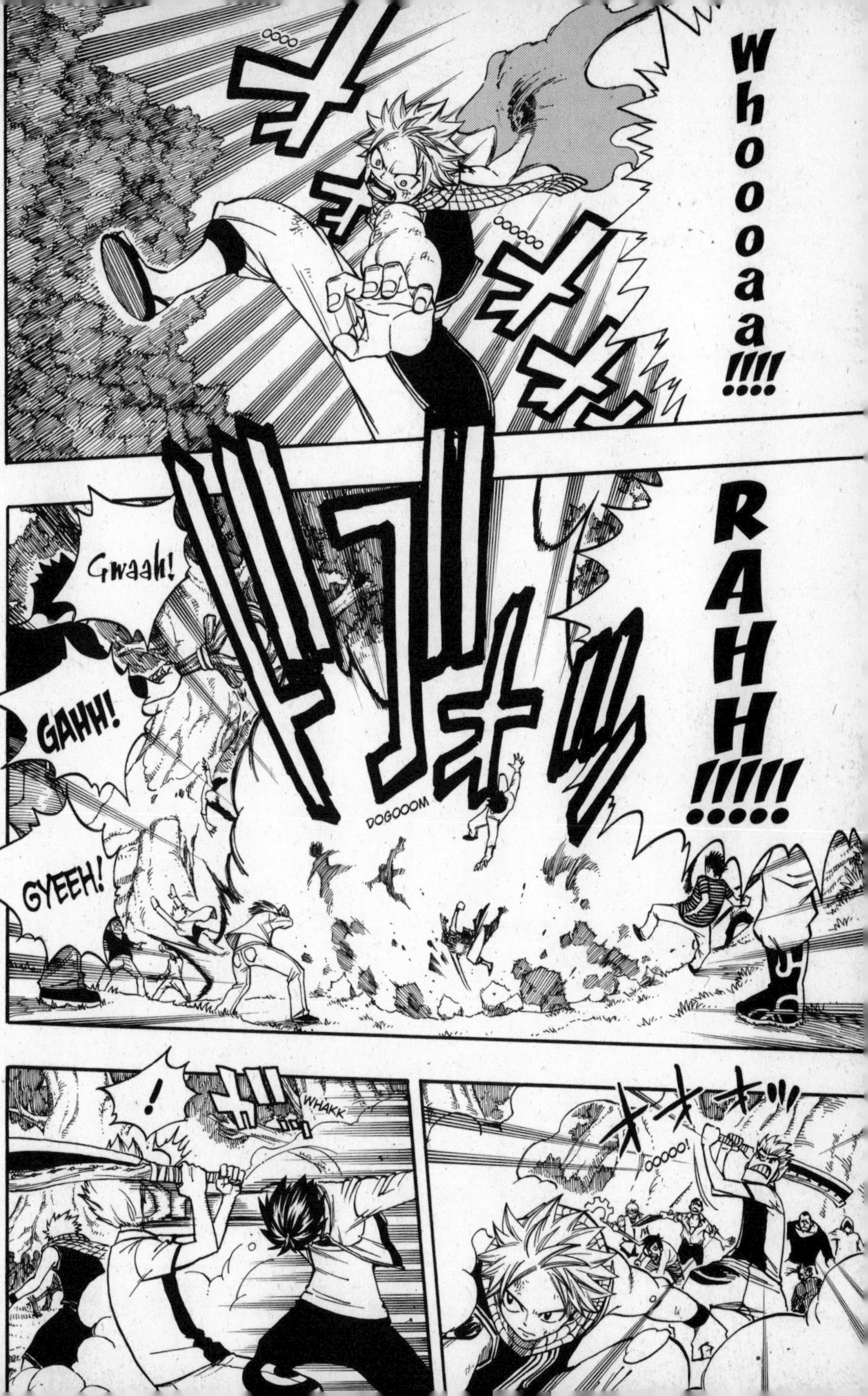
oooo
Whoooaa!!!!
oooooo
RAHH!!!!!
Gwaah!
GAHH!
GYEEH!
DOGOOOM
ooooo!
!
WHAKK

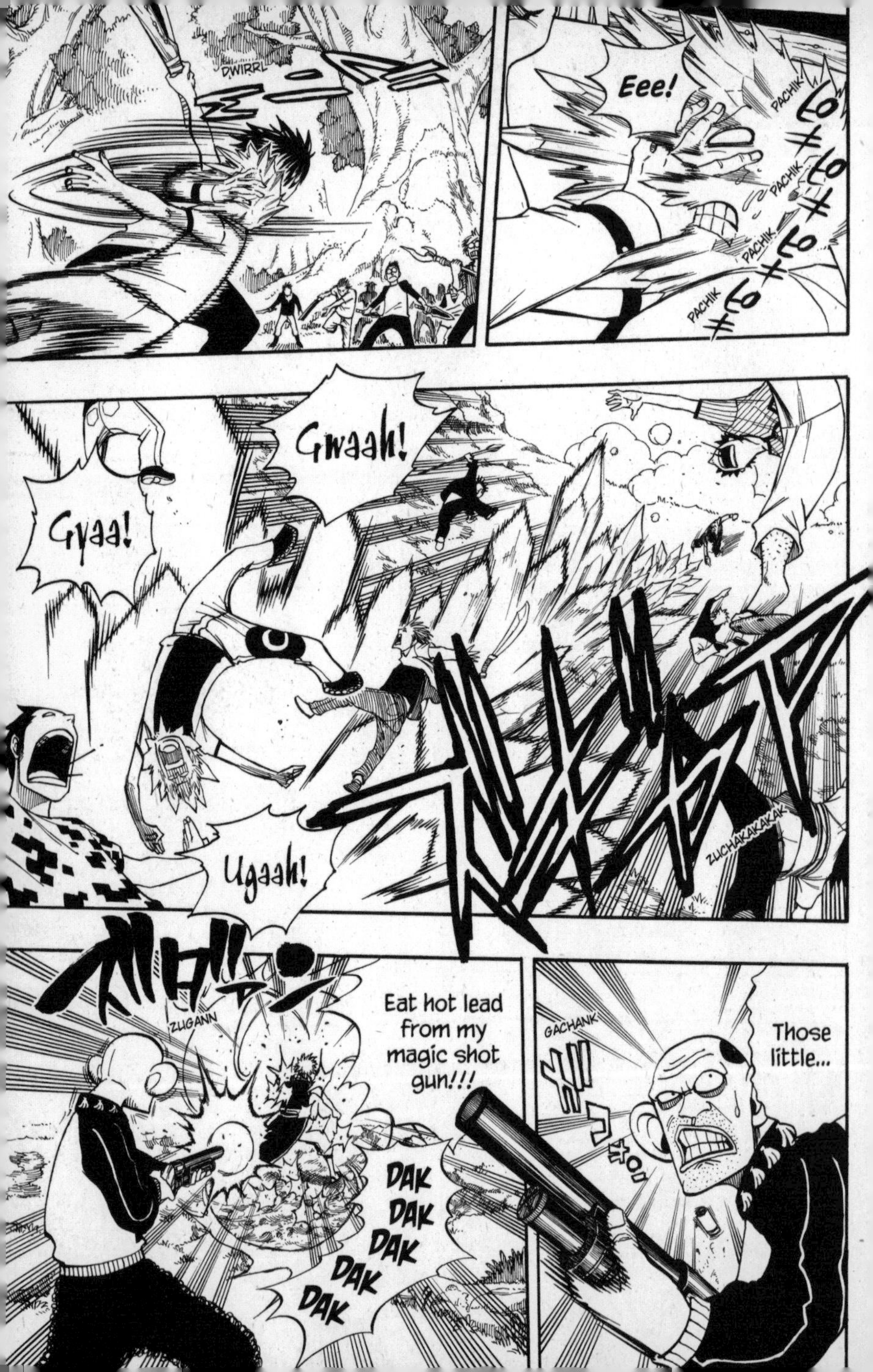
Eee!
PACHIK
PACHIK
PACHIK
PACHIK
DWIRRL
ZUCHAKAKAKAK
Gwaah!
Gyaa!
Ugaah!
Those little...
GACHANK
Eat hot lead from my magic shot gun!!!
ZUGANN
DAK
DAK
DAK
DAK
DAK

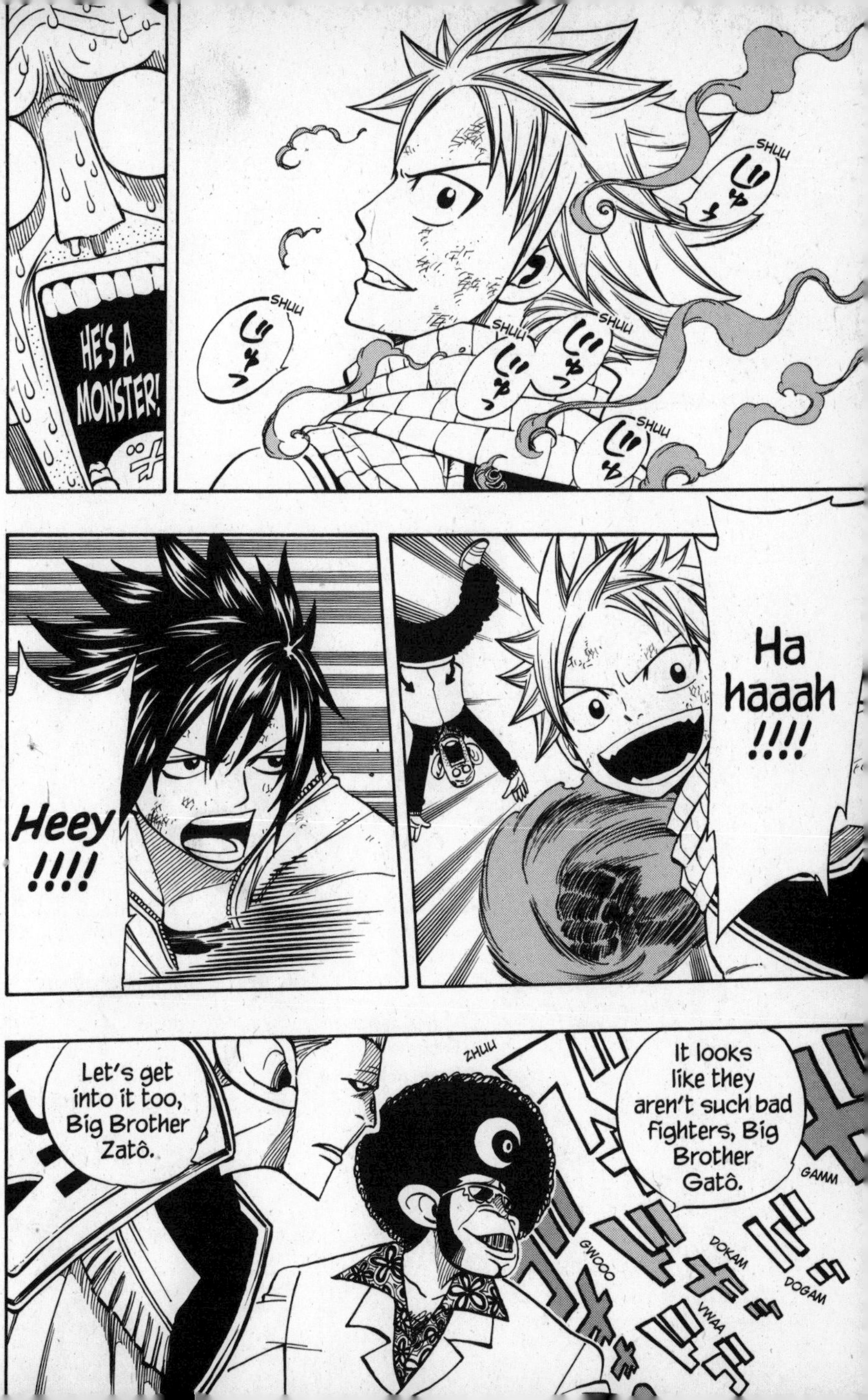
SHUU
SHUU
SHUU
SHUU
SHUU
HE'S A MONSTER!
Ha haaah!!!!
Heey!!!!
ZHUU
It looks like they aren't such bad fighters, Big Brother Gatô.
Let's get into it too, Big Brother Zatô.
GAMM
DOKAM
DOGAM
VWAA
GWOOO

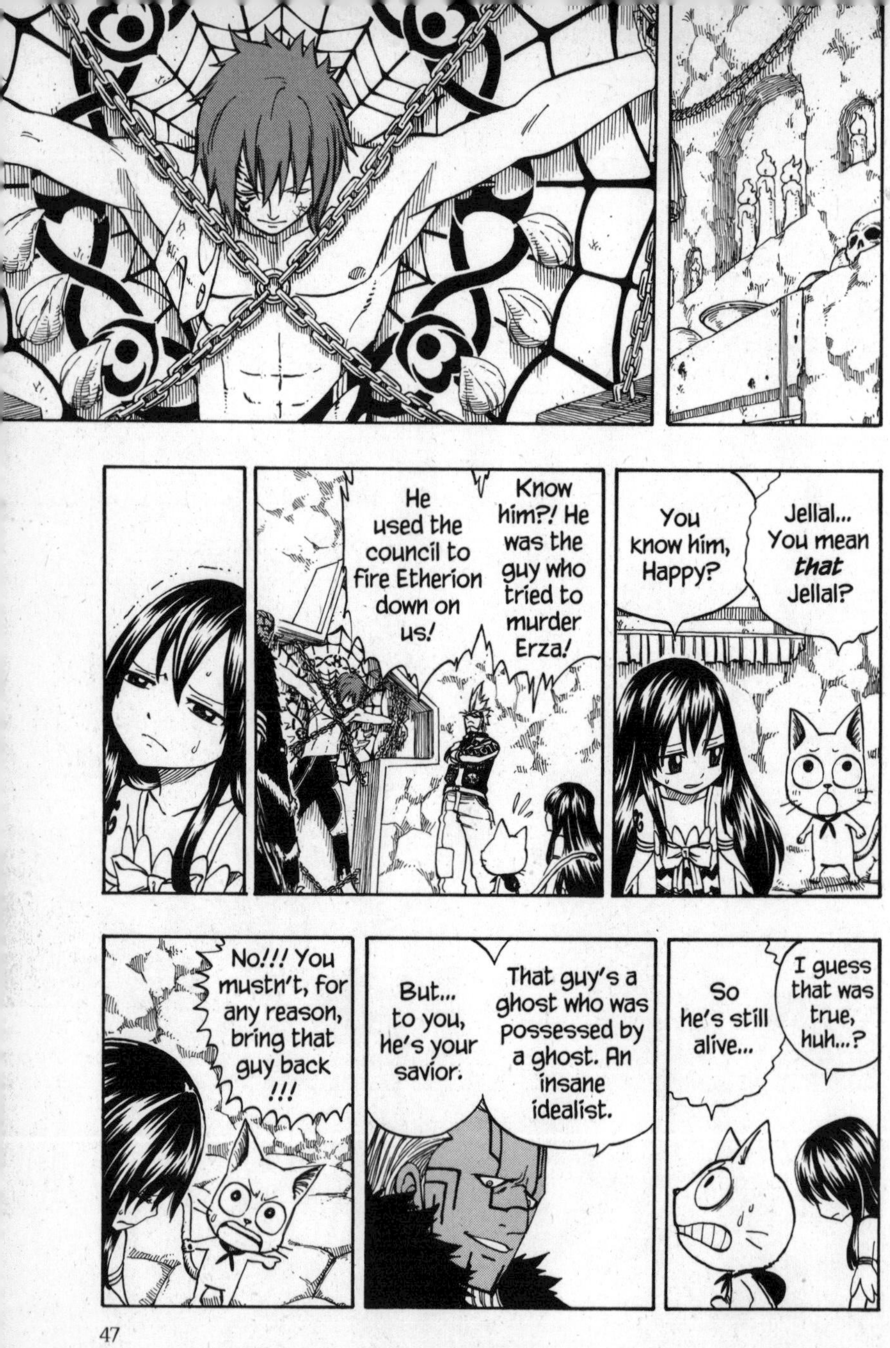
Jellal... You mean *that* Jellal?
You know him, Happy?
Know him?! He was the guy who tried to murder Erza!
He used the council to fire Etherion down on us!
I guess that was true, huh...?
So he's still alive...
That guy's a ghost who was possessed by a ghost. An insane idealist.
But... to you, he's your savior.
No!!! You mustn't, for any reason, bring that guy back!!!

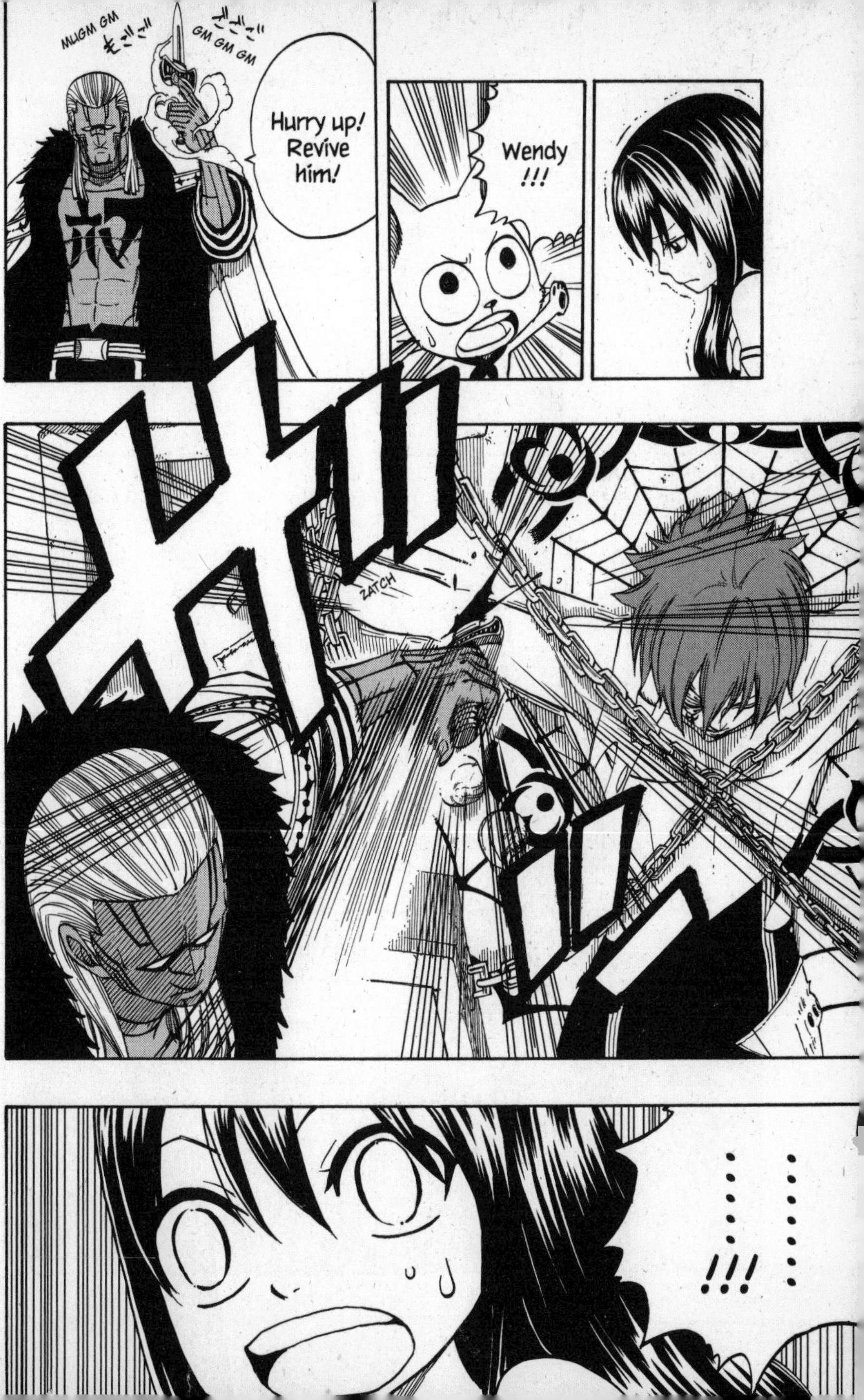
Wendy !!!
MUGM GM
GM GM GM
Hurry up! Revive him!
ZATCH
......!!!

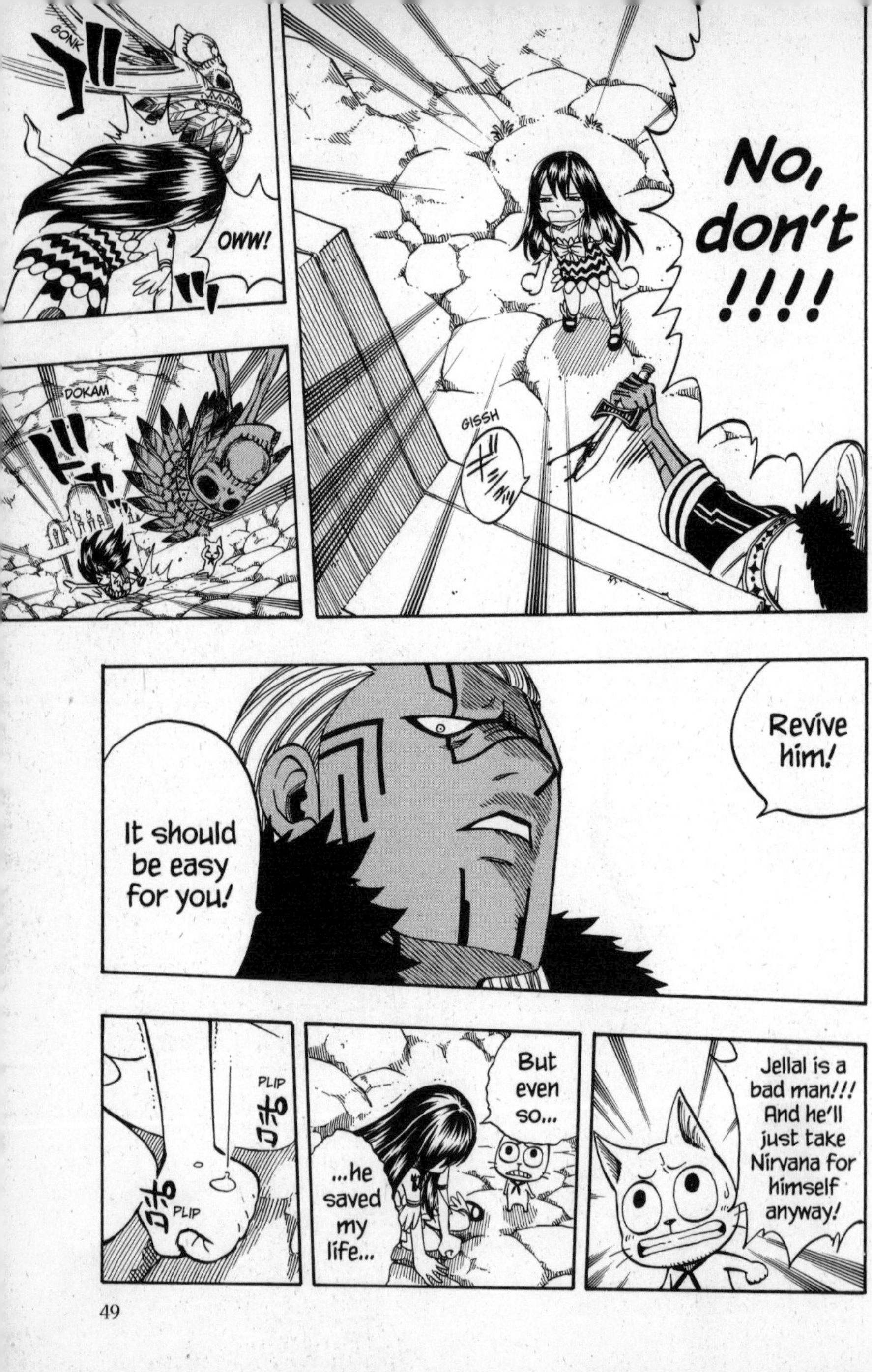
No, don't !!!!
GISSH
GONK
OWW!
DOKAM
Revive him!
It should be easy for you!
Jellal is a bad man!!! And he'll just take Nirvana for himself anyway!
But even so...
...he saved my life...
PLIP
PLIP

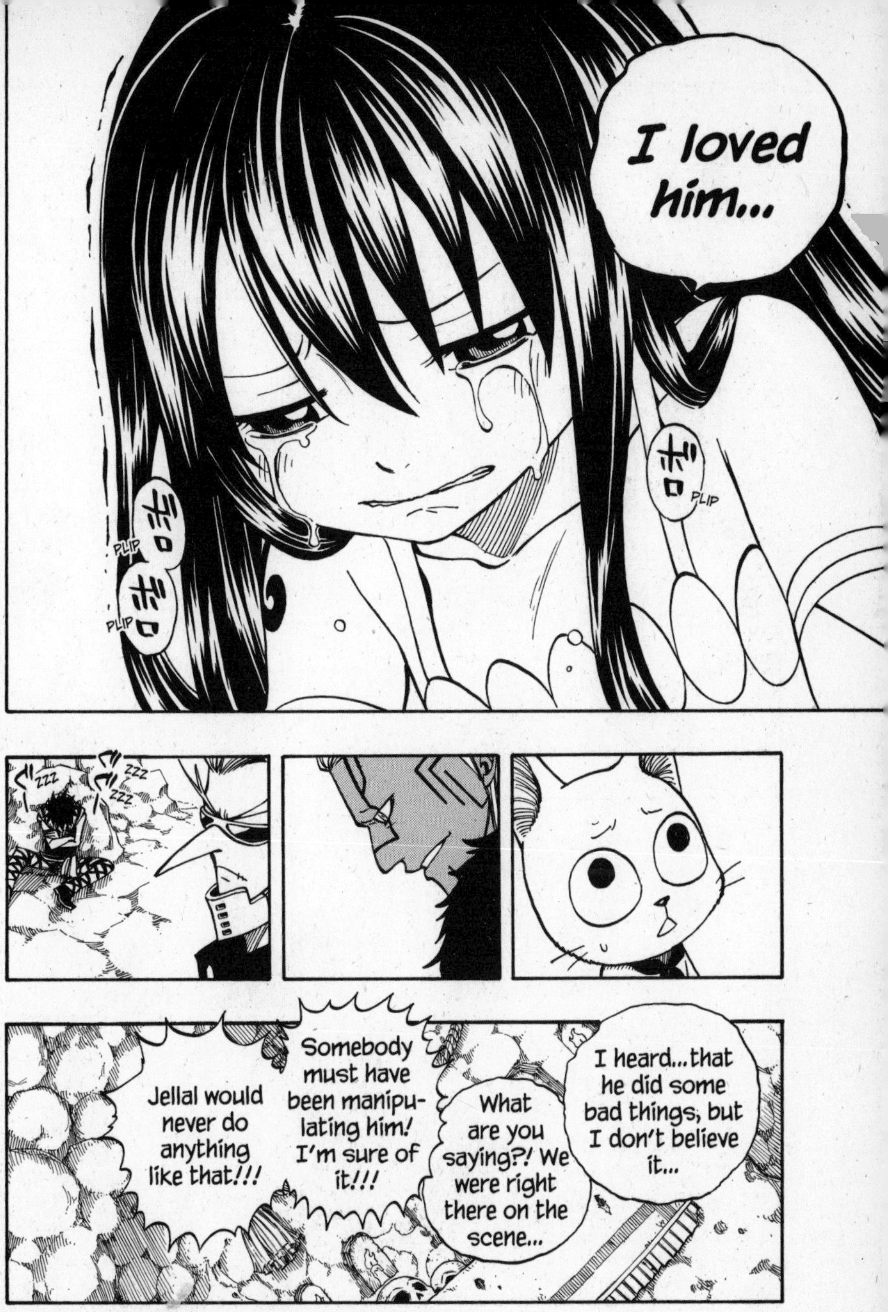
I loved him...
ボロ
PLIP
ボロ
PLIP
ボロ
PLIP
ZZZ
ZZZ
ZZZ
I heard...that he did some bad things, but I don't believe it...
What are you saying?! We were right there on the scene...
Somebody must have been manipulating him! I'm sure of it!!!
Jellal would never do anything like that!!!

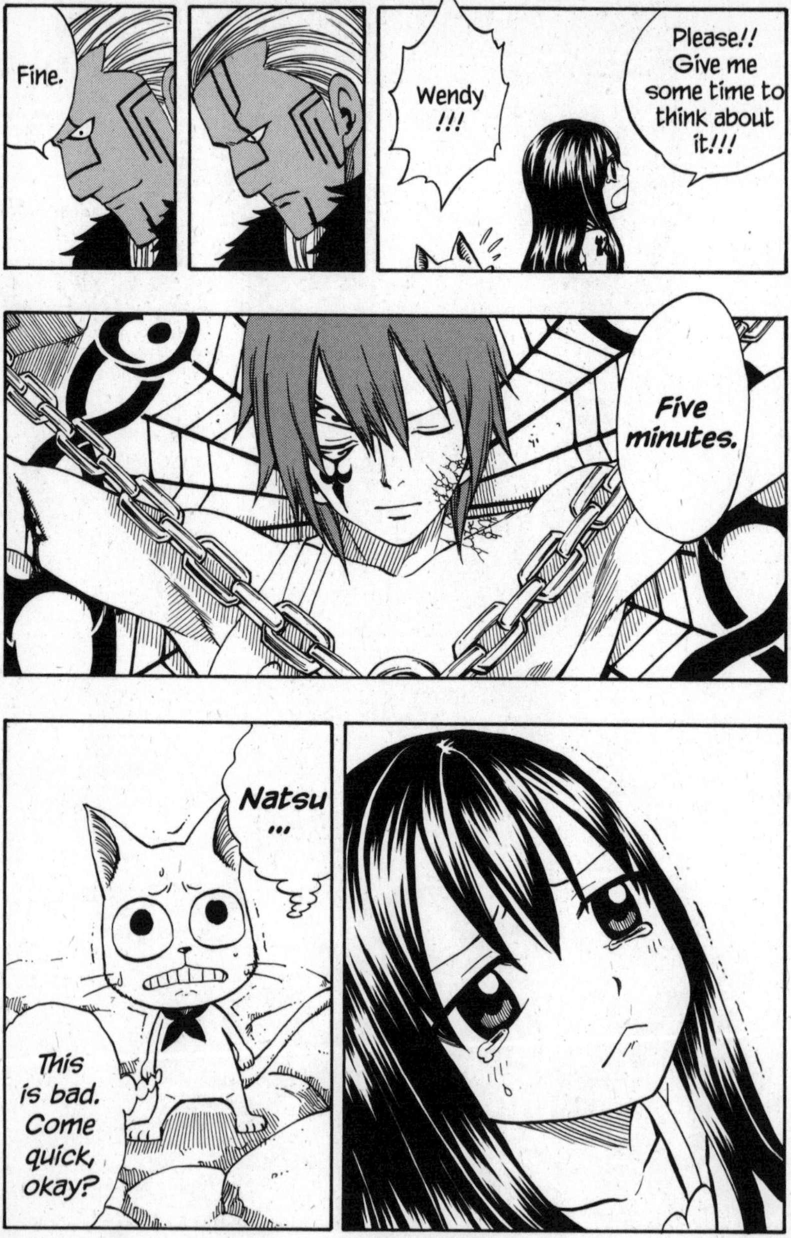
Please!! Give me some time to think about it!!!
Wendy !!!
Fine.
Five minutes.
Natsu ...
This is bad. Come quick, okay?

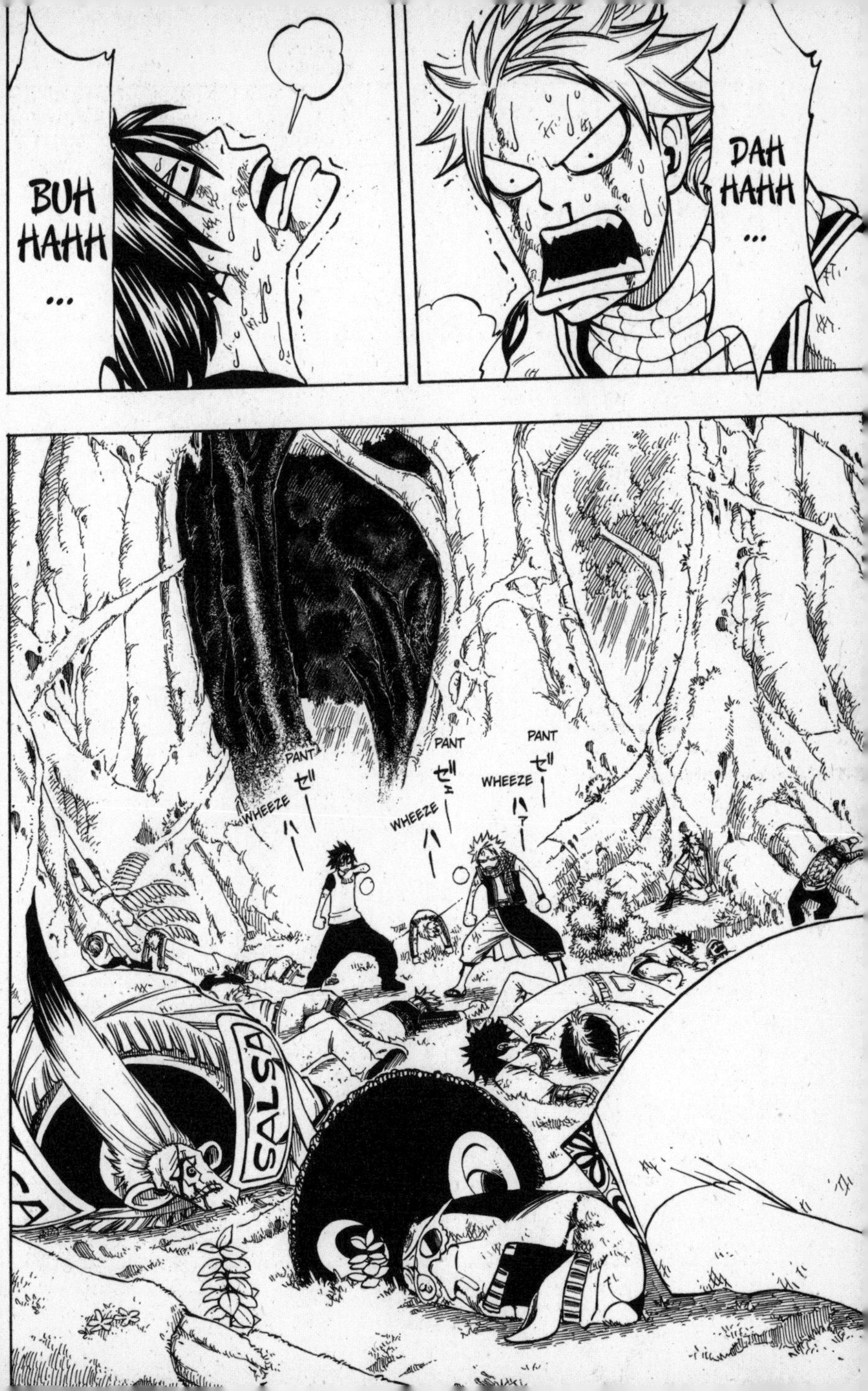
DAH HAHH ...
BUH HAHH ...
PANT
ゼー
WHEEZE
ハァー
PANT
ゼェ
WHEEZE
ハー
PANT
ゼー
WHEEZE
ハー
SALSA

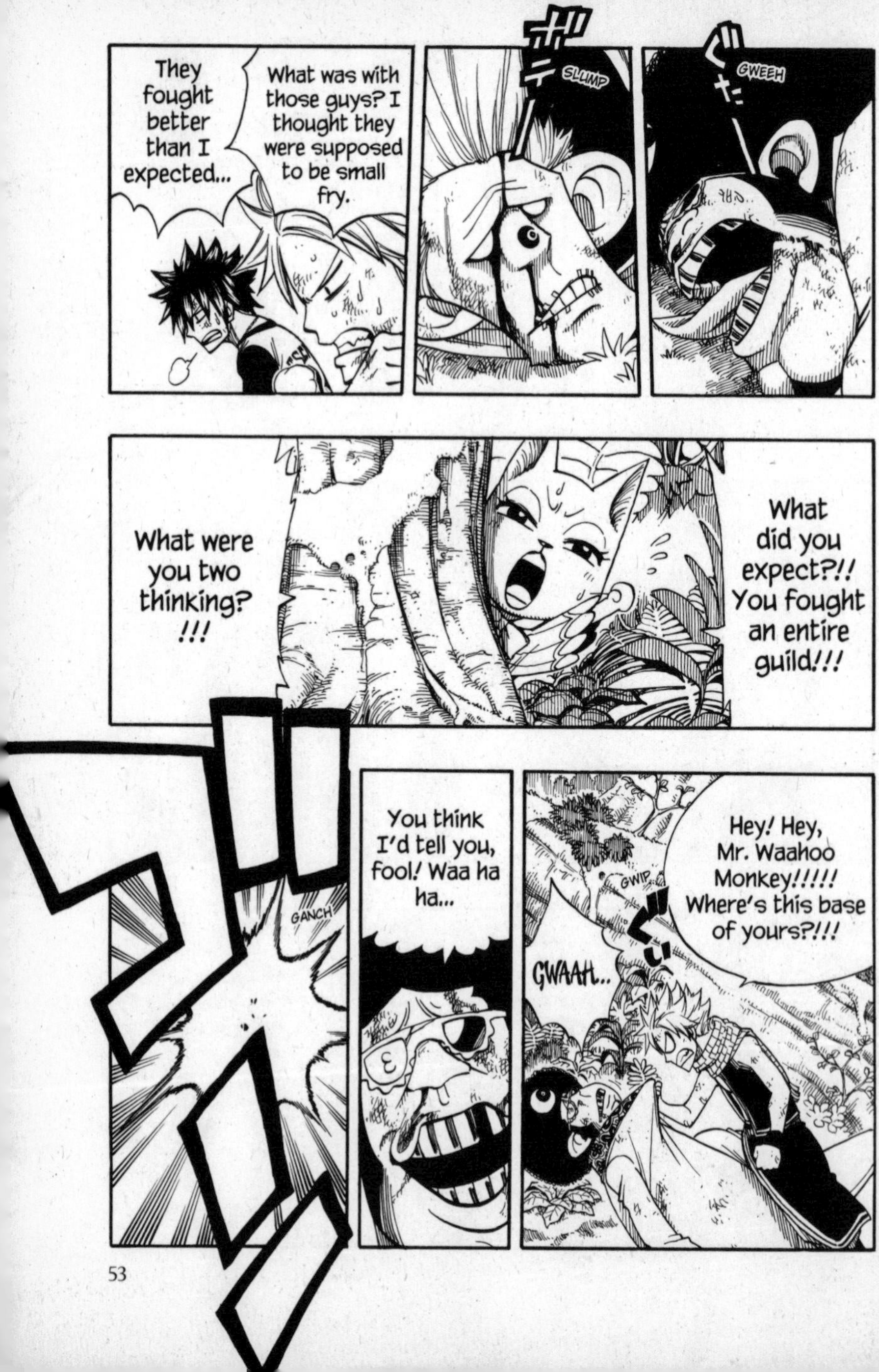
GWEEH
SLUMP
What was with those guys? I thought they were supposed to be small fry.
They fought better than I expected...
What did you expect?!! You fought an entire guild!!!
What were you two thinking?!!!
Hey! Hey, Mr. Waahoo Monkey!!!!! Where's this base of yours?!!!
GWIP
GWAAH...
You think I'd tell you, fool! Waa ha ha...
GANCH

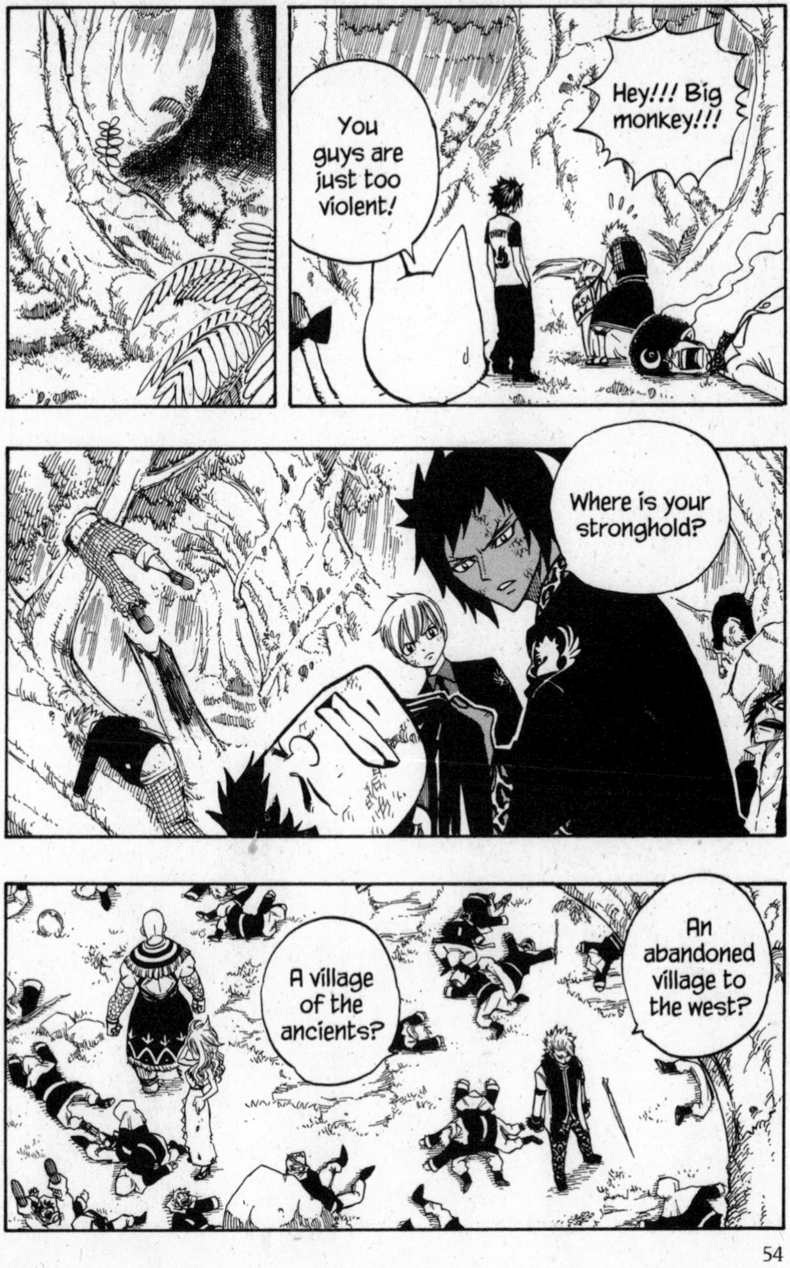
Hey!!! Big monkey!!!
You guys are just too violent!
Where is your stronghold?
An abandoned village to the west?
A village of the ancients?

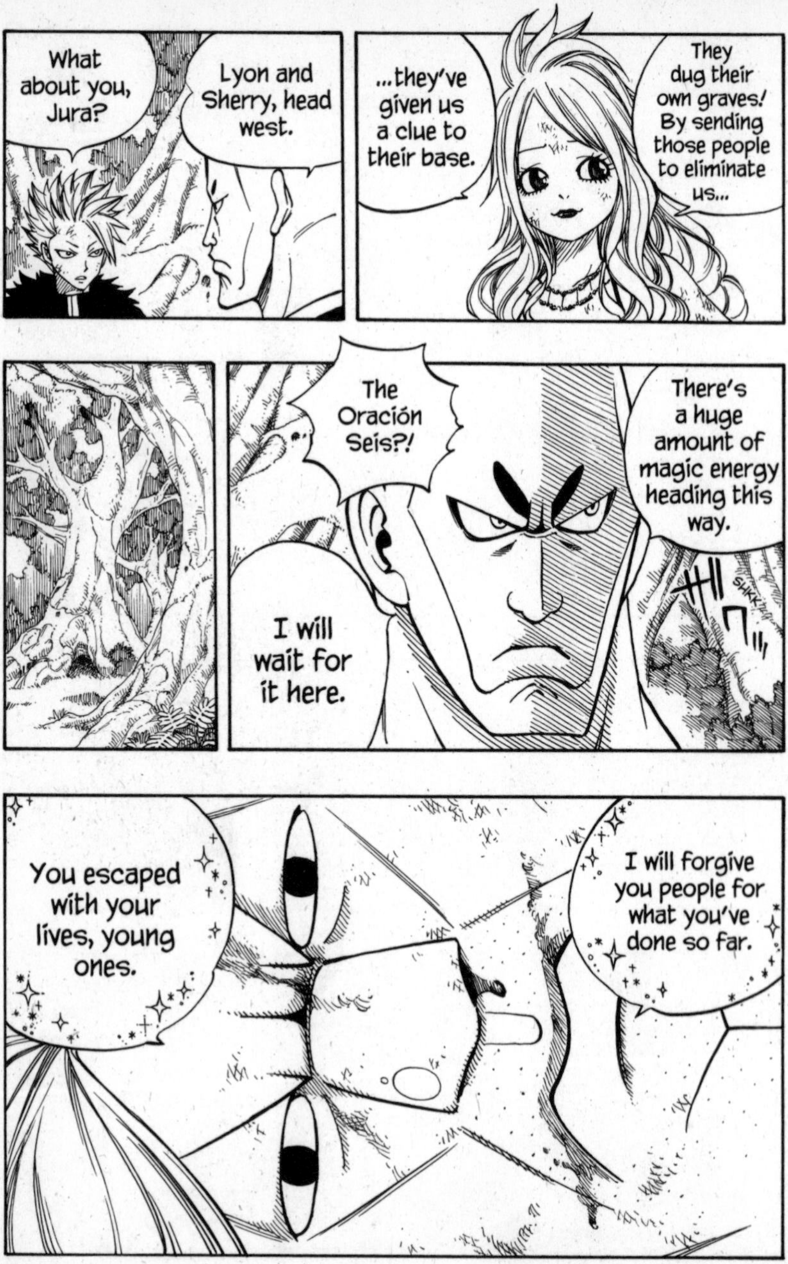
They dug their own graves! By sending those people to eliminate us...
...they've given us a clue to their base.
Lyon and Sherry, head west.
What about you, Jura?
There's a huge amount of magic energy heading this way.
SHKK
The Oración Seis?!
I will wait for it here.
I will forgive you people for what you've done so far.
You escaped with your lives, young ones.

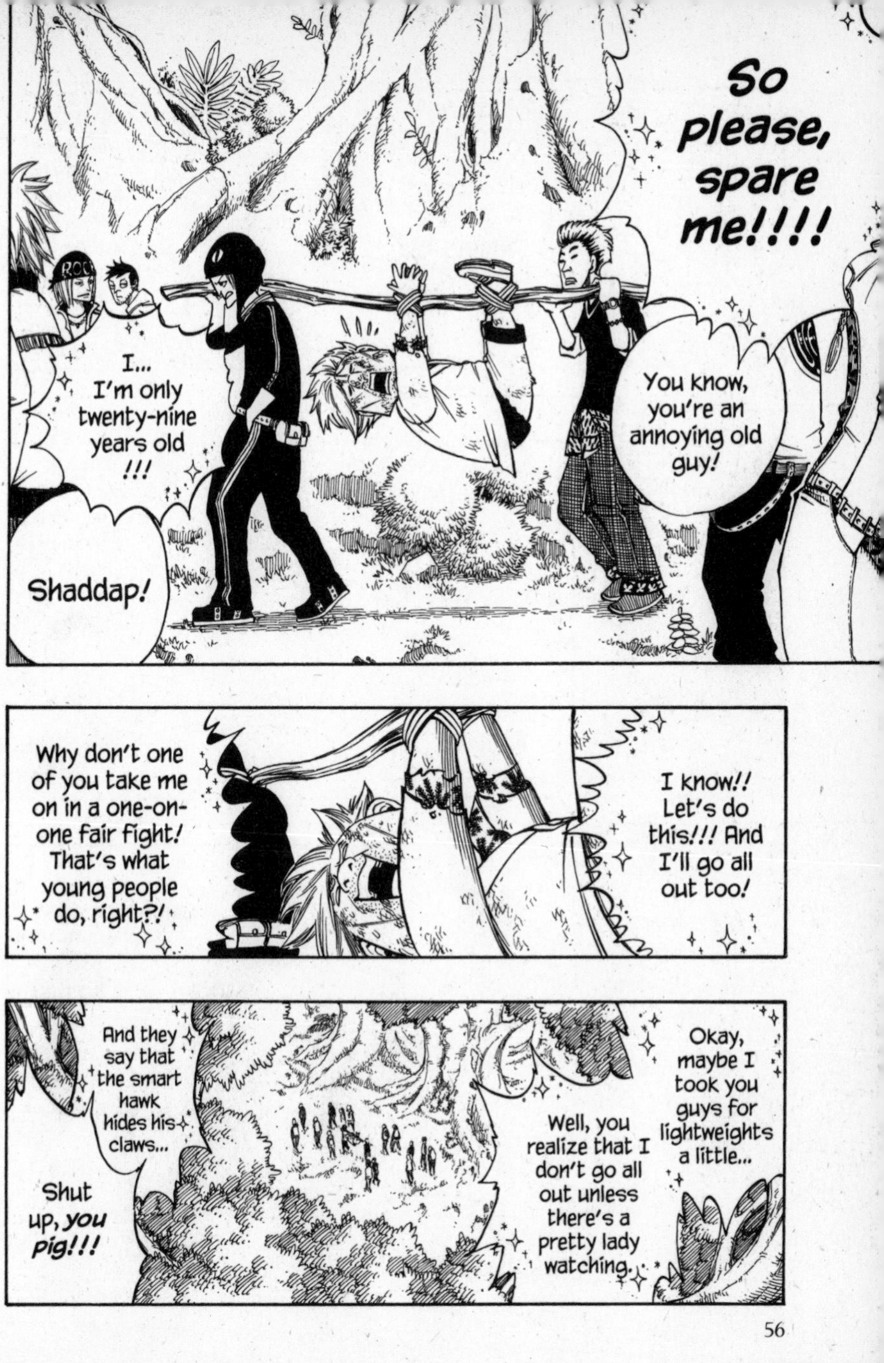
So please, spare me!!!!
You know, you're an annoying old guy!
I... I'm only twenty-nine years old!!!
Shaddap!
I know!! Let's do this!!! And I'll go all out too!
Why don't one of you take me on in a one-on-one fair fight! That's what young people do, right?!
Okay, maybe I took you guys for lightweights a little...
Well, you realize that I don't go all out unless there's a pretty lady watching.
And they say that the smart hawk hides his claws...
Shut up, *you pig!!!*

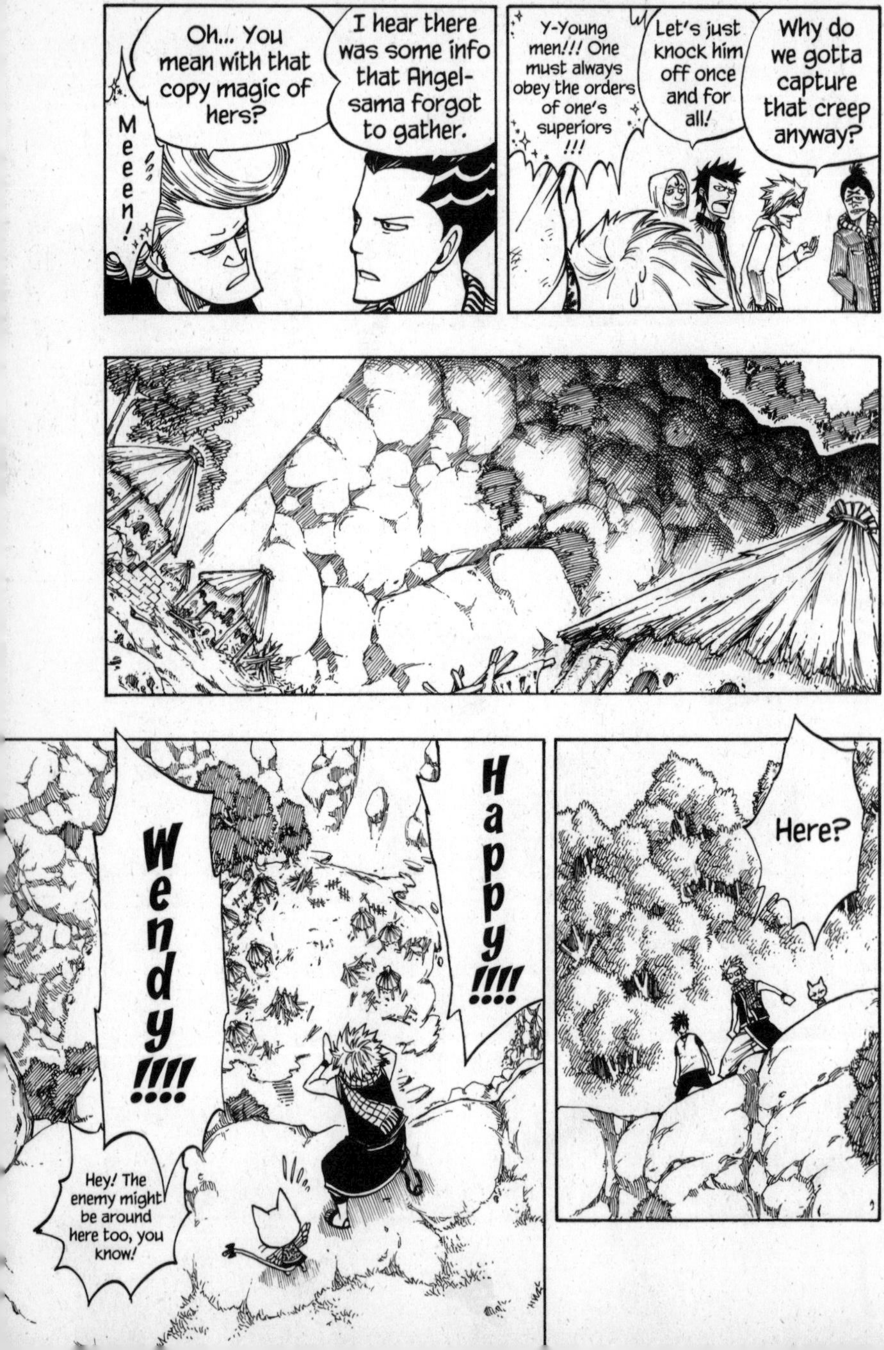
Why do we gotta capture that creep anyway?
Let's just knock him off once and for all!
Y-Young men!!! One must always obey the orders of one's superiors!!!
I hear there was some info that Angel-sama forgot to gather.
Oh... You mean with that copy magic of hers?
Meeen!
Here?
Happy!!!!
Wendy!!!!
Hey! The enemy might be around here too, you know!

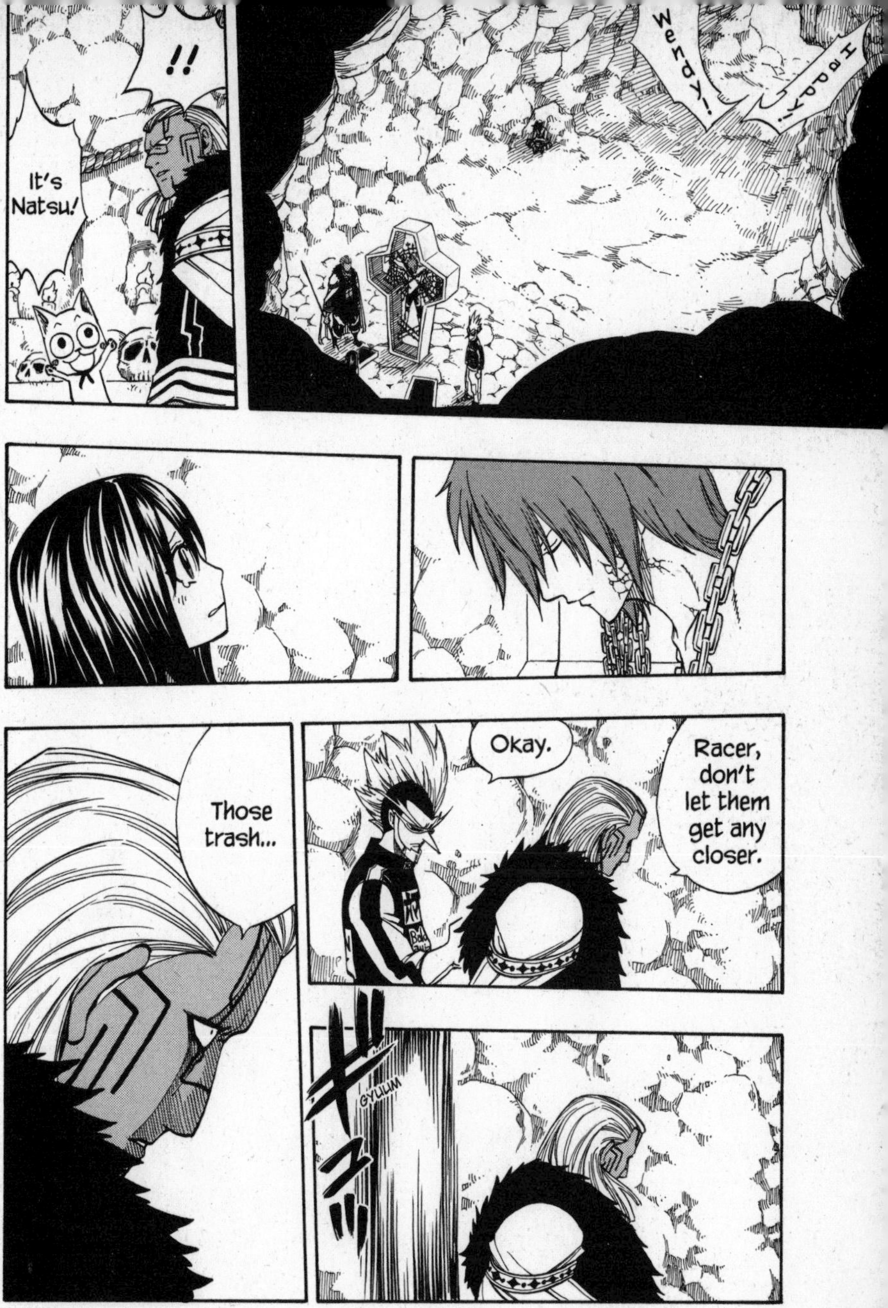
Happy!
Wendy!
!!
It's Natsu!
Racer, don't let them get any closer.
Okay.
GYUUM
Those trash...

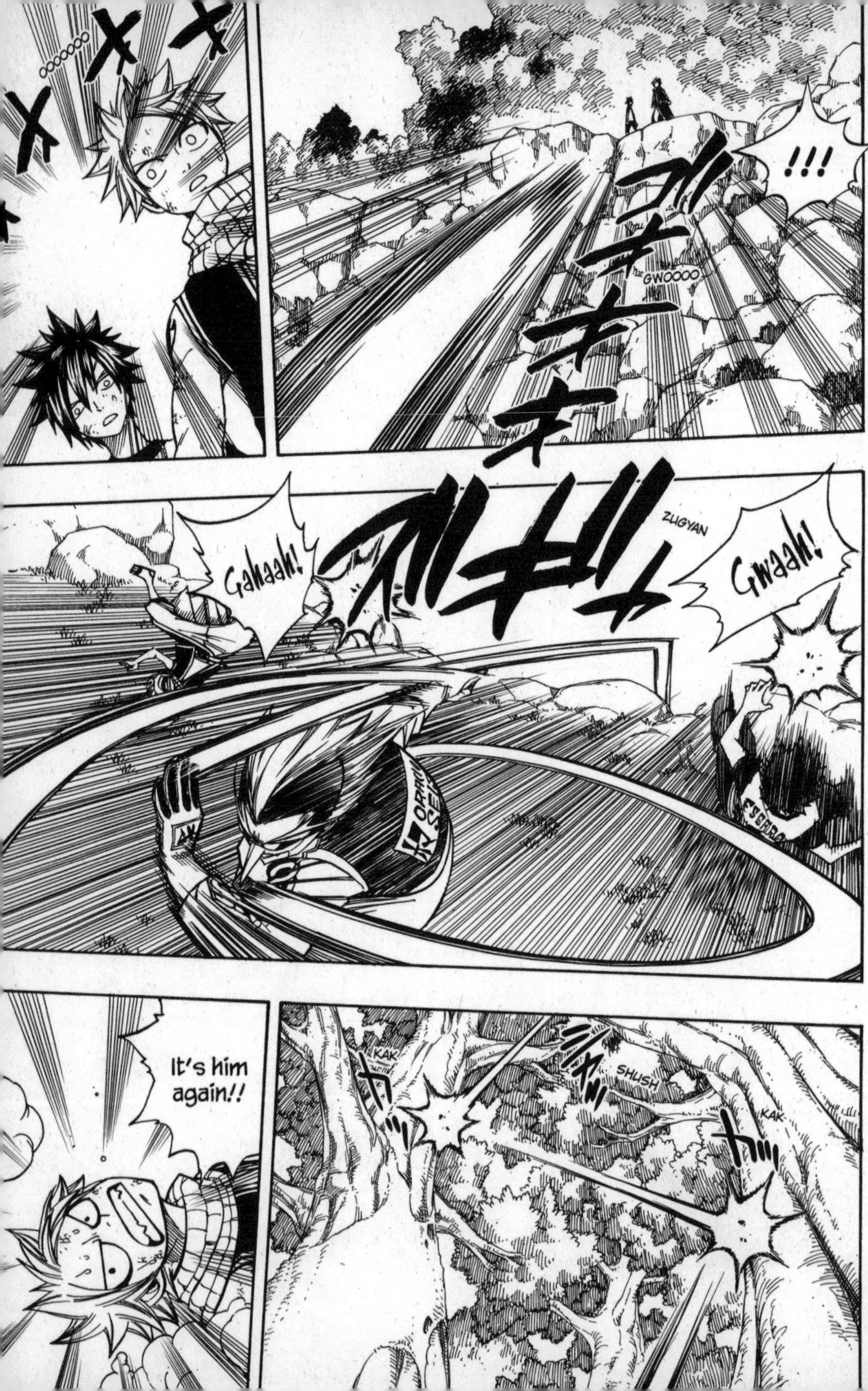
!!!
GWOOOO
Gwaah!
ZUGYAN
Gahaah!
KAK
SHUSH
KAK
It's him again!!

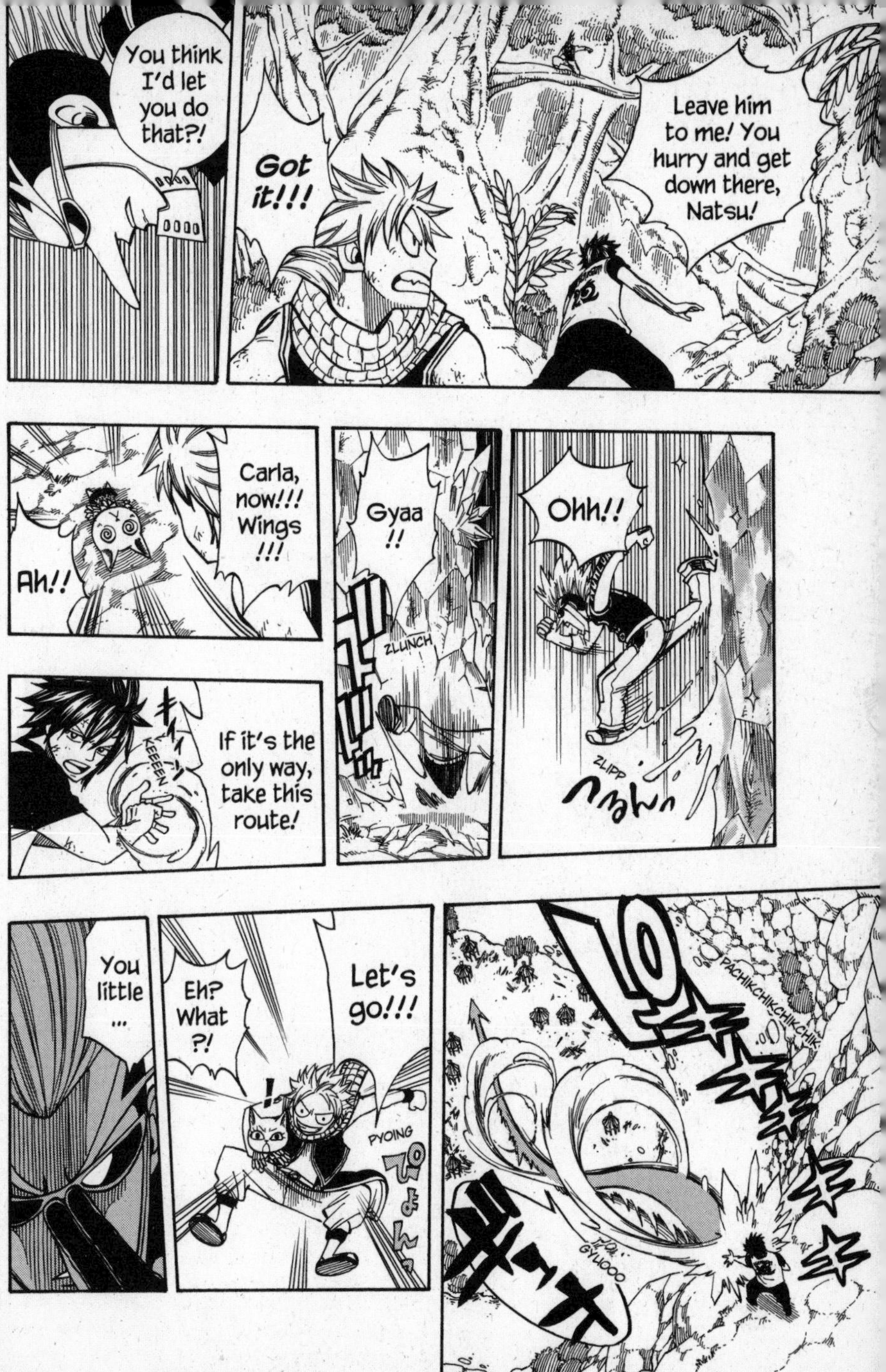
Leave him to me! You hurry and get down there, Natsu!
Got it!!!
You think I'd let you do that?!
Ohh!!
ZLIPP
Gyaa !!
ZLUNCH
Carla, now!!! Wings!!!
Ah!!
KEEEEN
If it's the only way, take this route!
PACHIKCHIKCHIKCHIK
GYUOOO
Let's go!!!
Eh? What?!
PYOING
You little ...

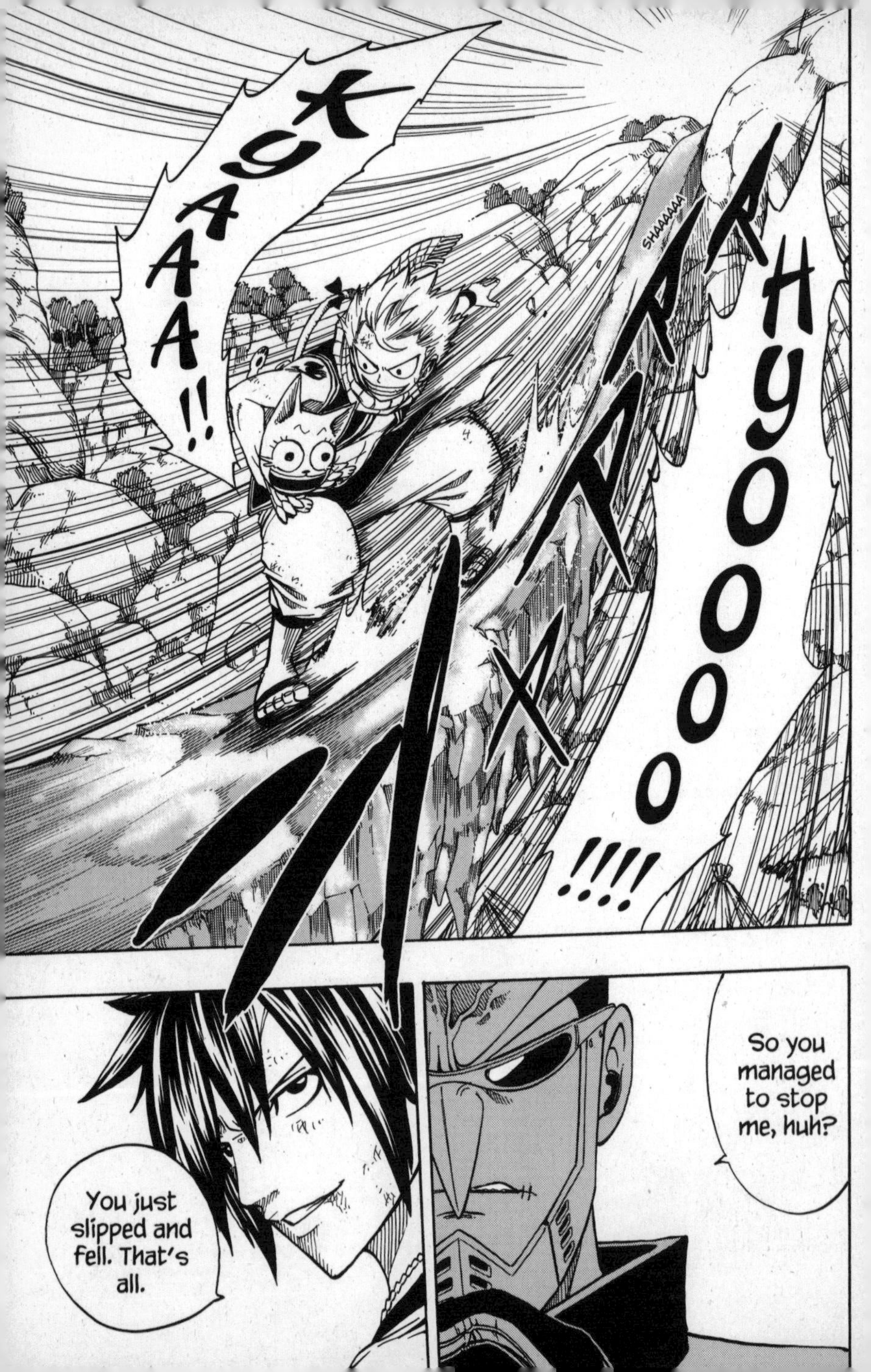
HYOOOOO!!!!
SHAAAAAA
KYAAA!!
So you managed to stop me, huh?
You just slipped and fell. That's all.

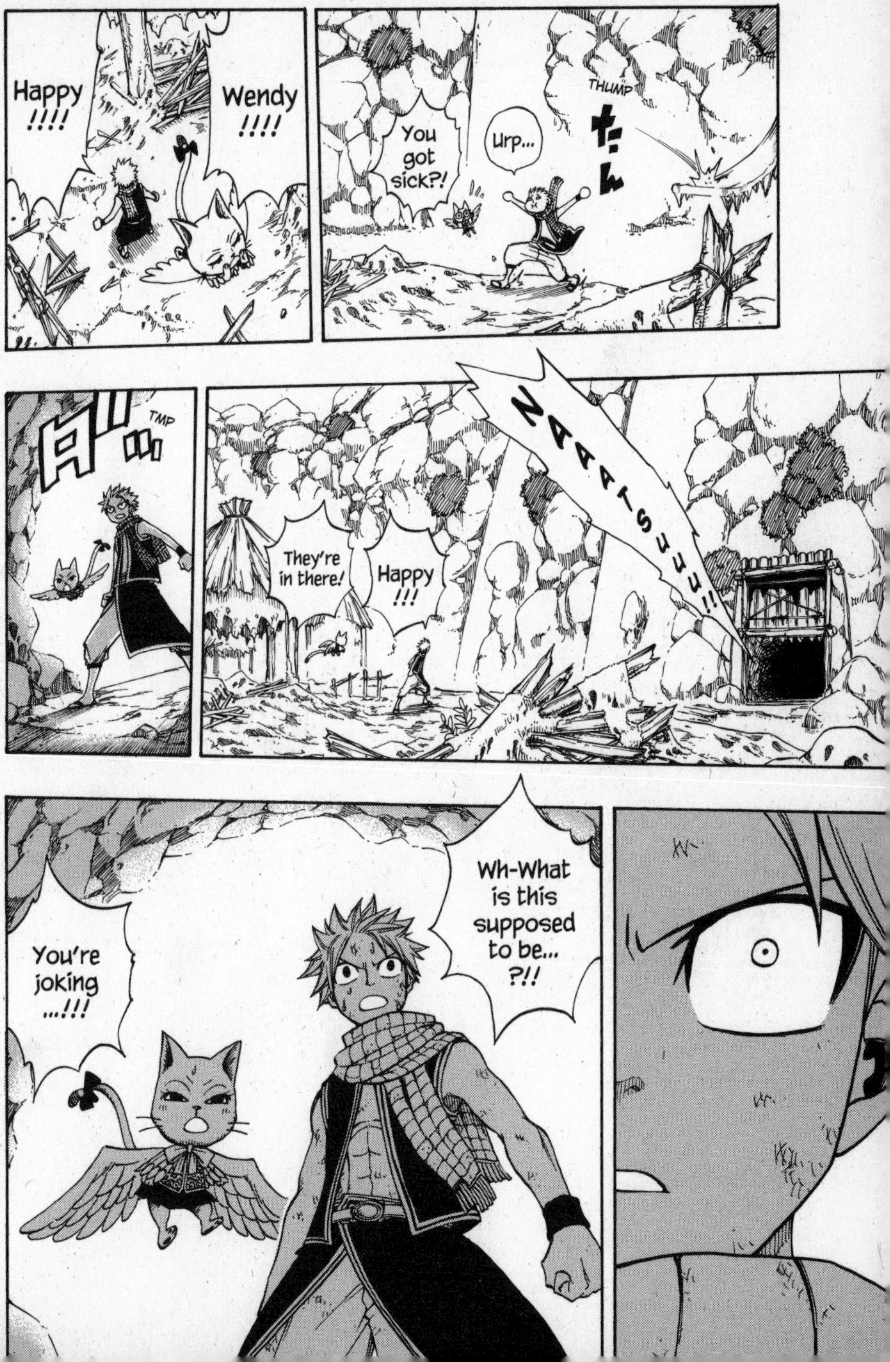
THUMP
Urp...
You got sick?!
Wendy !!!!
Happy !!!!
NAAATSUUUU!!
Happy !!!
They're in there!
TMP
Wh-What is this supposed to be... ?!!
You're joking ...!!!

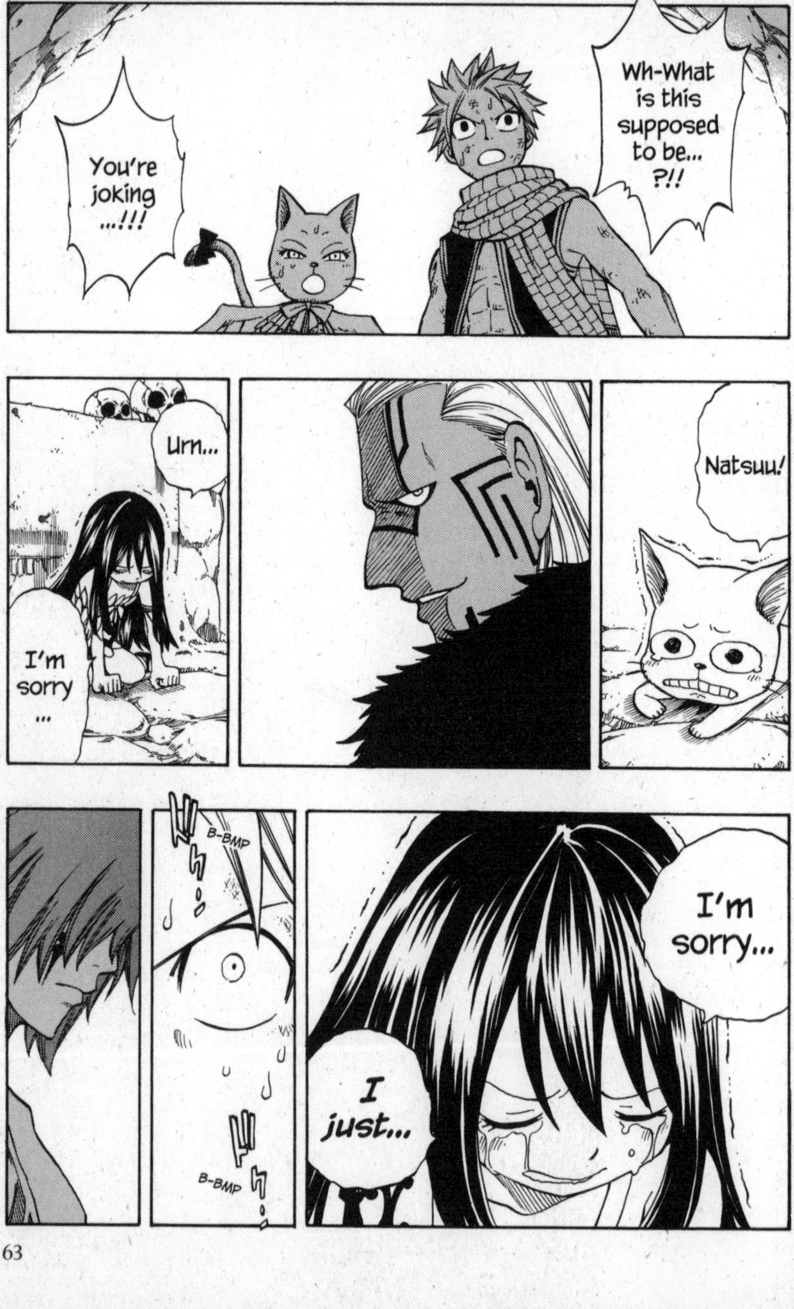
Wh-What is this supposed to be...?!!
You're joking...!!!
Natsuu!
Urn...
I'm sorry...
I'm sorry...
I just...
B-BMP
B-BMP

Chapter 138, Didn't Count On...

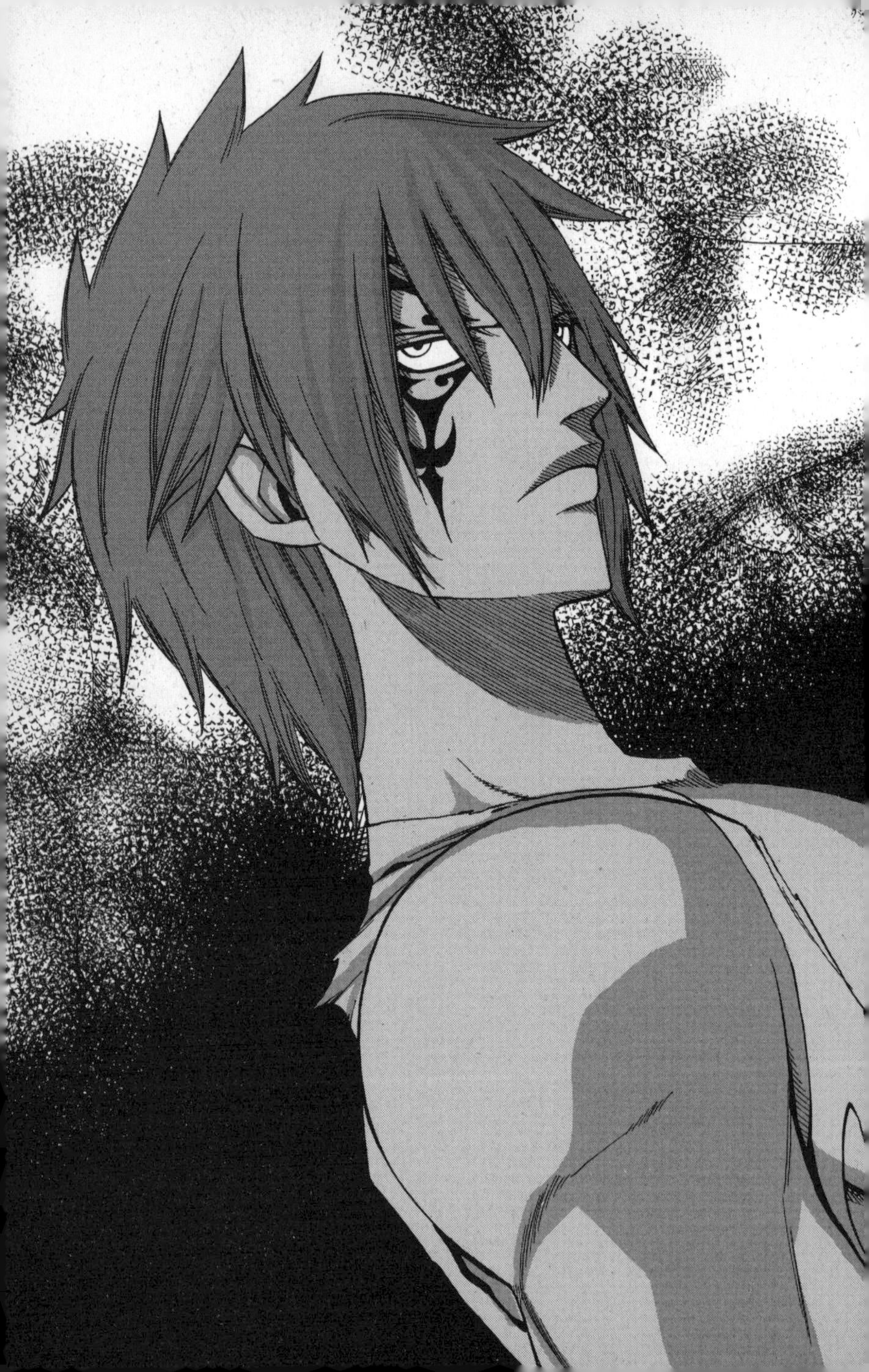

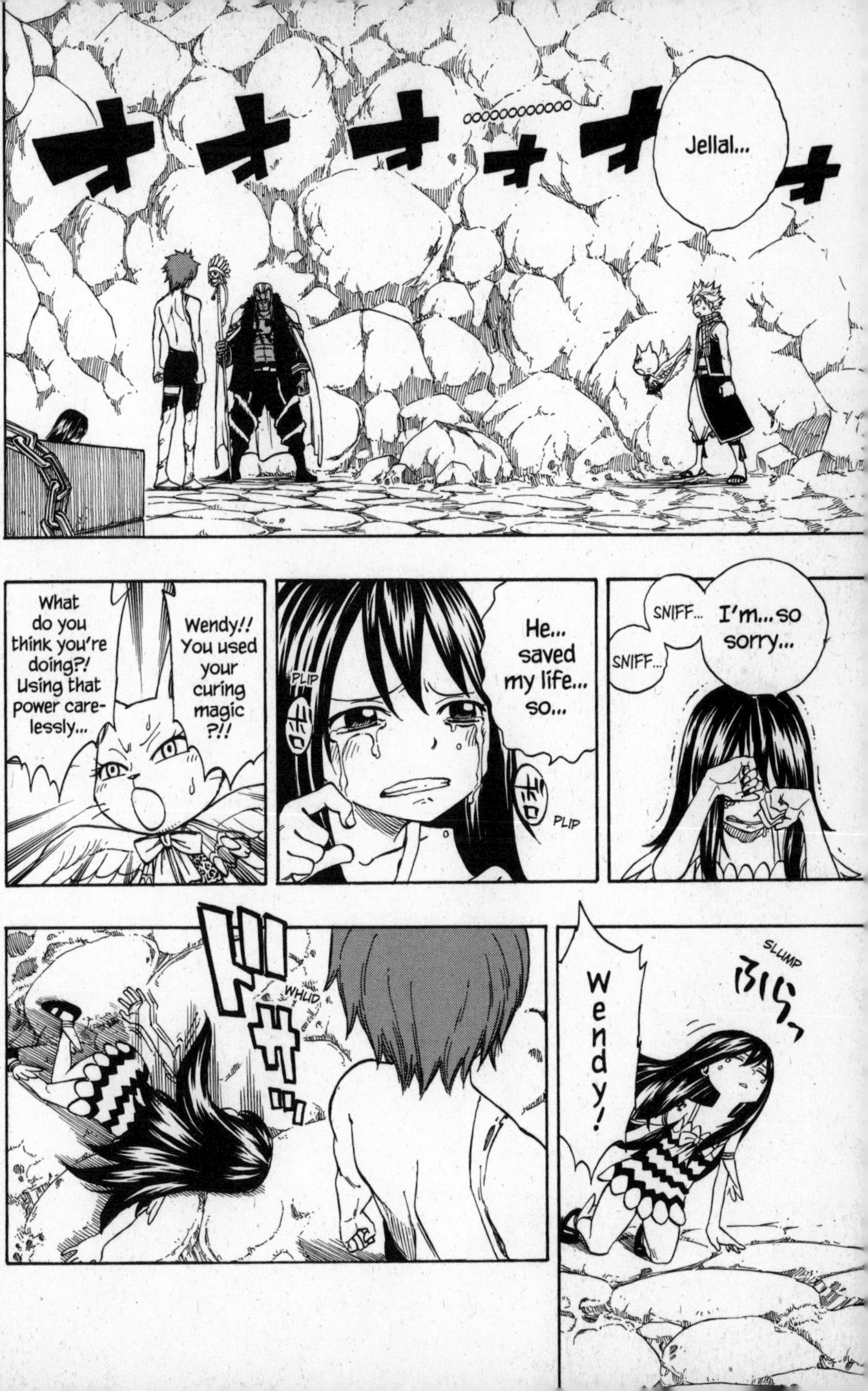
Jellal...
OOOOOOOOOOOO
I'm...so sorry...
SNIFF...
SNIFF...
He... saved my life... so...
PLIP
PLIP
Wendy!! You used your curing magic?!!
What do you think you're doing?! Using that power carelessly...
SLUMP
Wendy!
WHUD

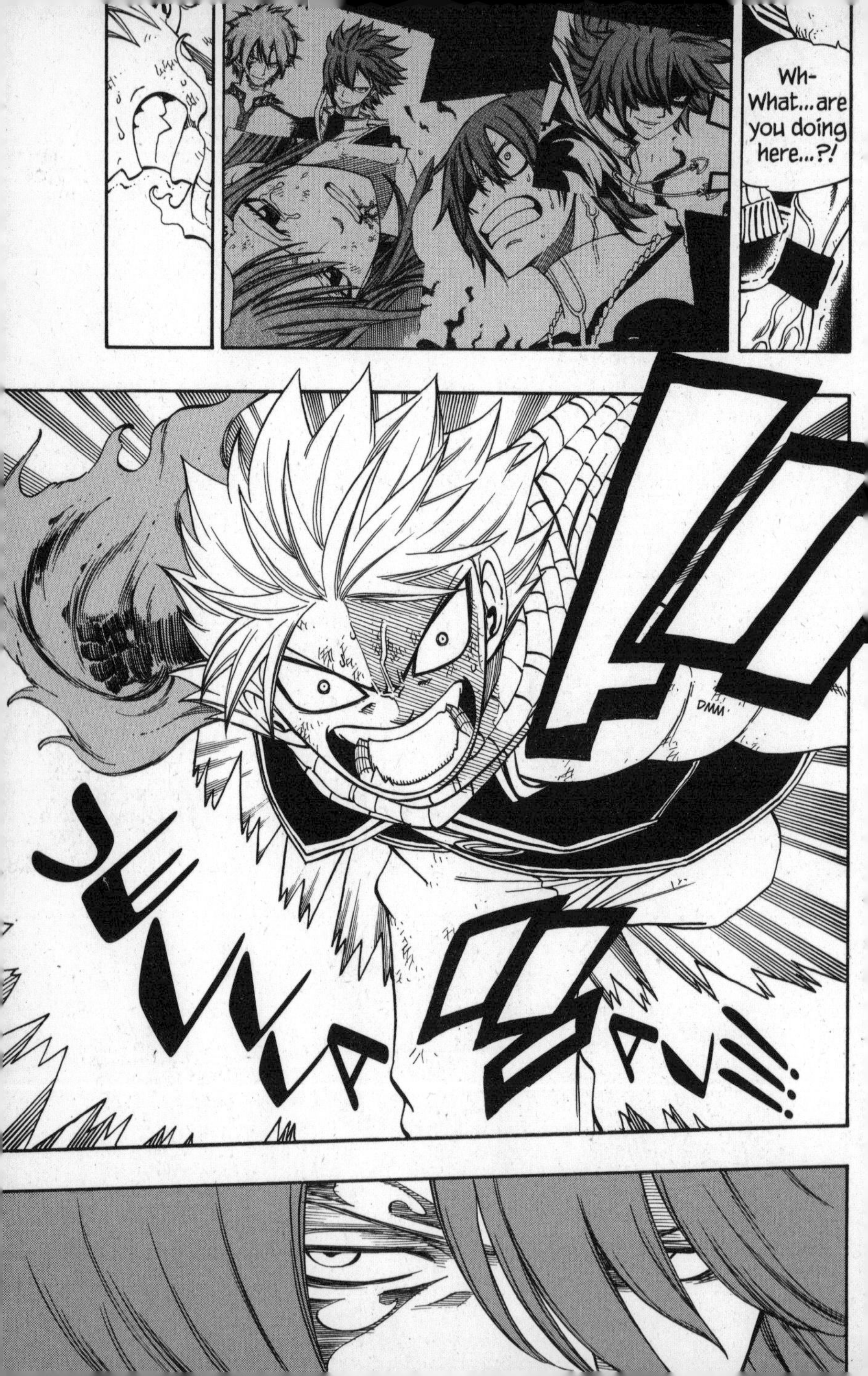

Wh- What...are you doing here...?!
DMM
JELLAL!!!

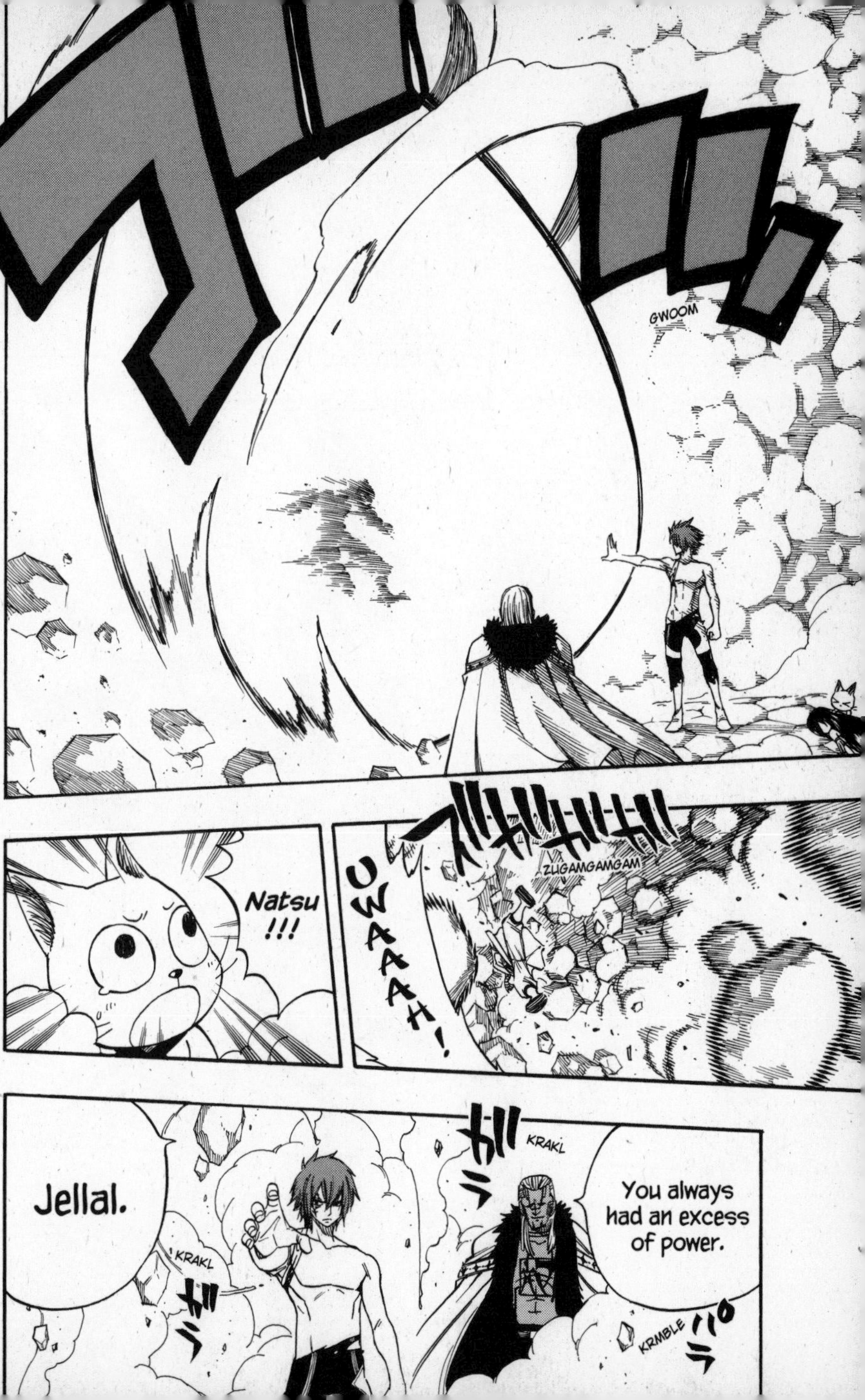
GWOOM
ZUGAMGAMGAM
UWAAAAH!
Natsu !!!
KRAKL
You always had an excess of power.
KRMBLE
Jellal.
KRAKL

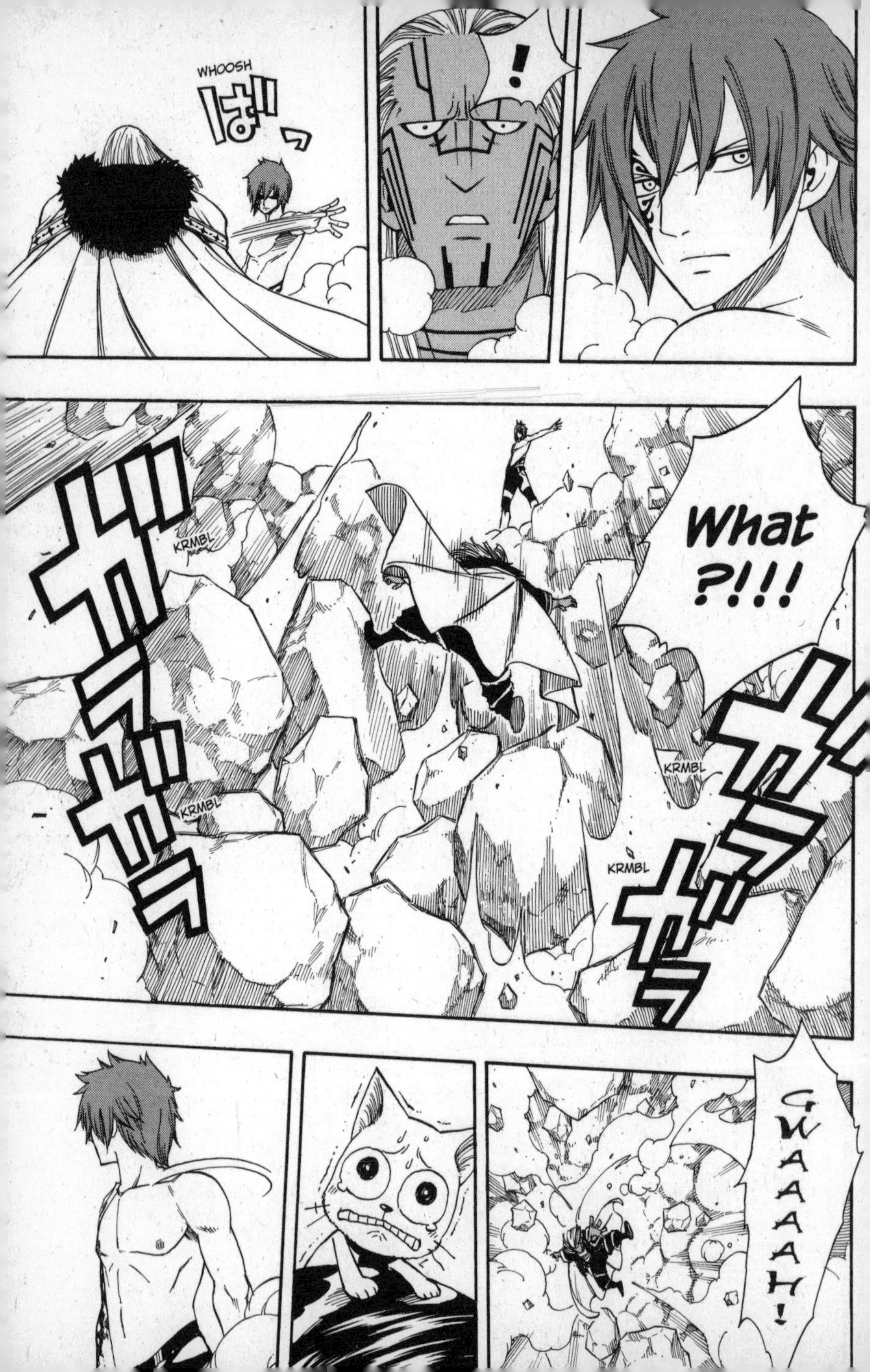
!
WHOOSH
What ?!!!
KRMBL
KRMBL
KRMBL
KRMBL
GWAAAAH!

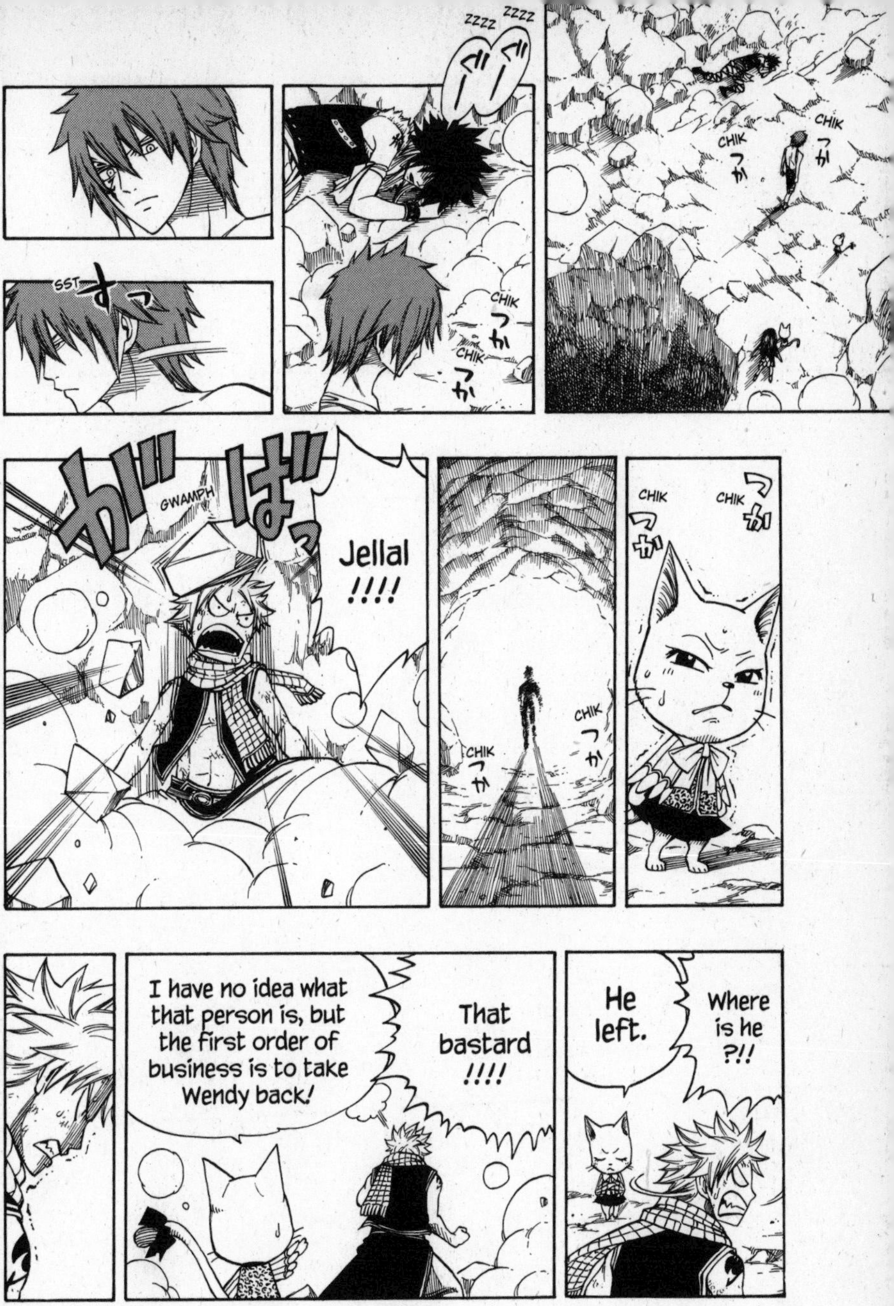
CHIK
CHIK
ZZZZ
ZZZZ
CHIK
CHIK
SST
CHIK
CHIK
CHIK
CHIK
GWAMPH
Jellal!!!!
Where is he?!!
He left.
That bastard!!!!
I have no idea what that person is, but the first order of business is to take Wendy back!

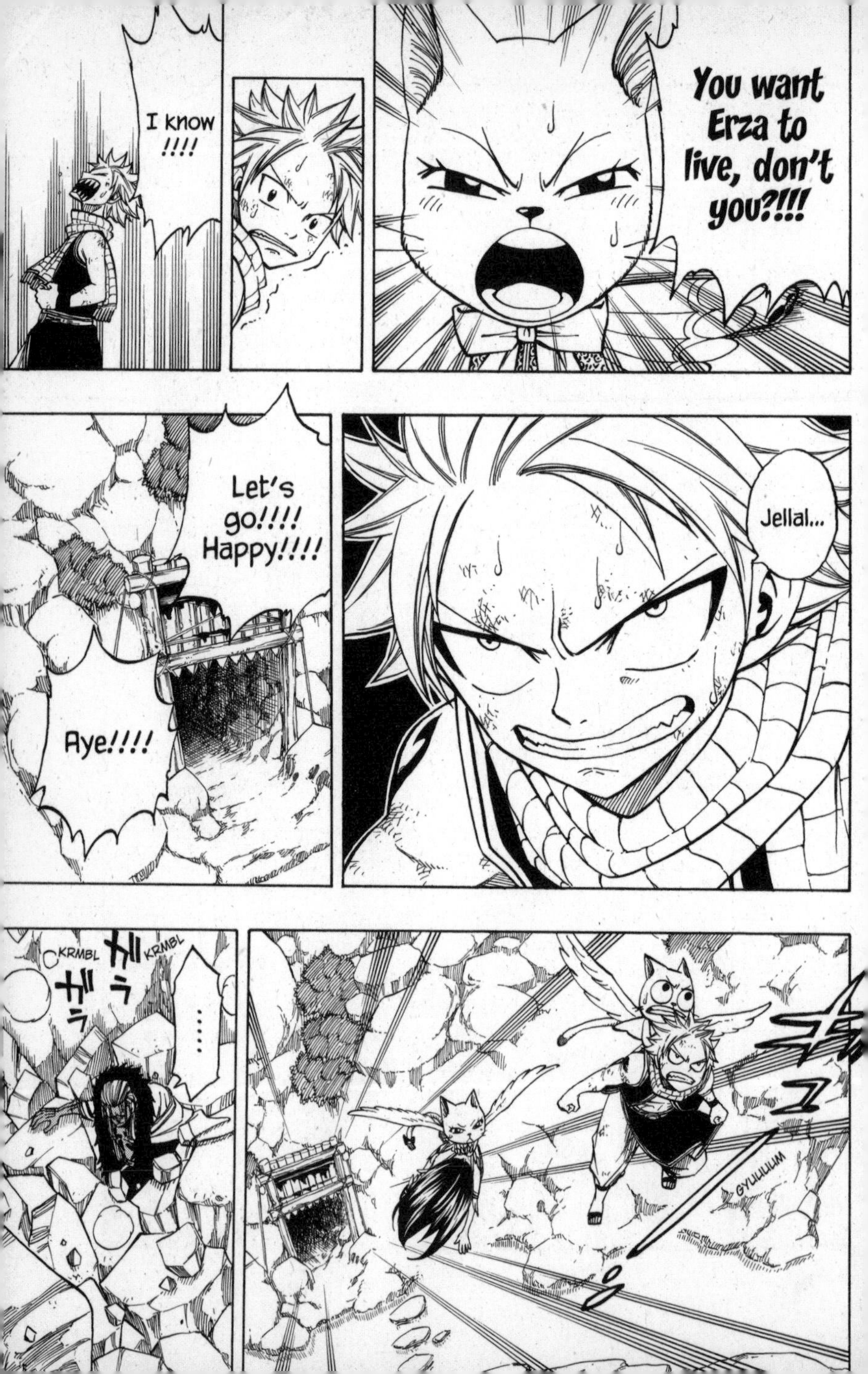
You want Erza to live, don't you?!!!
I know !!!!
Jellal...
Let's go!!!! Happy!!!!
Aye!!!!
GYUUUUM
KRMBL KRMBL
ガラ ガラ
......

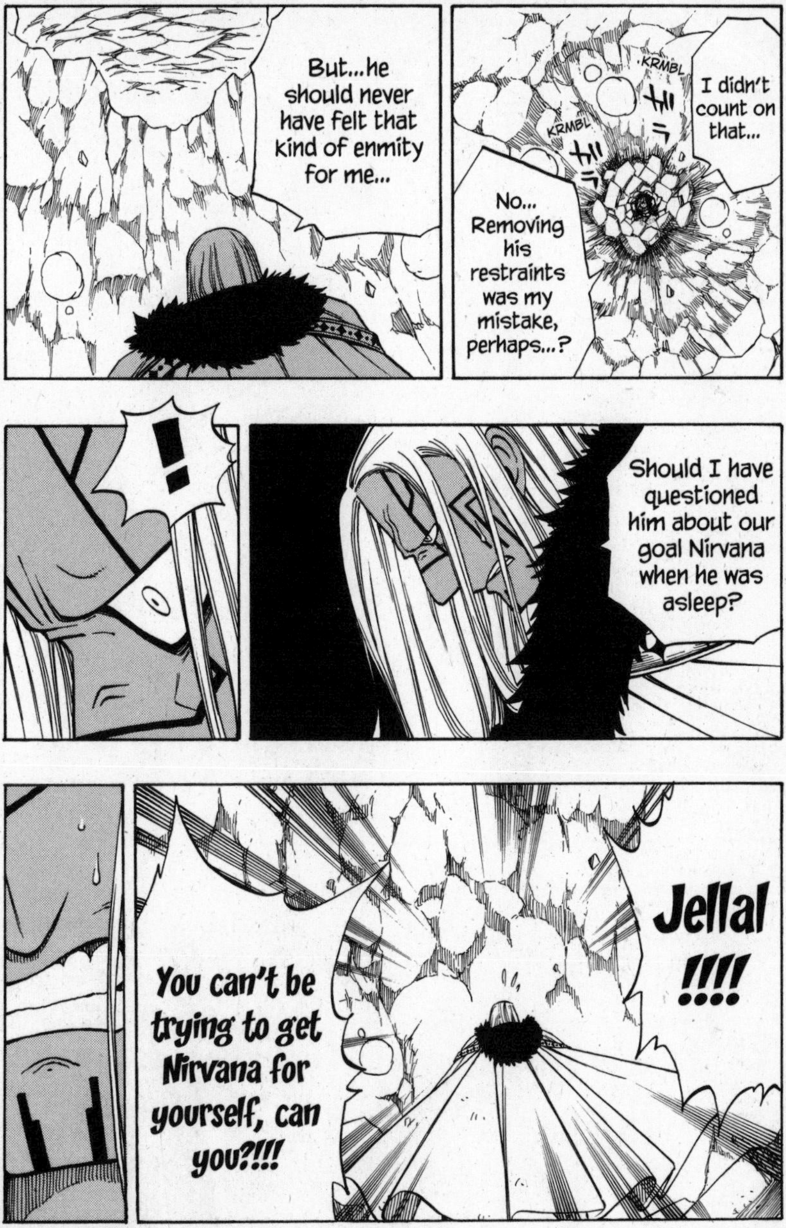
I didn't count on that...
KRMBL
KRMBL
No... Removing his restraints was my mistake, perhaps...?
But...he should never have felt that kind of enmity for me...
Should I have questioned him about our goal Nirvana when he was asleep?
!
Jellal!!!!
You can't be trying to get Nirvana for yourself, can you?!!!

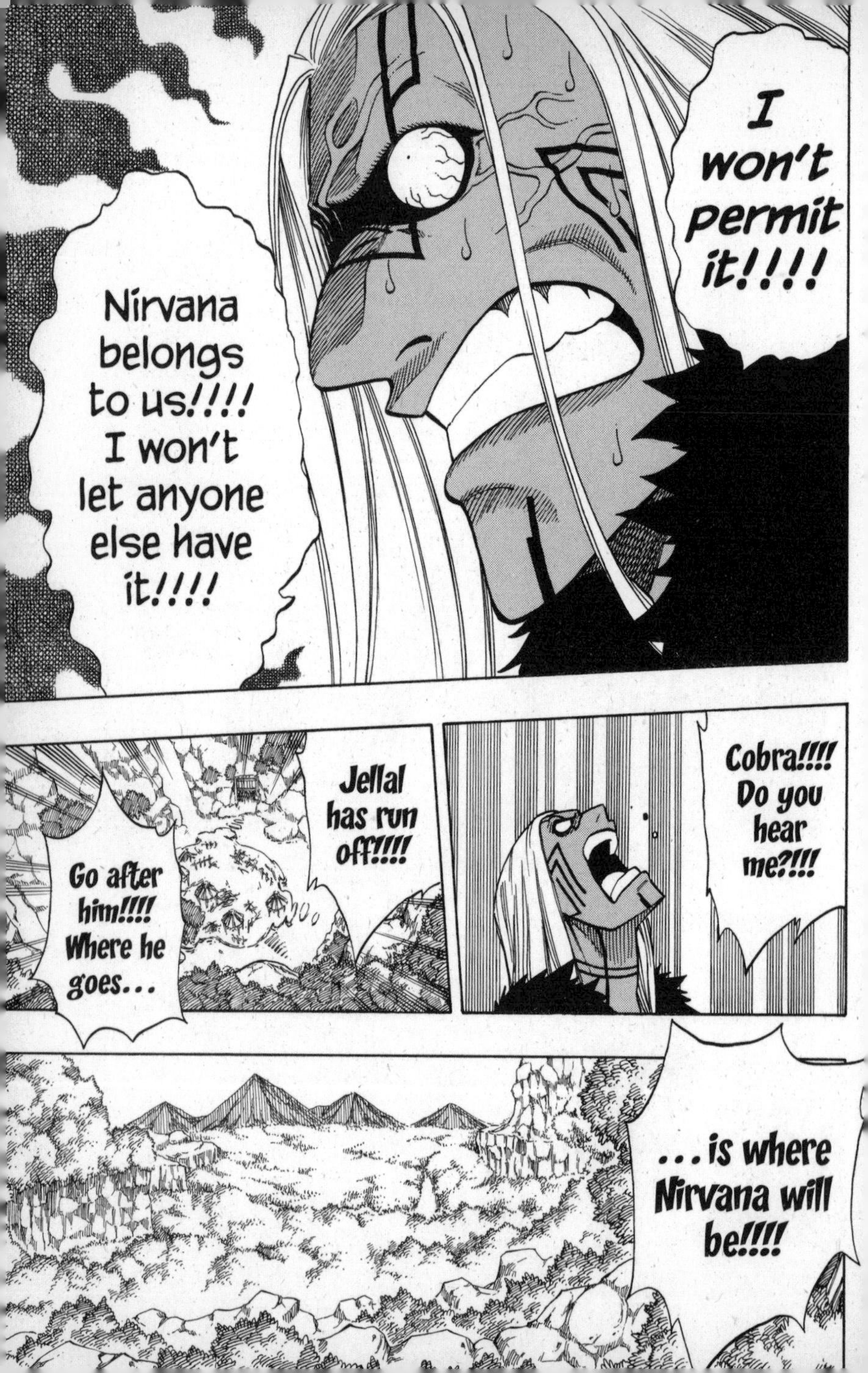
I won't permit it!!!!
Nirvana belongs to us!!!! I won't let anyone else have it!!!!
Cobra!!!! Do you hear me?!!!
Jellal has run off!!!!
Go after him!!!! Where he goes...
...is where Nirvana will be!!!!

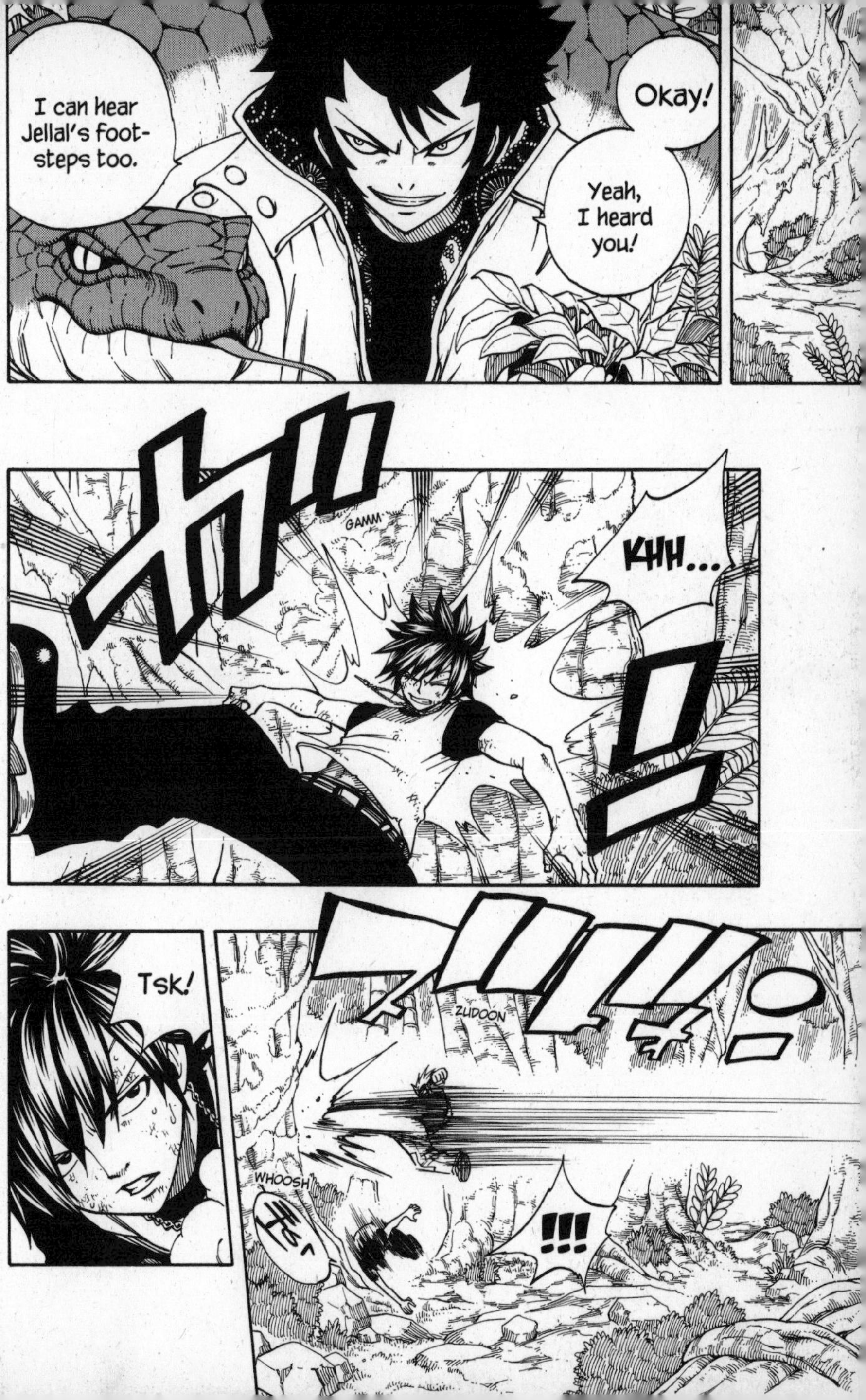
Okay!
Yeah, I heard you!
I can hear Jellal's foot-steps too.
GAMM
KHH...
ZUDOON
WHOOSH
!!!
Tsk!

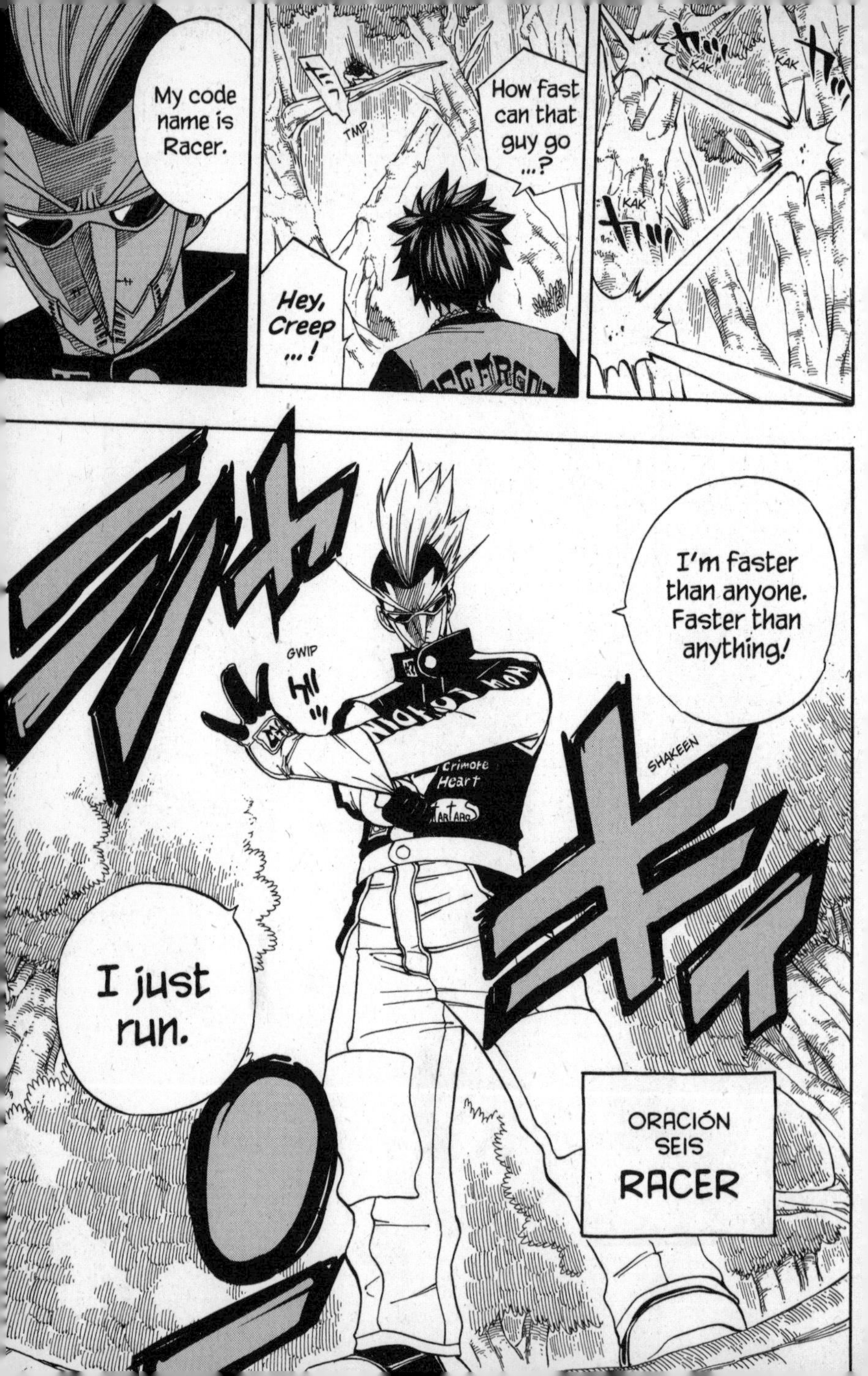
KAK
KAK
KAK
How fast can that guy go ...?
TMP
Hey, Creep ...!
My code name is Racer.
I'm faster than anyone. Faster than anything!
SHAKEEN
GWIP
ORACIÓN SEIS
RACER
I just run.

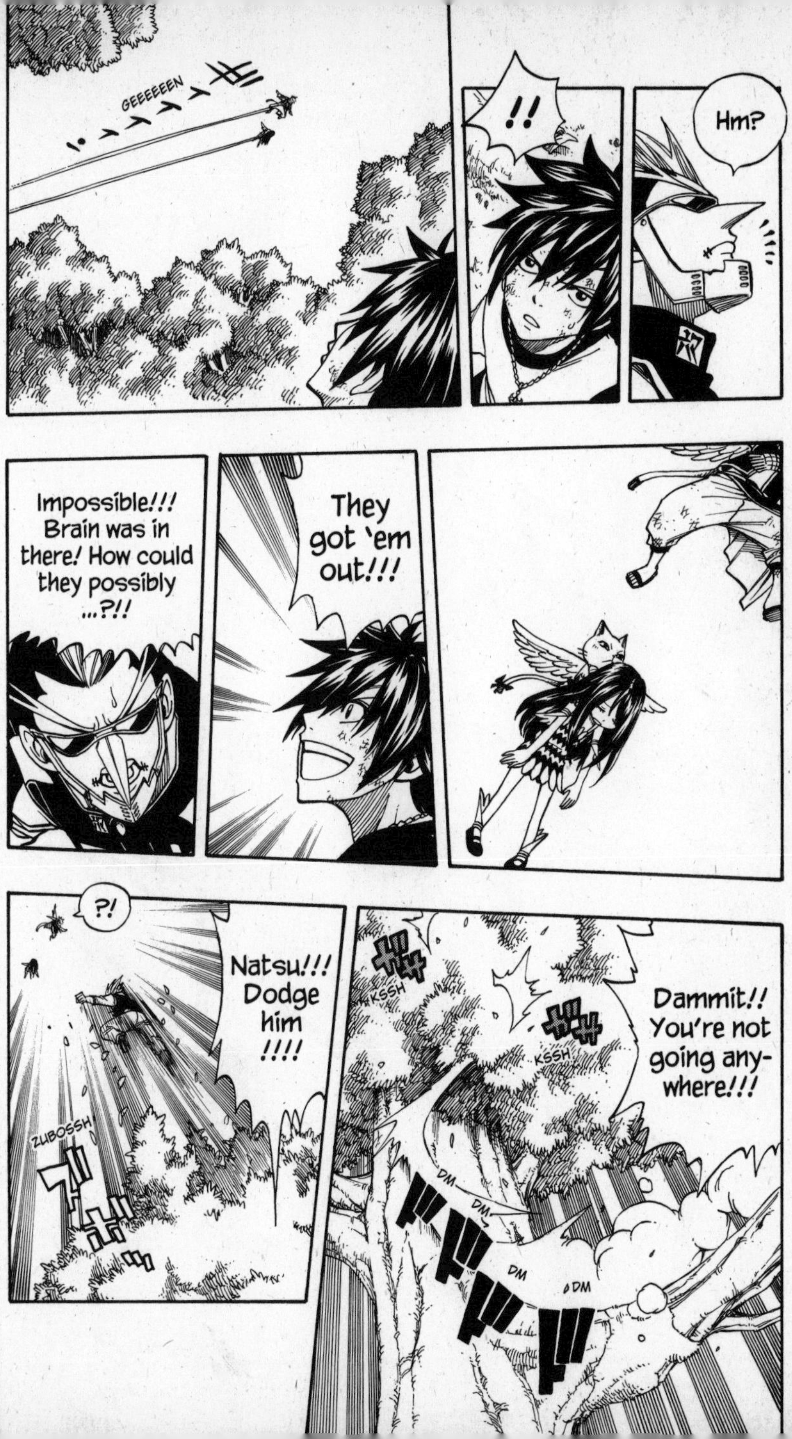
Hm?
!!
GEEEEEEN
They got 'em out!!!
Impossible!!! Brain was in there! How could they possibly ...?!!
KSSH
KSSH
Dammit!! You're not going any-where!!!
DM
DM
DM
DM
?!
Natsu!!! Dodge him !!!!
ZUBOSSH

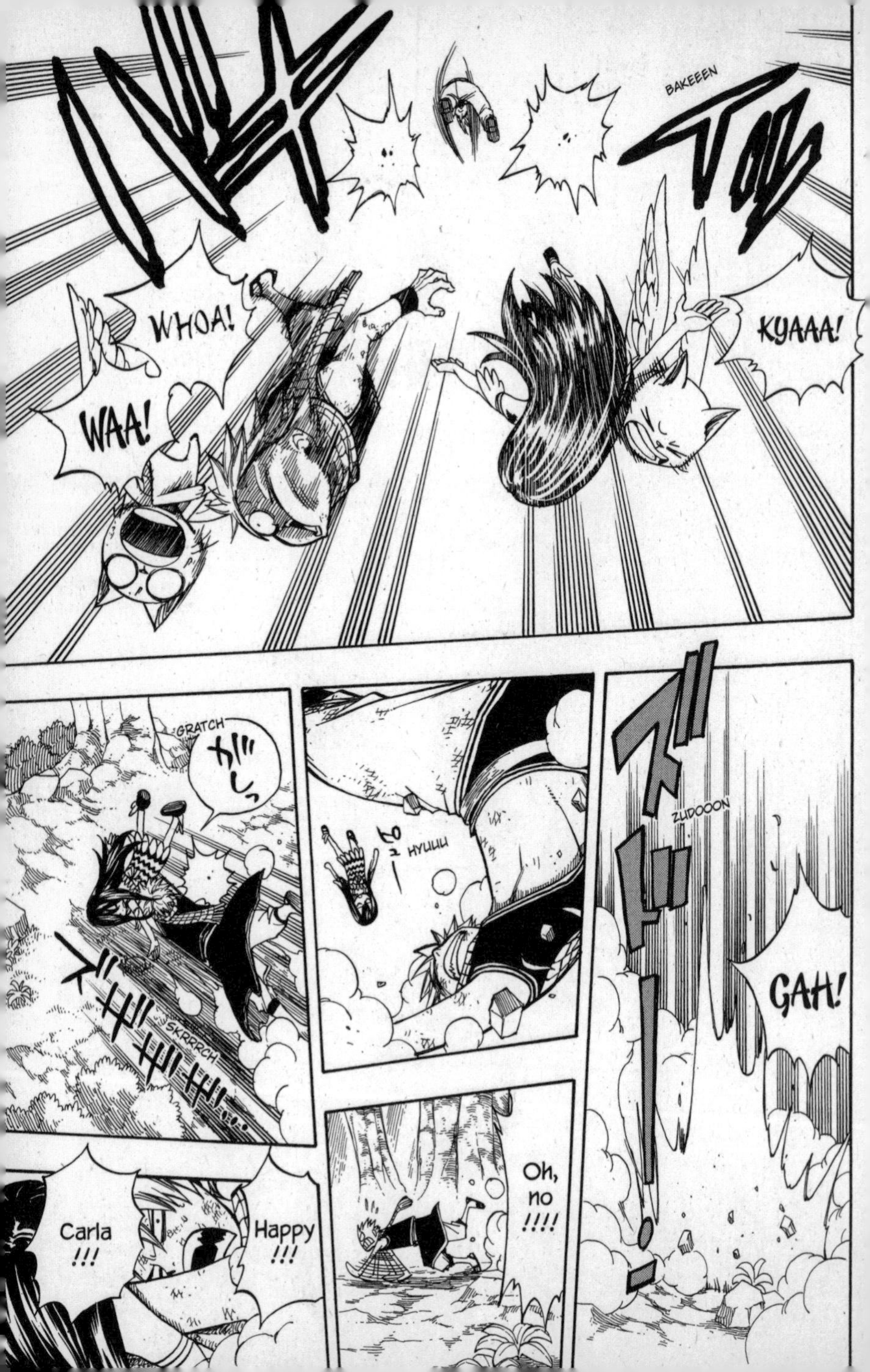
BAKEEEN
KYAAA!
WHOA!
WAA!
ZUDOOON
GAH!
HYUUU
GRATCH
がしっ
SKRRRCH
Oh, no!!!!
Happy!!!
Carla!!!

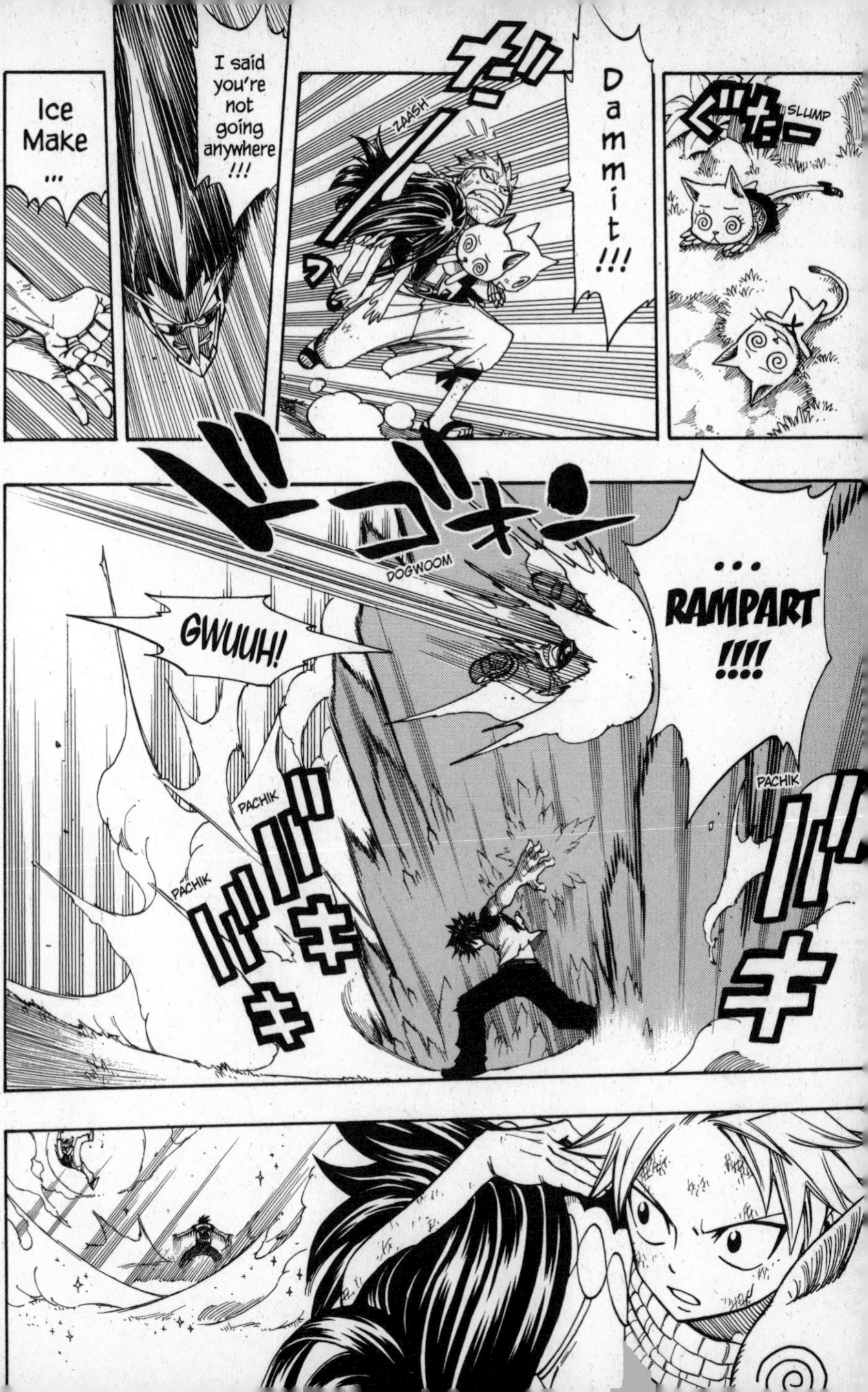

SLUMP
ZAASH
Dammit!!!
I said you're not going anywhere!!!
Ice Make ...
DOGWOOM
... RAMPART!!!!
GWUUH!
PACHIK
PACHIK
PACHIK

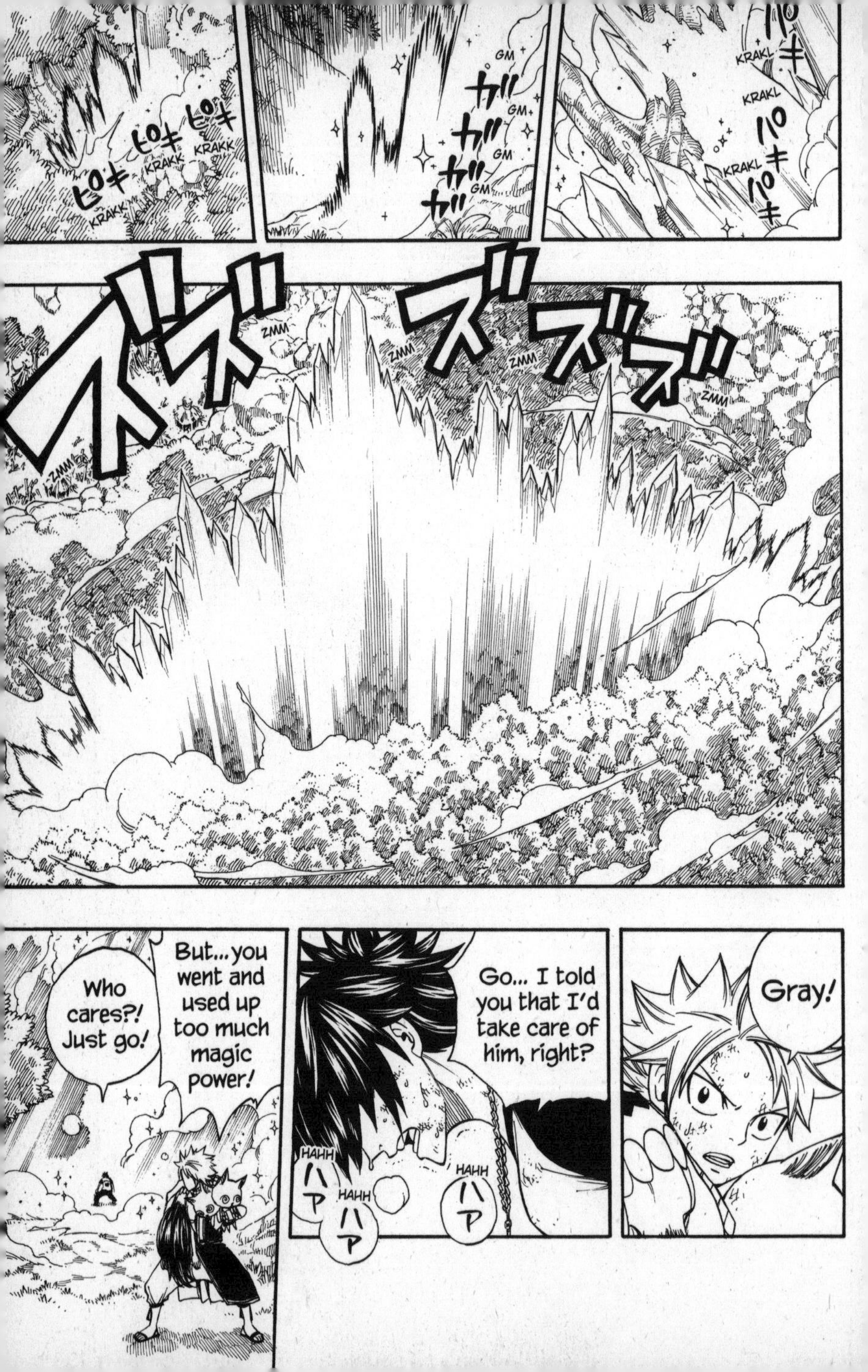
KRAKL
KRAKL
KRAKL
GM
GM
GM
GM
KRAKK
KRAKK
KRAKK
ZMM
ZMM
ZMM
ZMM
ZMM
Gray!
Go... I told you that I'd take care of him, right?
HAHH
HAHH
HAHH
But...you went and used up too much magic power!
Who cares?! Just go!

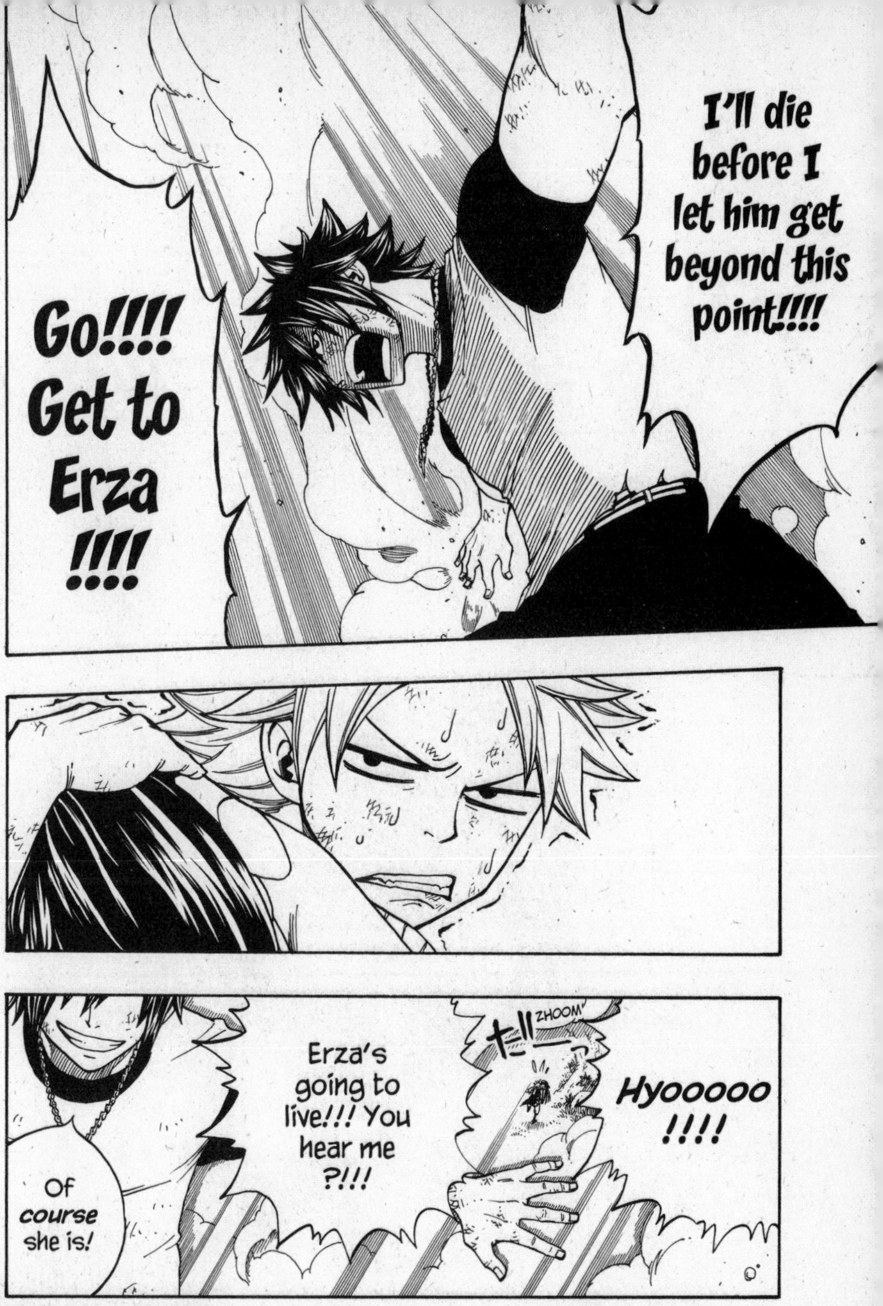

I'll die before I let him get beyond this point!!!!
Go!!!! Get to Erza!!!!
ZHOOM
Hyoooooo!!!!
Erza's going to live!!! You hear me?!!!
Of course she is!

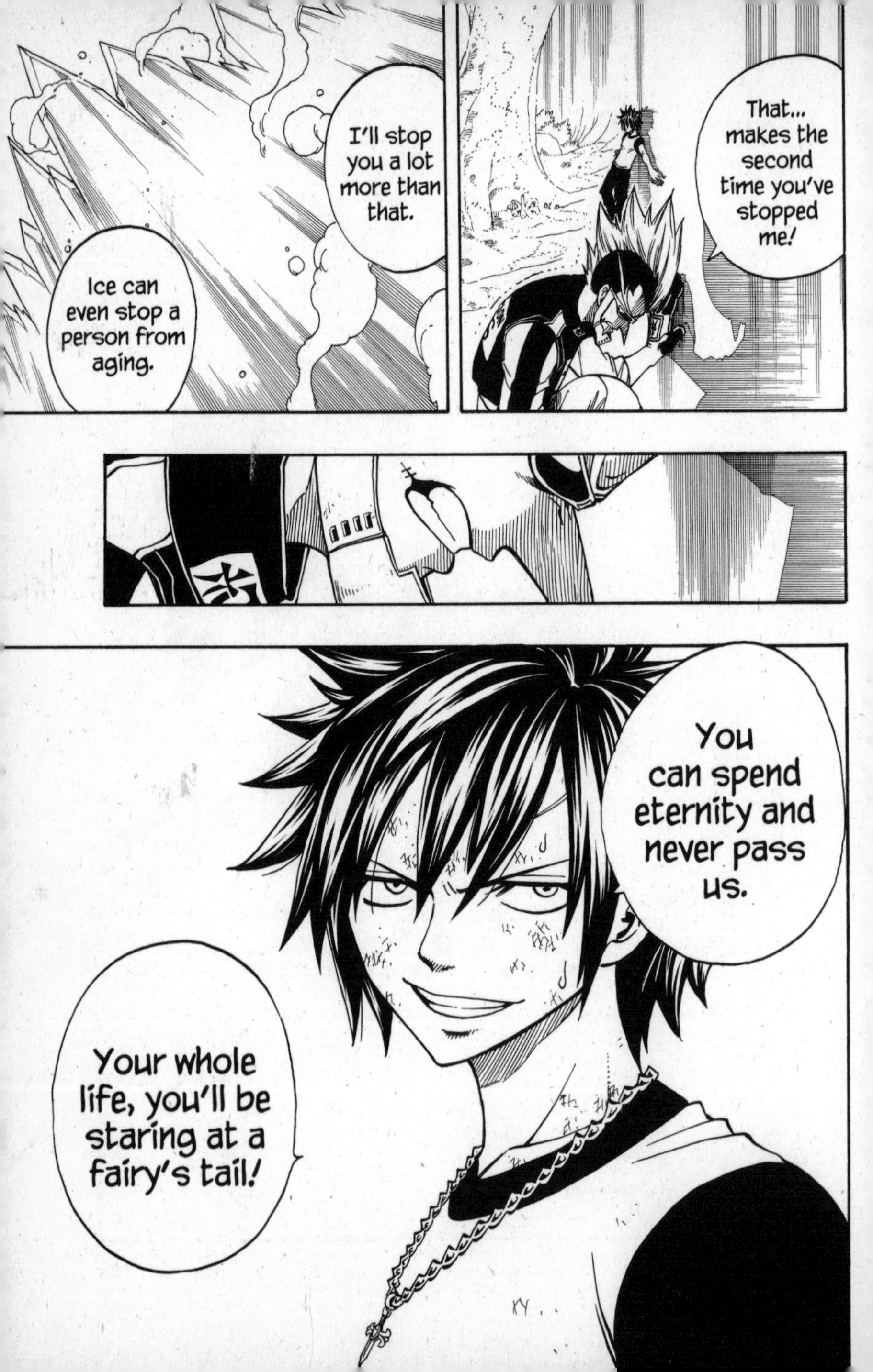
That... makes the second time you've stopped me!
I'll stop you a lot more than that.
Ice can even stop a person from aging.
You can spend eternity and never pass us.
Your whole life, you'll be staring at a fairy's tail!

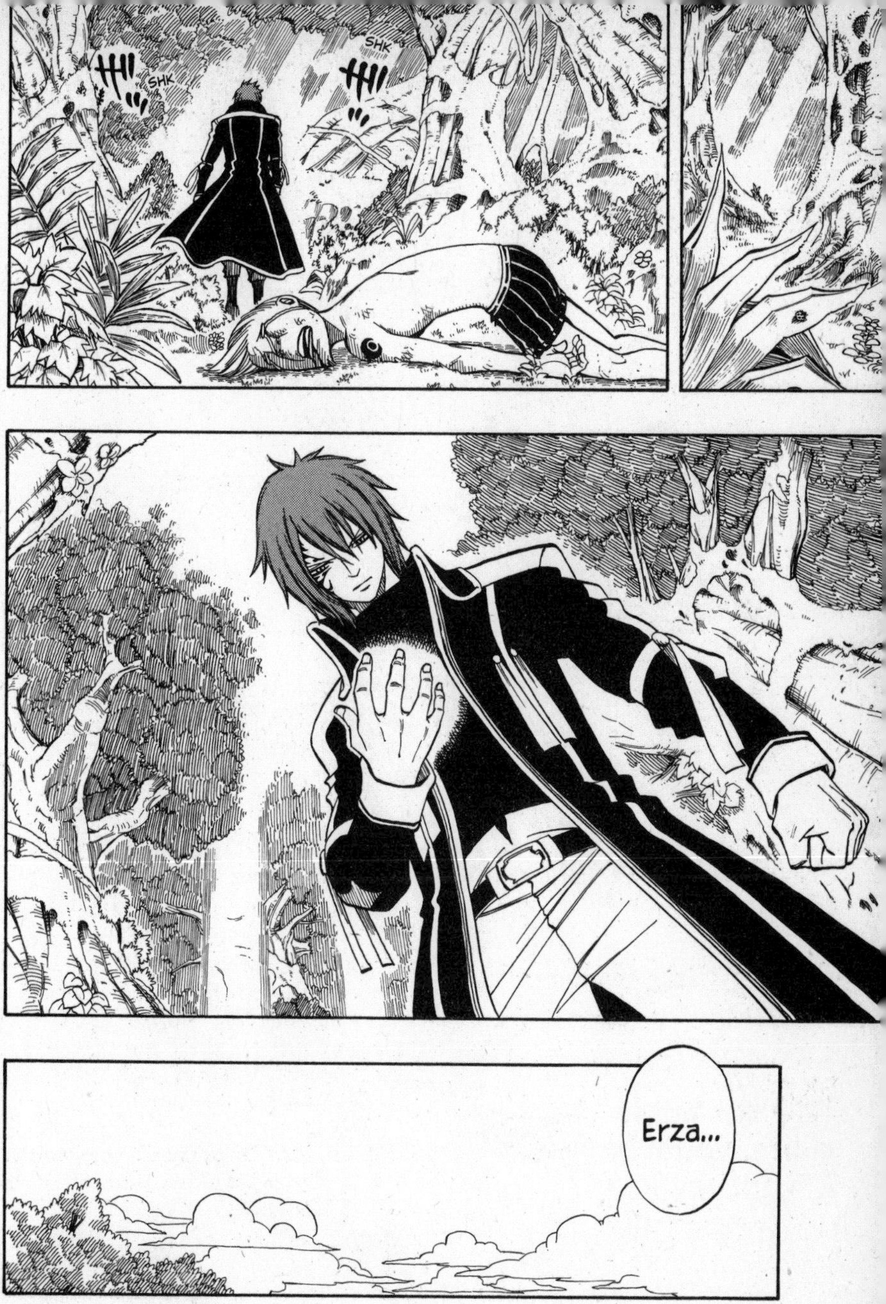
SHK
SHK
Erza...

FAIRY TAIL

フェアリーテイル

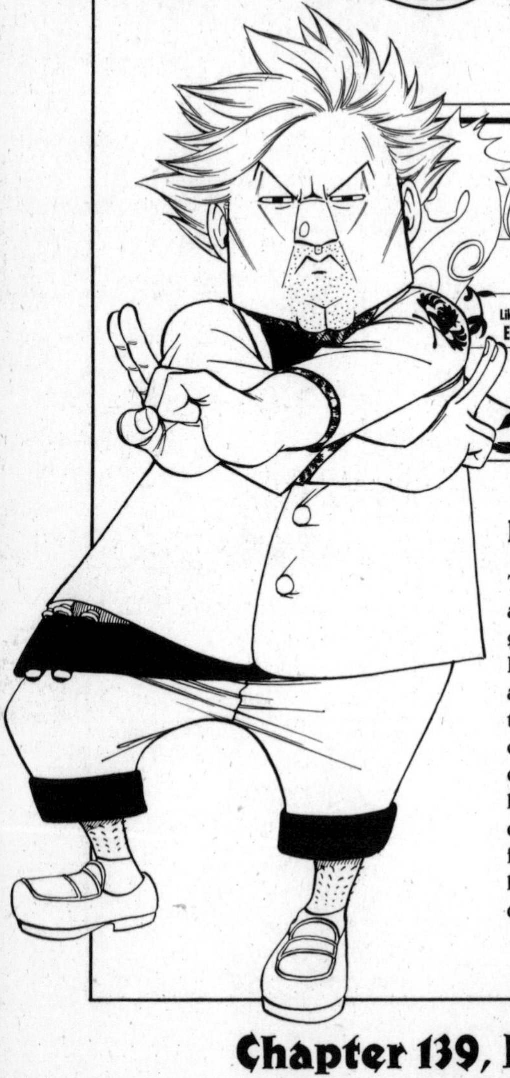

BLUE PEGASUS

Name:
Ichiya Vandalay Kotobuki (29)

Magic: **Perfume Magic**

Likes:
Every woman in the world

Dislikes:
Stinky things

WIZARD GUILD

Remarks

The black sheep of Blue Pegasus, a guild famous for gathering together beautiful men and women. His magic creates scents with all kinds of effects and he keeps these perfumes in flasks that he carries with him. Considered an effective wizard in his guild, he loves it when the junior members call him by respectful names. He fell in love with Erza the moment he saw her at a guild masters' dinner.

Chapter 139, Dead Grand Prix

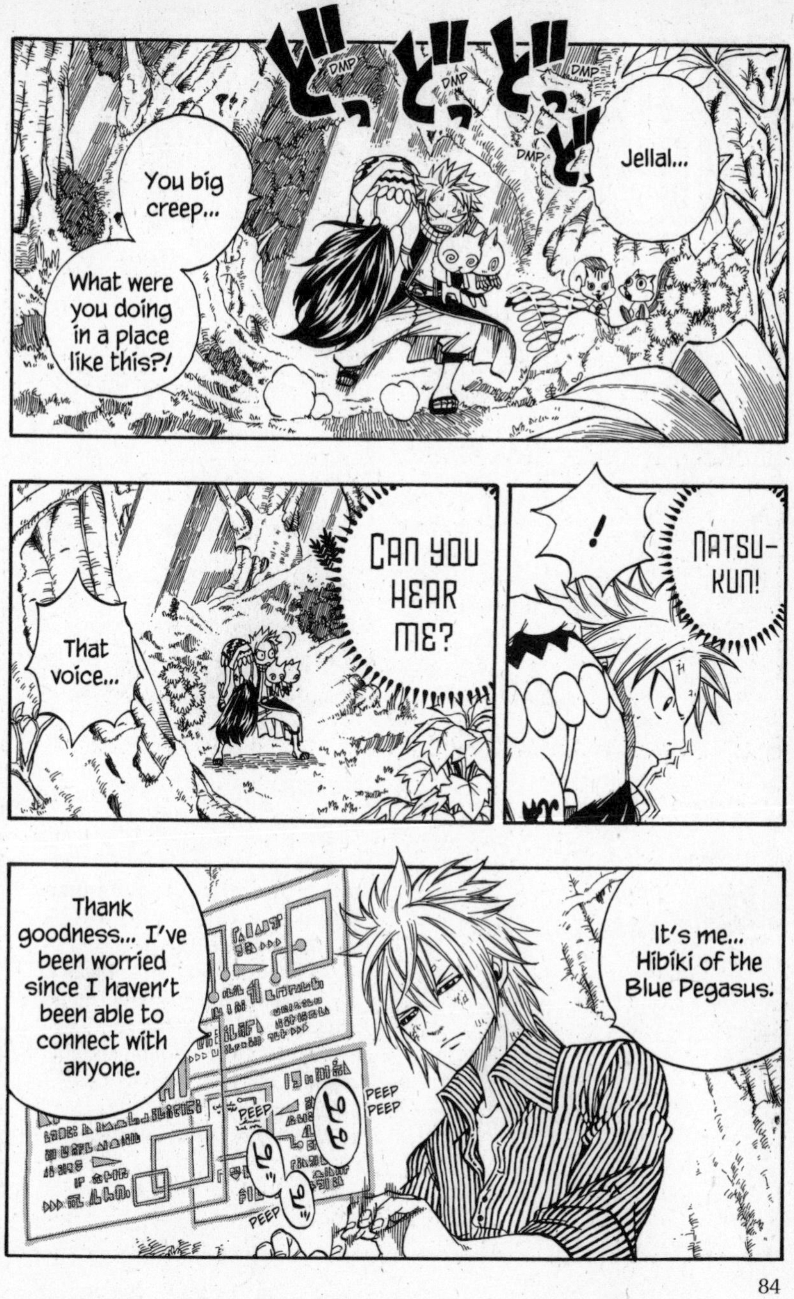
DMP
DMP
DMP
DMP
Jellal...
You big creep...
What were you doing in a place like this?!
!
NATSU-KUN!
CAN YOU HEAR ME?
That voice...
It's me... Hibiki of the Blue Pegasus.
Thank goodness... I've been worried since I haven't been able to connect with anyone.
PEEP PEEP
PEEP
PEEP

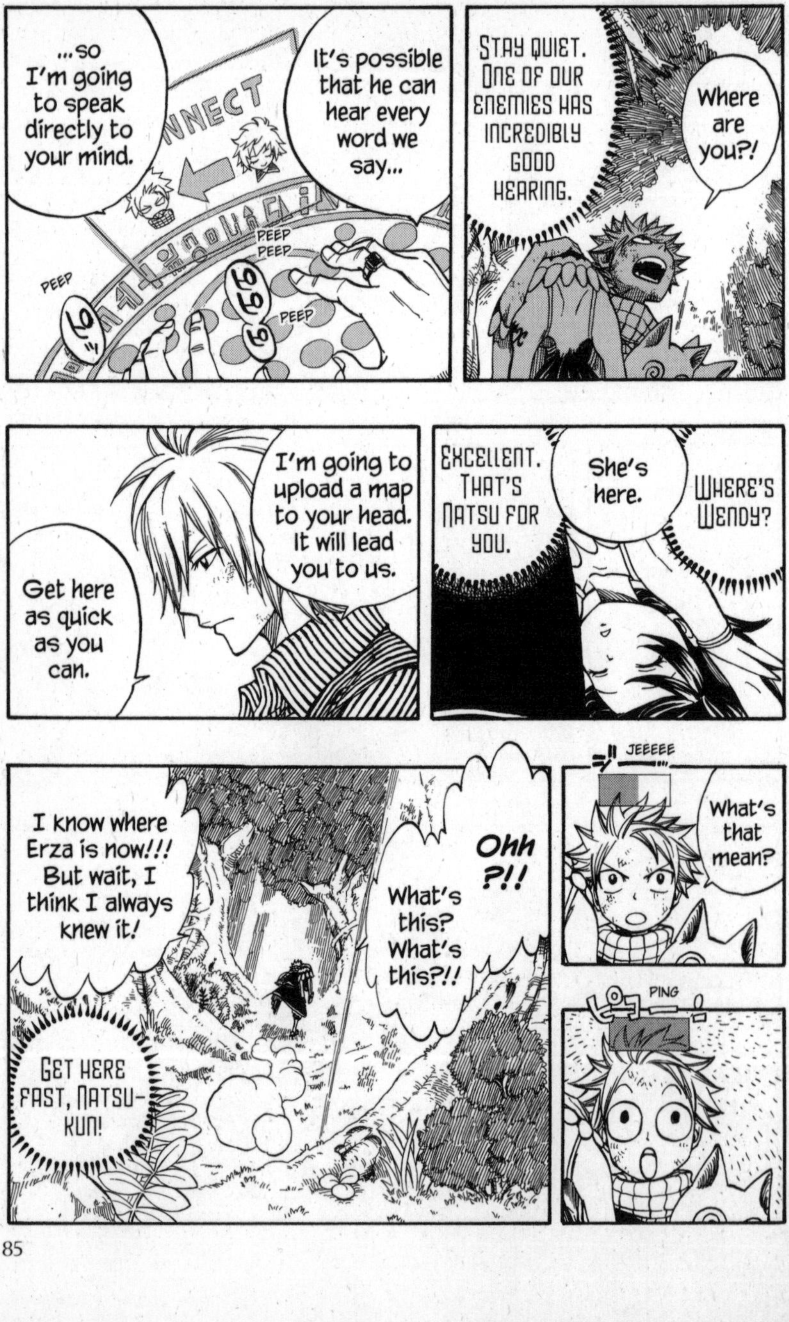
Where are you?!
STAY QUIET. ONE OF OUR ENEMIES HAS INCREDIBLY GOOD HEARING.
It's possible that he can hear every word we say...
...so I'm going to speak directly to your mind.
PEEP PEEP
PEEP
PEEP
WHERE'S WENDY?
She's here.
EXCELLENT. THAT'S NATSU FOR YOU.
I'm going to upload a map to your head. It will lead you to us.
Get here as quick as you can.
JEEEEE
What's that mean?
PING
Ohh ?!!
What's this? What's this?!!
I know where Erza is now!!! But wait, I think I always knew it!
GET HERE FAST, NATSU-KUN!

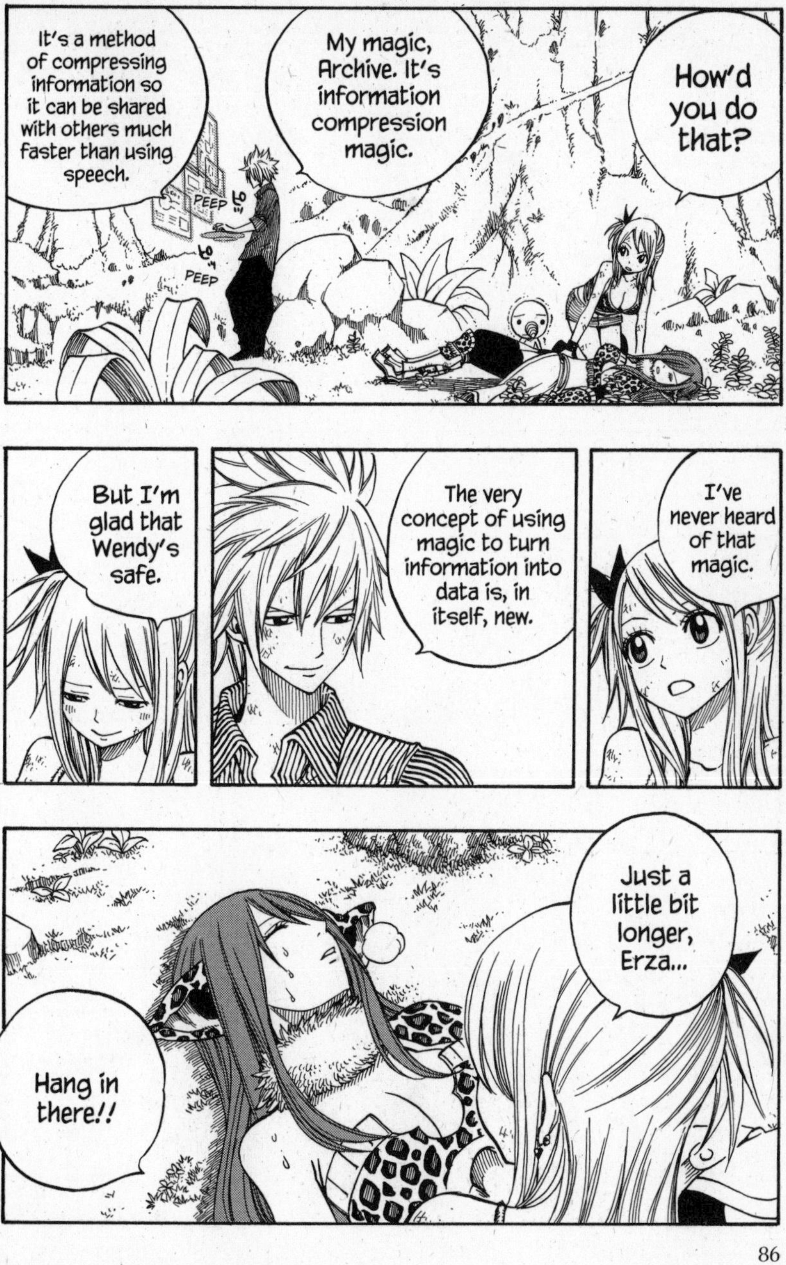
How'd you do that?
My magic, Archive. It's information compression magic.
It's a method of compressing information so it can be shared with others much faster than using speech.
PEEP
PEEP
I've never heard of that magic.
The very concept of using magic to turn information into data is, in itself, new.
But I'm glad that Wendy's safe.
Just a little bit longer, Erza...
Hang in there!!

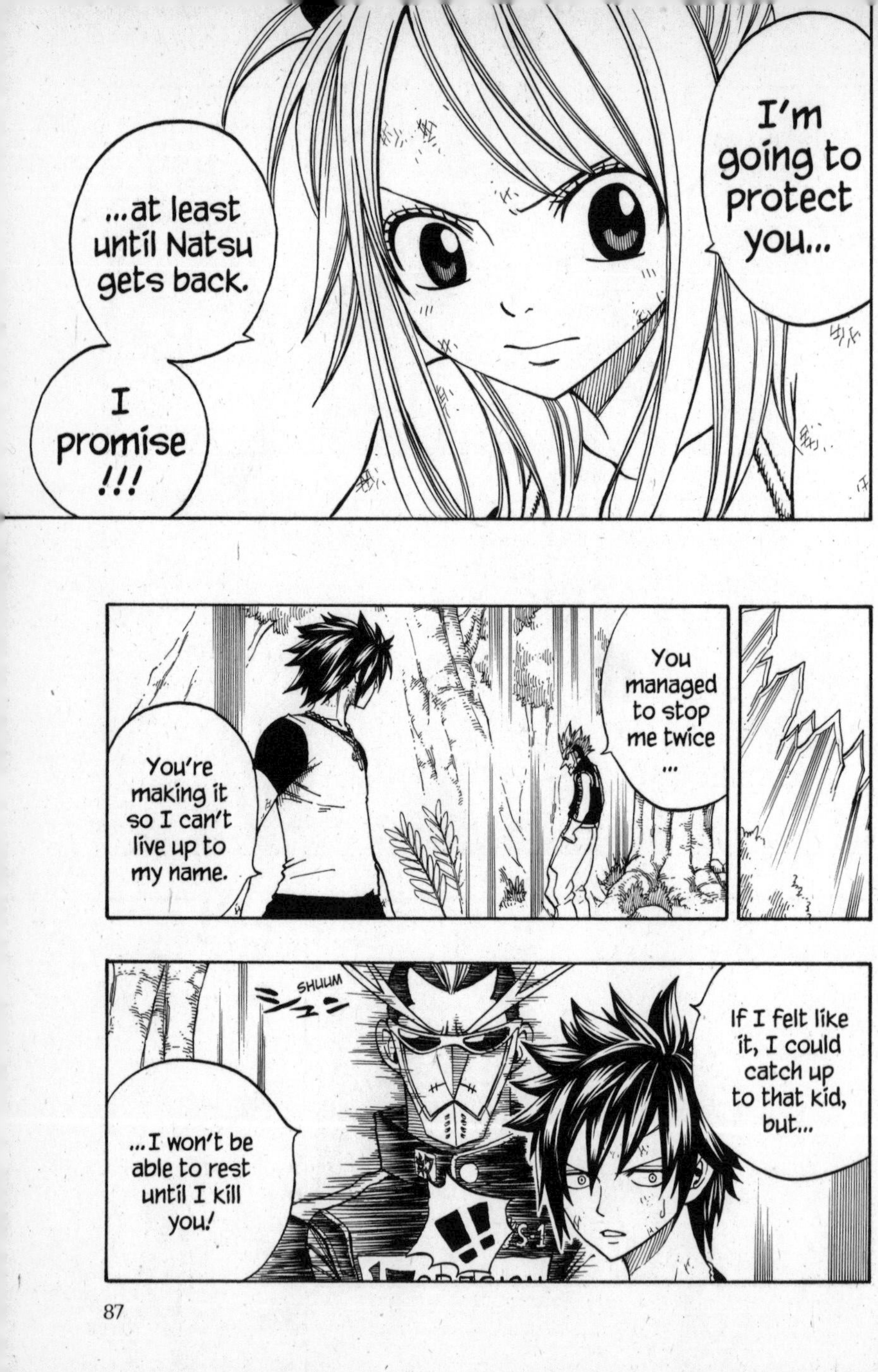
I'm going to protect you...
...at least until Natsu gets back.
I promise!!!
You managed to stop me twice ...
You're making it so I can't live up to my name.
If I felt like it, I could catch up to that kid, but...
SHUUM
...I won't be able to rest until I kill you!

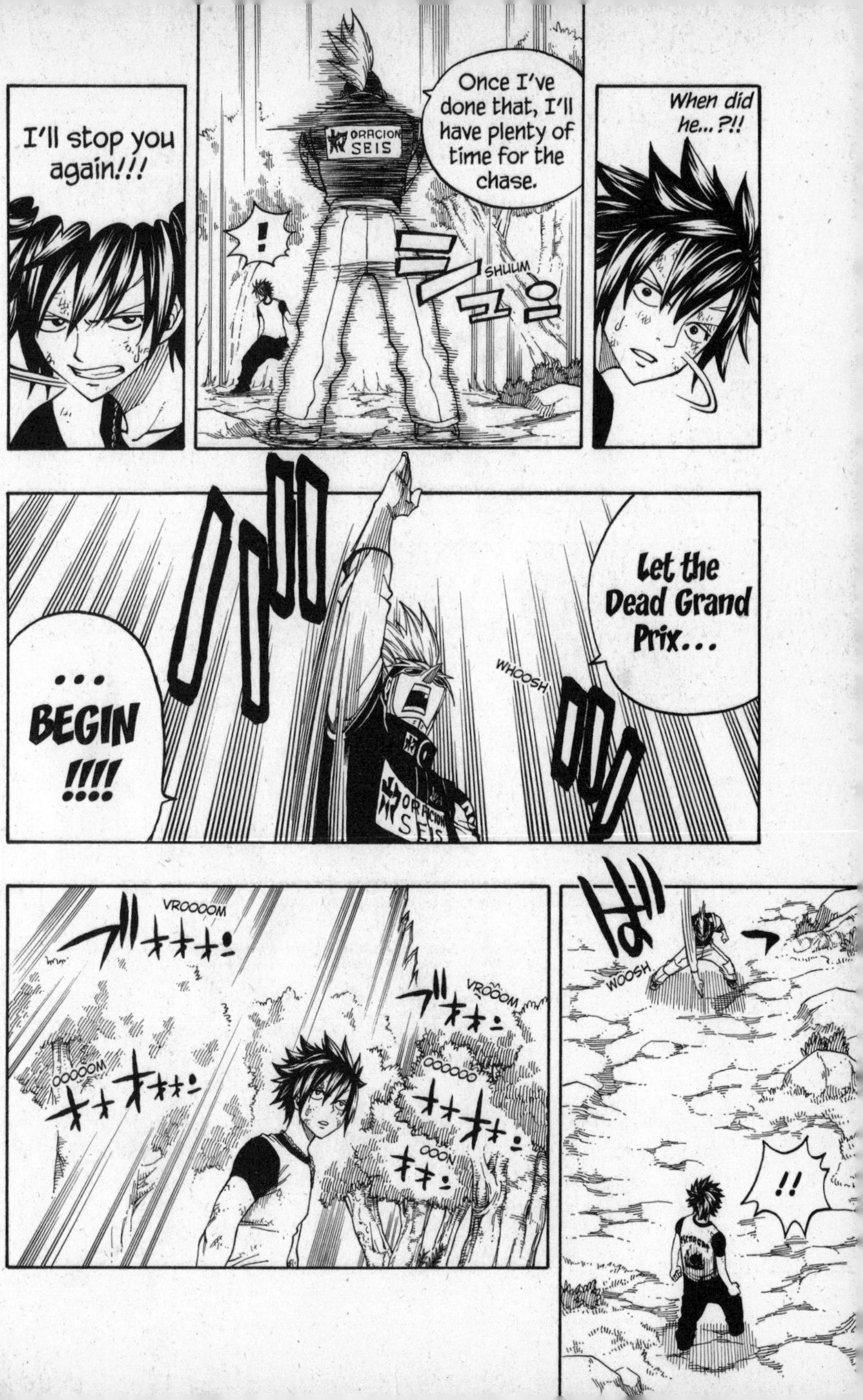
When did he...?!!
Once I've done that, I'll have plenty of time for the chase.
!
SHULUM
ORACION SEIS
I'll stop you again!!!
Let the Dead Grand Prix...
WHOOSH
ORACION SEIS
...BEGIN!!!!
WOOSH
!!
VROOOOM
VROOOM
OOOOOO
OOON
OOOOOOM

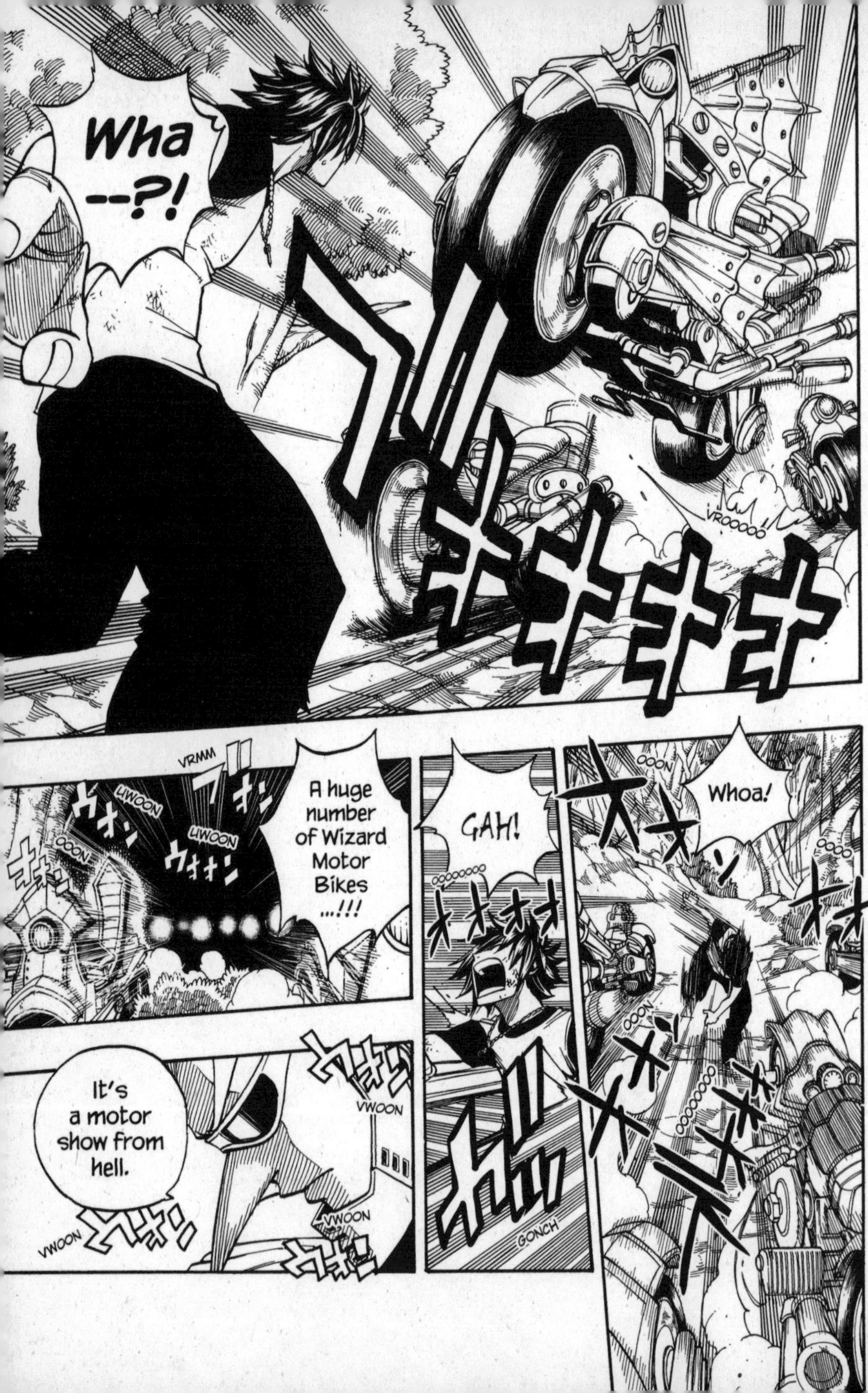
Wha --?!
VROOOOO
OOON
Whoa!
OOOO
OOON
GAH!
OOOOOOOO
GONCH
A huge number of Wizard Motor Bikes ...!!!
VRMM
UWOON
UWOON
OOON
It's a motor show from hell.
VWOON
VWOON
VWOON

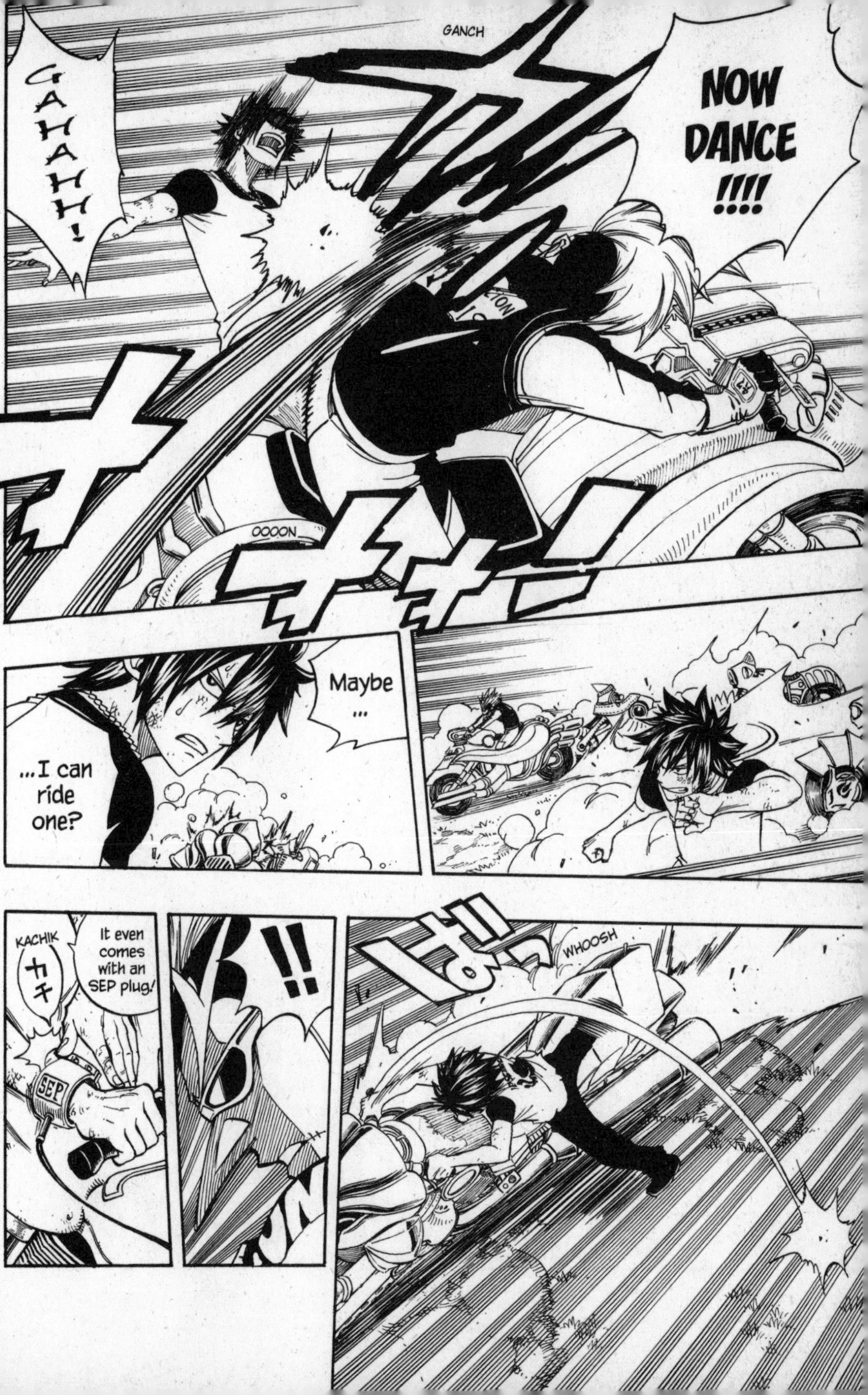
NOW DANCE !!!!
GANCH
GAHAHH!
OOOON
Maybe ...
...I can ride one?
WHOOSH
!!
It even comes with an SEP plug!
KACHIK
カチ
SEP

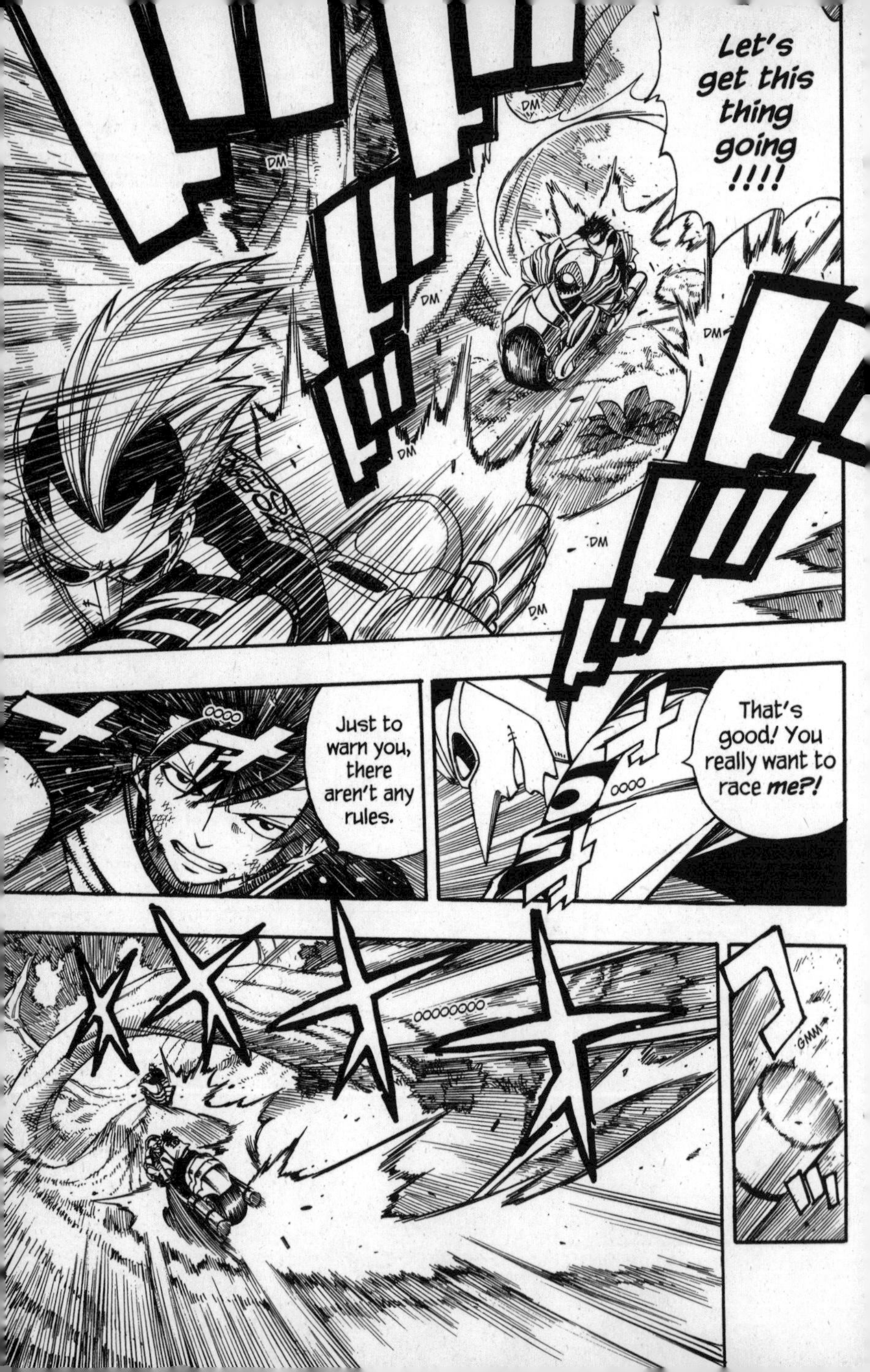
Let's get this thing going !!!!
DM
That's good! You really want to race me?!
Just to warn you, there aren't any rules.
GMM

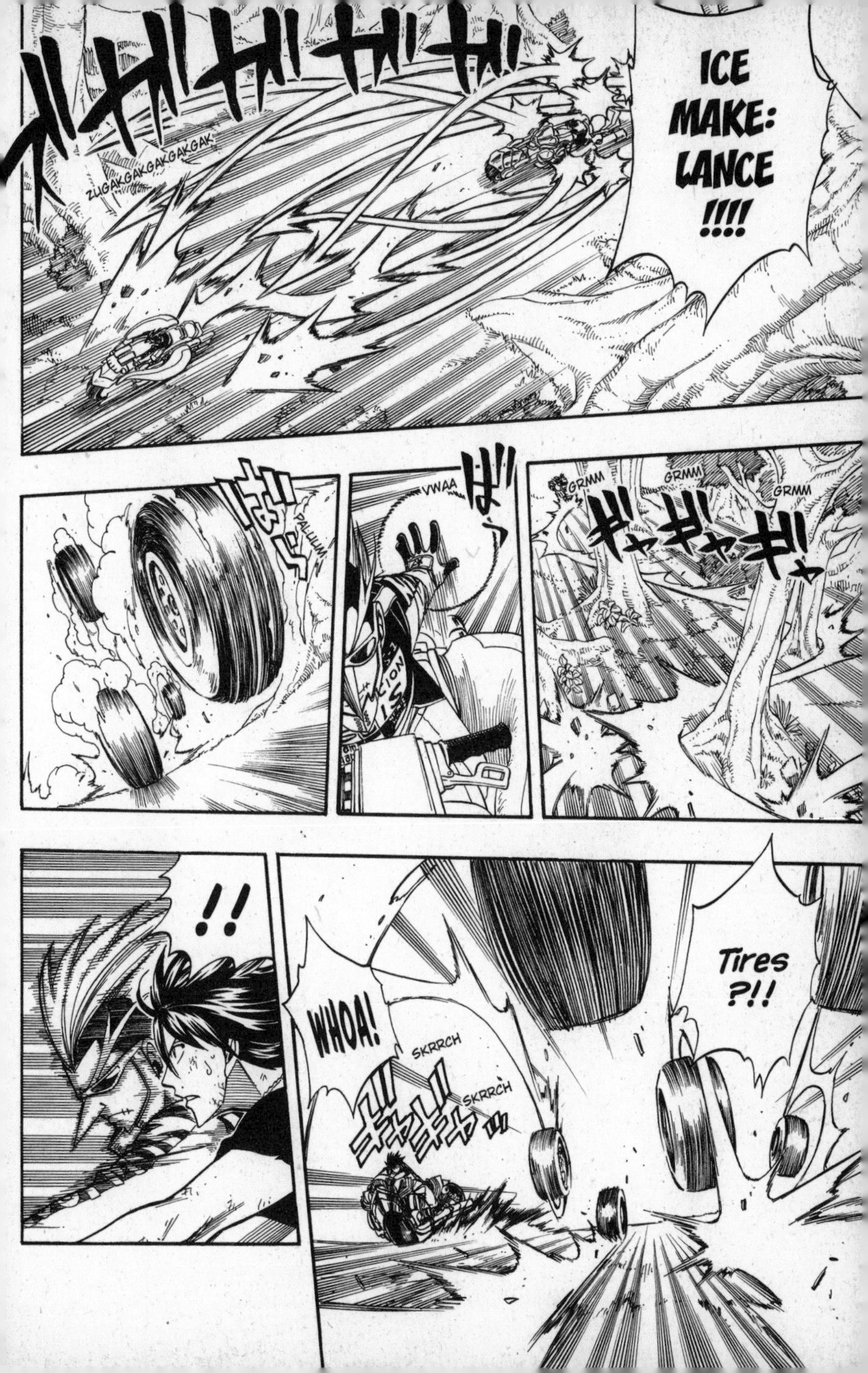
ICE MAKE: LANCE !!!!
ZUGAKGAKGAKGAK
GRMM
GRMM
GRMM
VWAA
PALLUUM
Tires ?!!
WHOA!
SKRRCH
SKRRCH
!!

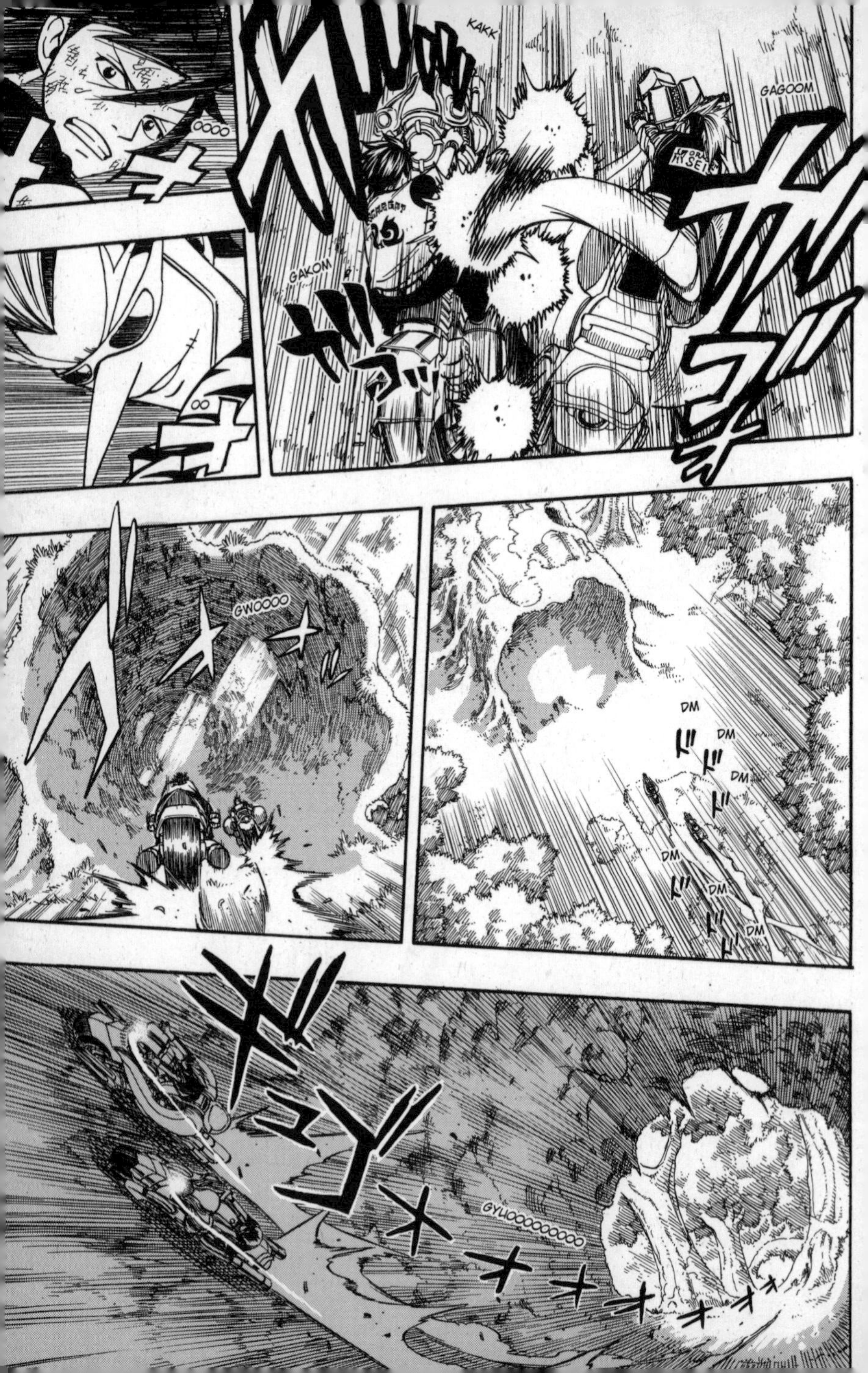
GAGOOM
KAKK
GAKOM
OOOO
DM
DM
DM
DM
DM
DM
GWOOOO
GYUOOOOOOOOOO

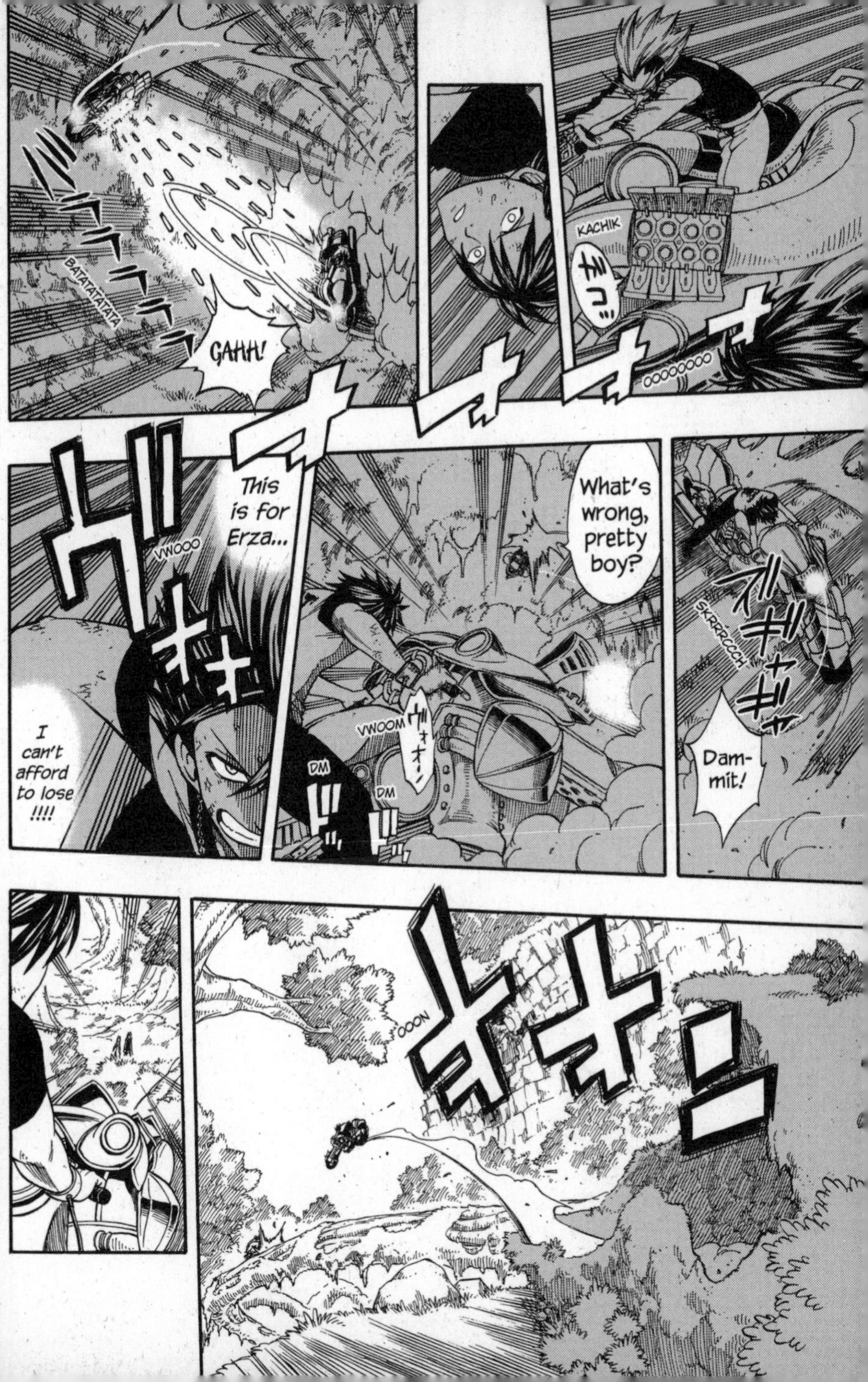
KACHIK
OOOOOOOO
BATATATATATA
GAHH!
SKRRRCCCH
Dam-mit!
What's wrong, pretty boy?
VWOOM
DM
DM
This is for Erza...
VWOOO
I can't afford to lose !!!!
OOON

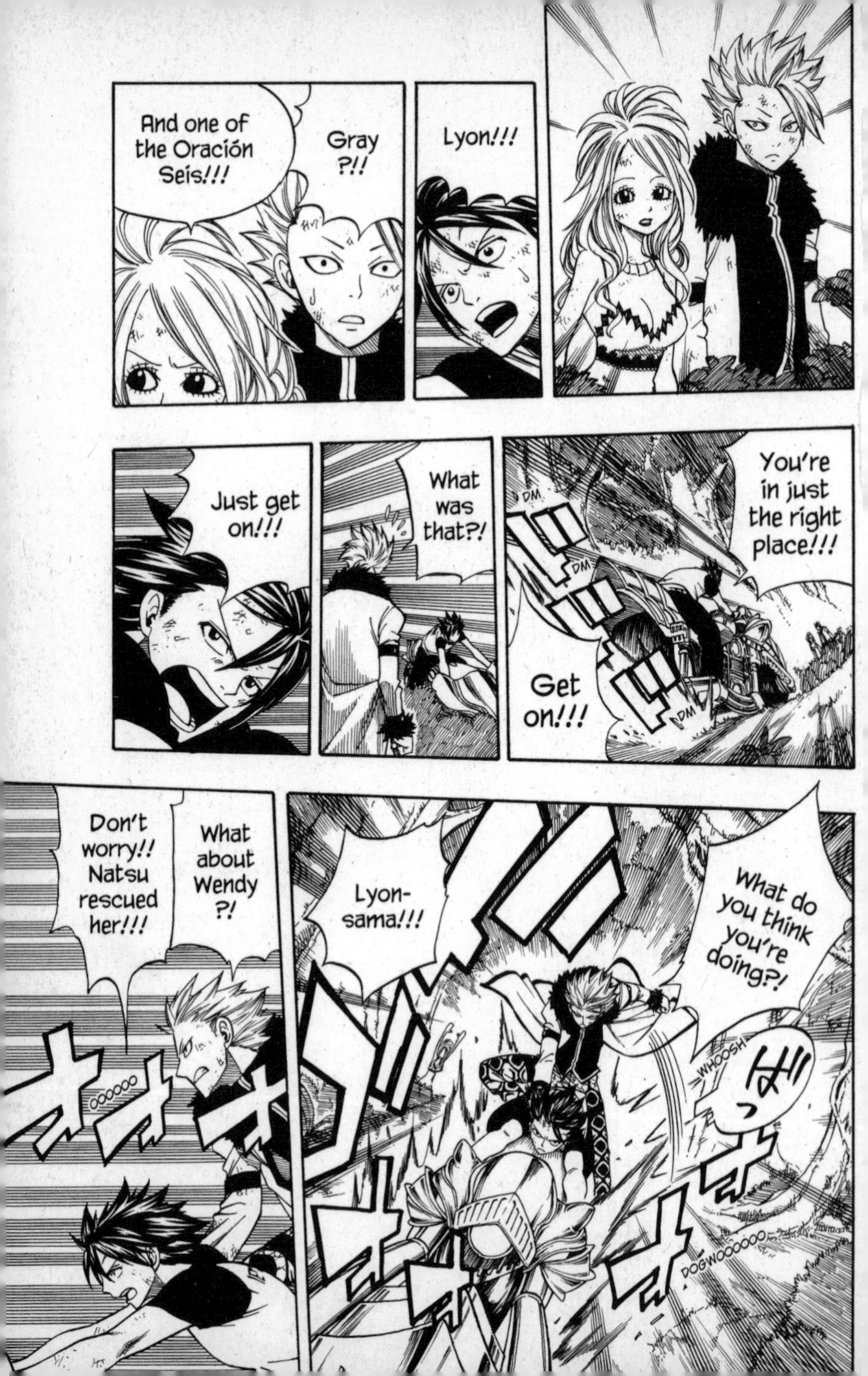
Lyon!!!
Gray ?!!
And one of the Oración Seis!!!
You're in just the right place!!!
DM
DM
DM
Get on!!!
What was that?!
Just get on!!!
What do you think you're doing?!
Lyon-sama!!!
WHOOSH
DOGWOOOOOOO
What about Wendy ?!
Don't worry!! Natsu rescued her!!!
OOOOOO

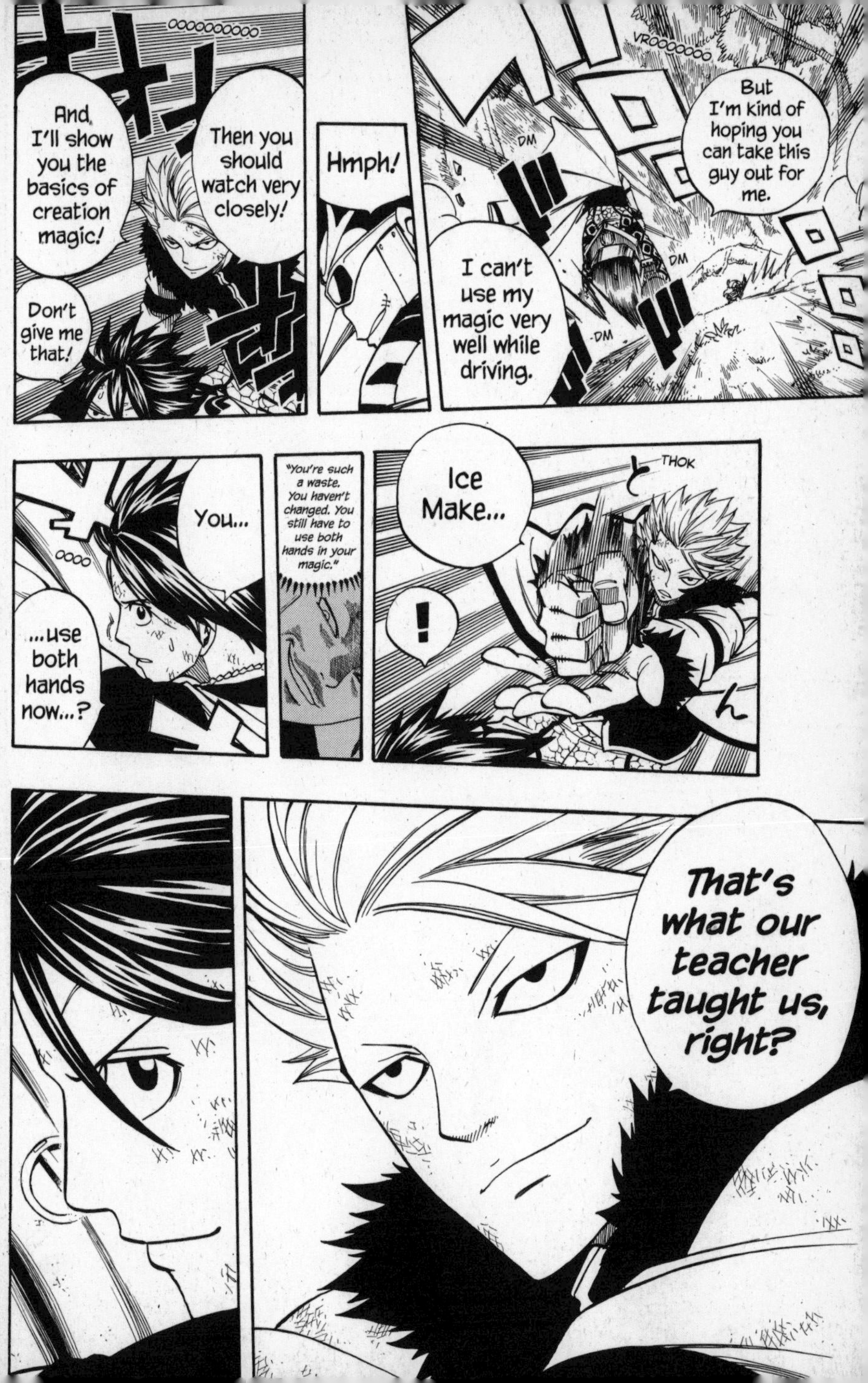
VROOOOOOOO
But I'm kind of hoping you can take this guy out for me.
DM
I can't use my magic very well while driving.
DM
DM
Hmph!
OOOOOOOOOO
Then you should watch very closely!
And I'll show you the basics of creation magic!
Don't give me that!
THOK
Ice Make...
!
"You're such a waste. You haven't changed. You still have to use both hands in your magic."
You...
OOOO
...use both hands now...?
That's what our teacher taught us, right?

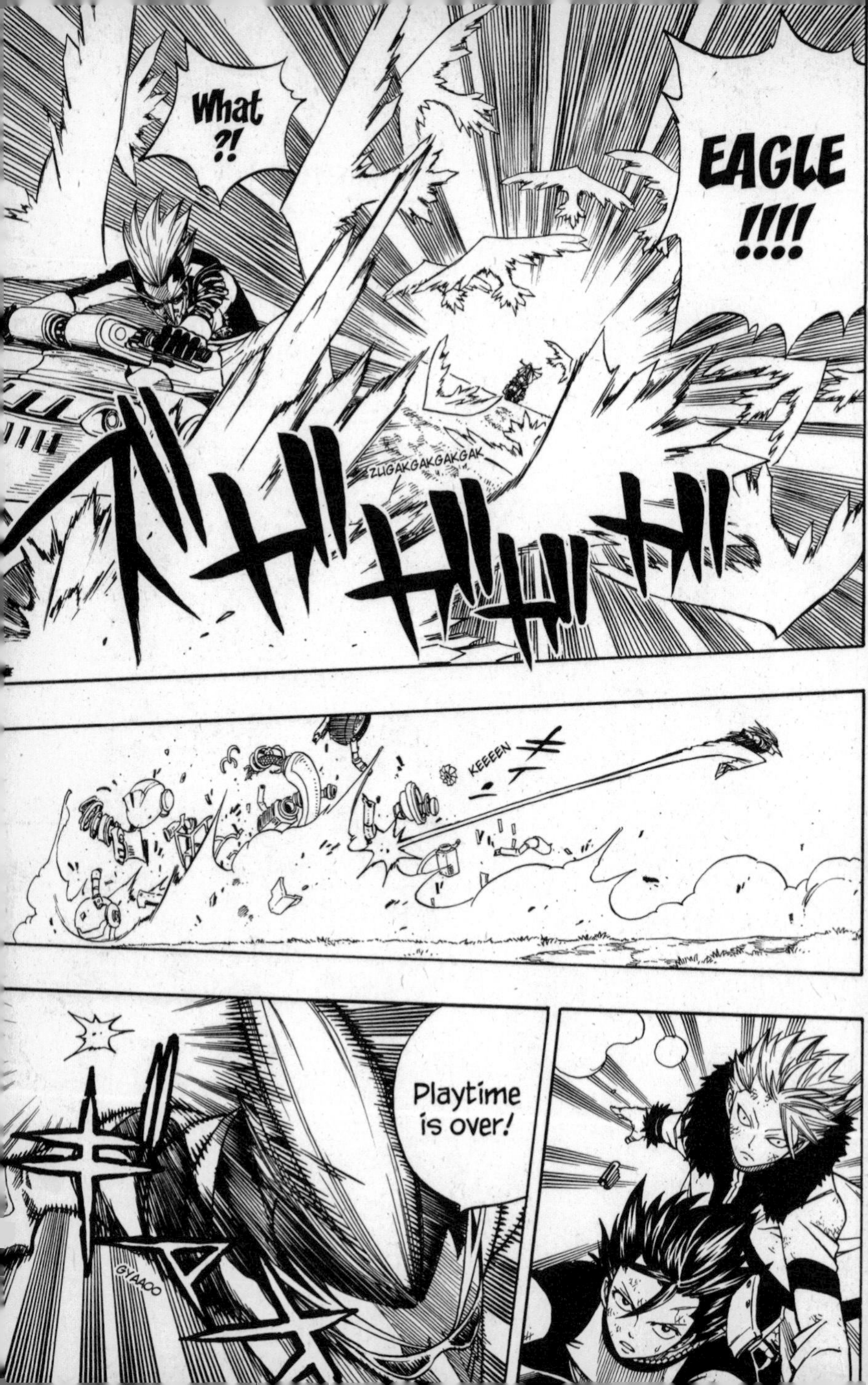
EAGLE !!!!
What ?!
ZUGAKGAKGAKGAK
KEEEEN
Playtime is over!
GYAAOO

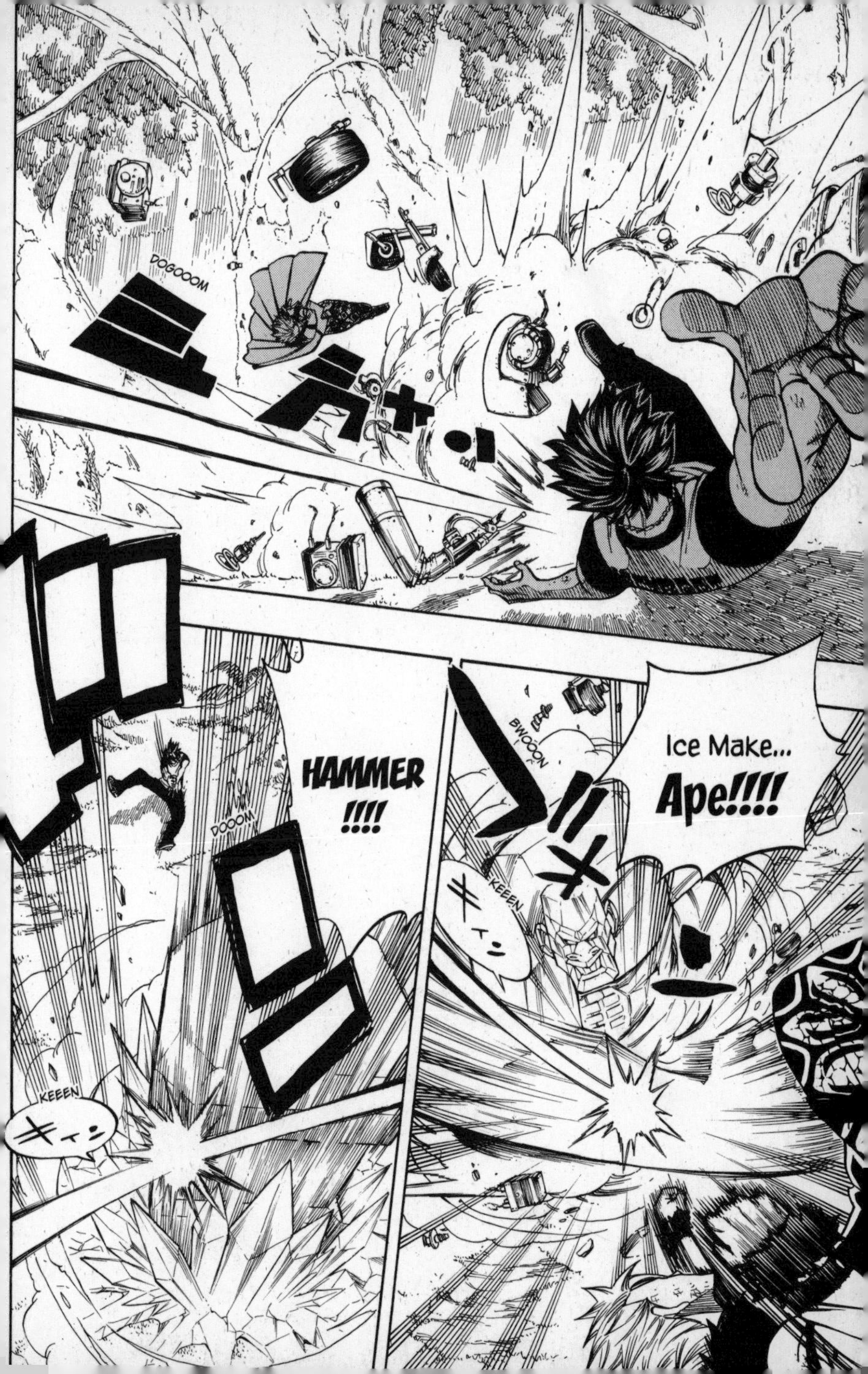
DOGOOOM
BWOOON
Ice Make... Ape!!!!
KEEEN
DOOOM
HAMMER!!!!
KEEEN

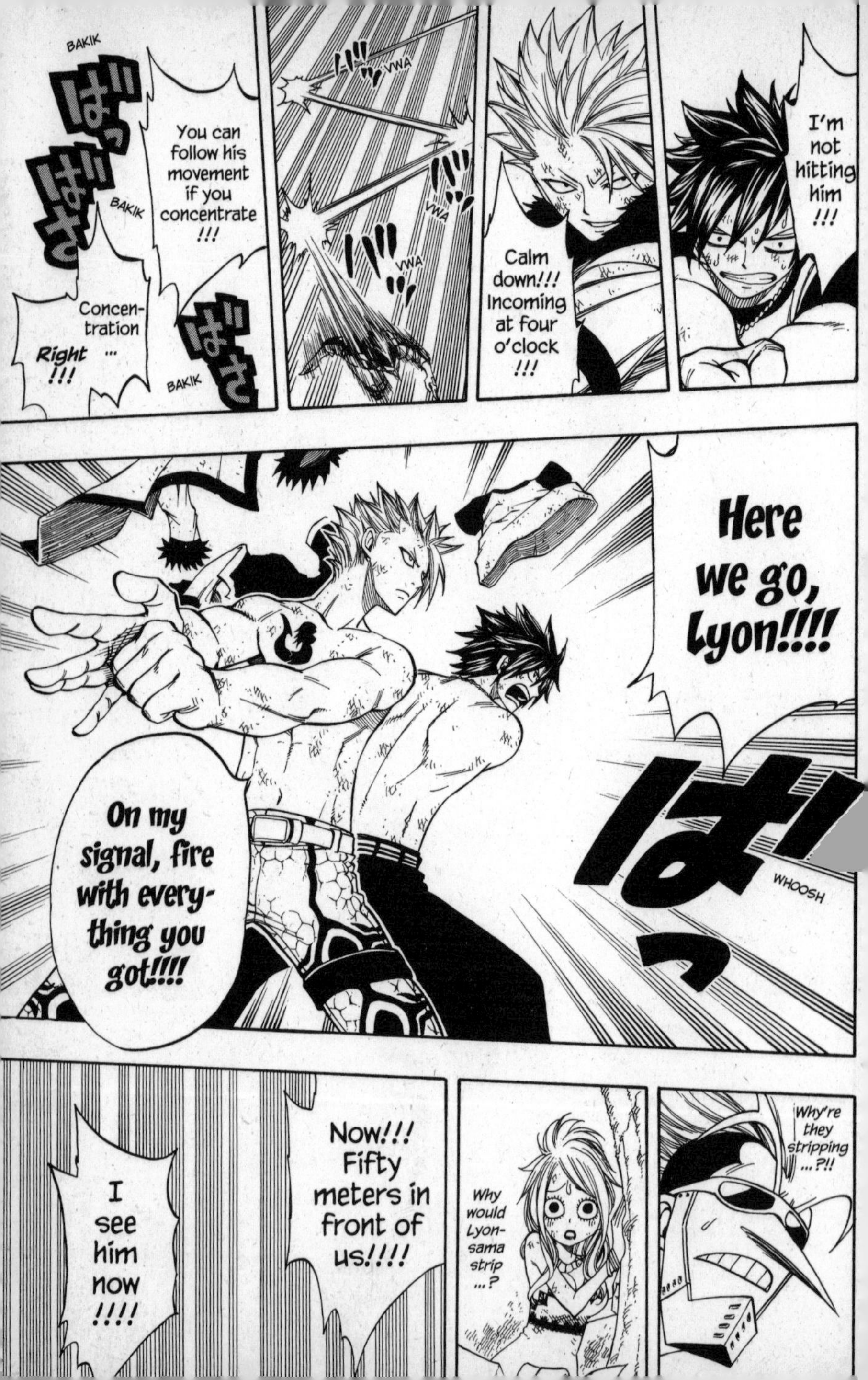
I'm not hitting him!!!
Calm down!!! Incoming at four o'clock!!!
VWA
VWA
VWA
You can follow his movement if you concentrate!!!
BAKIK
BAKIK
BAKIK
Concen-tration... Right!!!
Here we go, Lyon!!!!
WHOOSH
On my signal, fire with every-thing you got!!!!
Why're they stripping...?!!
Why would Lyon-sama strip...?
Now!!! Fifty meters in front of us!!!!
I see him now!!!!

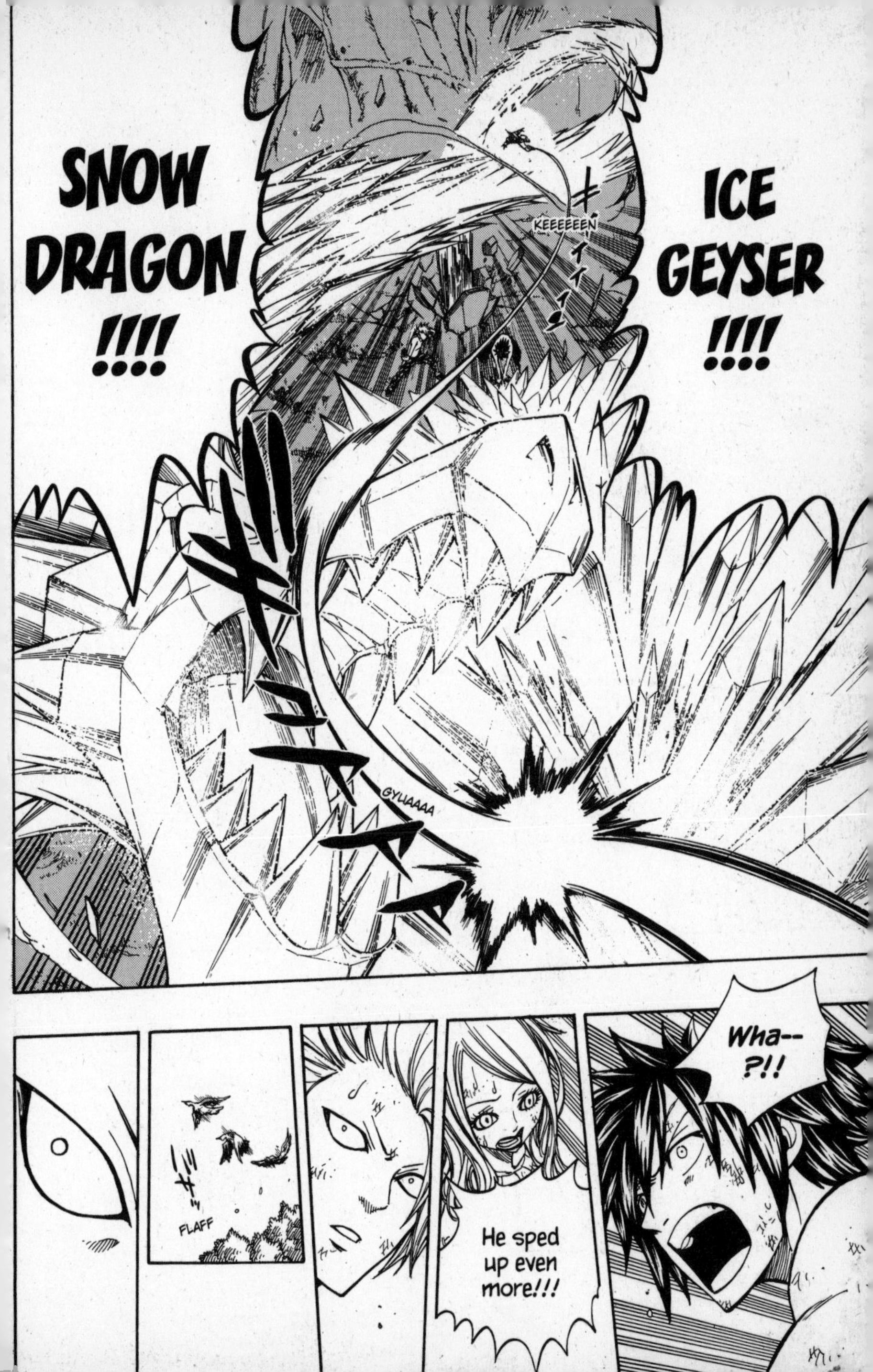
ICE GEYSER!!!!
SNOW DRAGON!!!!
KEEEEEEN
GYUAAAA
Wha--?!!
He sped up even more!!!
FLAFF

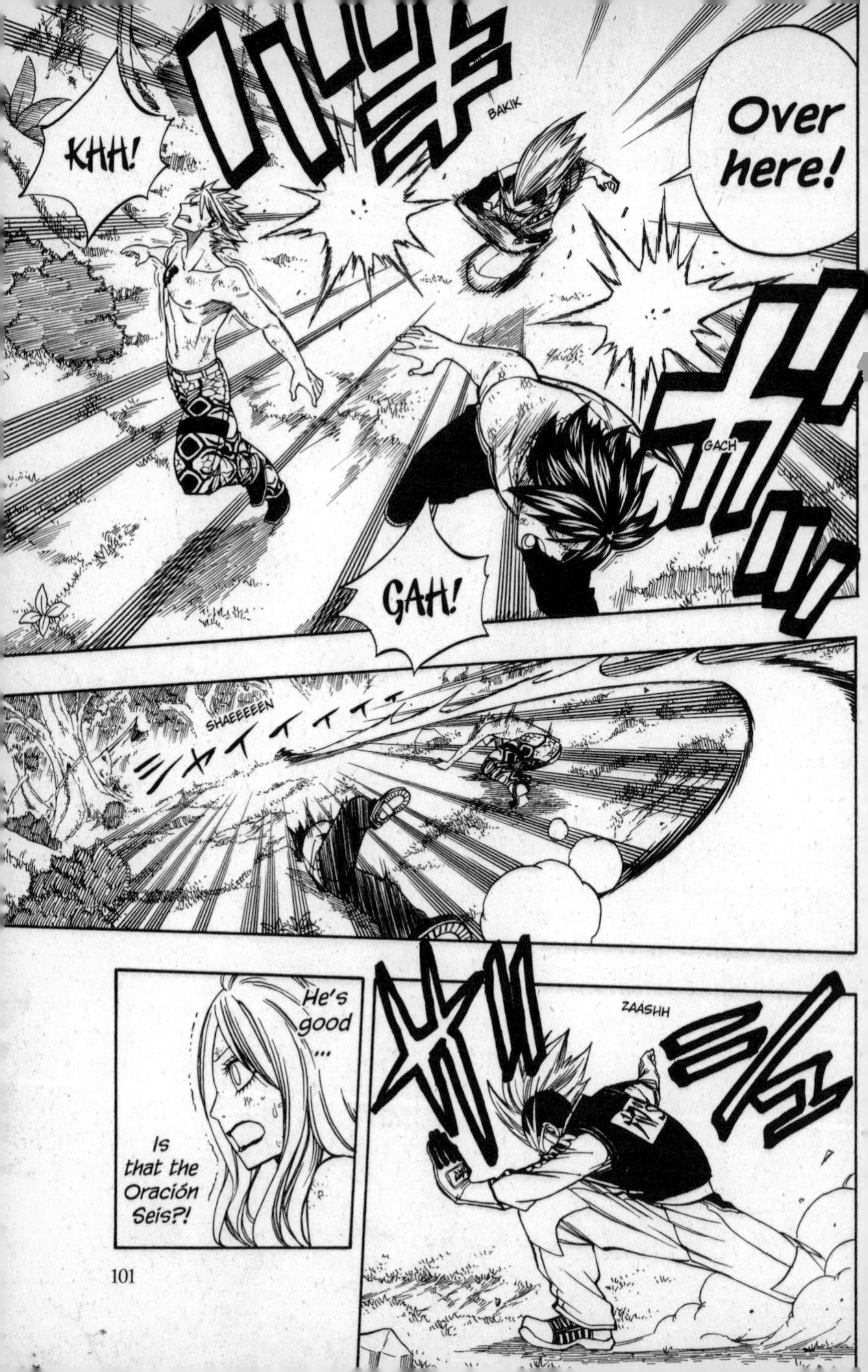
Over here!
BAKIK
KHH!
GACH
GAH!
SHAEEEEEN
ZAASHH
He's good ...
Is that the Oración Seis?!

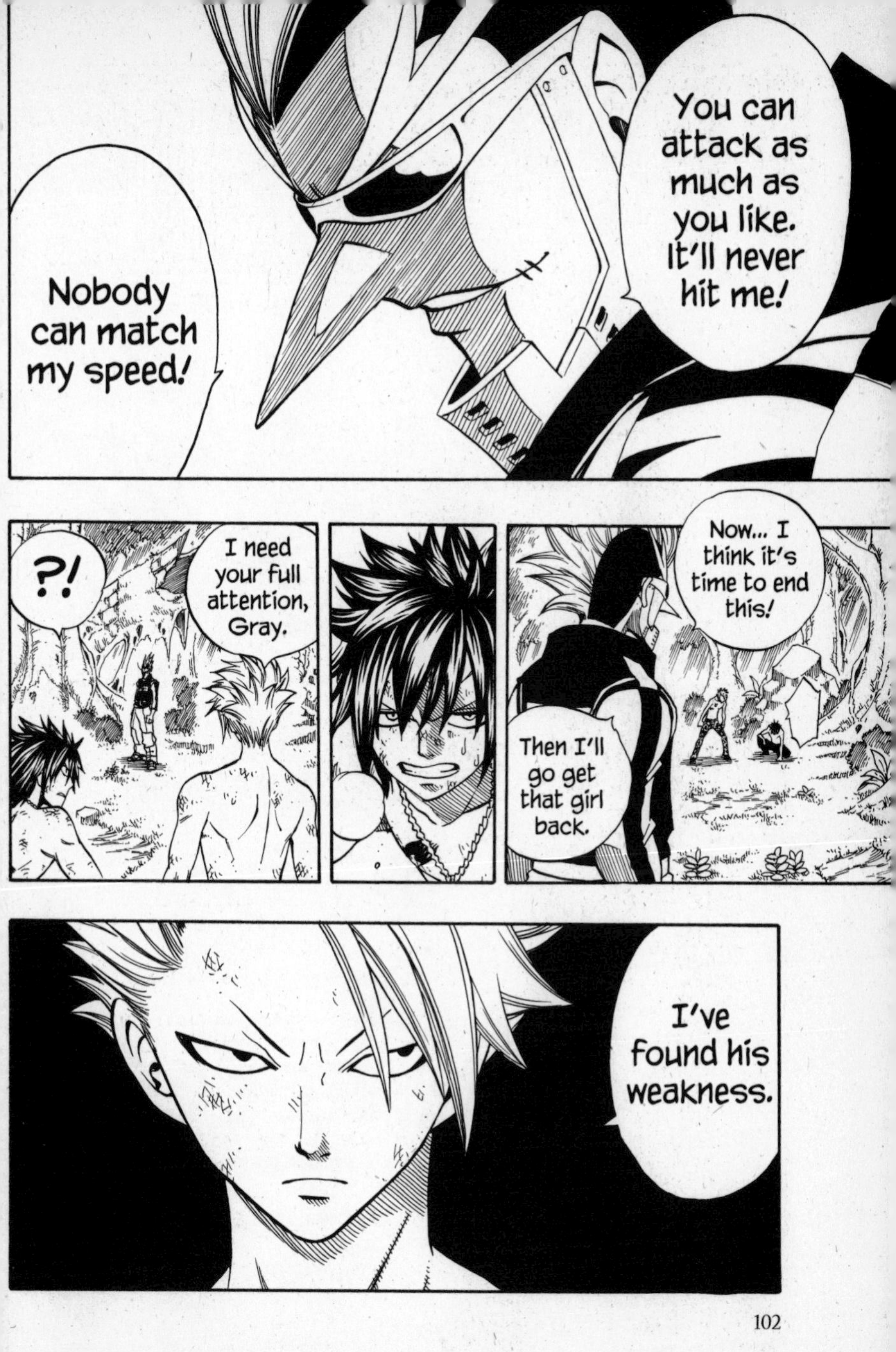
You can attack as much as you like. It'll never hit me!
Nobody can match my speed!
Now... I think it's time to end this!
Then I'll go get that girl back.
I need your full attention, Gray.
?!
I've found his weakness.

FAIRY TAIL

フェアリーテイル

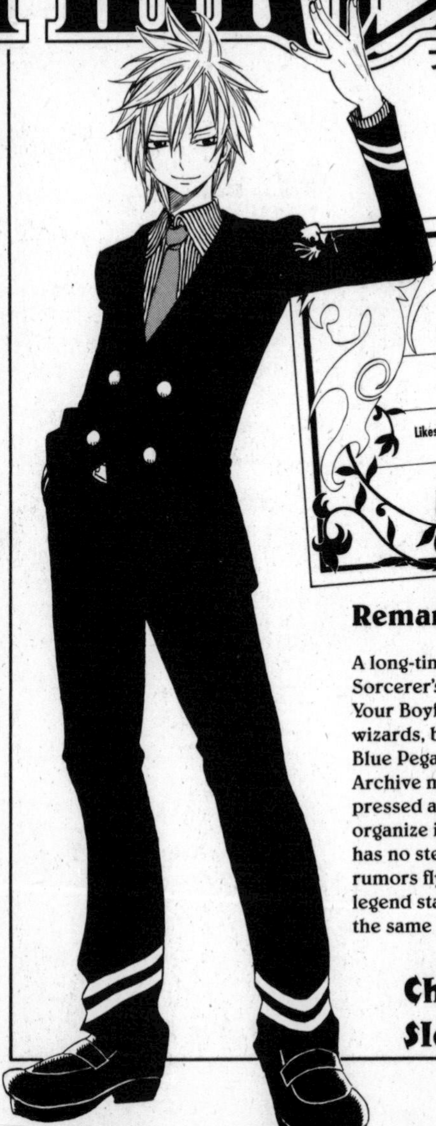

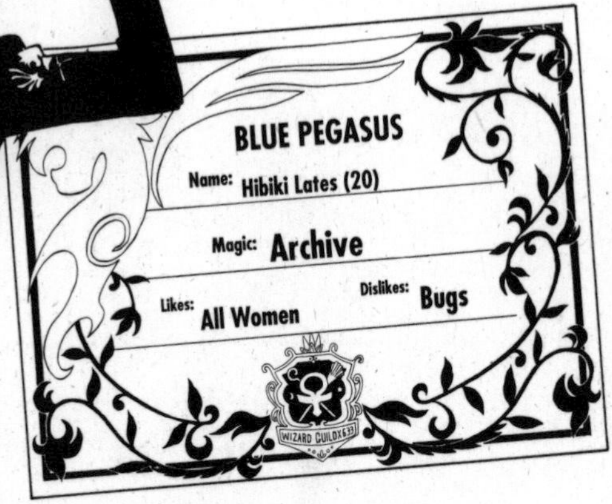
BLUE PEGASUS
Name: Hibiki Lates (20)
Magic: Archive
Likes: All Women
Dislikes: Bugs
WIZARD GUILD X633

Remarks

A long-time top-ranker in the Weekly Sorcerer's poll of "Wizards You Wish Were Your Boyfriend." It's said that many female wizards, bewitched by his looks, try to join Blue Pegasus.
Archive magic lets information be compressed and sent to a recipient. He can also organize information and oversee battles. He has no steady girlfriend, but there are always rumors flying around who he's seeing. A legend states that he once dated 18 women at the same time (the truth is unconfirmed).

Chapter 140, Slow Speed World

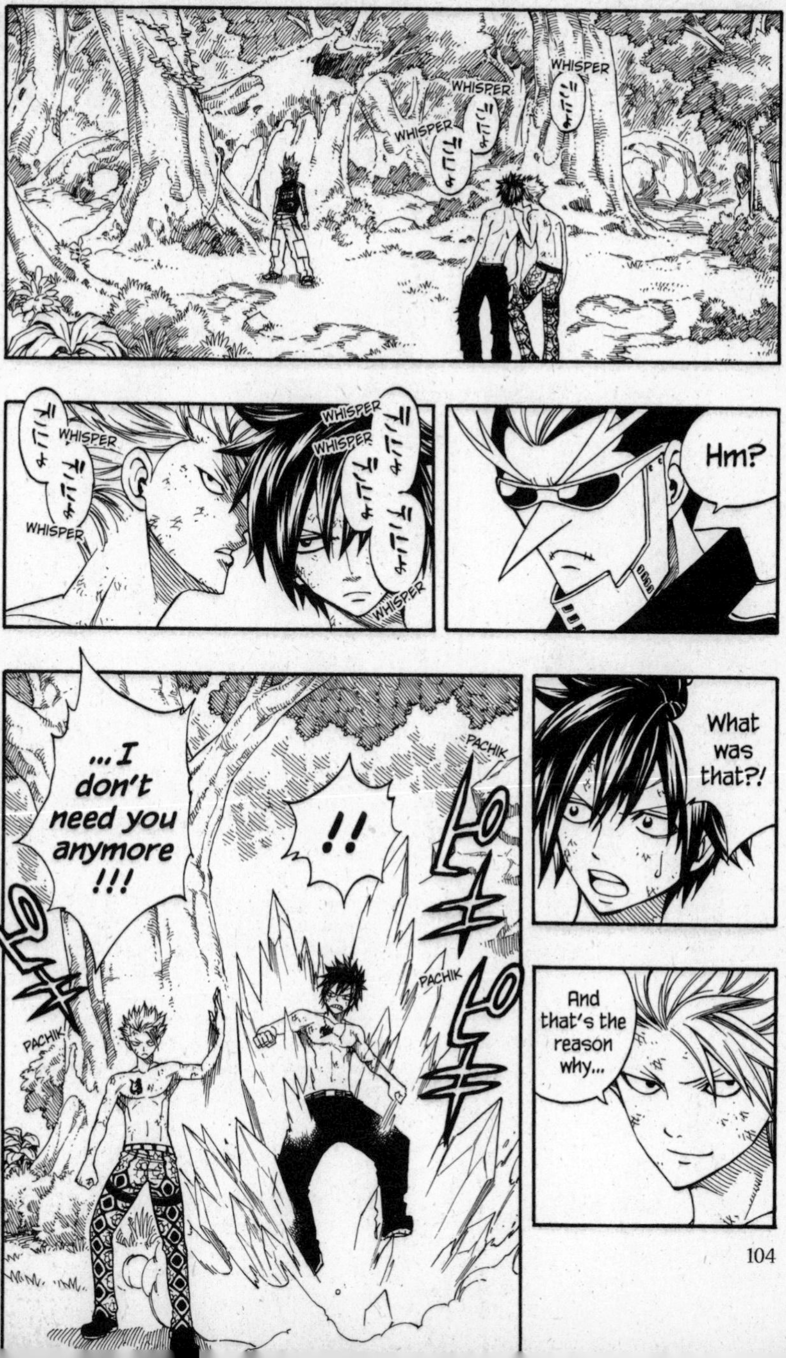
WHISPER
WHISPER
WHISPER
Hm?
WHISPER
WHISPER
WHISPER
WHISPER
What was that?!
And that's the reason why...
...I don't need you anymore!!!
!!
PACHIK
PACHIK
PACHIK

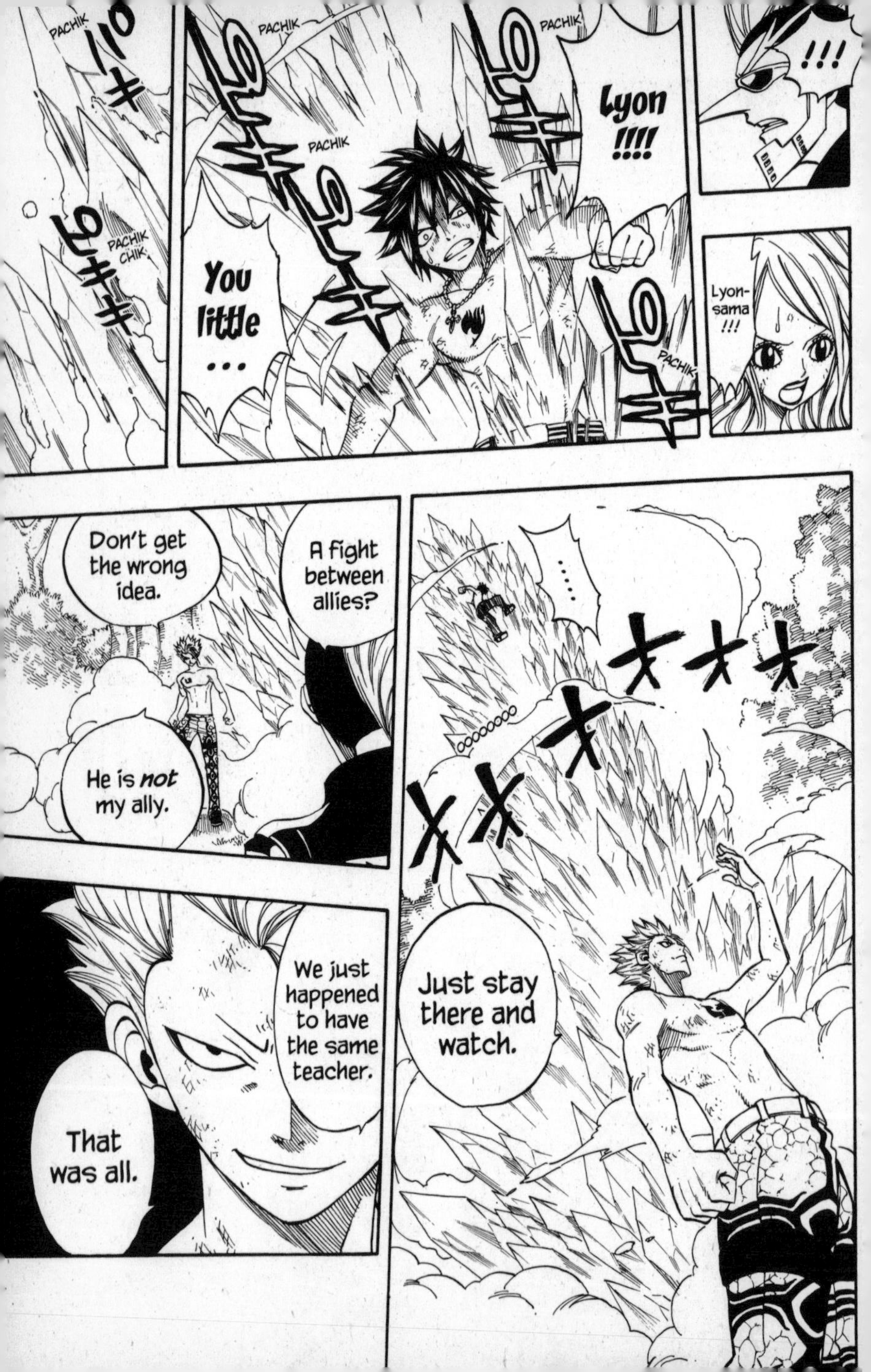
!!!
Lyon-sama !!!
PACHIK
Lyon !!!!
PACHIK
PACHIK
You little ...
PACHIK
PACHIK
PACHIK CHIK
......
Just stay there and watch.
A fight between allies?
Don't get the wrong idea.
He is *not* my ally.
We just happened to have the same teacher.
That was all.

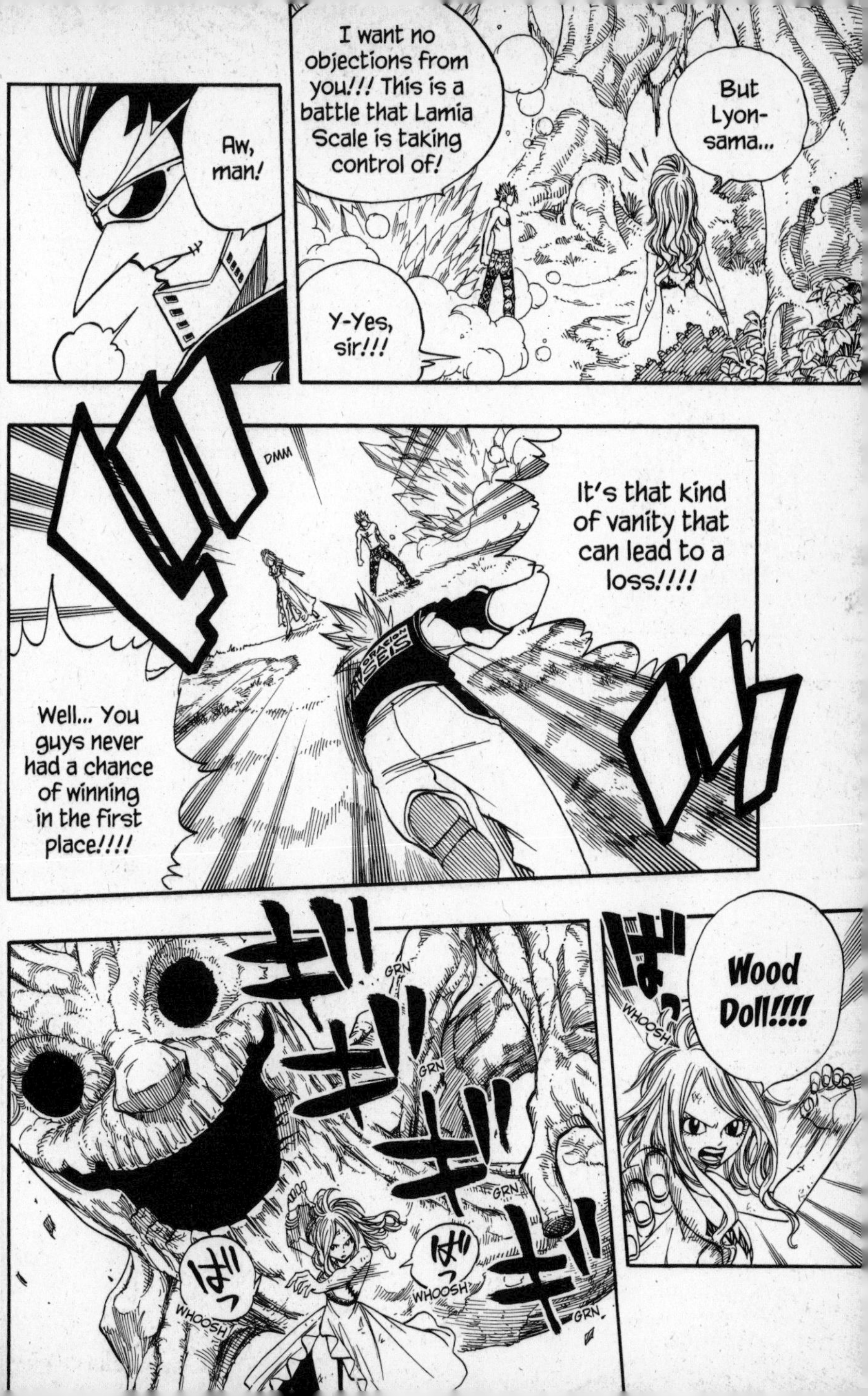
But Lyon-sama...
I want no objections from you!!! This is a battle that Lamia Scale is taking control of!
Y-Yes, sir!!!
Aw, man!
DMM
It's that kind of vanity that can lead to a loss!!!!
Well... You guys never had a chance of winning in the first place!!!!
WHOOSH
Wood Doll!!!!
GRN
GRN
GRN
WHOOSH
GRN
WHOOSH

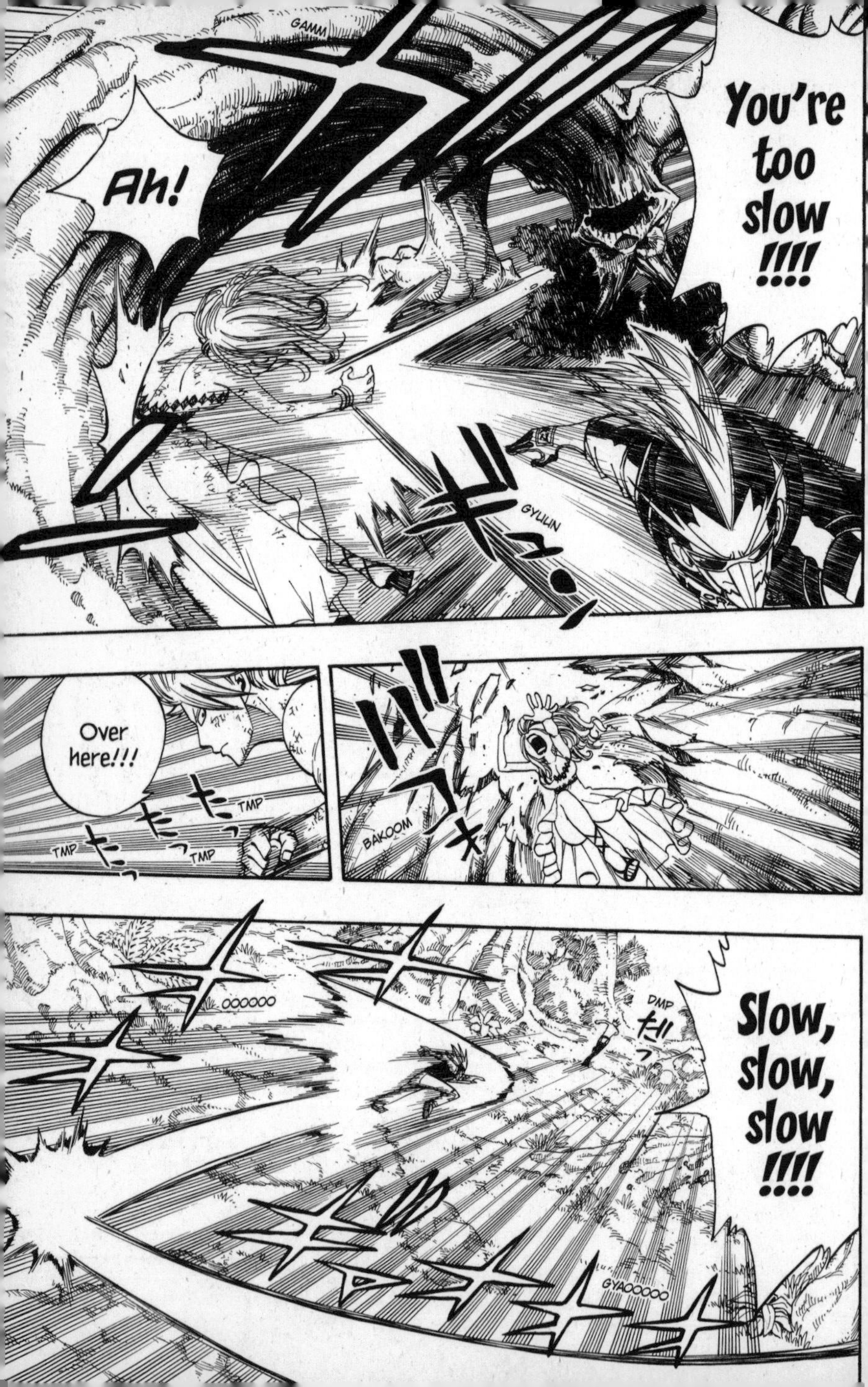

You're too slow!!!!
GAMM
Ah!
GYUUN
BAKOOM
Over here!!!
TMP
TMP
TMP
Slow, slow, slow!!!!
DMP
OOOOOO
GYAOOOOO

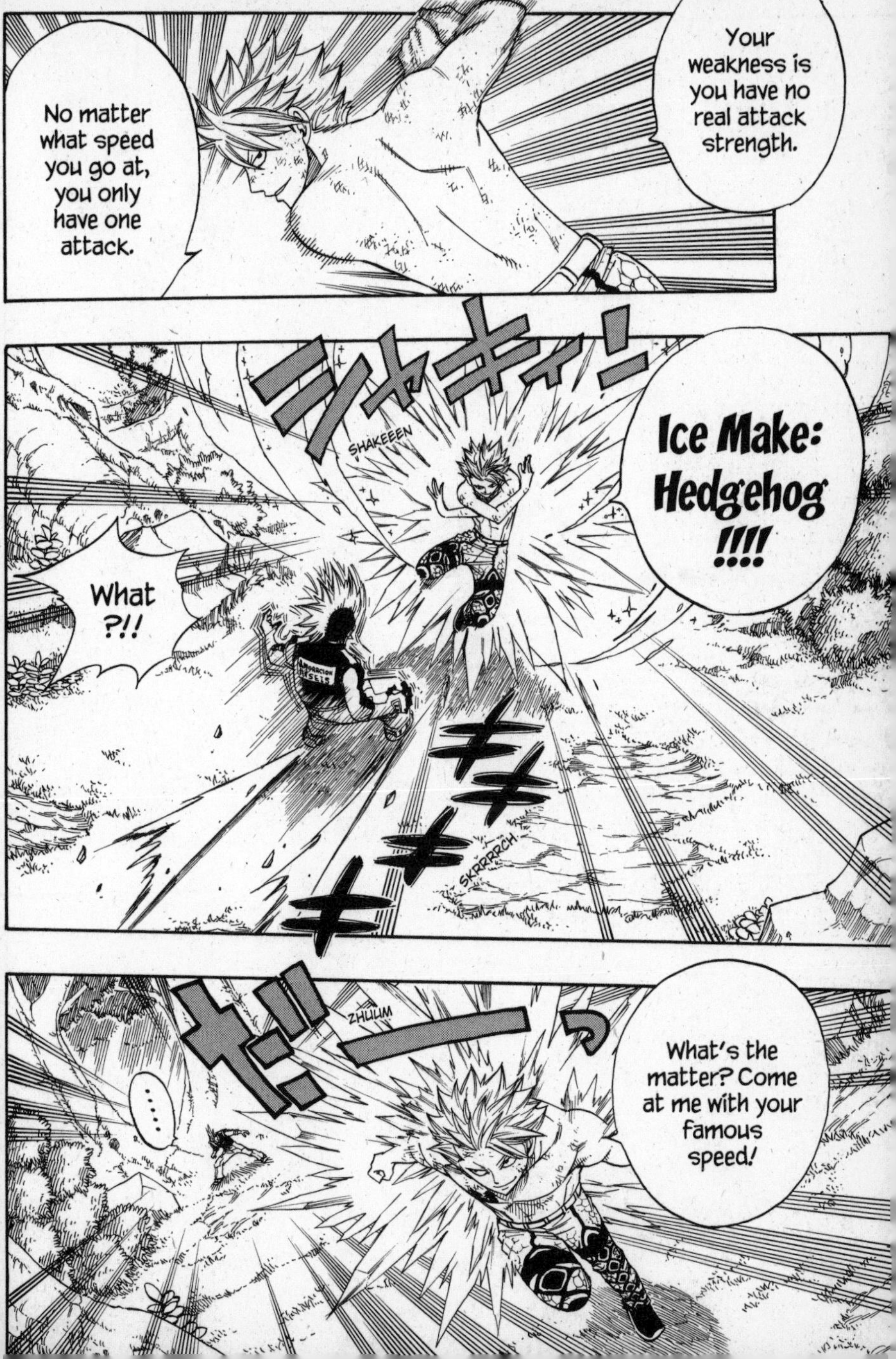
Your weakness is you have no real attack strength.
No matter what speed you go at, you only have one attack.
SHAKEEEN
Ice Make: Hedgehog !!!!
What ?!!
SKRRRRCH
ZHULUM
What's the matter? Come at me with your famous speed!
......

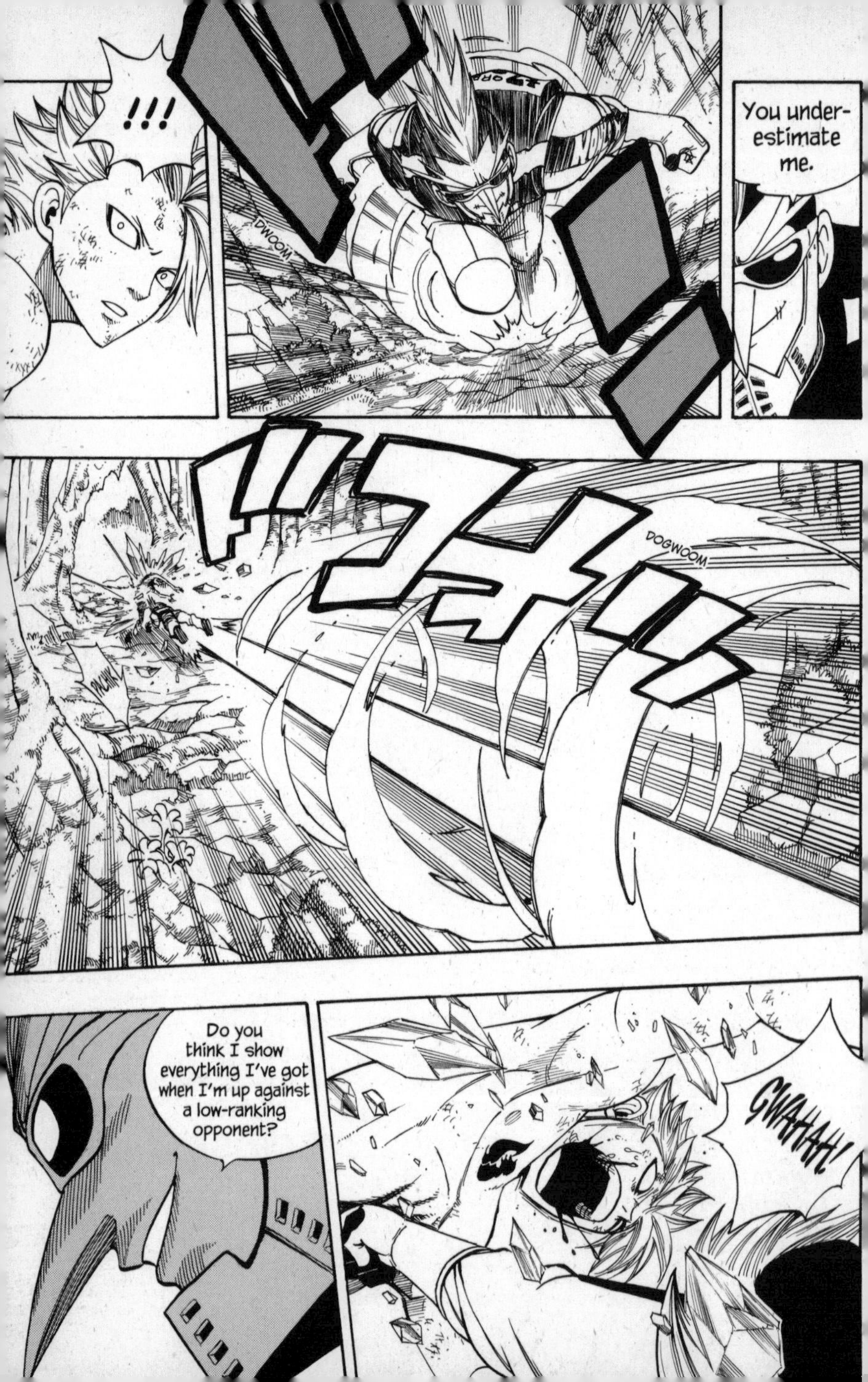
You under-estimate me.
DWOOM
!!!
DOGWOOM
PACHK
GWAHAH!
Do you think I show everything I've got when I'm up against a low-ranking opponent?

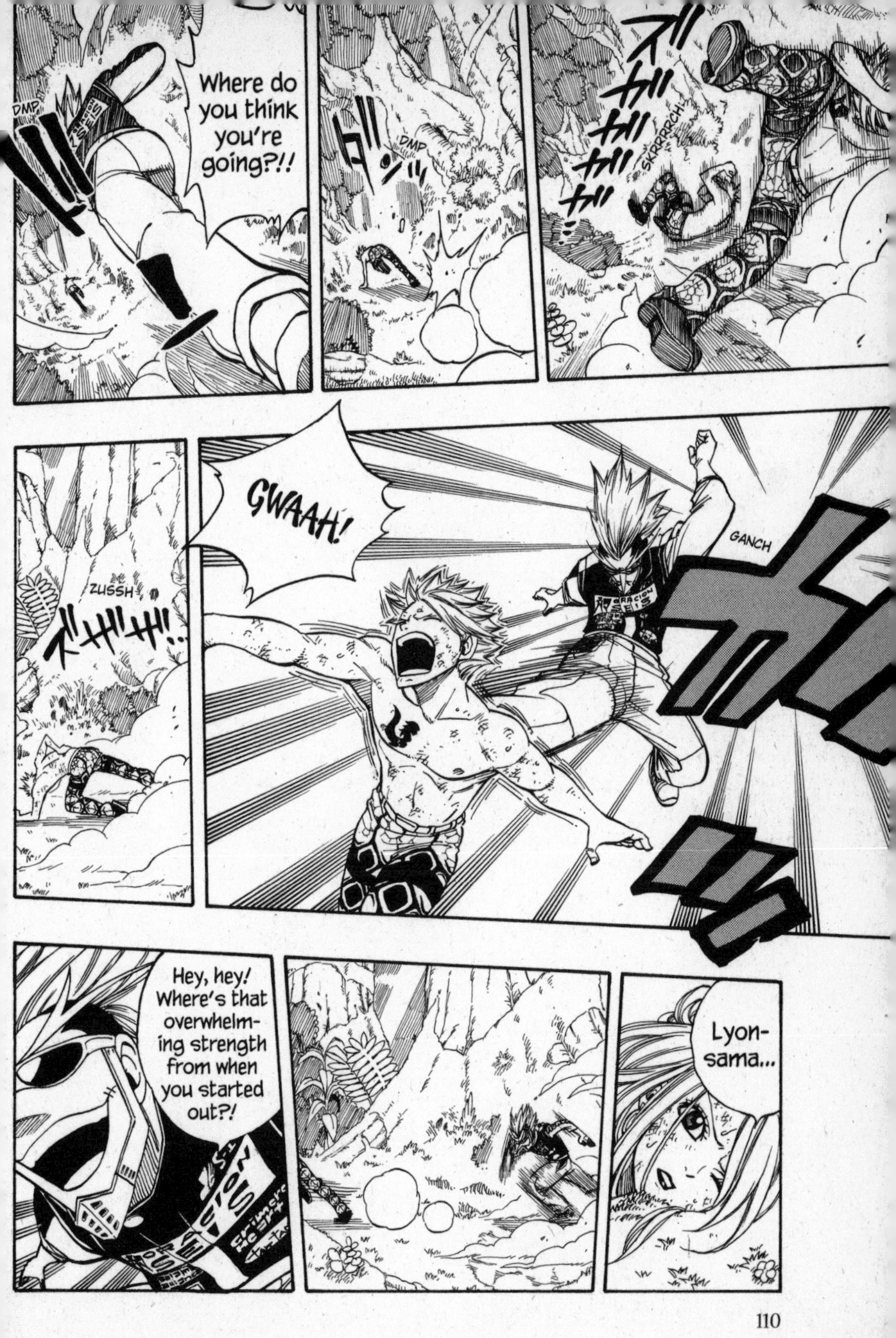
SKRRRCH
DMP
DMP
Where do you think you're going?!!
GANCH
GWAAH!
ZUSSH
Lyon-sama...
Hey, hey! Where's that overwhelming strength from when you started out?!

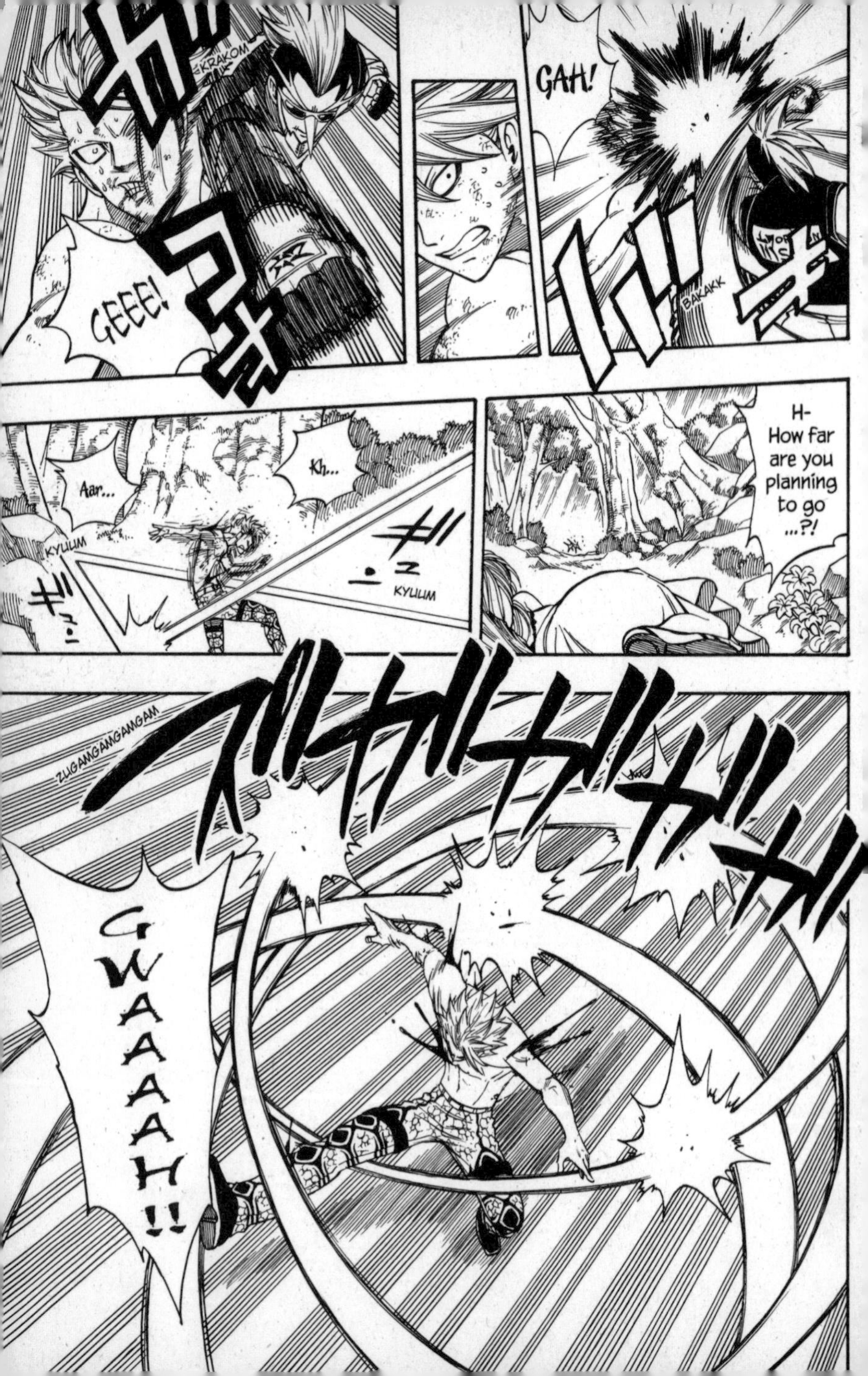
GAH!
BAKAKK
KRAKOM
GEEE!
H-
How far are you planning to go ...?!
Kh...
KYUUM
Aar...
KYUUM
ZUGANGANGANGAM
GWAAAAAH!!

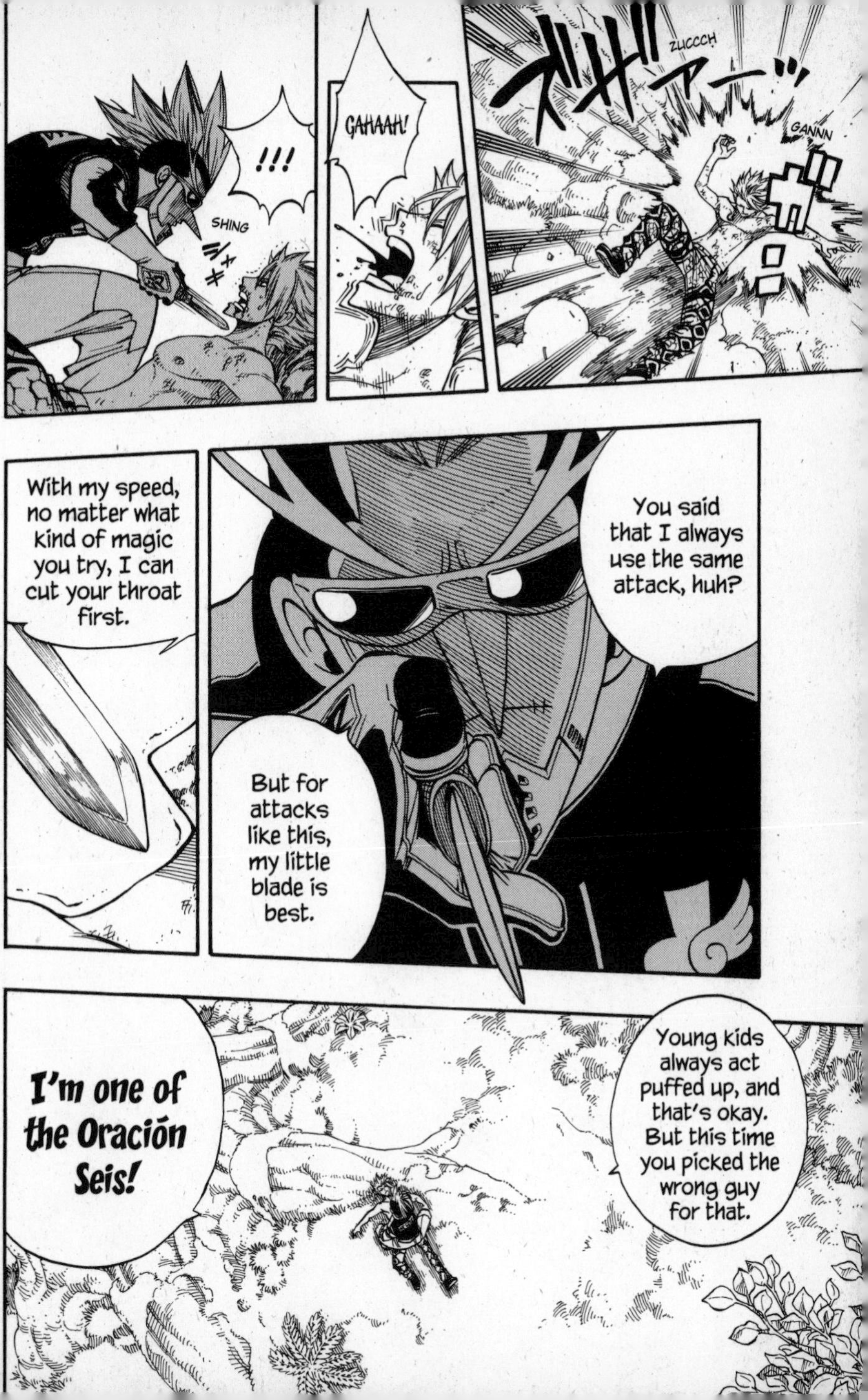
ZUCCCH
GANNN
GAHAAH!
!!!
SHING
You said that I always use the same attack, huh?
But for attacks like this, my little blade is best.
With my speed, no matter what kind of magic you try, I can cut your throat first.
Young kids always act puffed up, and that's okay. But this time you picked the wrong guy for that.
I'm one of the Oración Seis!

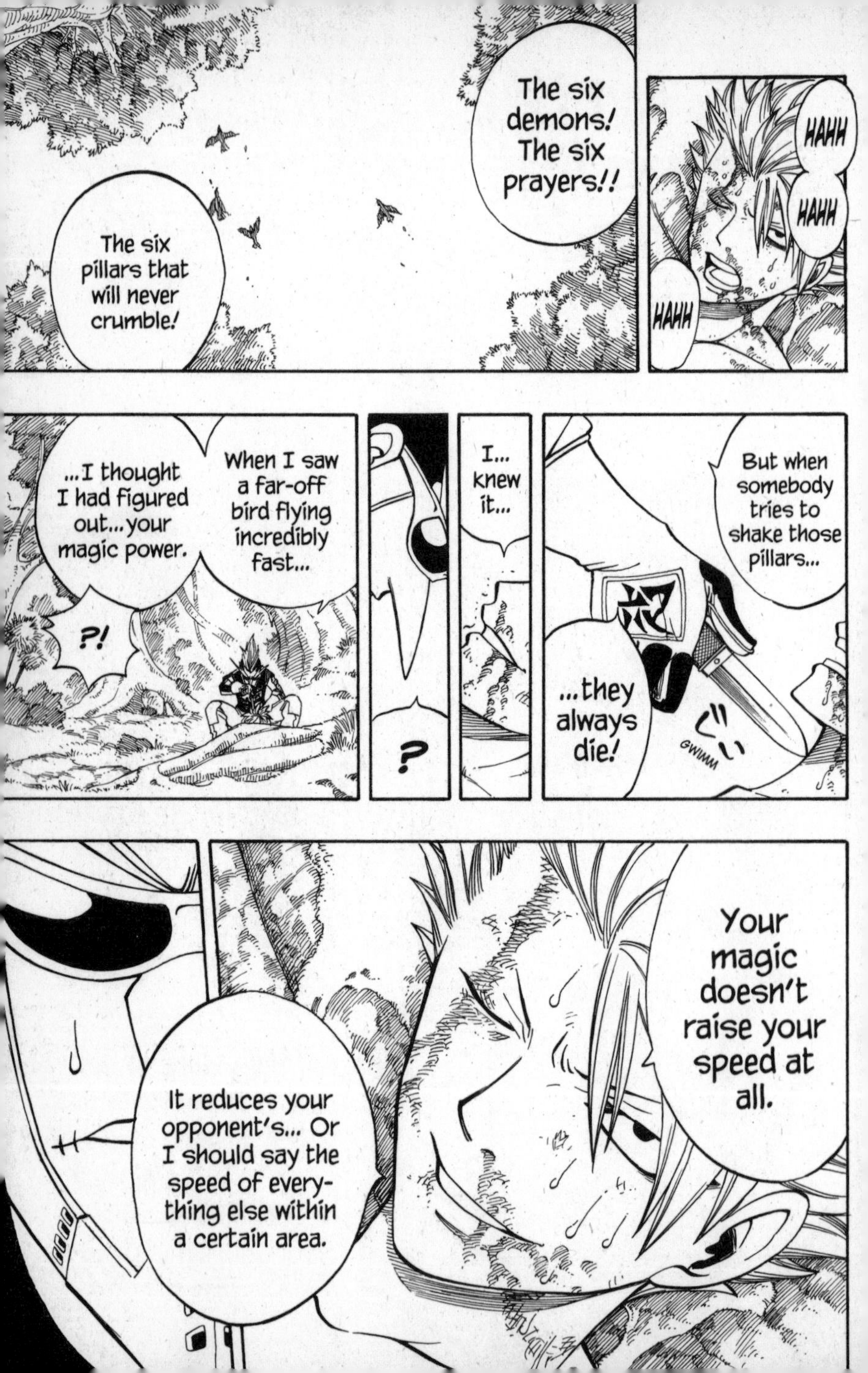
HAHH
HAHH
HAHH
The six demons! The six prayers!!
The six pillars that will never crumble!
But when somebody tries to shake those pillars...
...they always die!
GWIMM
I... knew it...
?
When I saw a far-off bird flying incredibly fast...
...I thought I had figured out...your magic power.
?!
Your magic doesn't raise your speed at all.
It reduces your opponent's... Or I should say the speed of everything else within a certain area.

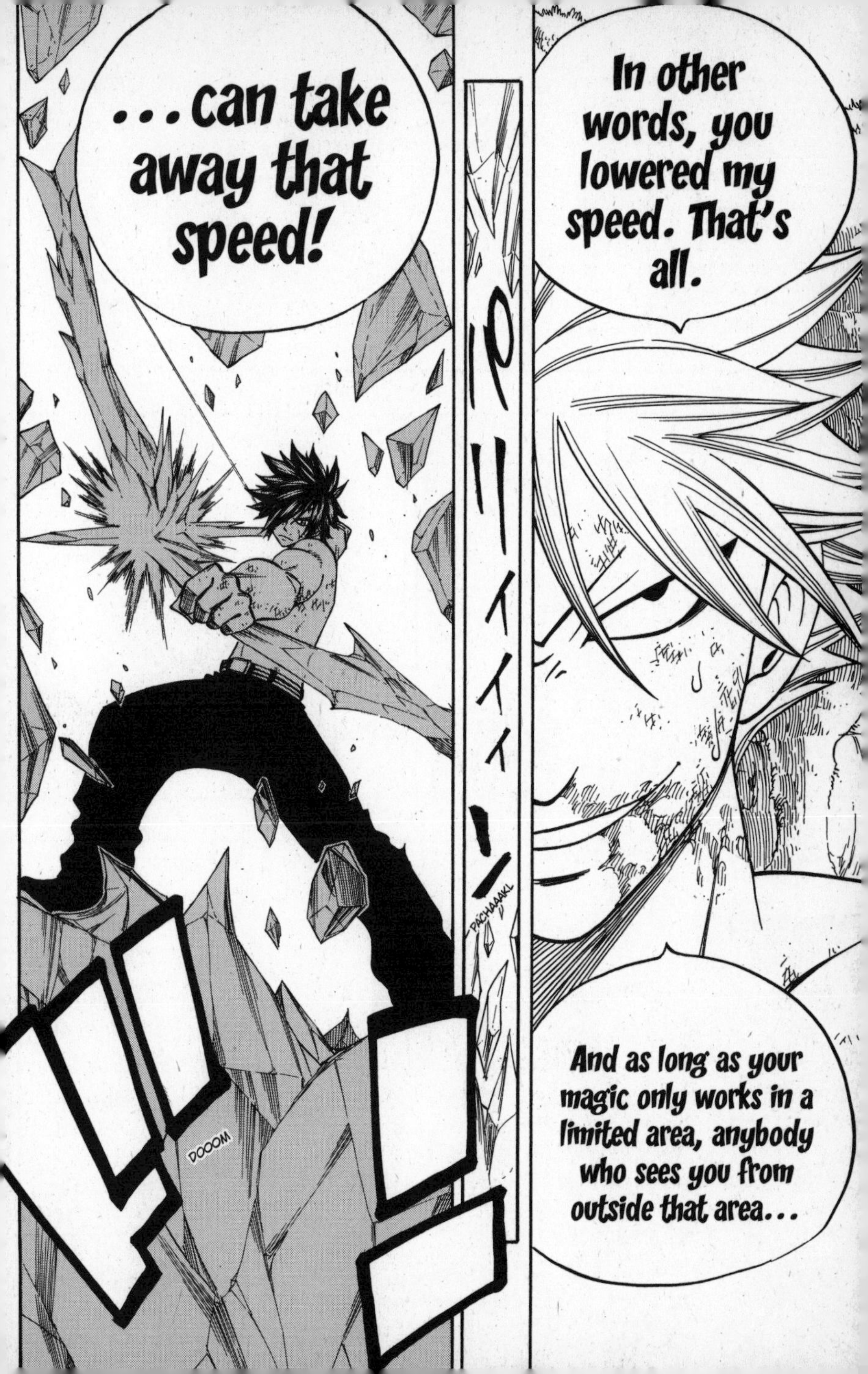
In other words, you lowered my speed. That's all.
And as long as your magic only works in a limited area, anybody who sees you from outside that area...
PACHAAAKL
...can take away that speed!
DOOOM

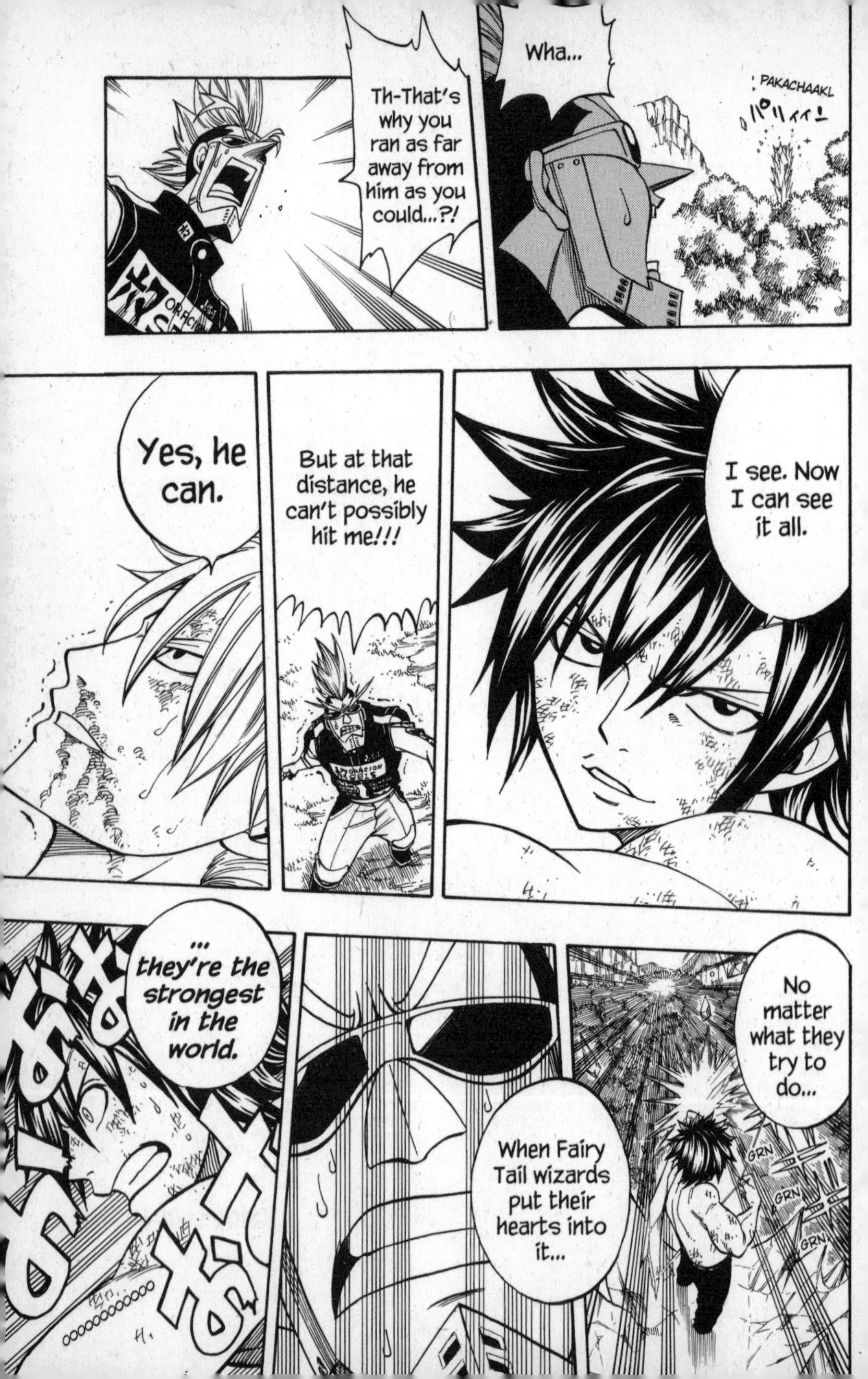
Wha...
PAKACHAAKL
Th-That's why you ran as far away from him as you could...?!
I see. Now I can see it all.
But at that distance, he can't possibly hit me!!!
Yes, he can.
No matter what they try to do...
When Fairy Tail wizards put their hearts into it...
GRN
GRN
GRN
...they're the strongest in the world.

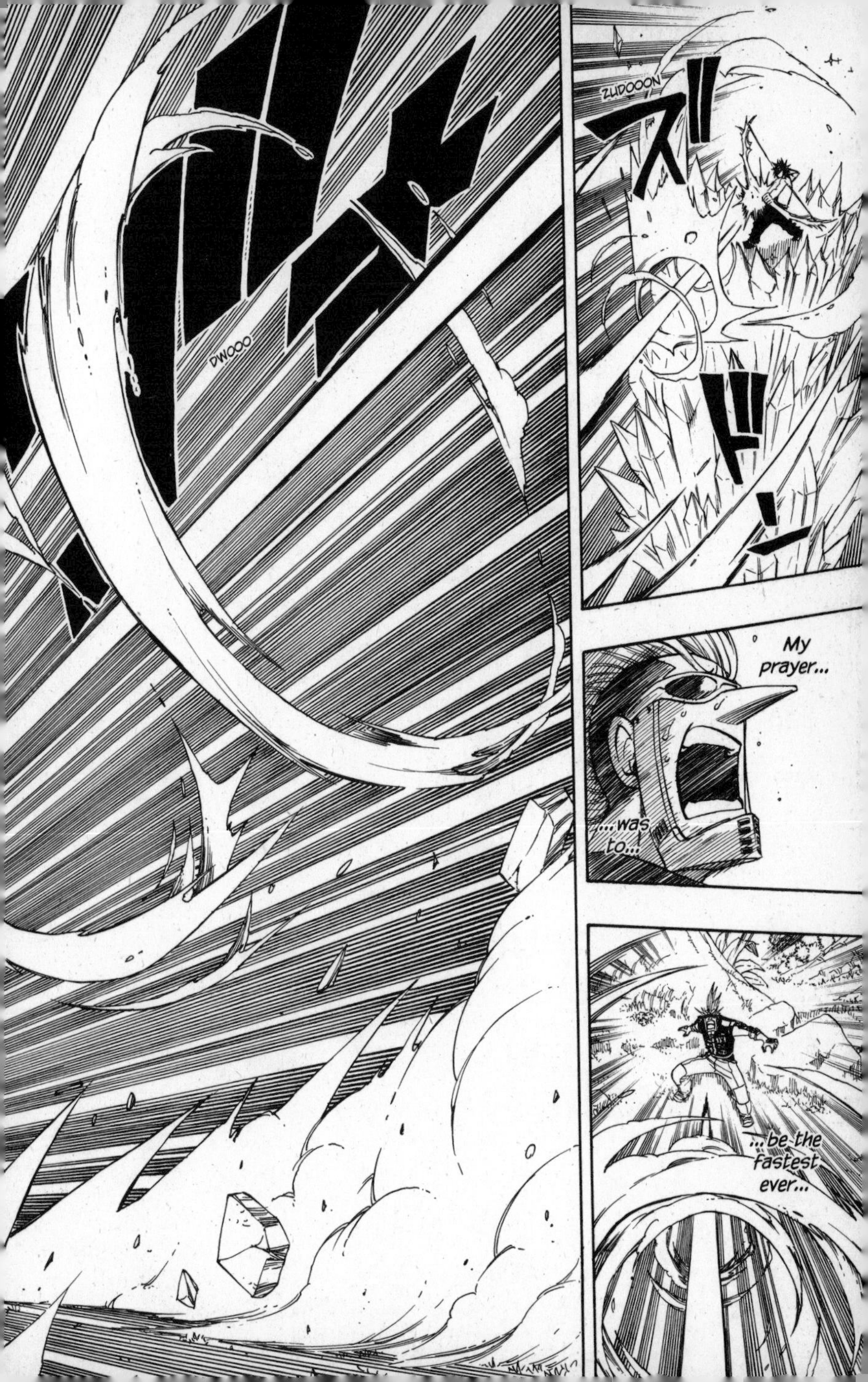
ZUDOOON
My prayer...
...was to...
...be the fastest ever...
DWOOO

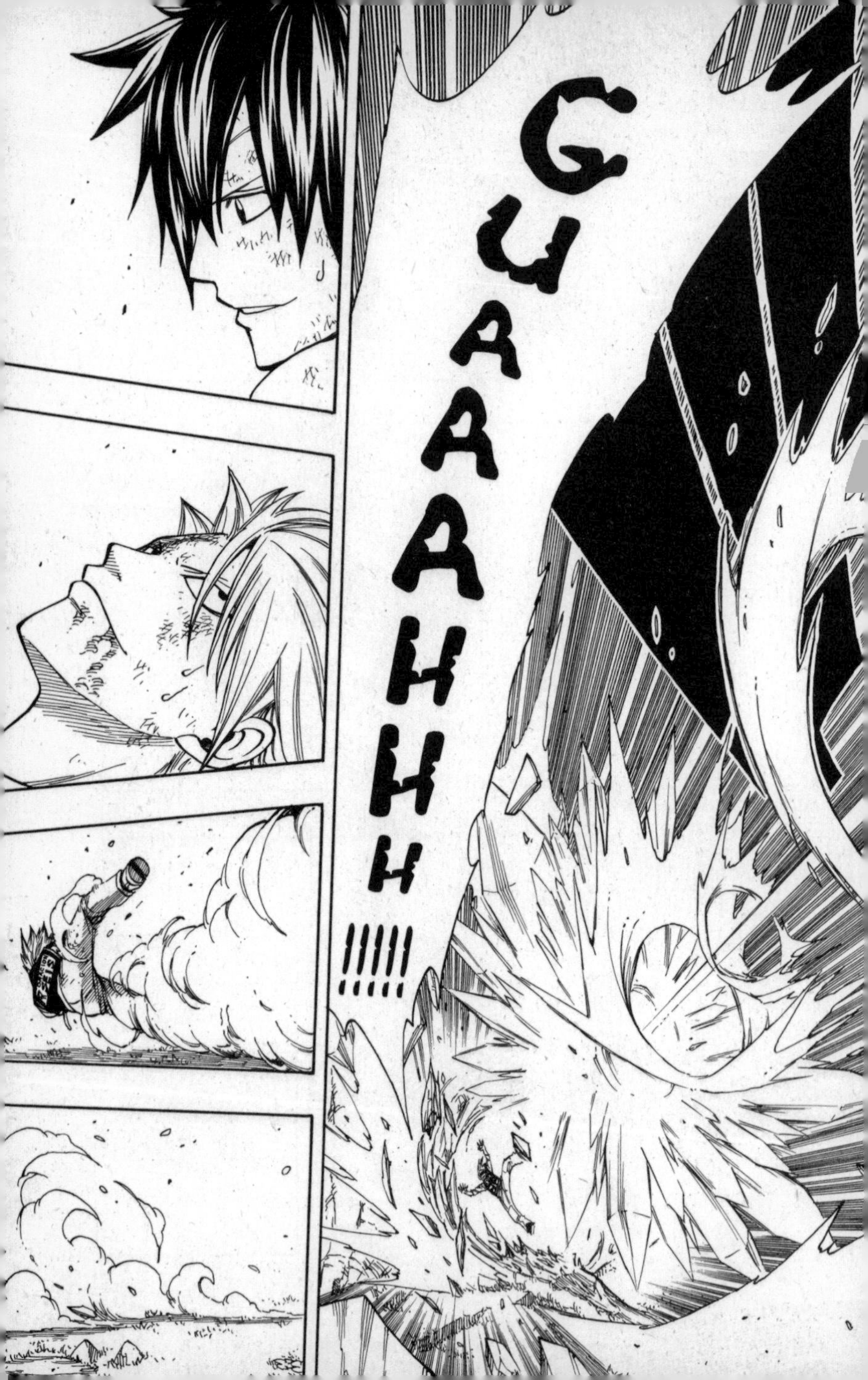
GUAAAHHH!!!!!

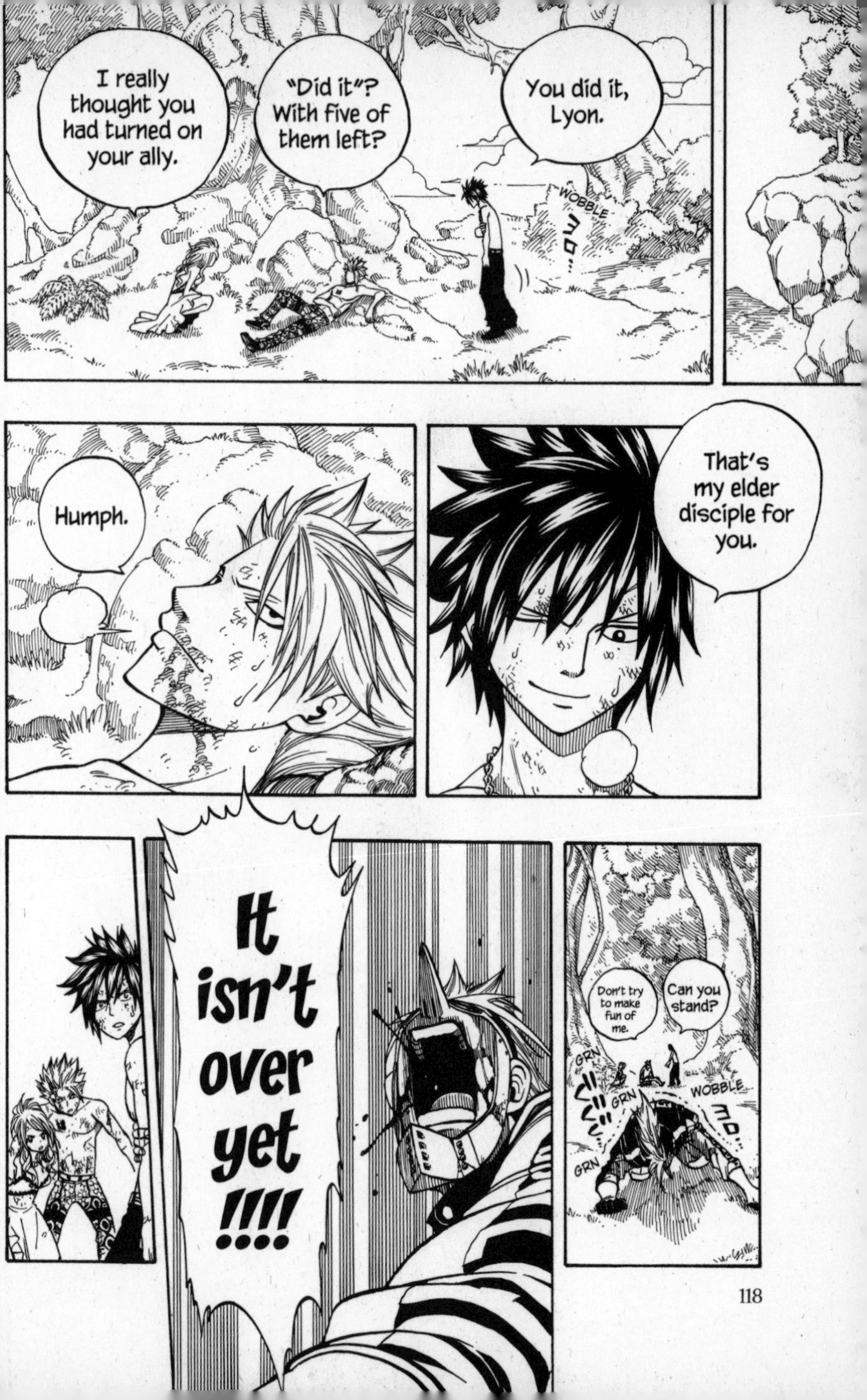

You did it, Lyon.
WOBBLE
"Did it"? With five of them left?
I really thought you had turned on your ally.
That's my elder disciple for you.
Humph.
Can you stand?
Don't try to make fun of me.
GRN
GRN
GRN
WOBBLE
It isn't over yet!!!!

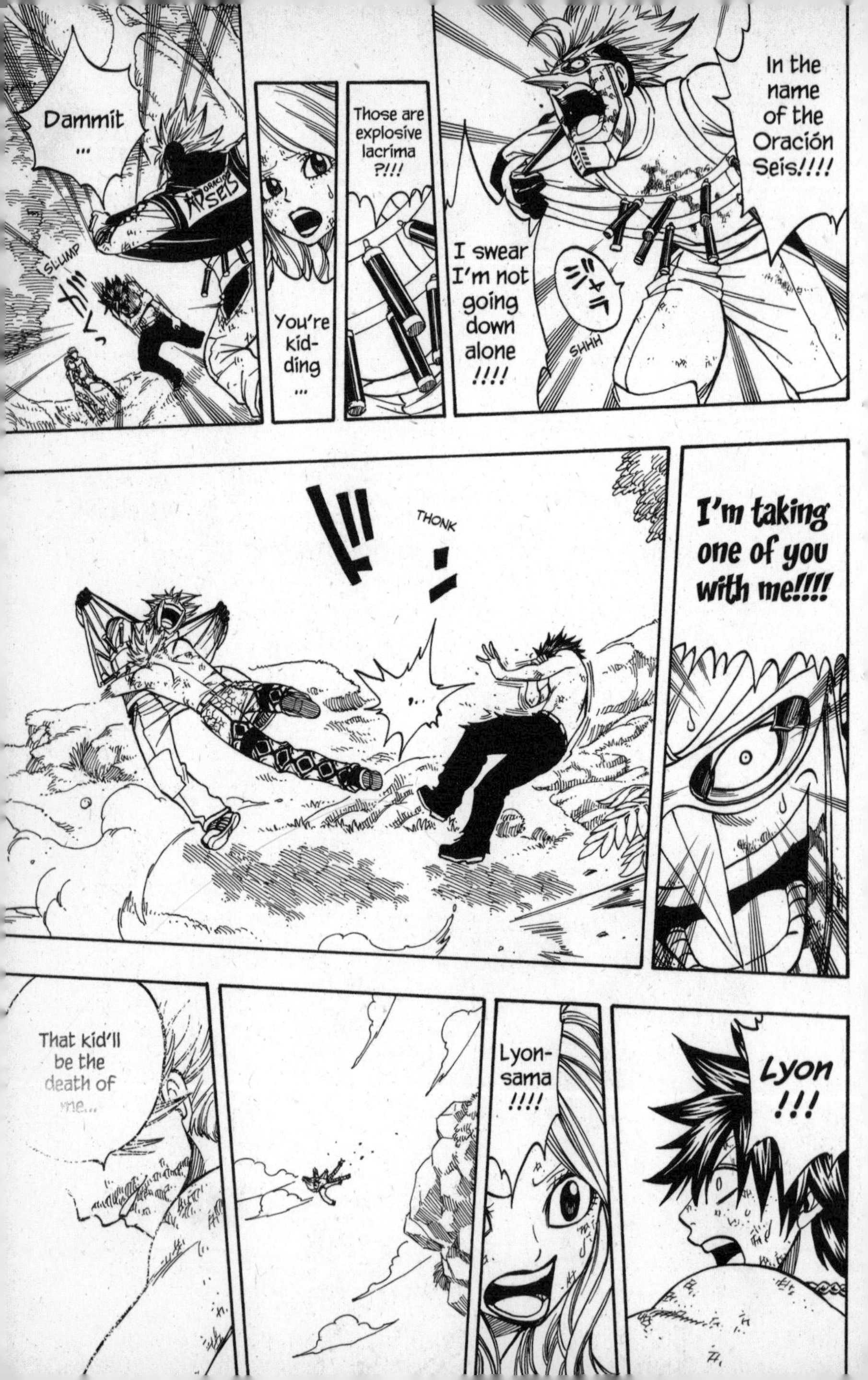
In the name of the Oración Seis!!!!
I swear I'm not going down alone!!!!
SHHH
Those are explosive lacrima ?!!!
You're kid-ding ...
Dammit ...
SLUMP
I'm taking one of you with me!!!!
THONK
Lyon !!!
Lyon-sama !!!!
That kid'll be the death of me...

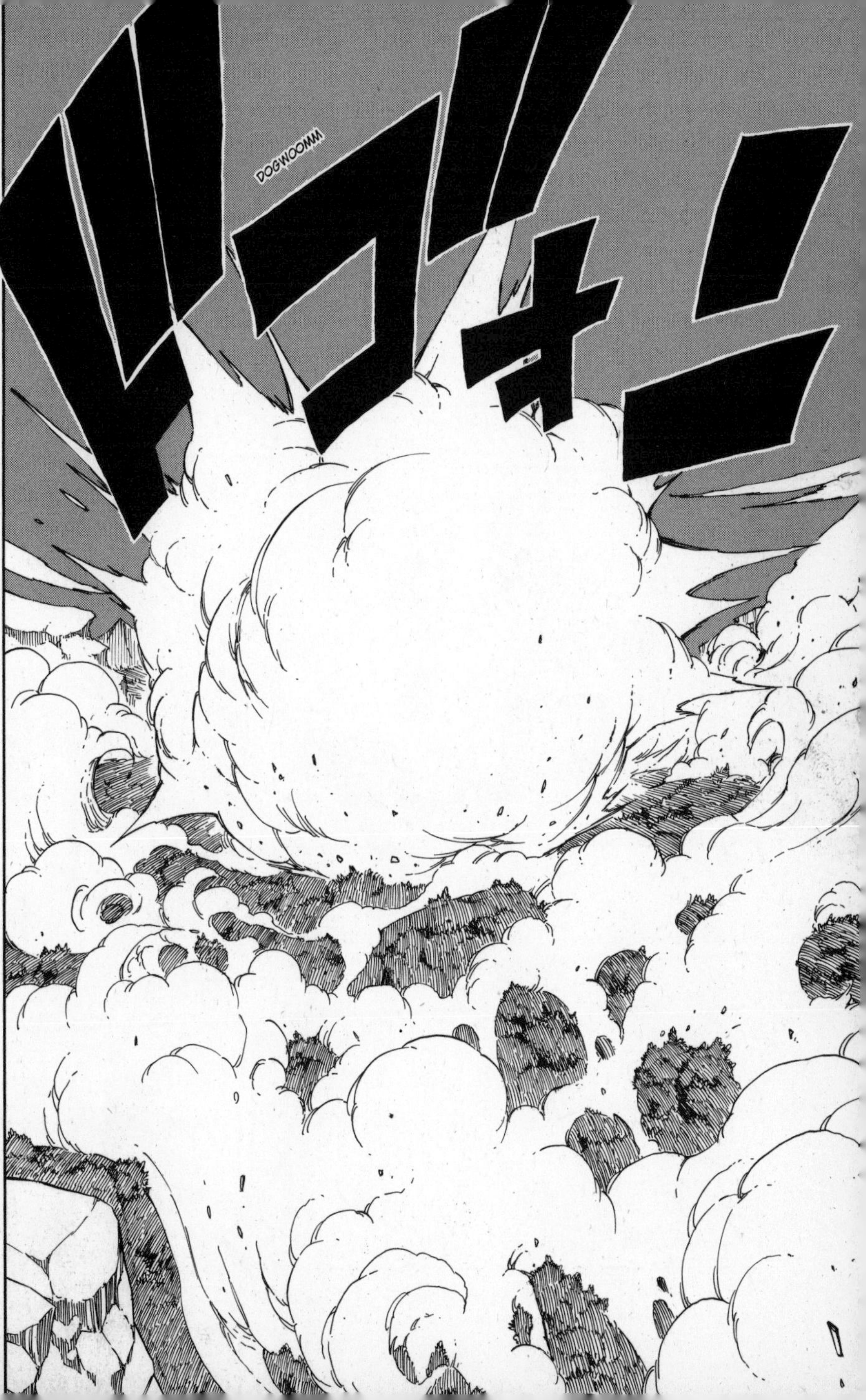
DOGWOOMM

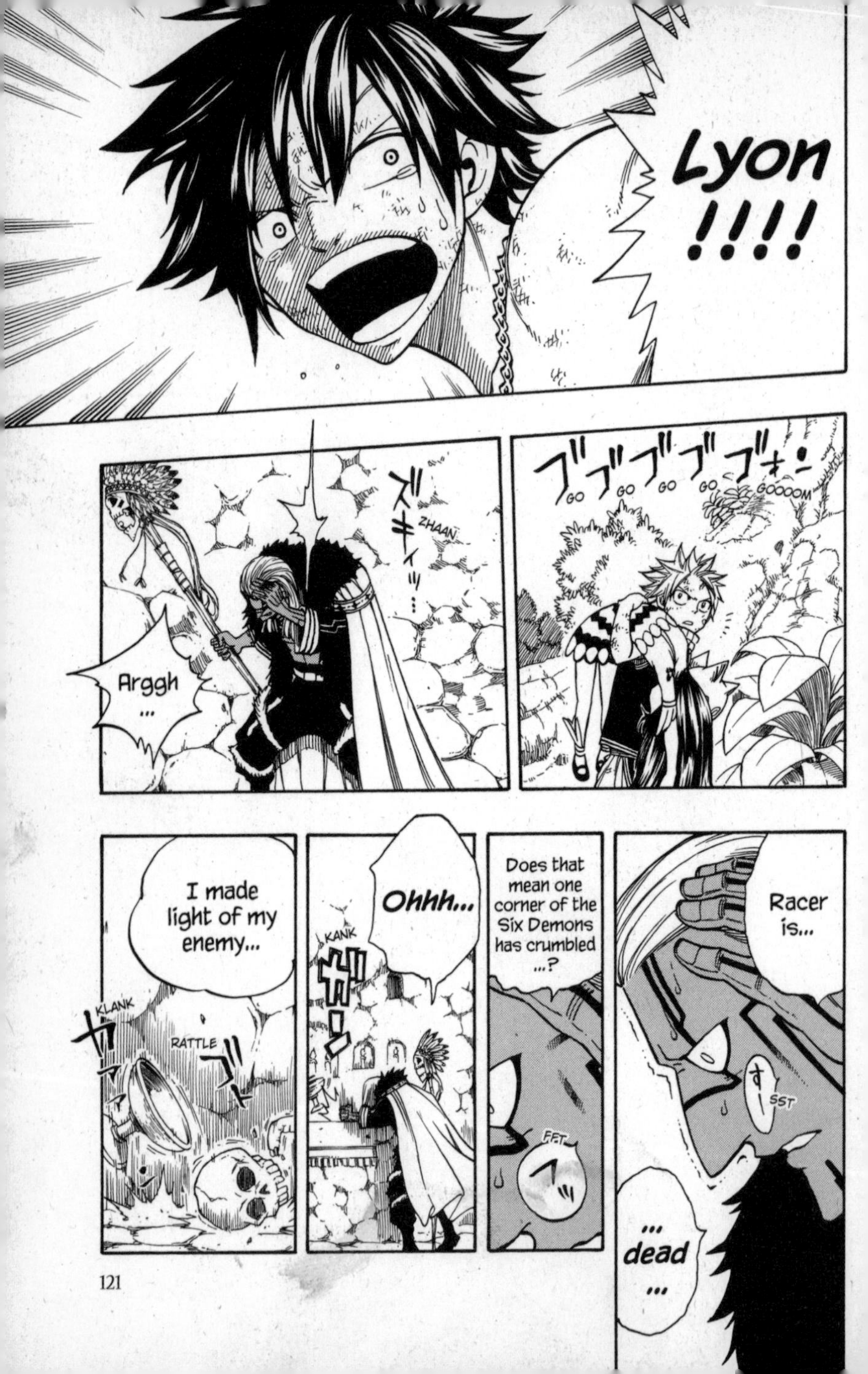
Lyon !!!!
GO GO GO GO GOOOOM
ZHAAN
Arggh ...
Racer is...
SST
... dead ...
Does that mean one corner of the Six Demons has crumbled ...?
FFT
Ohhh...
KANK
I made light of my enemy...
KLANK
RATTLE

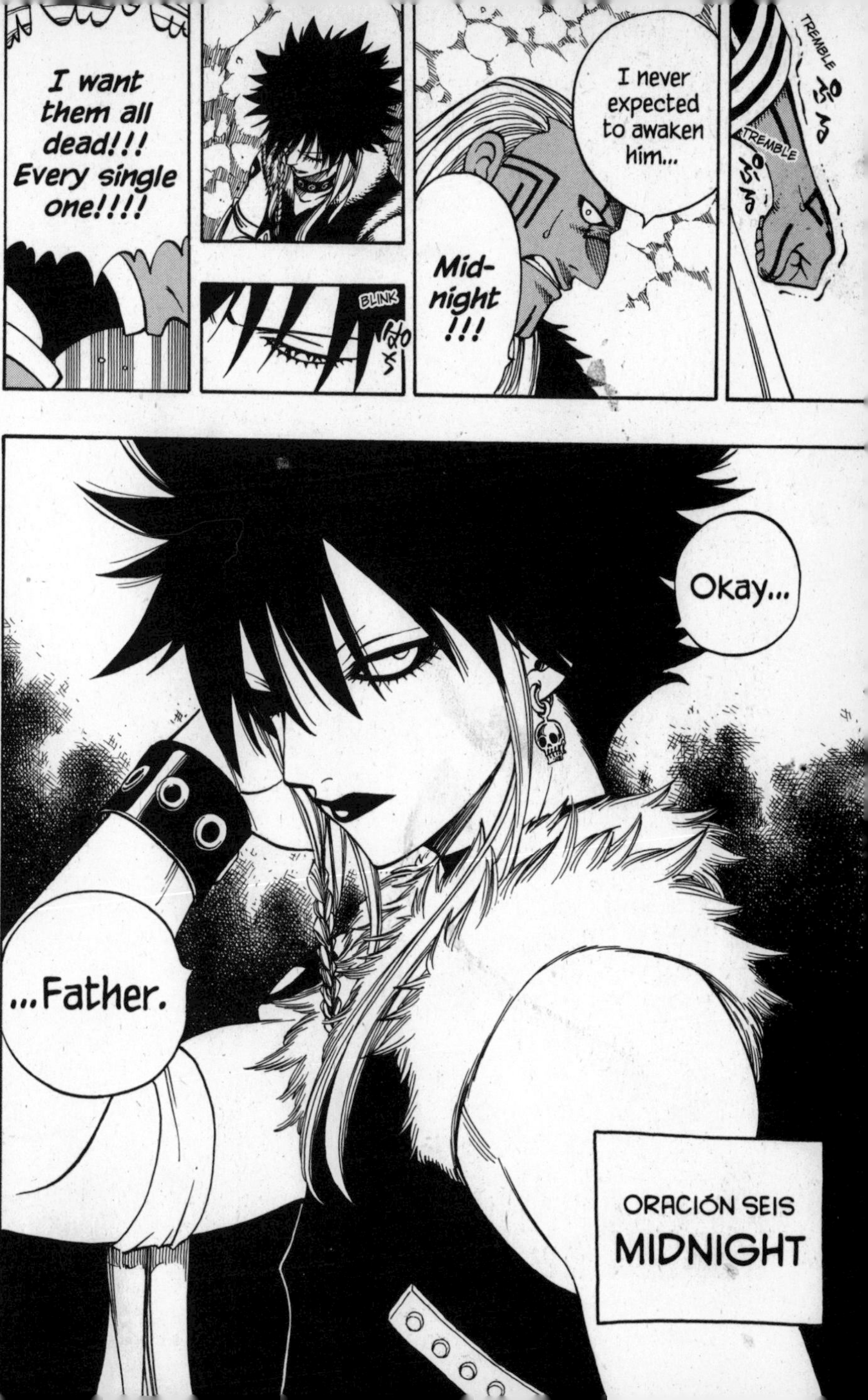
TREMBLE
TREMBLE
I never expected to awaken him...
Mid-night!!!
BLINK
I want them all dead!!! Every single one!!!!
Okay...
...Father.
ORACIÓN SEIS
MIDNIGHT

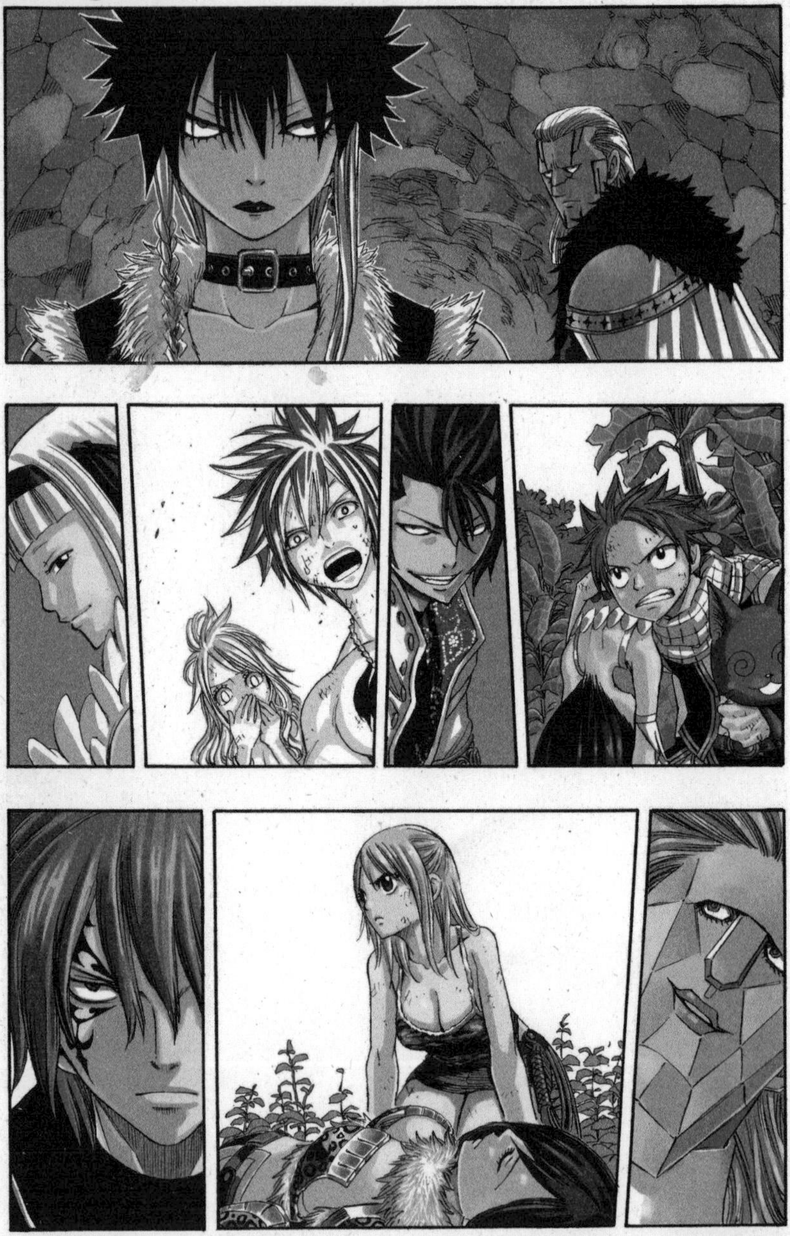

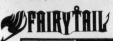

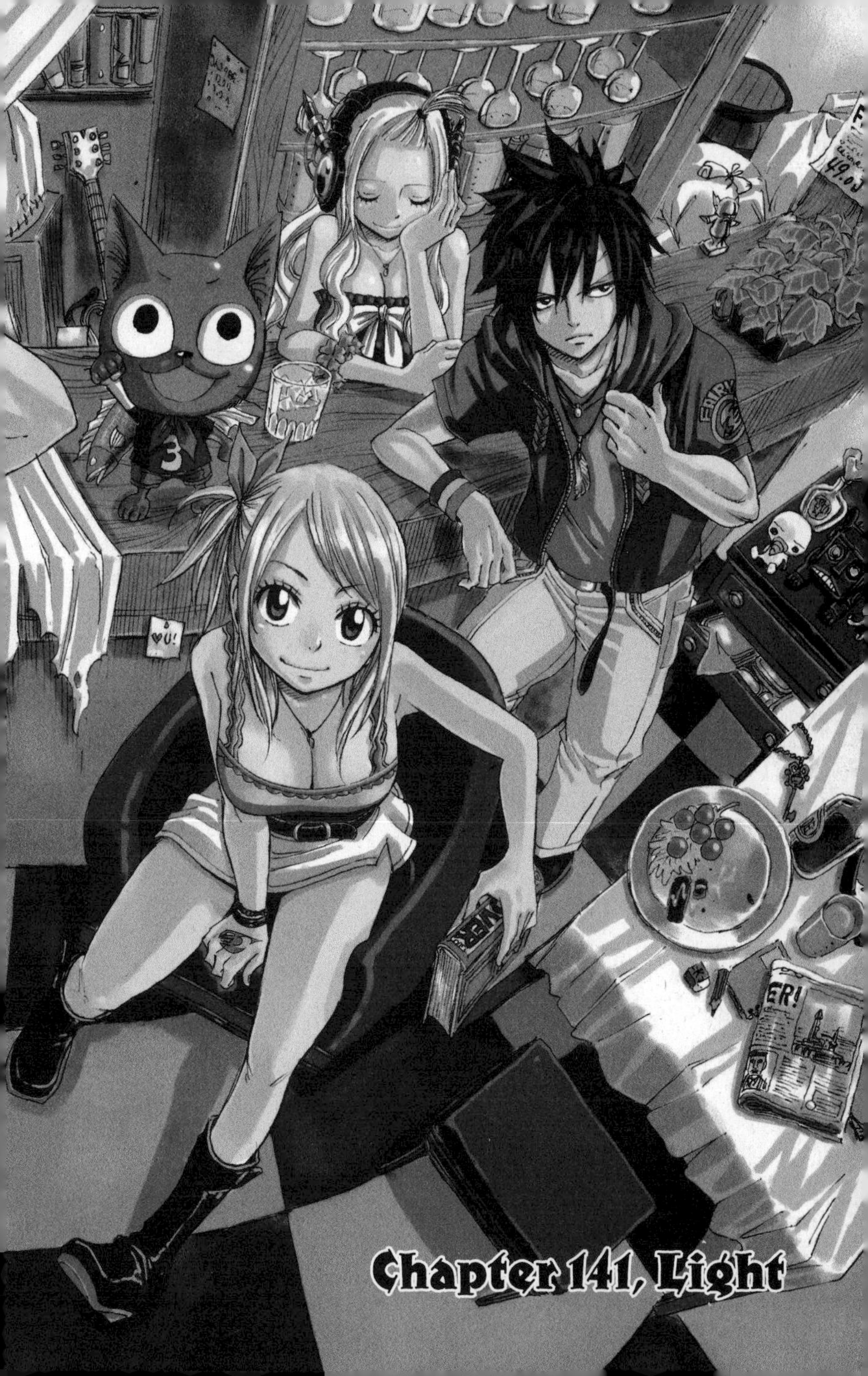
Chapter 141, Light

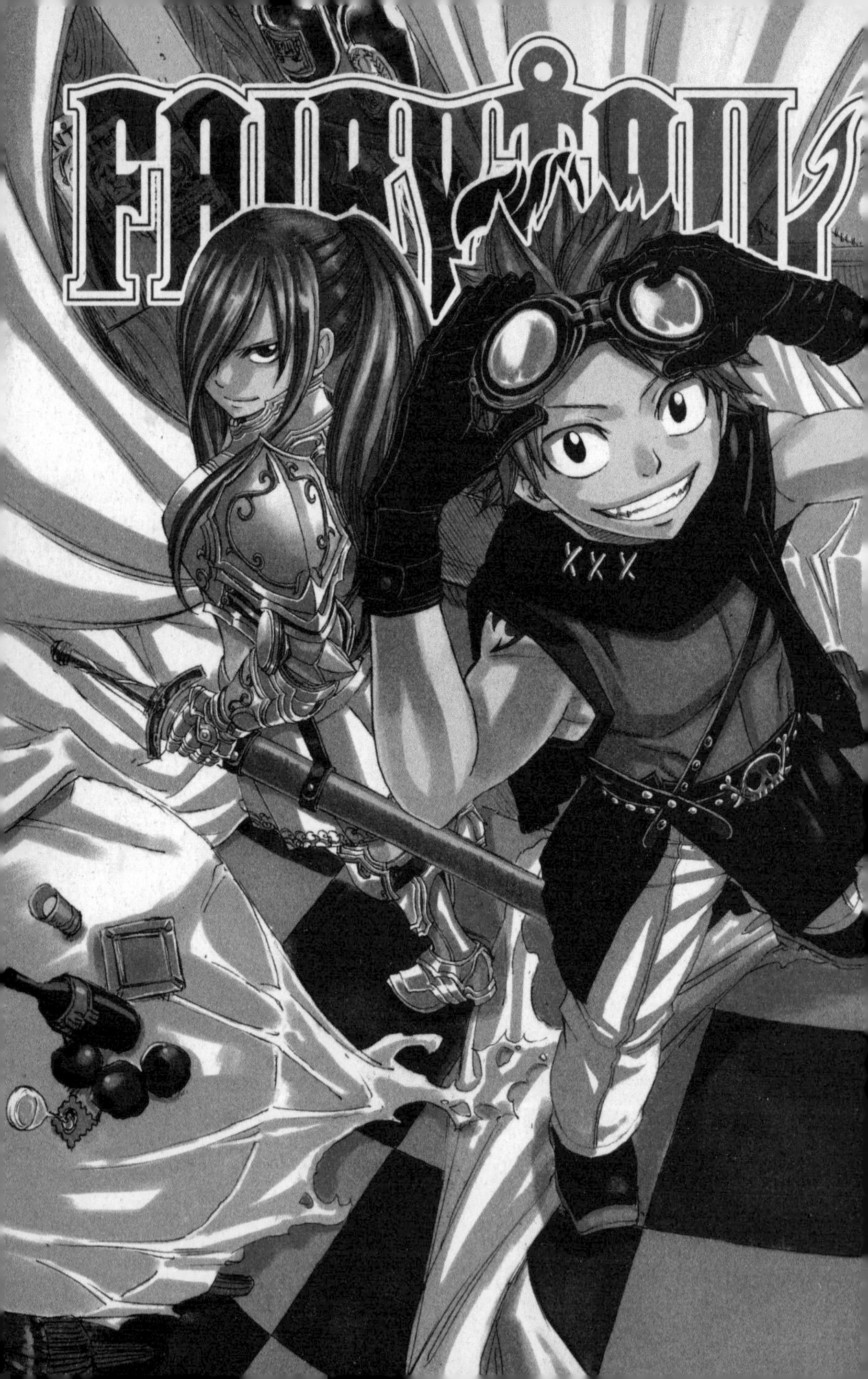
FAIRY TAIL

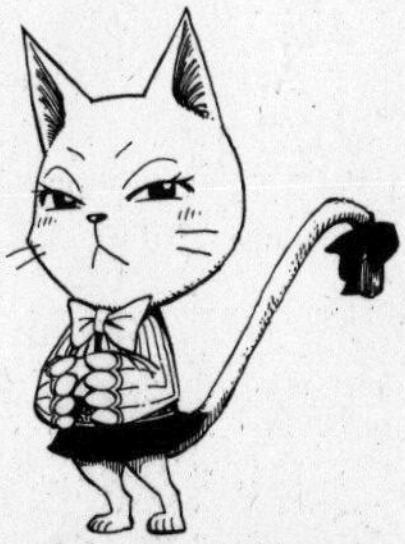

FAIRY TAIL

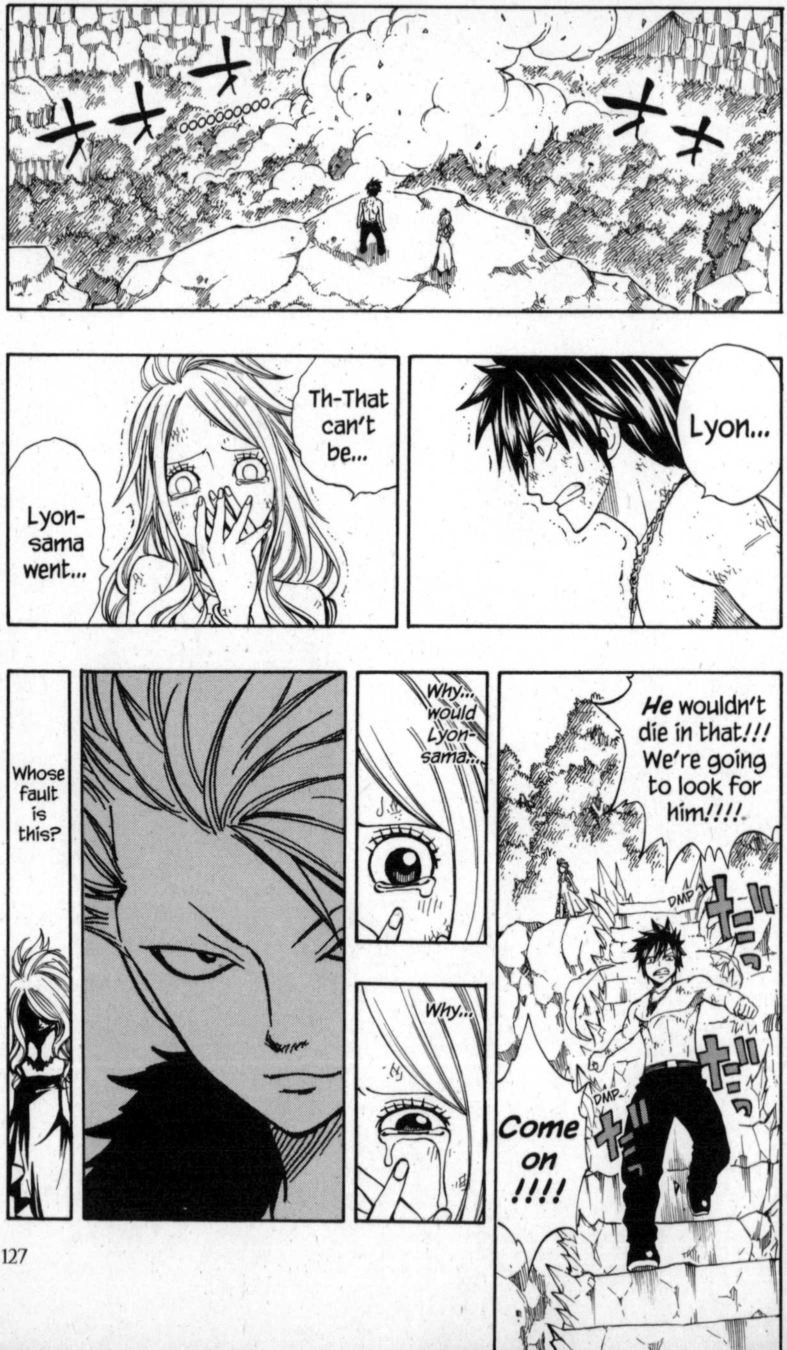

OOOOOOOOOO
Lyon...
Th-That can't be...
Lyon-sama went...
He wouldn't die in that!!! We're going to look for him!!!!
DMP
DMP
Come on !!!!
Why... would Lyon-sama...
Why...
Whose fault is this?

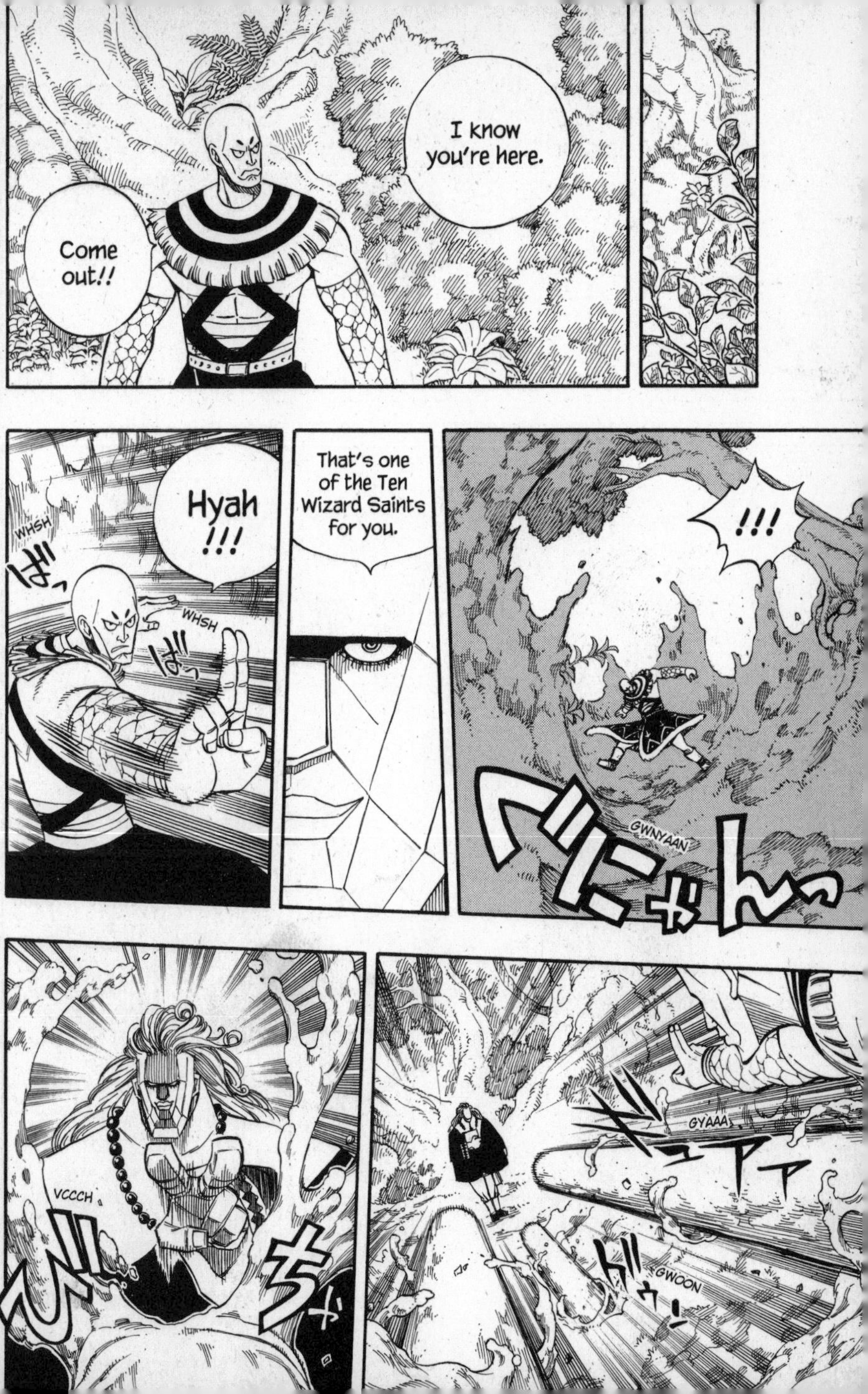
I know you're here.
Come out!!
!!!
GWNYAAN
That's one of the Ten Wizard Saints for you.
Hyah !!!
WHSH
WHSH
GYAAA
GWOON
VCCCH

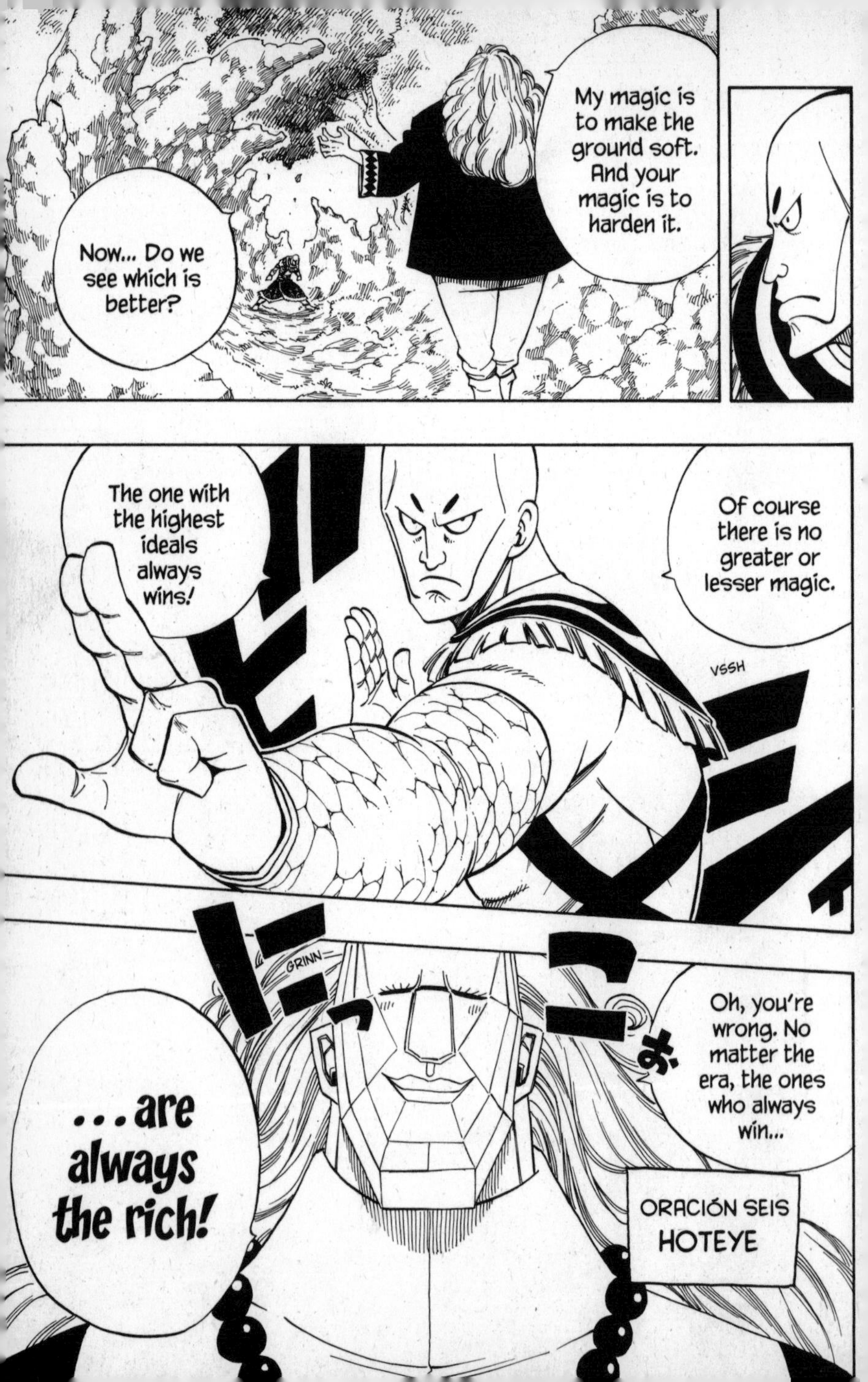
My magic is to make the ground soft. And your magic is to harden it.
Now... Do we see which is better?
Of course there is no greater or lesser magic.
The one with the highest ideals always wins!
VSSH
GRINN
Oh, you're wrong. No matter the era, the ones who always win...
...are always the rich!
ORACIÓN SEIS
HOTEYE

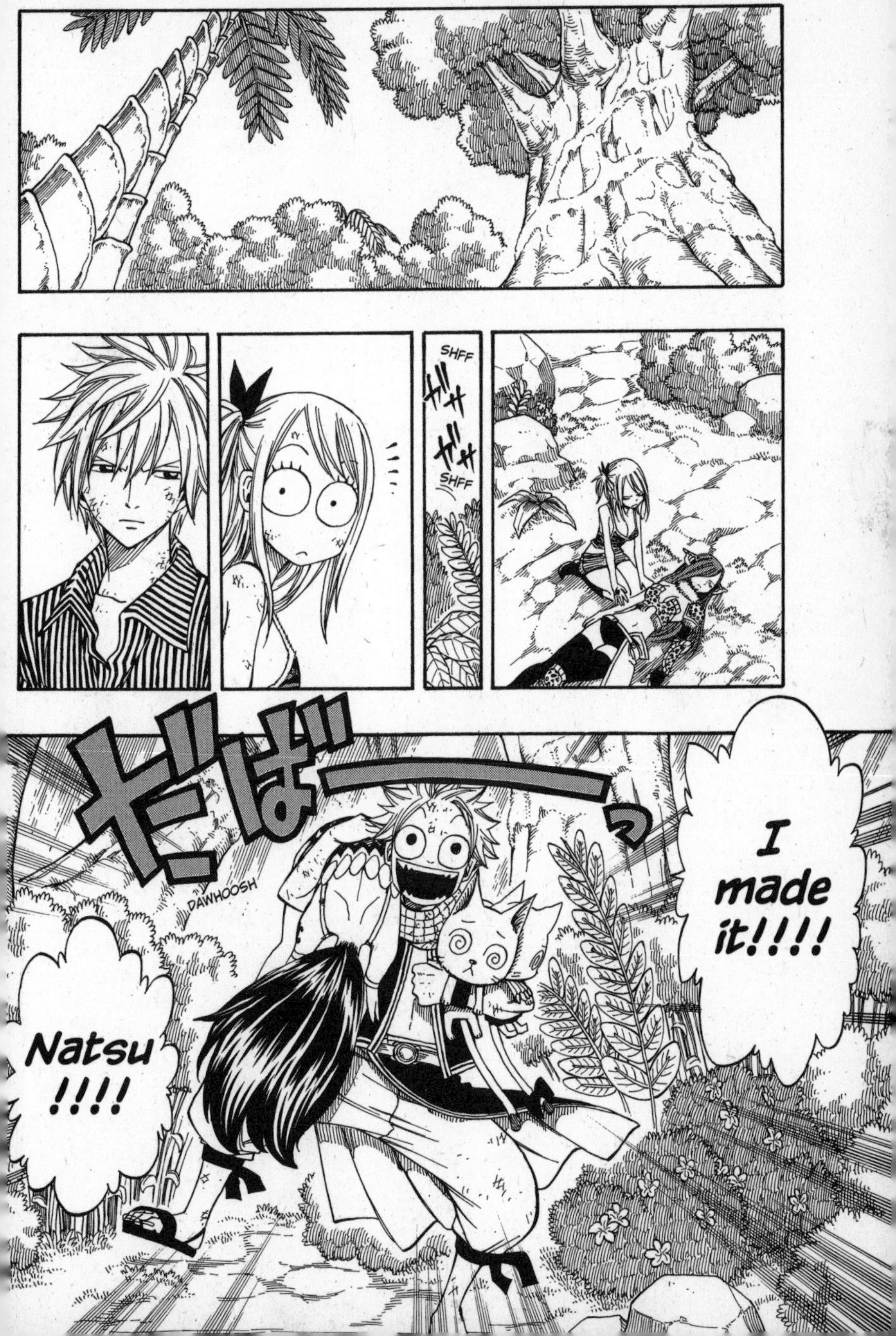
SHFF
SHFF
I made it!!!!
だばーっ
DAWHOOSH
Natsu !!!!

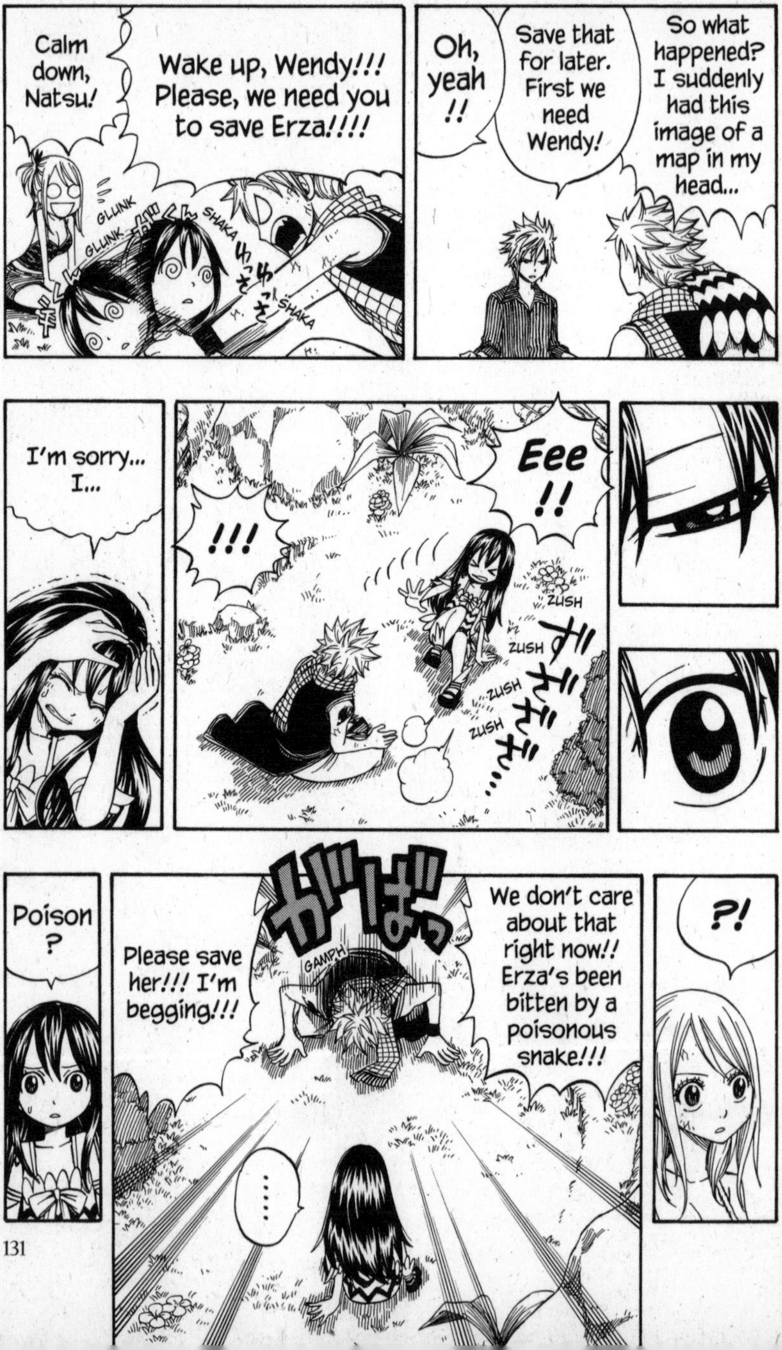
So what happened? I suddenly had this image of a map in my head...
Save that for later. First we need Wendy!
Oh, yeah !!
Wake up, Wendy!!! Please, we need you to save Erza!!!!
SHAKA
SHAKA
GLUNK
GLUNK
Calm down, Natsu!
Eee !!
ZUSH
ZUSH
ZUSH
ZUSH
!!!
I'm sorry... I...
?!
We don't care about that right now!! Erza's been bitten by a poisonous snake!!!
GAMPH
Please save her!!! I'm begging!!!
......
Poison ?

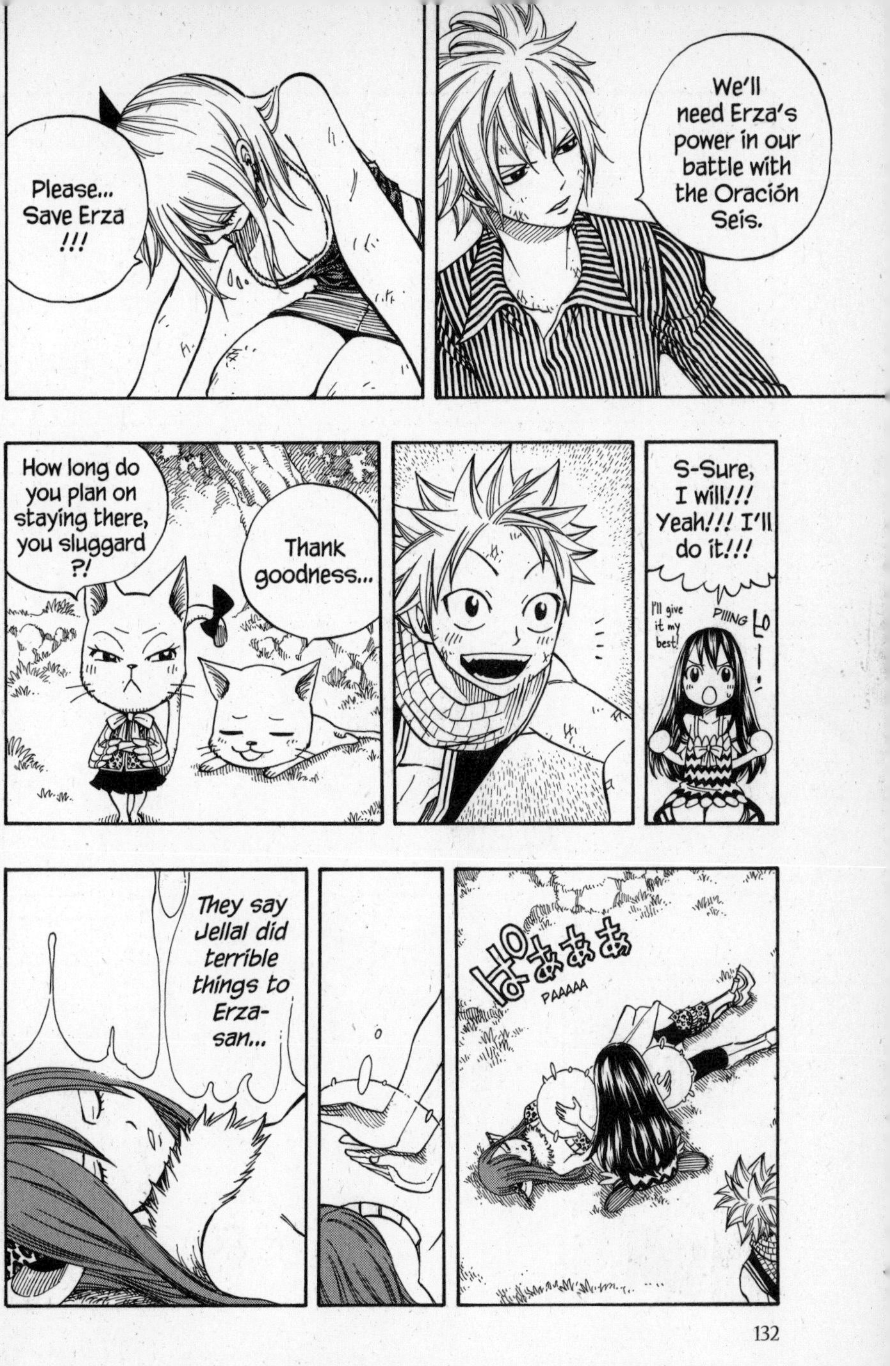
We'll need Erza's power in our battle with the Oración Seis.
Please... Save Erza !!!
S-Sure, I will!!! Yeah!!! I'll do it!!!
I'll give it my best!
PIIING
Thank goodness...
How long do you plan on staying there, you sluggard ?!
PAAAAA
They say Jellal did terrible things to Erza-san...

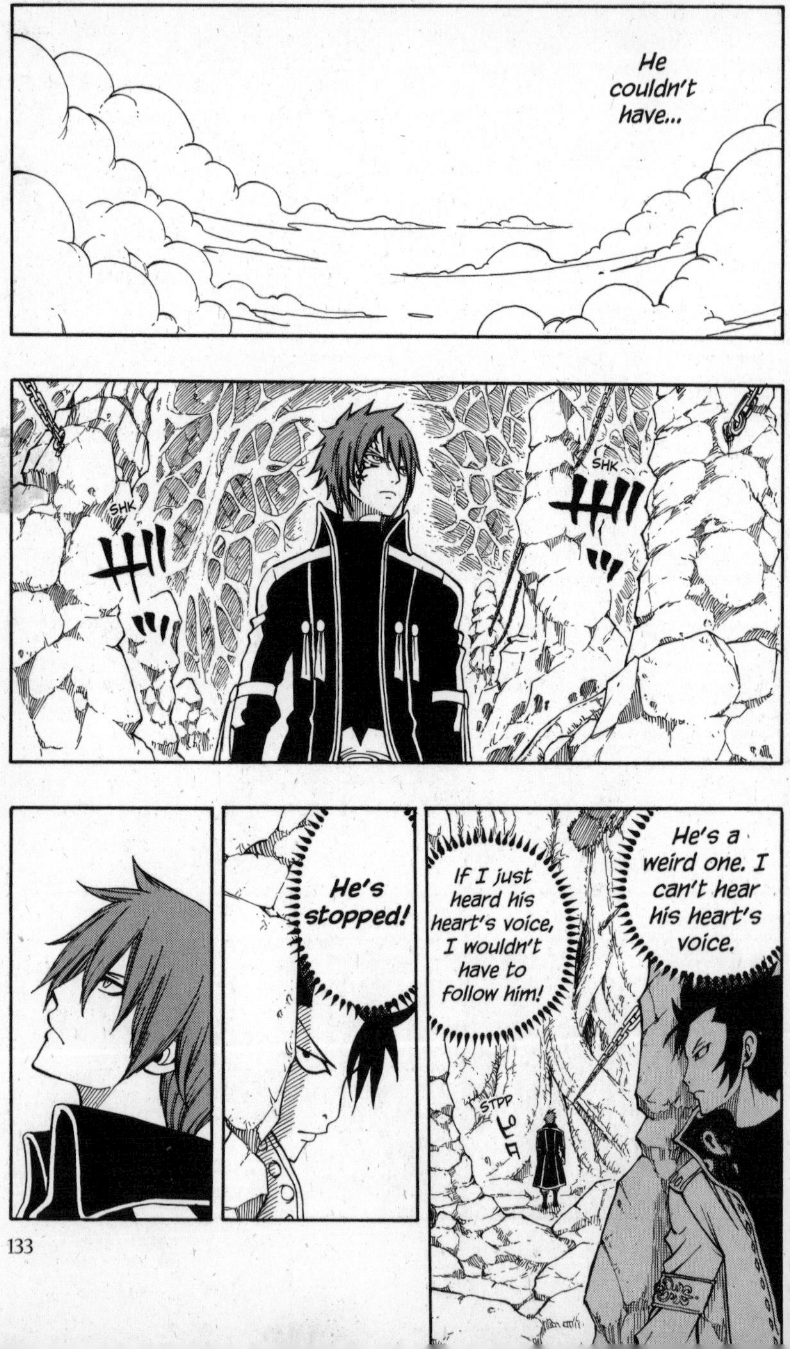
He couldn't have...
SHK
SHK
He's a weird one. I can't hear his heart's voice.
If I just heard his heart's voice, I wouldn't have to follow him!
STPP
He's stopped!

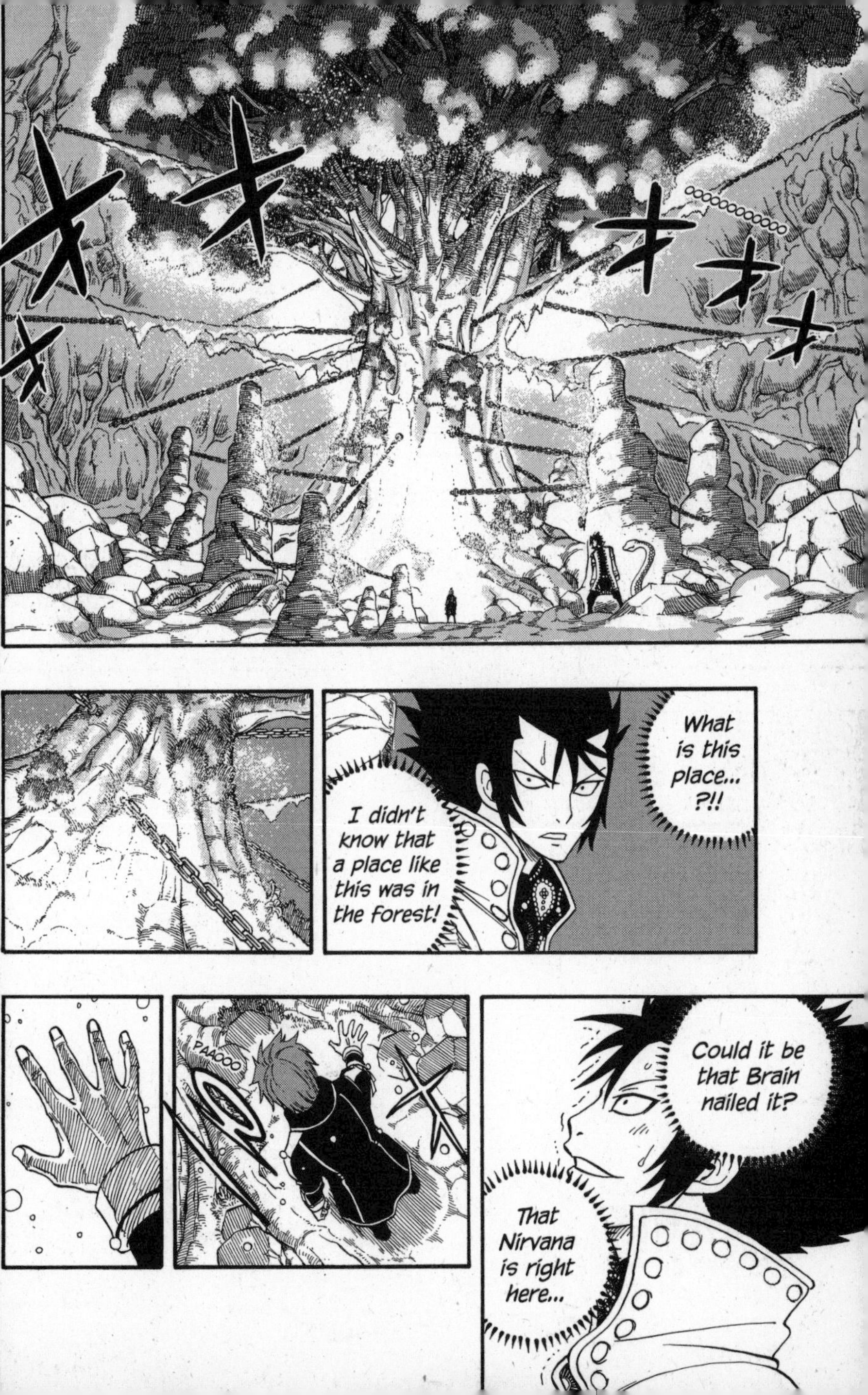
What is this place... ?!!
I didn't know that a place like this was in the forest!
Could it be that Brain nailed it?
That Nirvana is right here...
PAAOOO

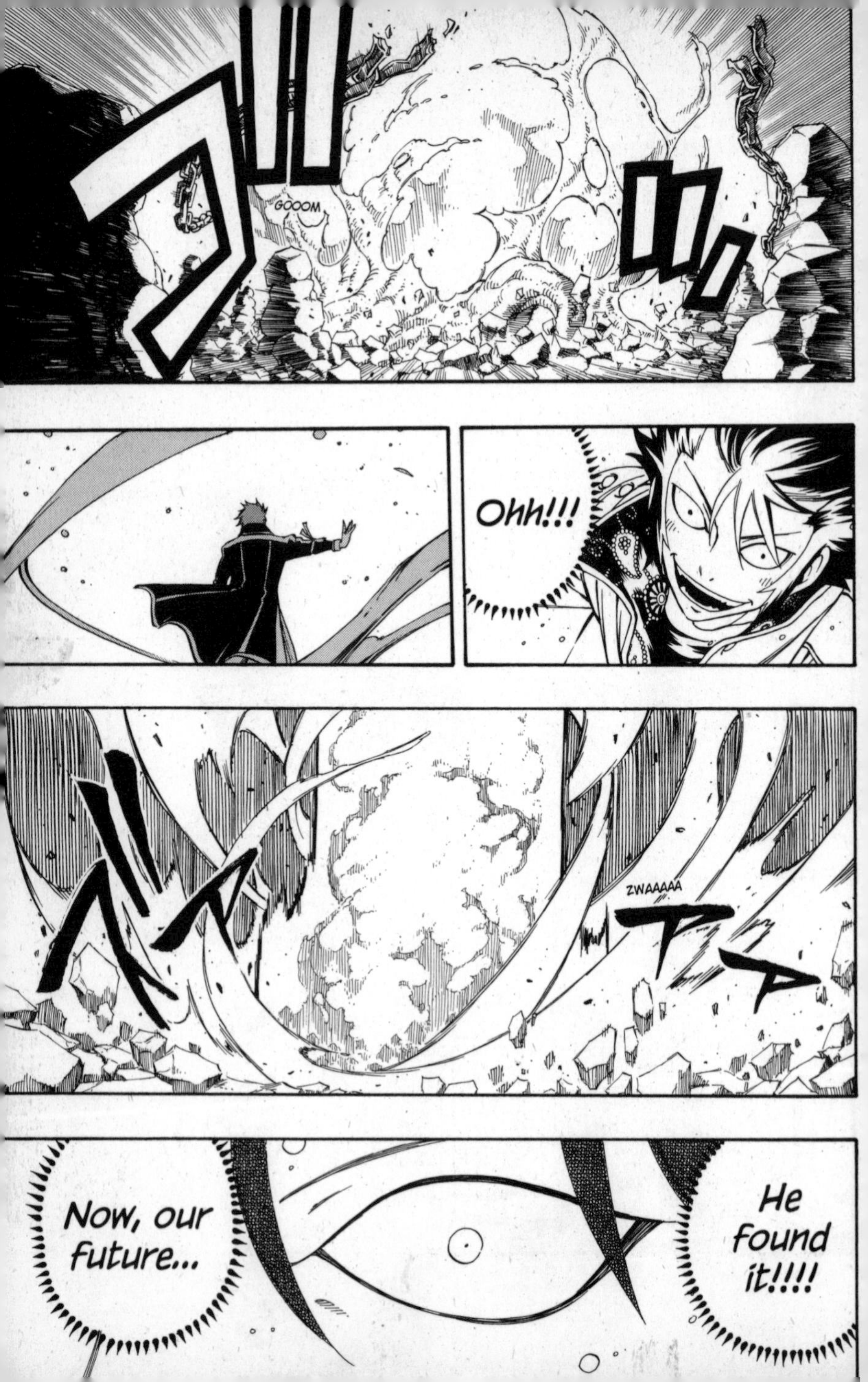
GOOOM
Ohh!!!
ZWAAAAA
He found it!!!!
Now, our future...

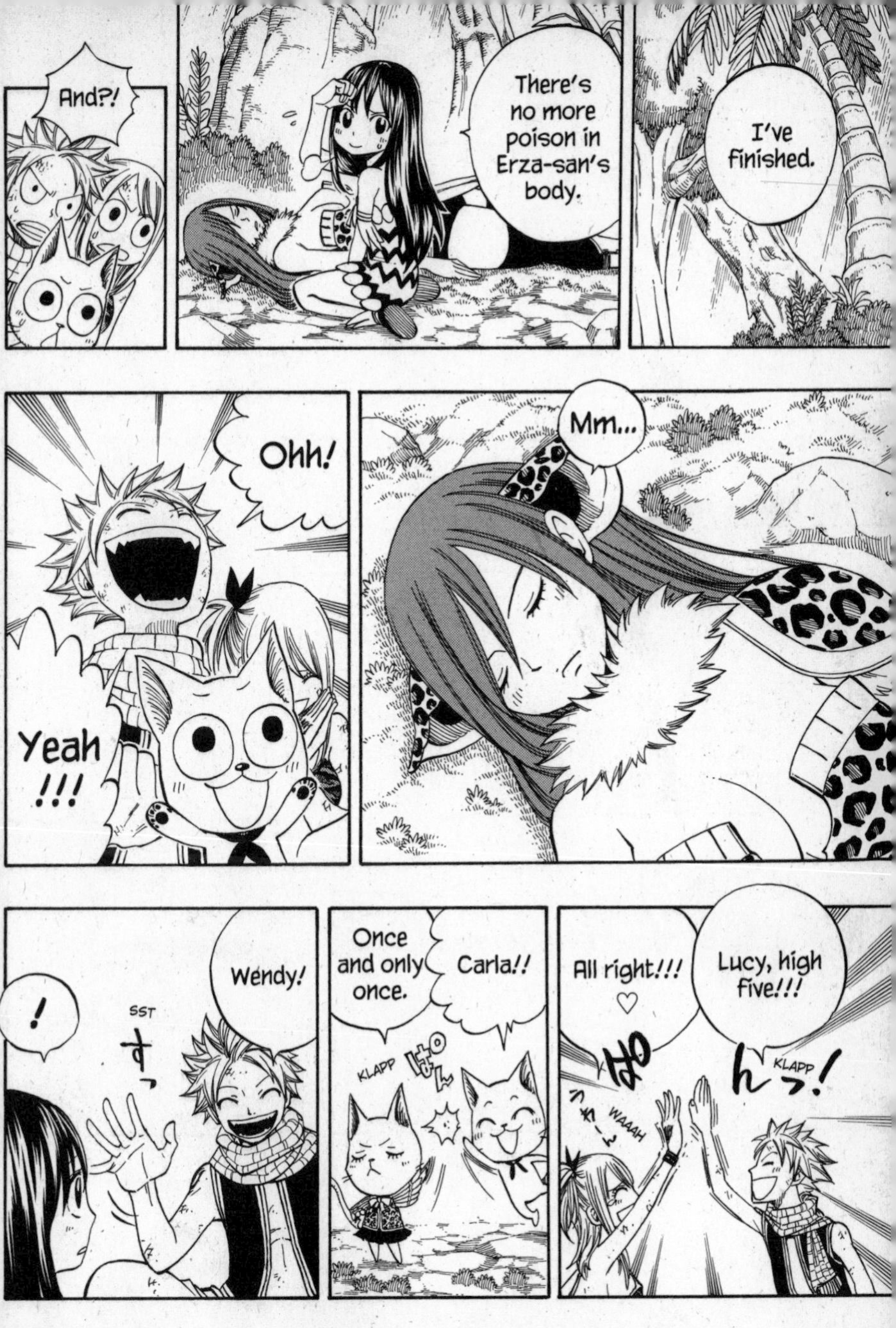
I've finished.
There's no more poison in Erza-san's body.
And?!
Mm...
Ohh!
Yeah !!!
Lucy, high five!!!
KLAPP
All right!!! ♡
WAAAH
Carla!!
Once and only once.
KLAPP
Wendy!
SST
!

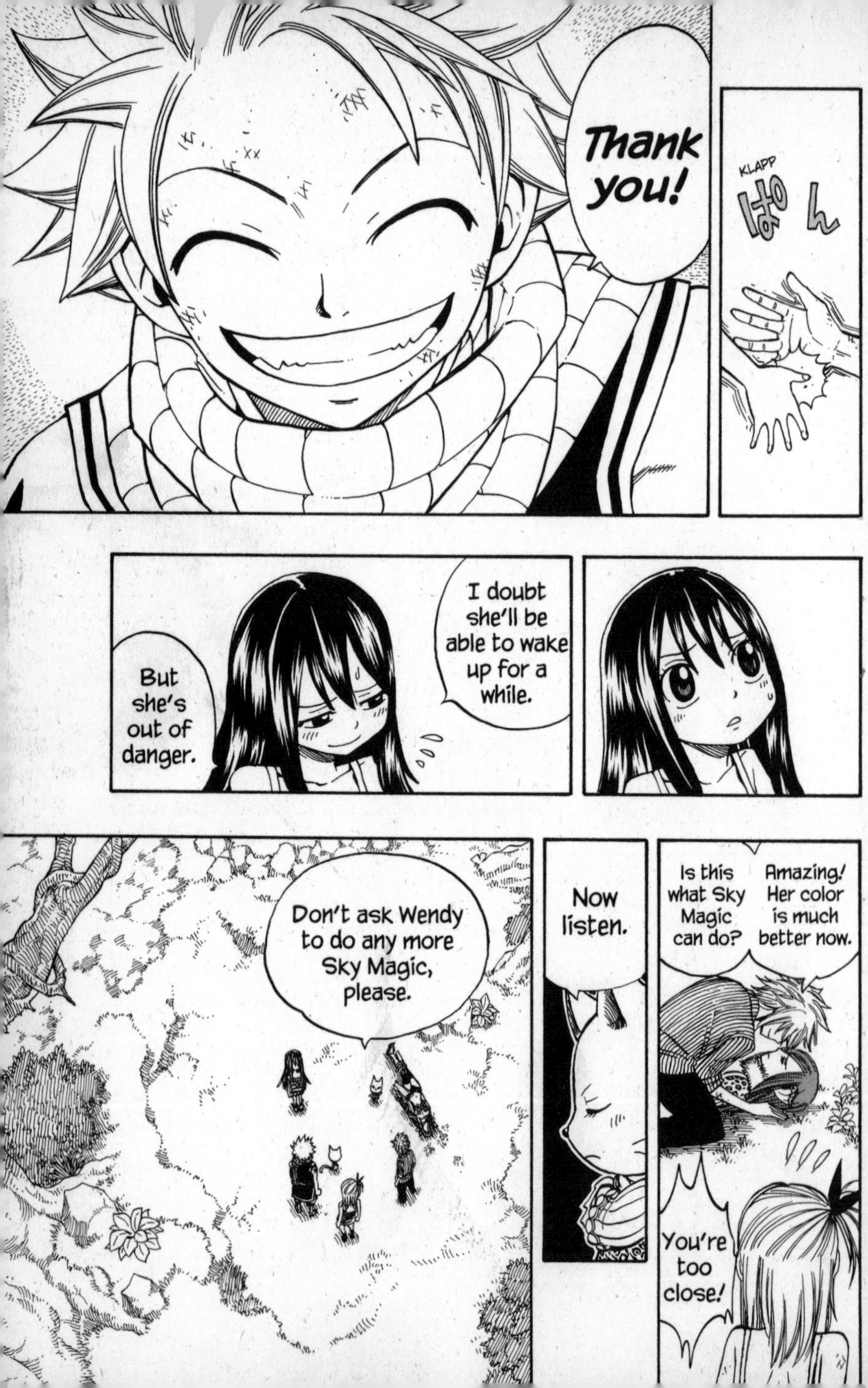
KLAPP
ぱん
Thank you!
I doubt she'll be able to wake up for a while.
But she's out of danger.
Amazing! Her color is much better now.
Is this what Sky Magic can do?
You're too close!
Now listen.
Don't ask Wendy to do any more Sky Magic, please.

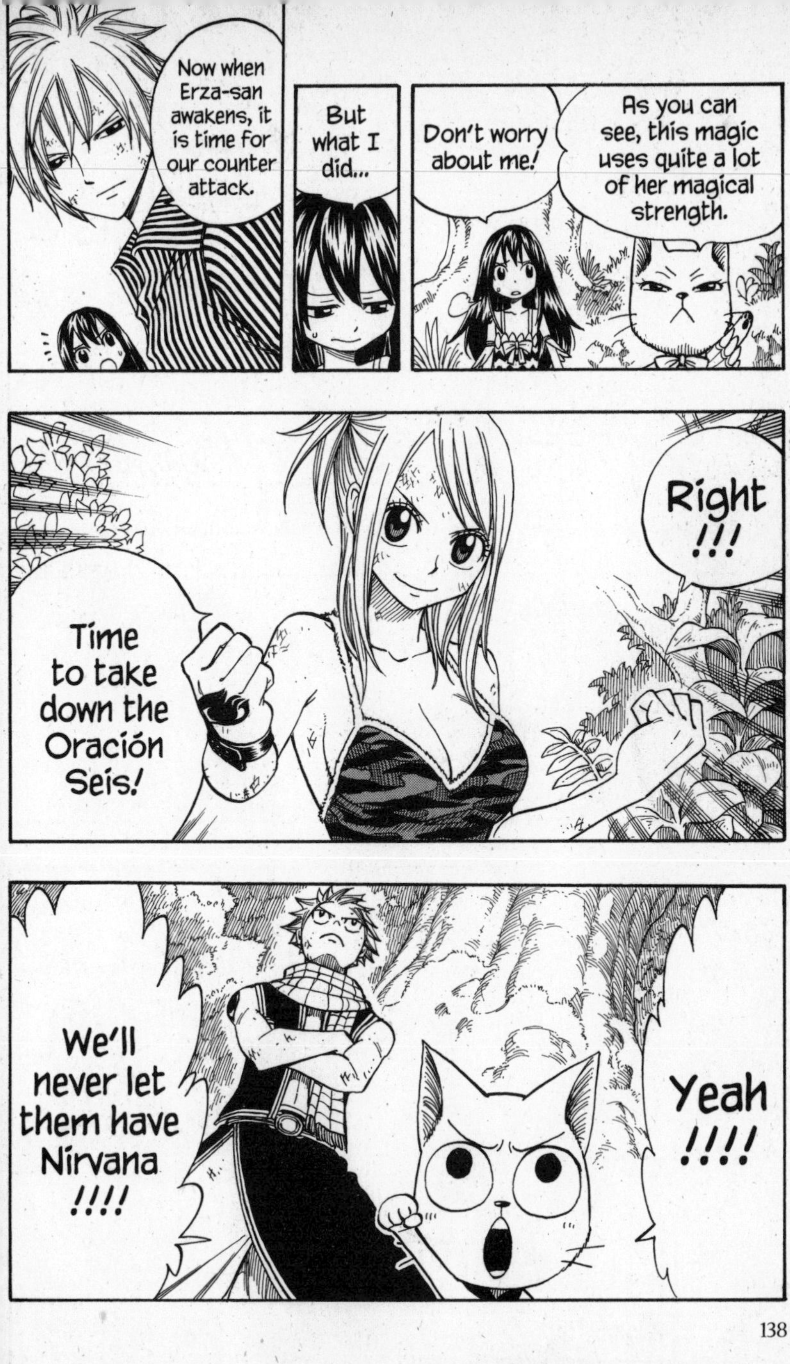

As you can see, this magic uses quite a lot of her magical strength.
Don't worry about me!
But what I did...
Now when Erza-san awakens, it is time for our counter attack.
Right !!!
Time to take down the Oración Seis!
Yeah !!!!
We'll never let them have Nirvana !!!!

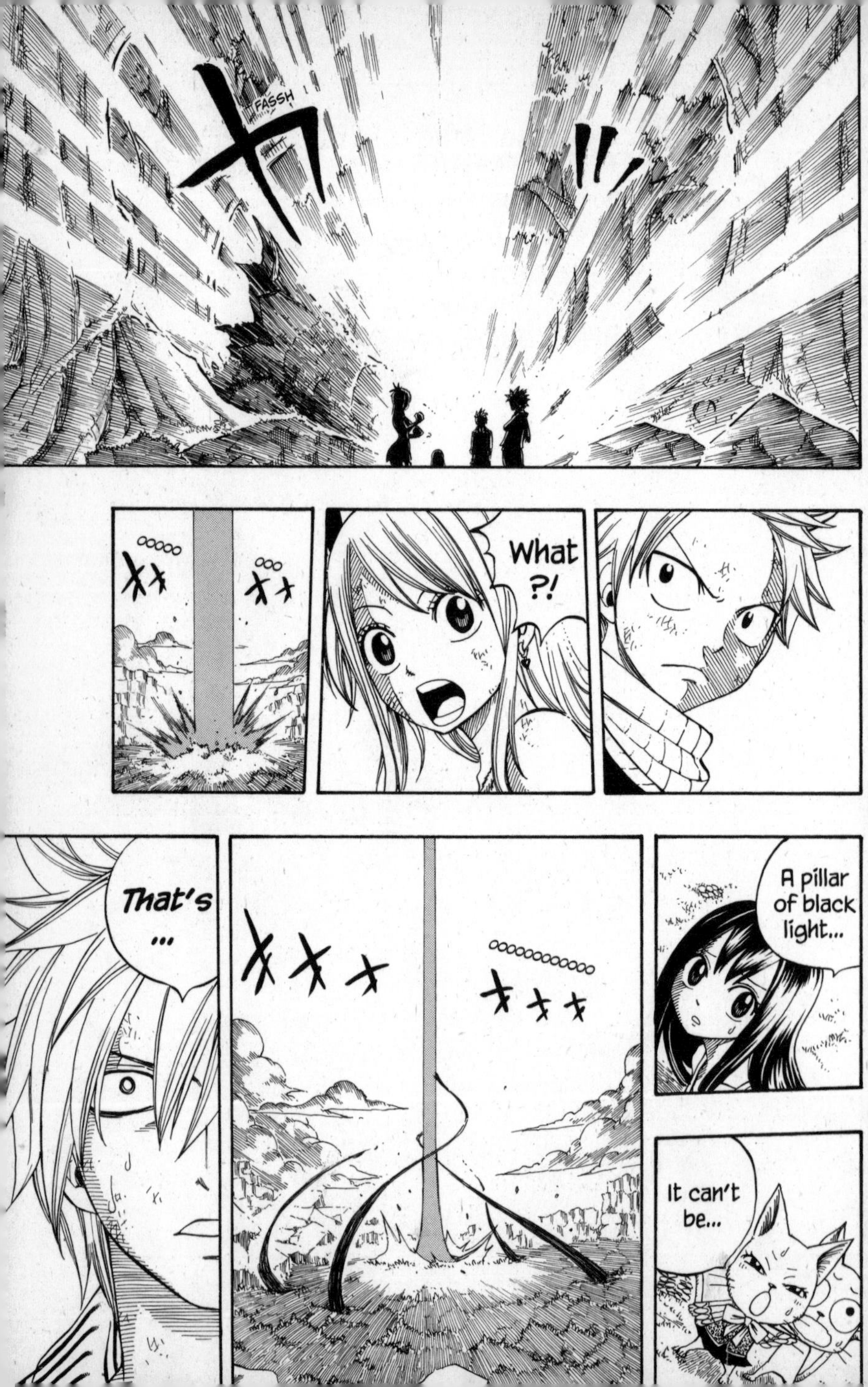
FASSH
What ?!
A pillar of black light...
It can't be...
That's ...

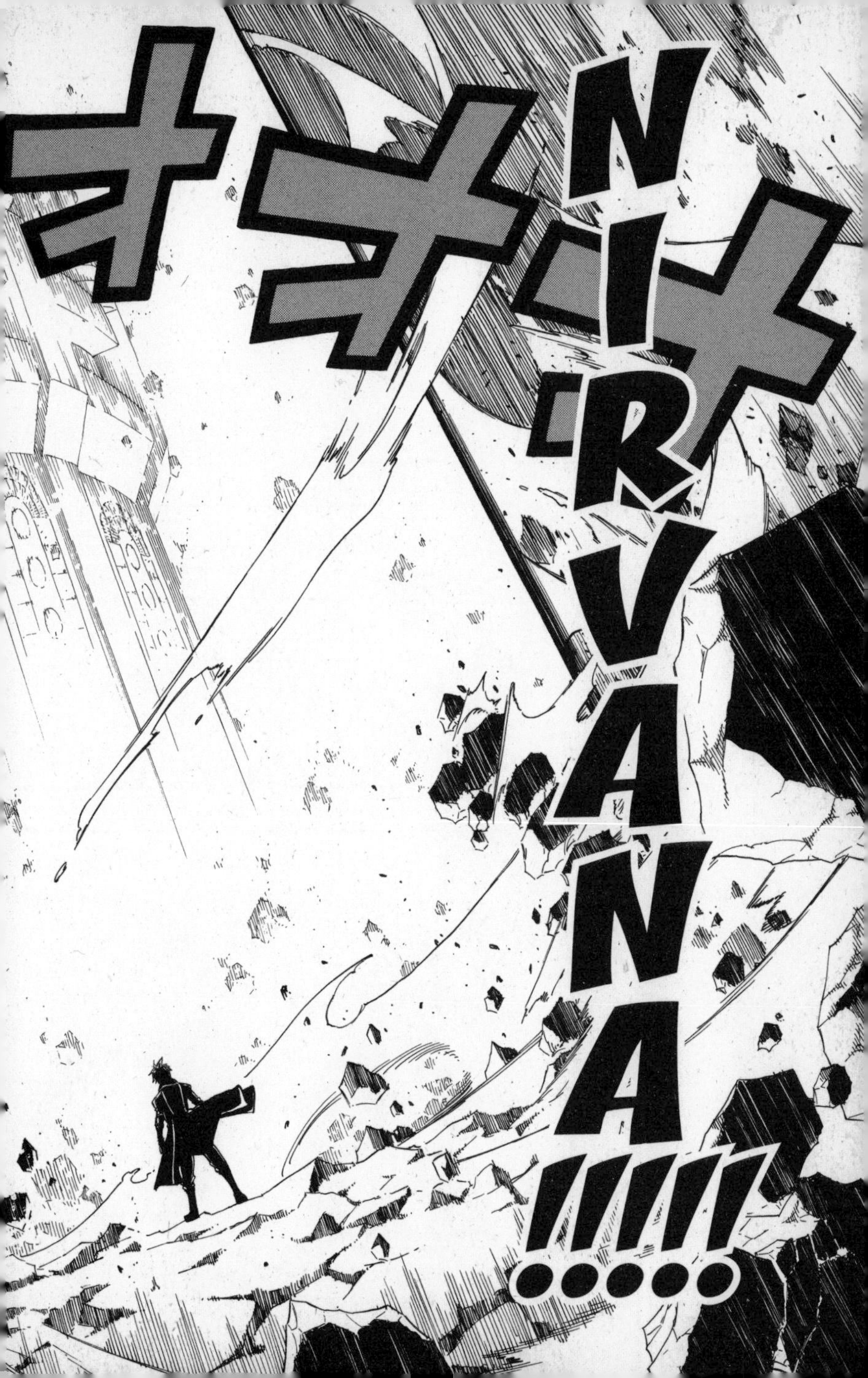
オオオオ
NIRVANA!!!!!.....

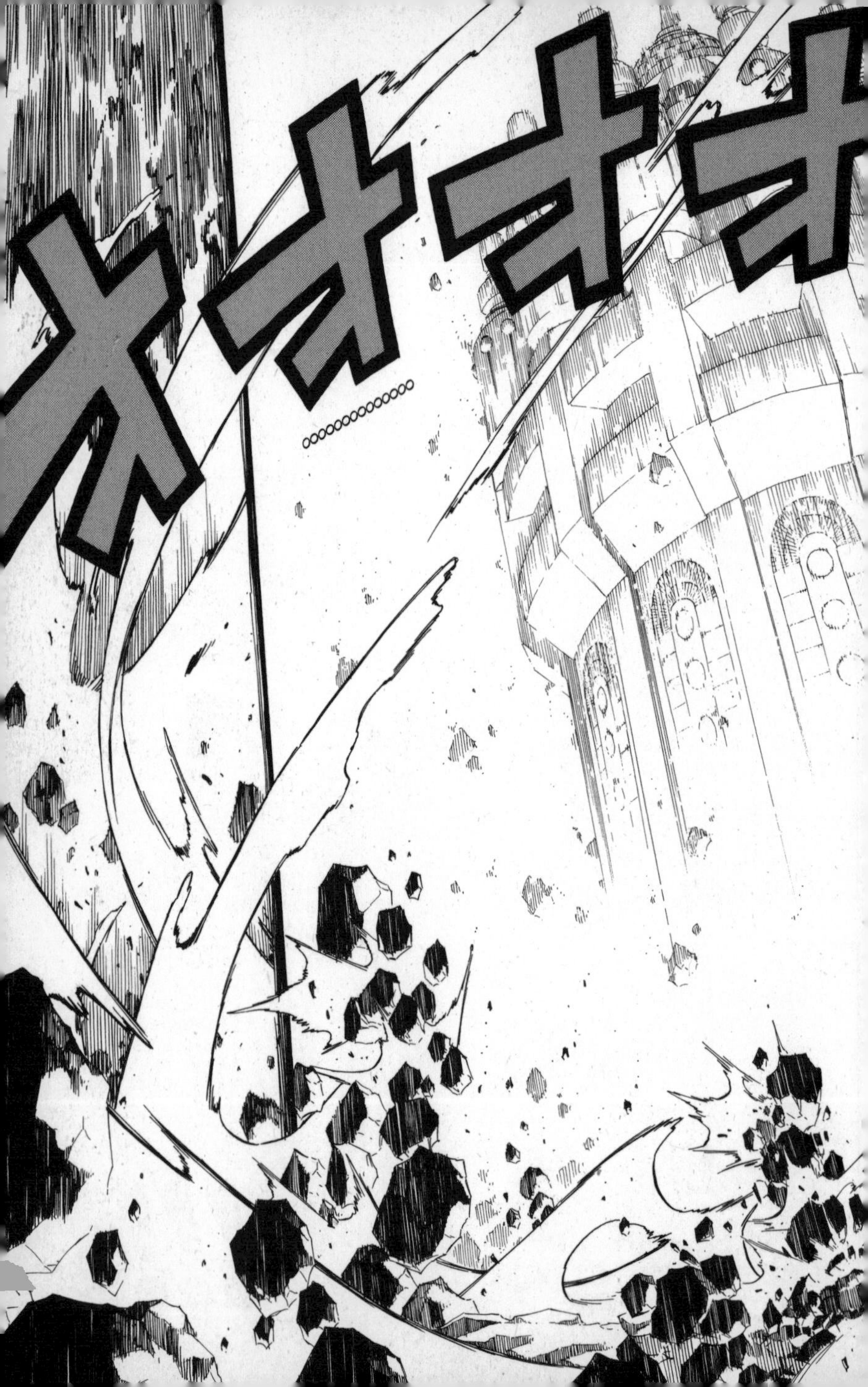
オオオオ

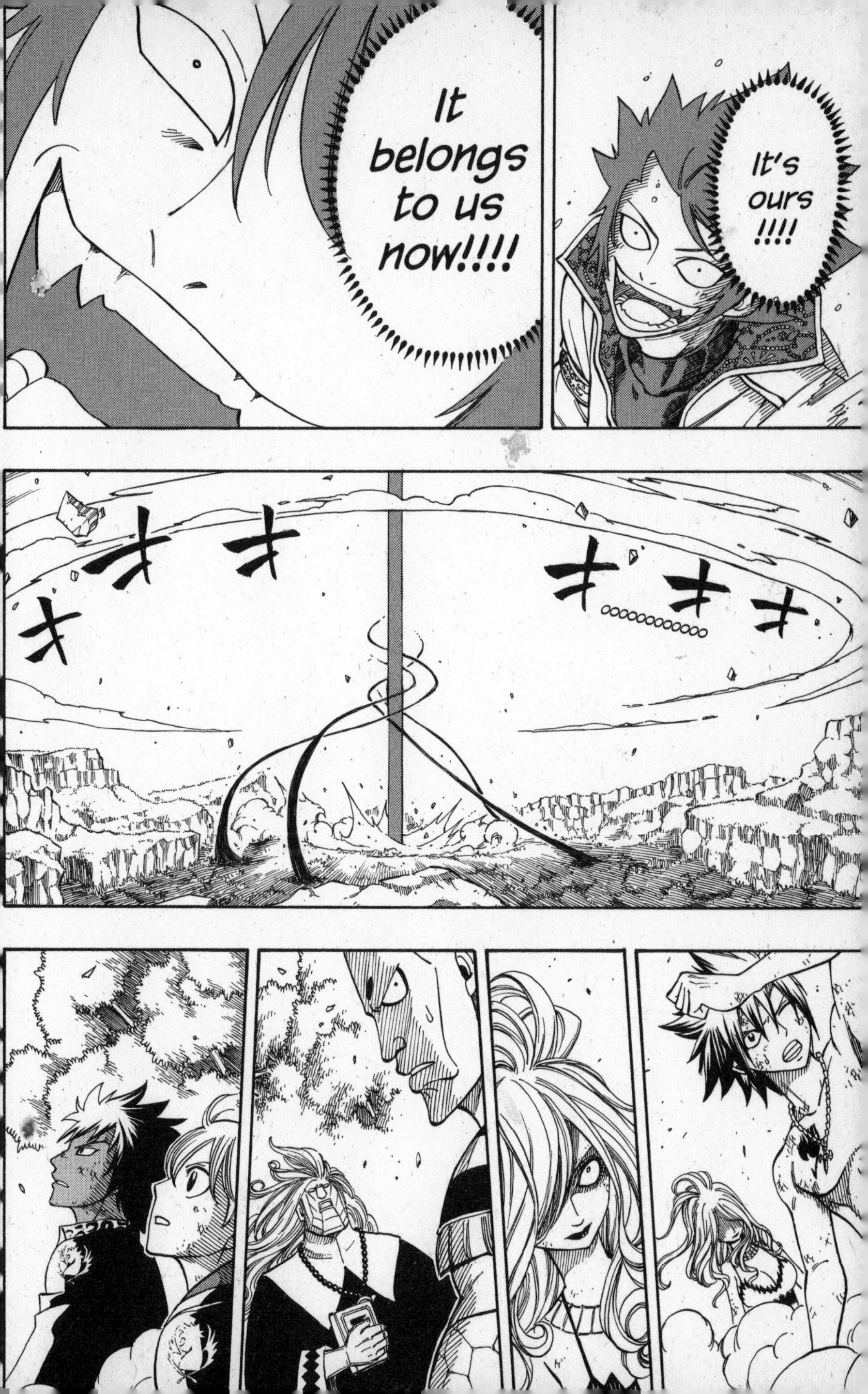
It's ours!!!!
It belongs to us now!!!!
oooooooooooo

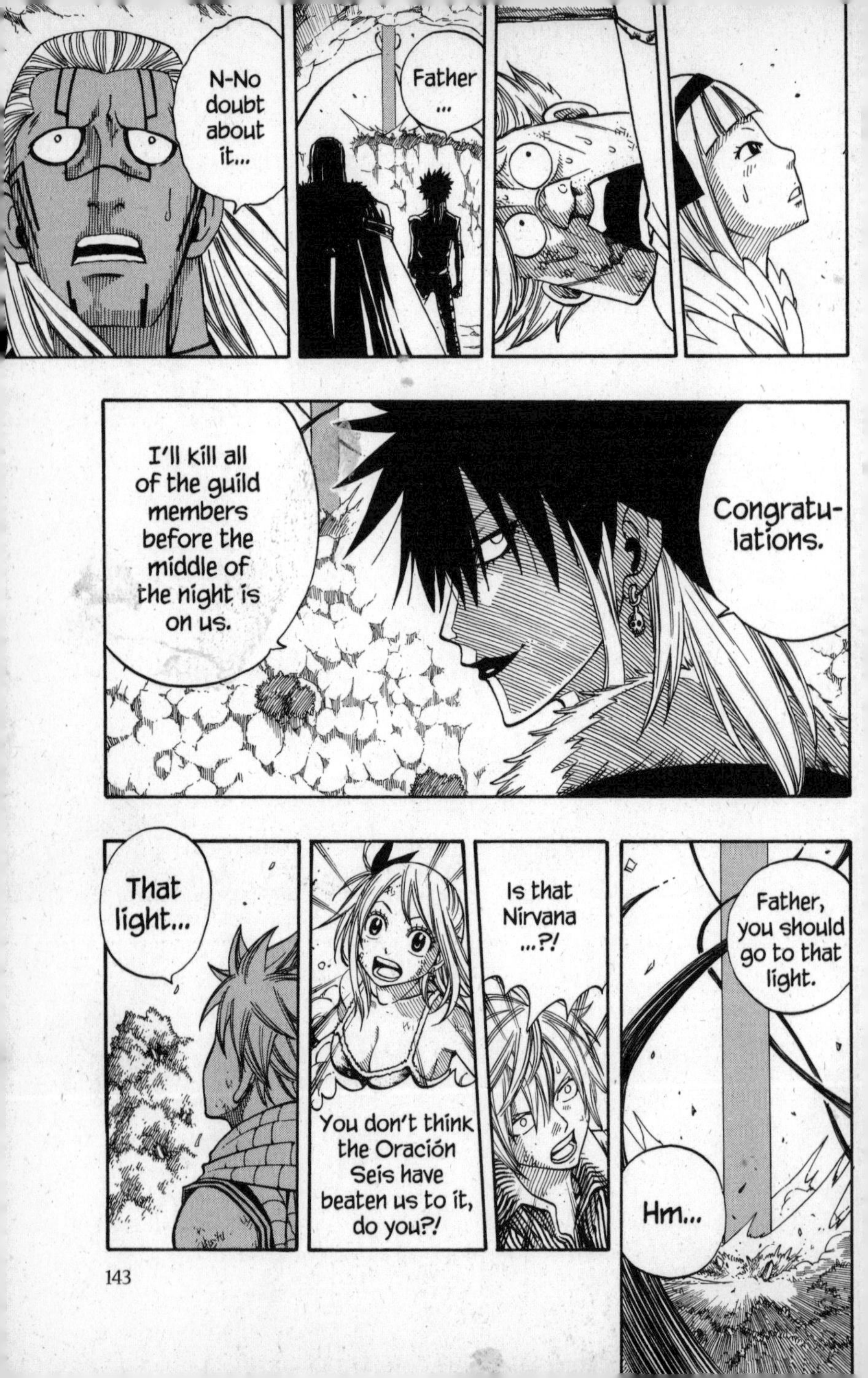
Father ...
N-No doubt about it...
Congratu-lations.
I'll kill all of the guild members before the middle of the night is on us.
Father, you should go to that light.
Hm...
Is that Nirvana ...?!
You don't think the Oración Seis have beaten us to it, do you?!
That light...

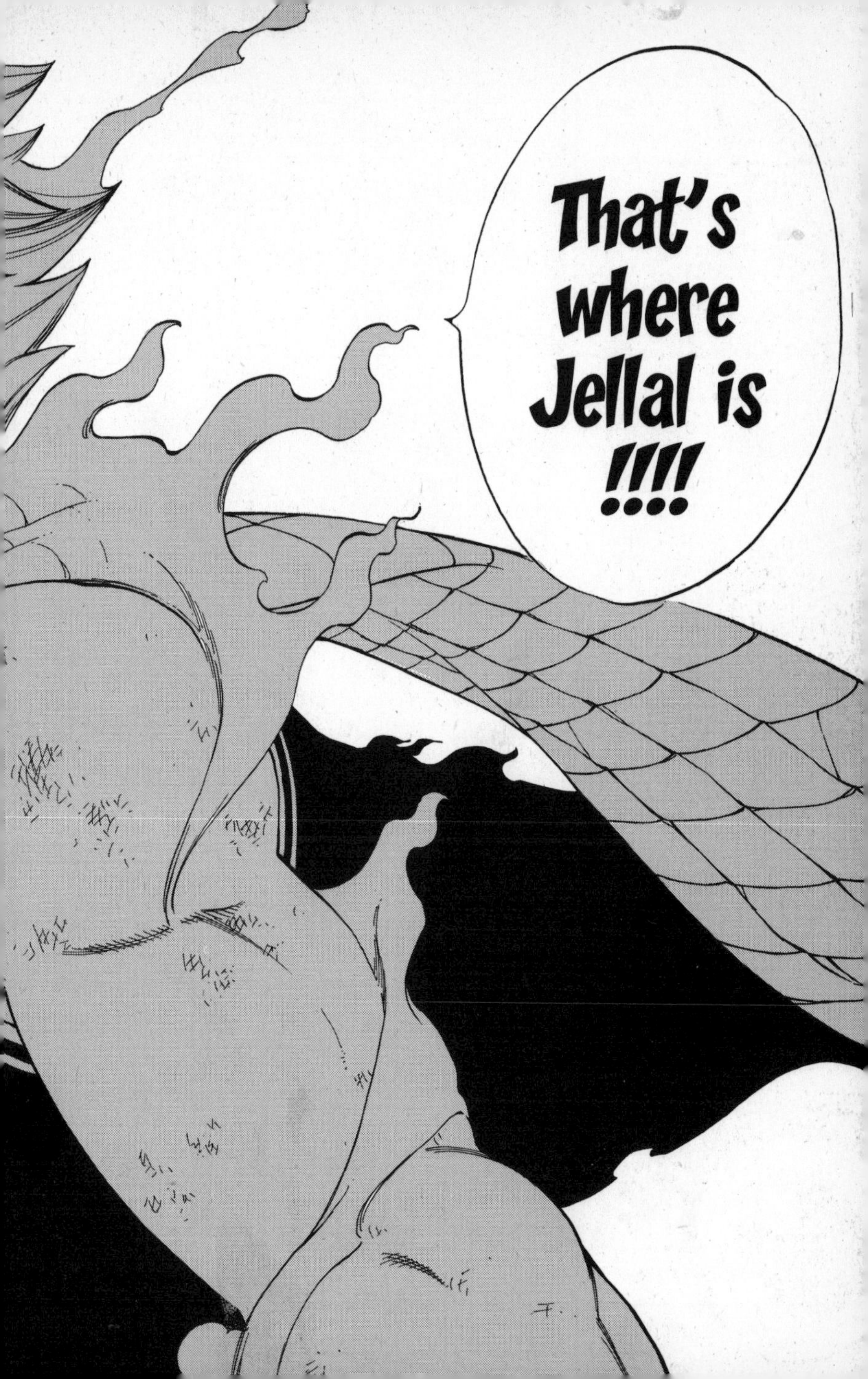
That's where Jellal is !!!!

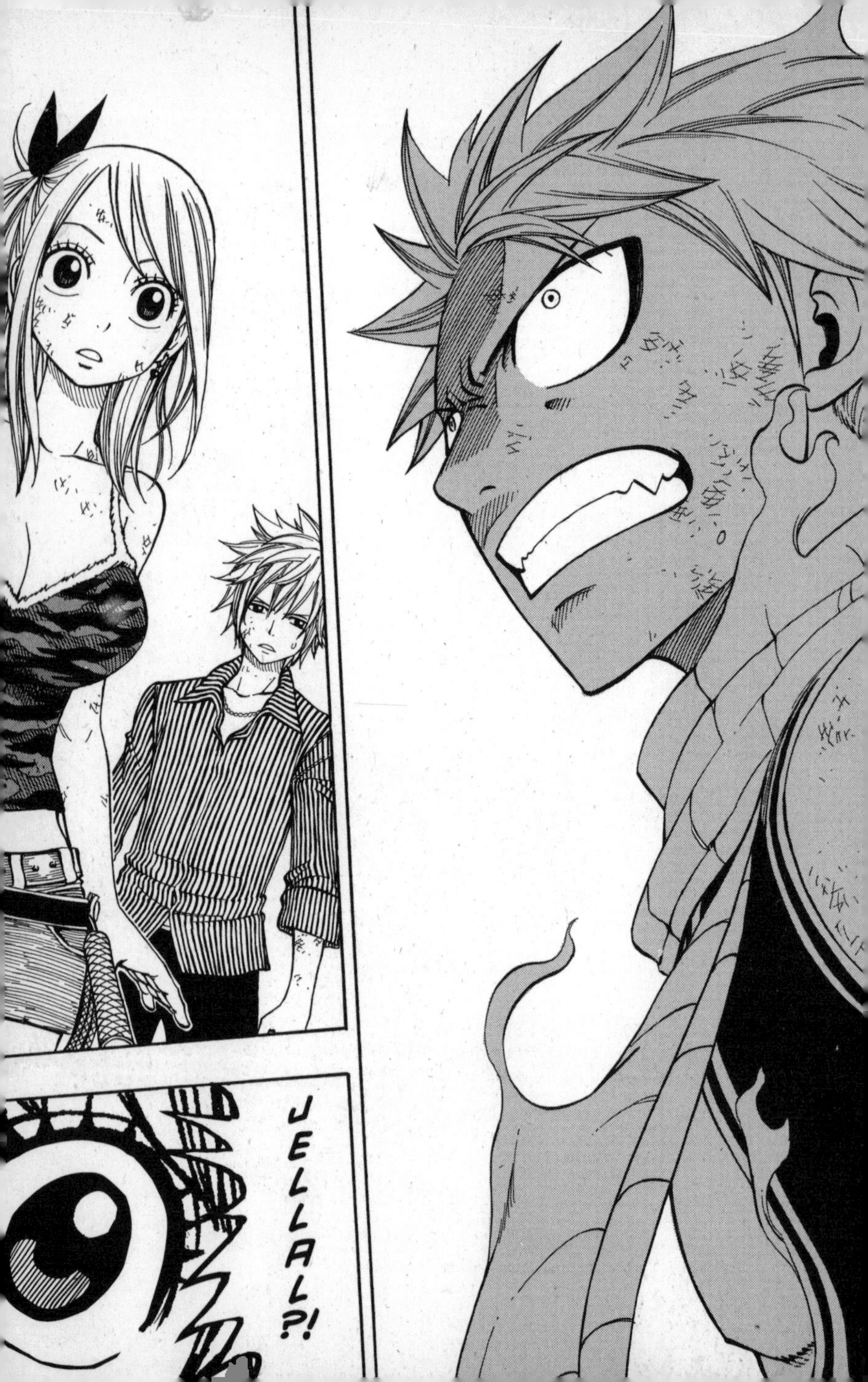
JELLAL?!

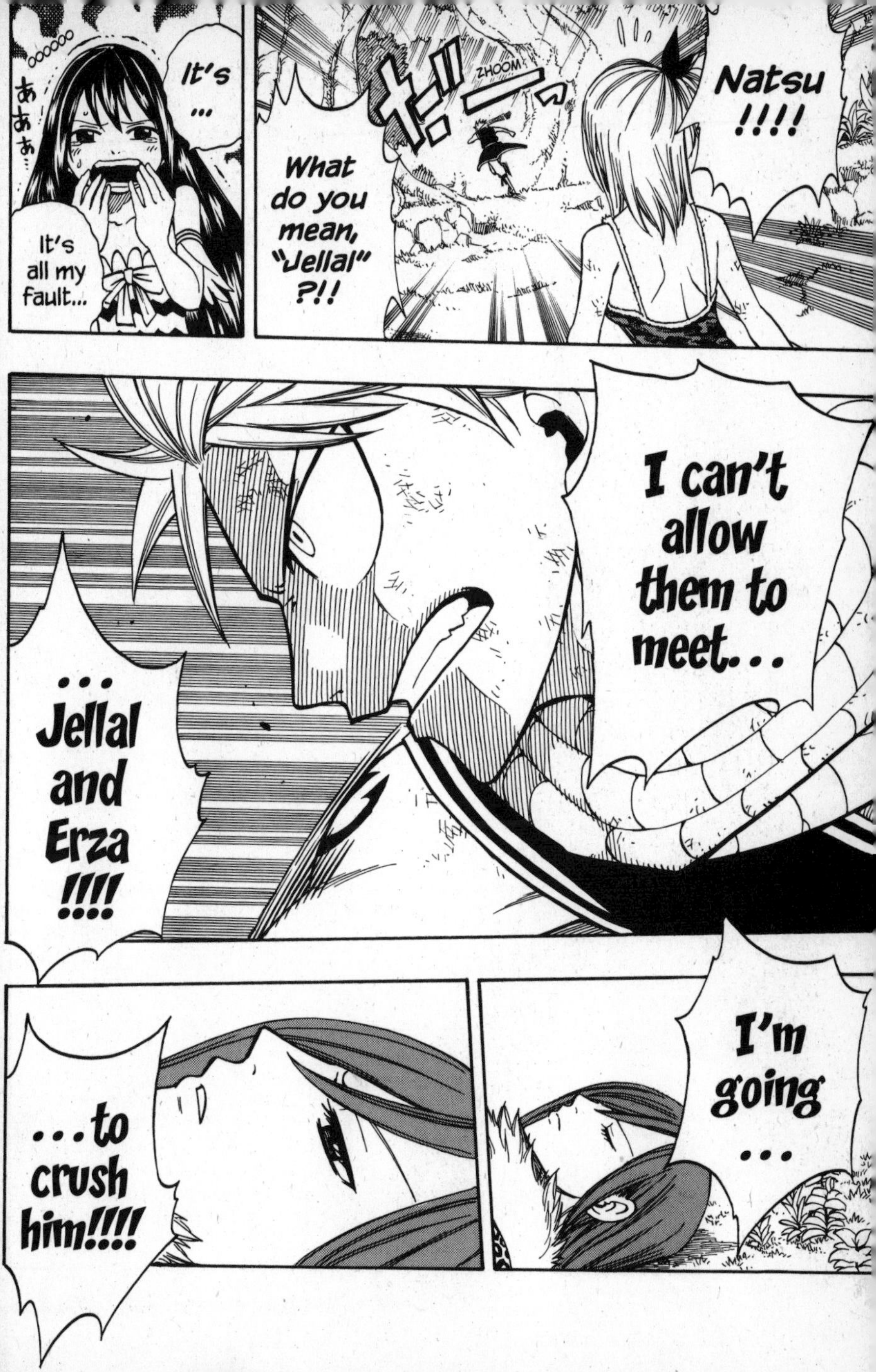
Natsu !!!!
ZHOOM
What do you mean, "Jellal" ?!!
It's ...
It's all my fault...
あああ…
oooooo
I can't allow them to meet...
...Jellal and Erza!!!!
I'm going ...
...to crush him!!!!

FAIRY TAIL

フェアリーテイル

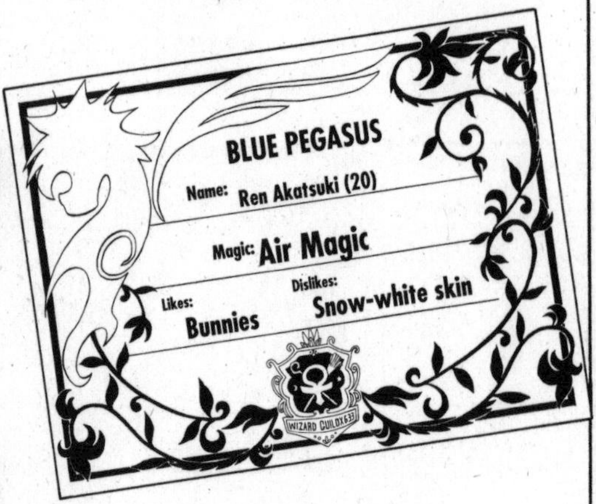
BLUE PEGASUS
Name: Ren Akatsuki (20)
Magic: Air Magic
Likes: Bunnies
Dislikes: Snow-white skin
WIZARD GUILD X633

Remarks

An Air Magic wizard working at the Blue Pegasus guild. Air Magic allows one to send waves of air, steal the oxygen out of the air around one's opponent and more. It's pretty difficult magic to face.
He placed tanning lacrima in the guild's training gym and sauna, so his perfect tan is due to the guild's support and lacrima crystals.
Tanning Lacrima is a magic item meant to give artificial sun tans. By adjusting the lacrima memory, you can tan to any shade you want in five minutes. The dial can be set to some mysterious number like 61, 63, or 65. Ren's is set to 61 - 61.5.

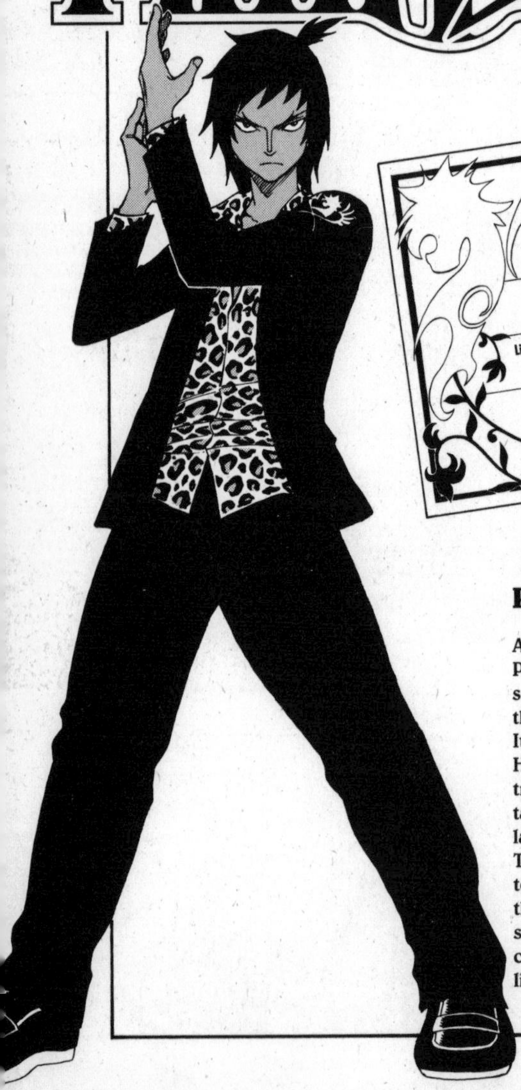

Chapter 142, Darkness

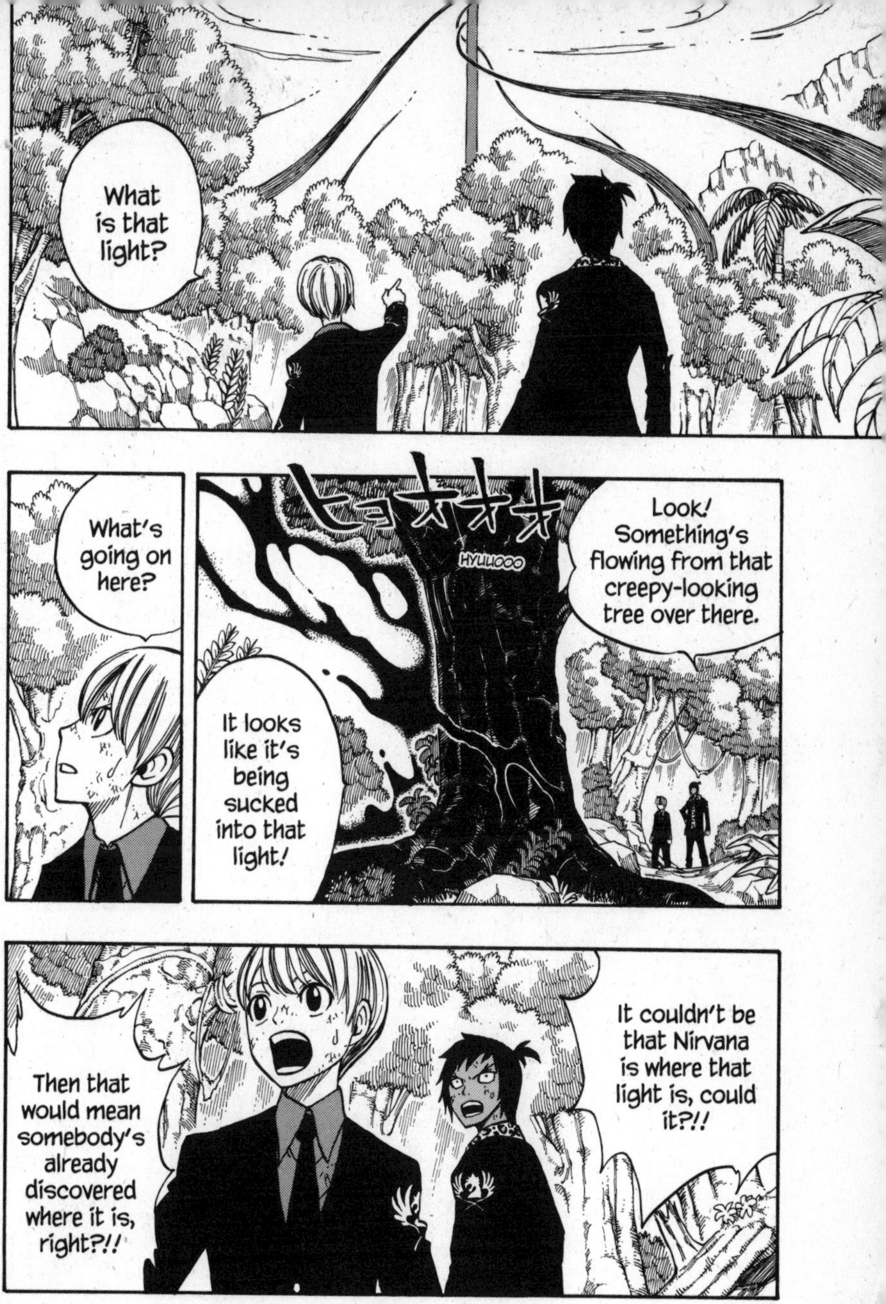
What is that light?
Look! Something's flowing from that creepy-looking tree over there.
ヒョオオオ
HYUUOOO
It looks like it's being sucked into that light!
What's going on here?
It couldn't be that Nirvana is where that light is, could it?!!
Then that would mean somebody's already discovered where it is, right?!!

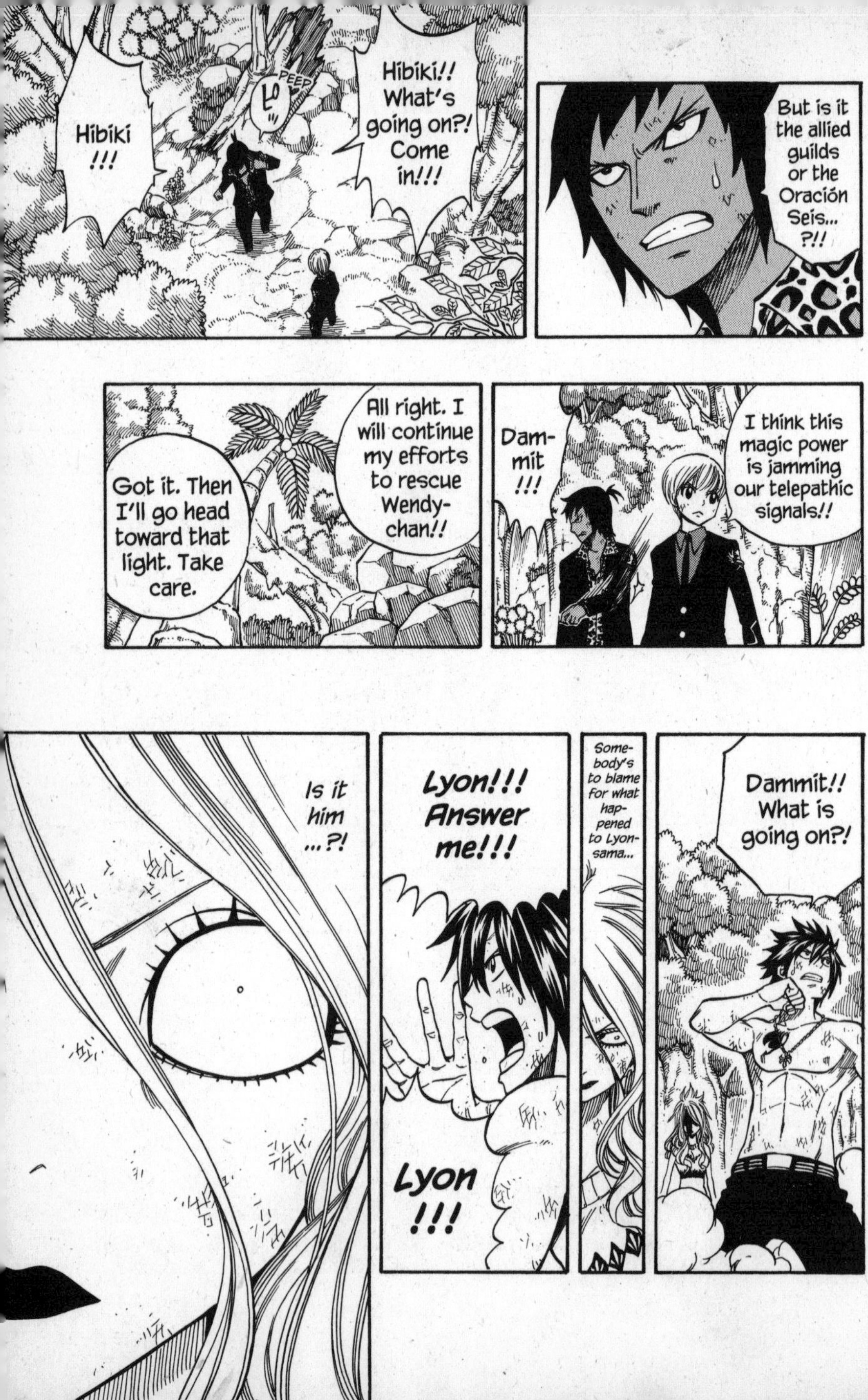
But is it the allied guilds or the Oración Seis...?!!
Hibiki!! What's going on?! Come in!!!
PEEP
Hibiki!!!
I think this magic power is jamming our telepathic signals!!
Dammit!!!
All right. I will continue my efforts to rescue Wendy-chan!!
Got it. Then I'll go head toward that light. Take care.
Dammit!! What is going on?!
Somebody's to blame for what happened to Lyon-sama...
Lyon!!! Answer me!!!
Lyon!!!
Is it him...?!

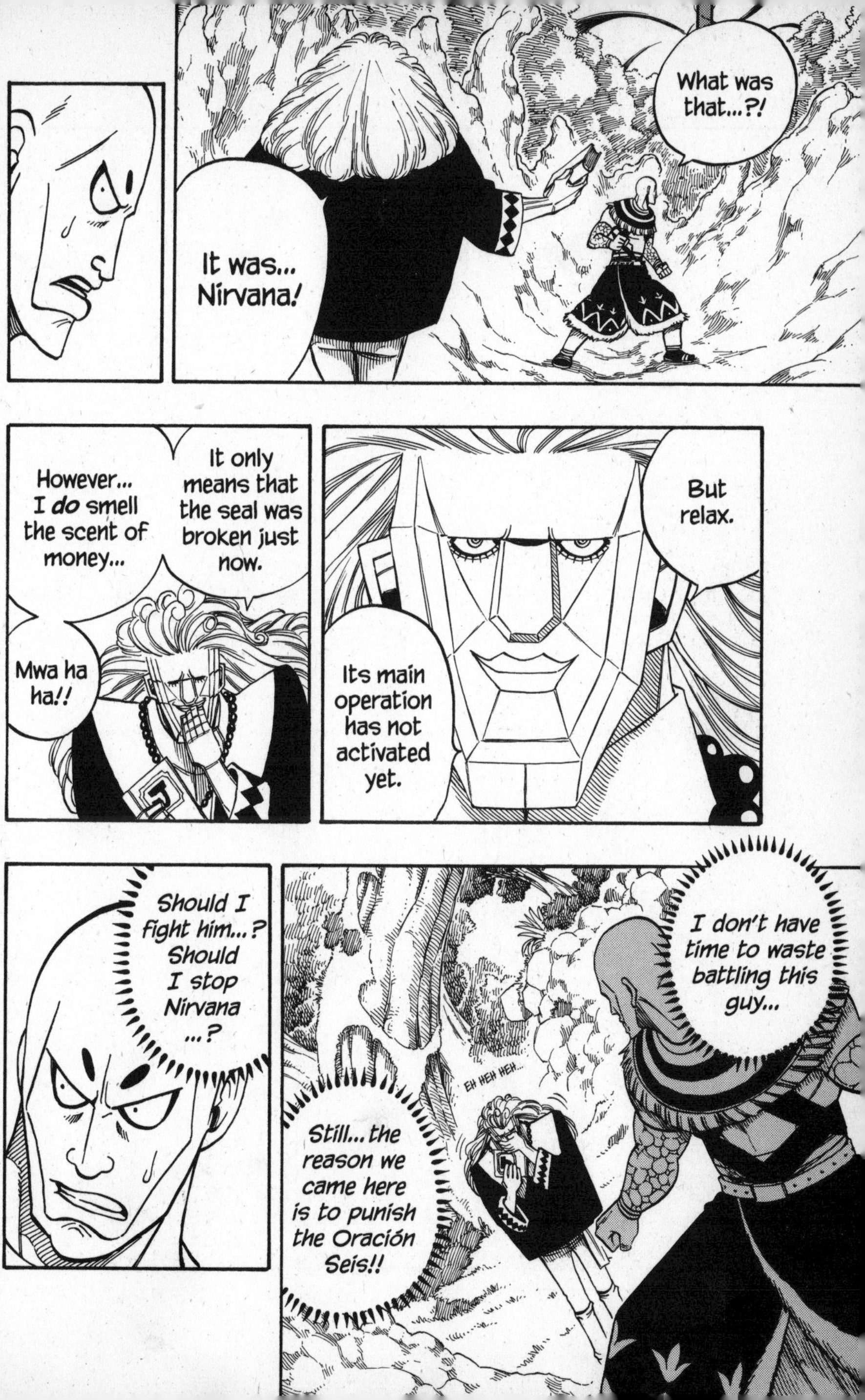
What was that...?!
It was... Nirvana!
But relax.
Its main operation has not activated yet.
It only means that the seal was broken just now.
However... I *do* smell the scent of money...
Mwa ha ha!!
I don't have time to waste battling this guy...
EH HEH HEH...
Still... the reason we came here is to punish the Oración Seis!!
Should I fight him...? Should I stop Nirvana...?

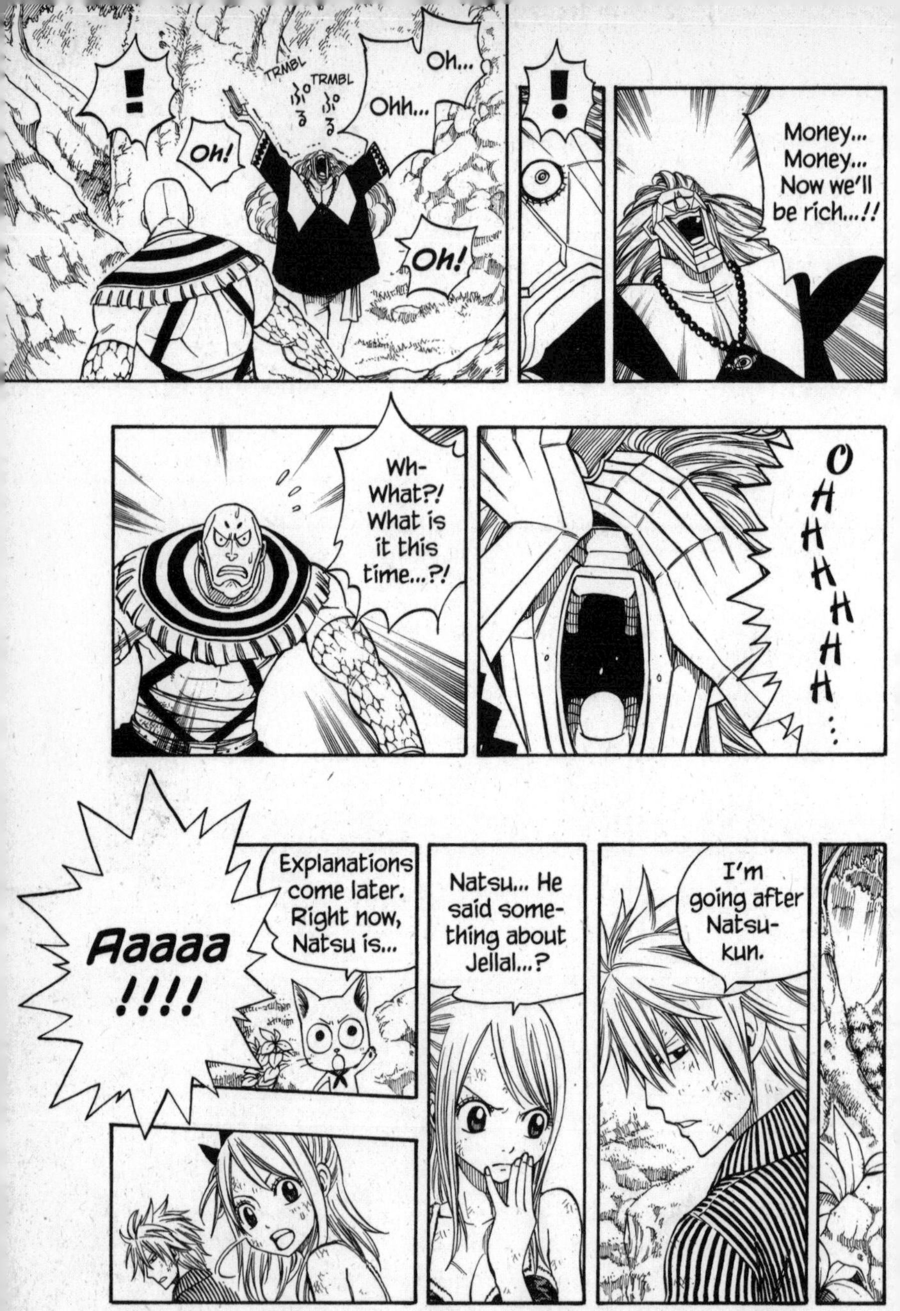
Money... Money... Now we'll be rich...!!
!
Oh...
Ohh...
TRMBL ぷる
TRMBL ぷる
!
Oh!
Oh!
OHHHHHH...
Wh- What?! What is it this time...?!
I'm going after Natsu-kun.
Natsu... He said some-thing about Jellal...?
Explanations come later. Right now, Natsu is...
Aaaaa !!!!

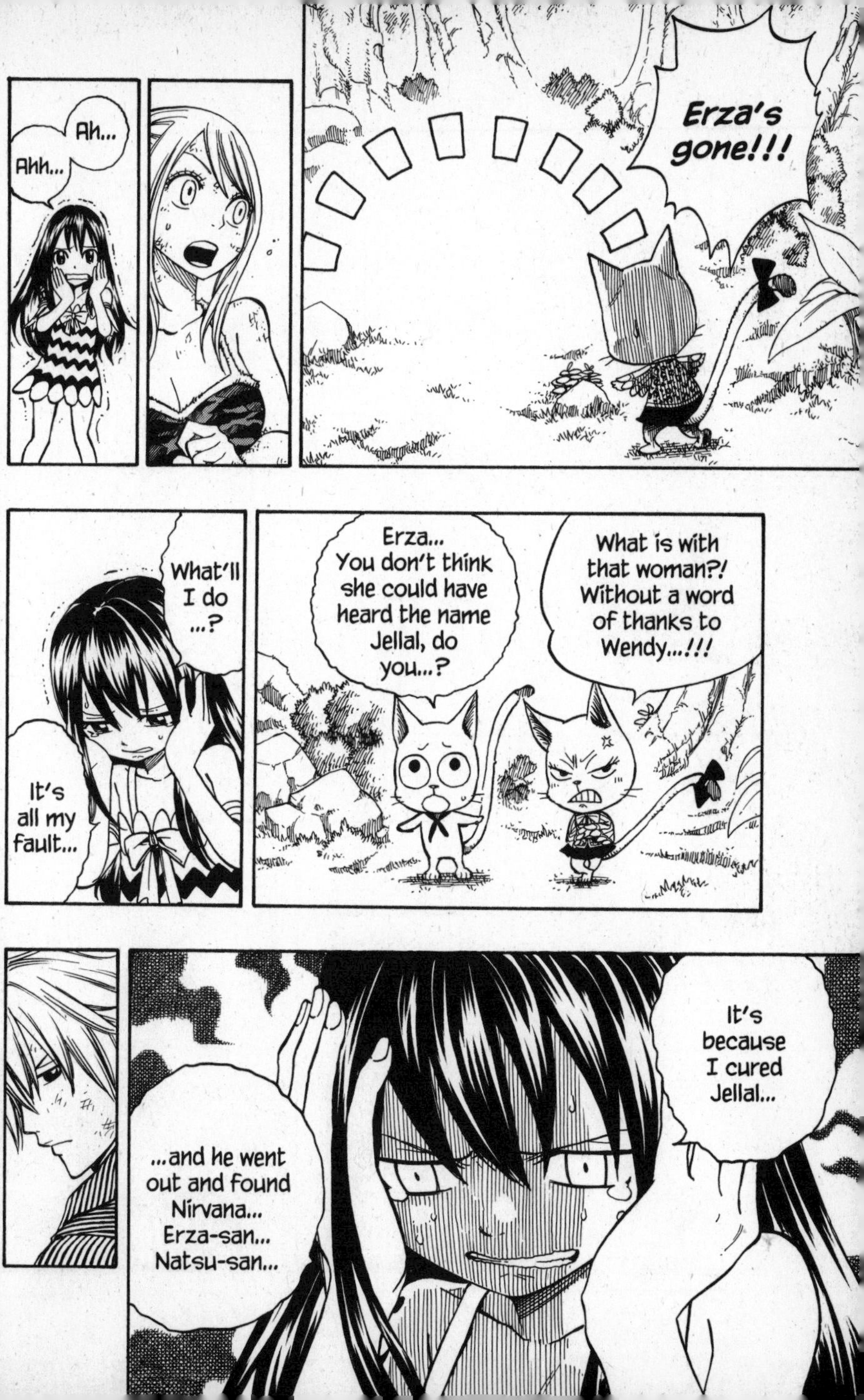
Erza's gone!!!
Ah...
Ahh...
What is with that woman?! Without a word of thanks to Wendy...!!!
Erza... You don't think she could have heard the name Jellal, do you...?
What'll I do ...?
It's all my fault...
It's because I cured Jellal...
...and he went out and found Nirvana... Erza-san... Natsu-san...

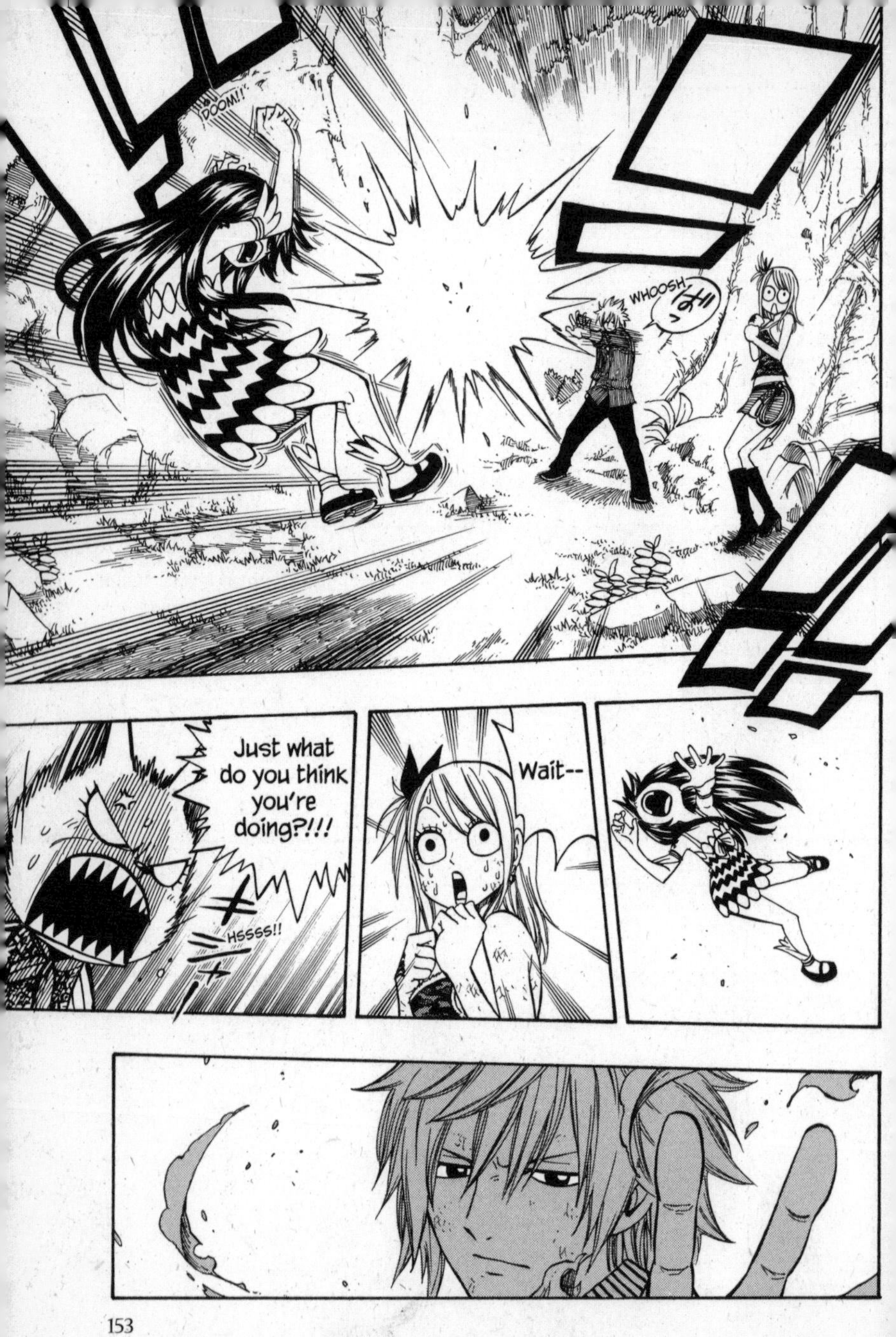
DOOM!!
WHOOSH
Wait--
Just what do you think you're doing?!!!
HSSSS!!

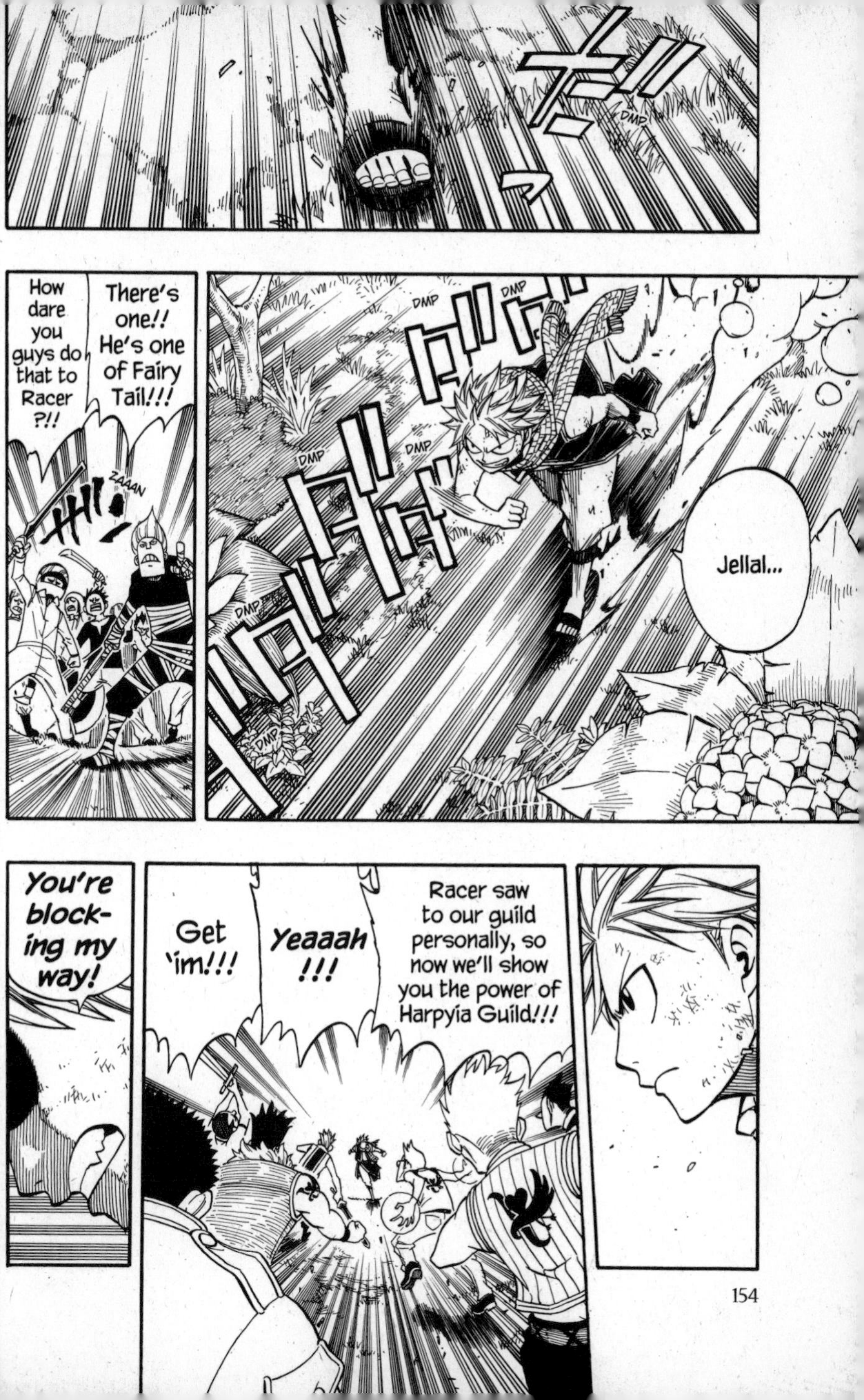
DMP
DMP
DMP
Jellal...
DMP
DMP
DMP
DMP
There's one!! He's one of Fairy Tail!!!
How dare you guys do that to Racer?!!
ZAAAN
Racer saw to our guild personally, so now we'll show you the power of Harpyia Guild!!!
Yeaaah!!!
Get 'im!!!
You're block-ing my way!

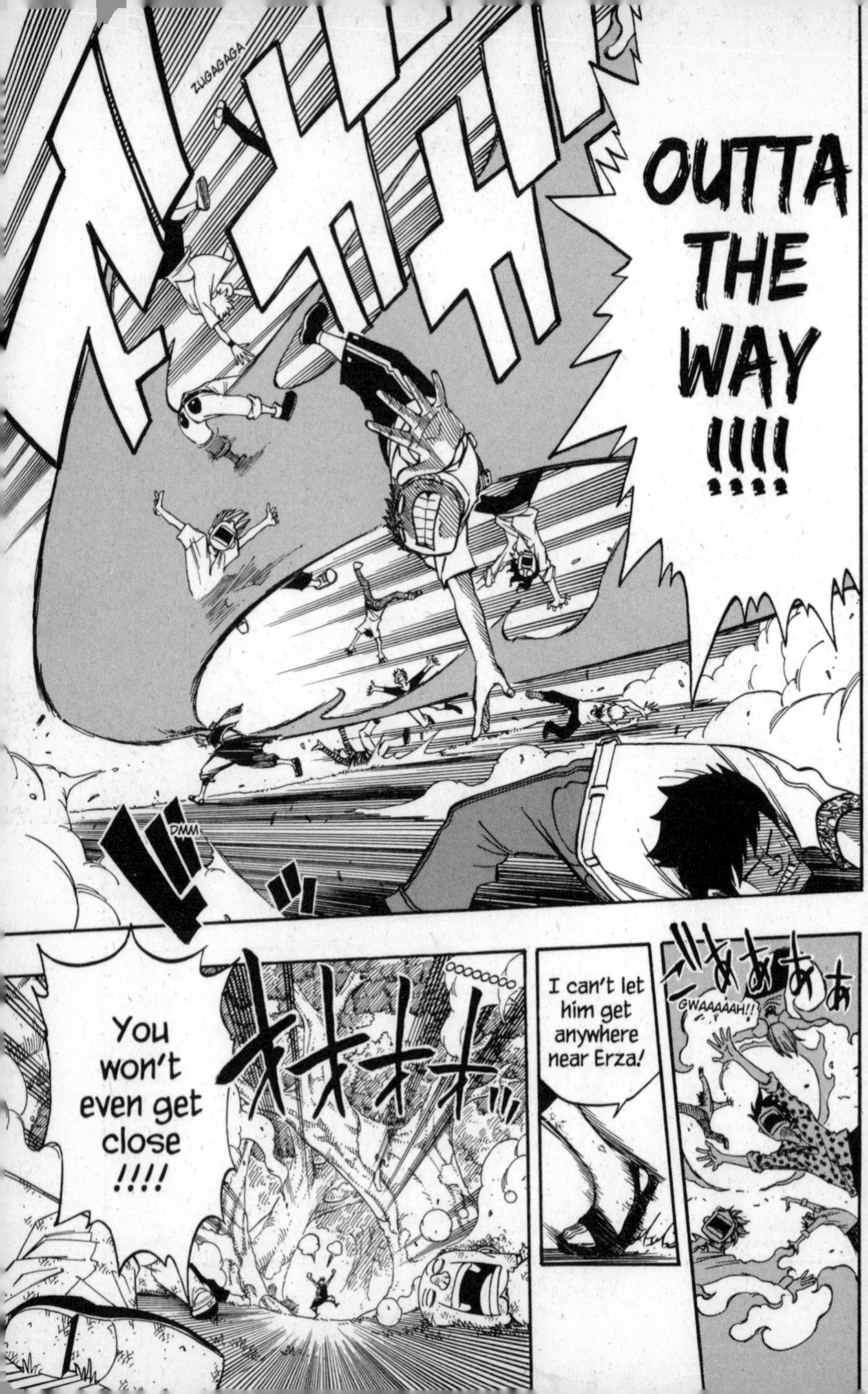
ZUGAGAGA
OUTTA THE WAY!!!!
DMM
GWAAAAAH!!
I can't let him get anywhere near Erza!
OOOOOOOO
You won't even get close!!!!

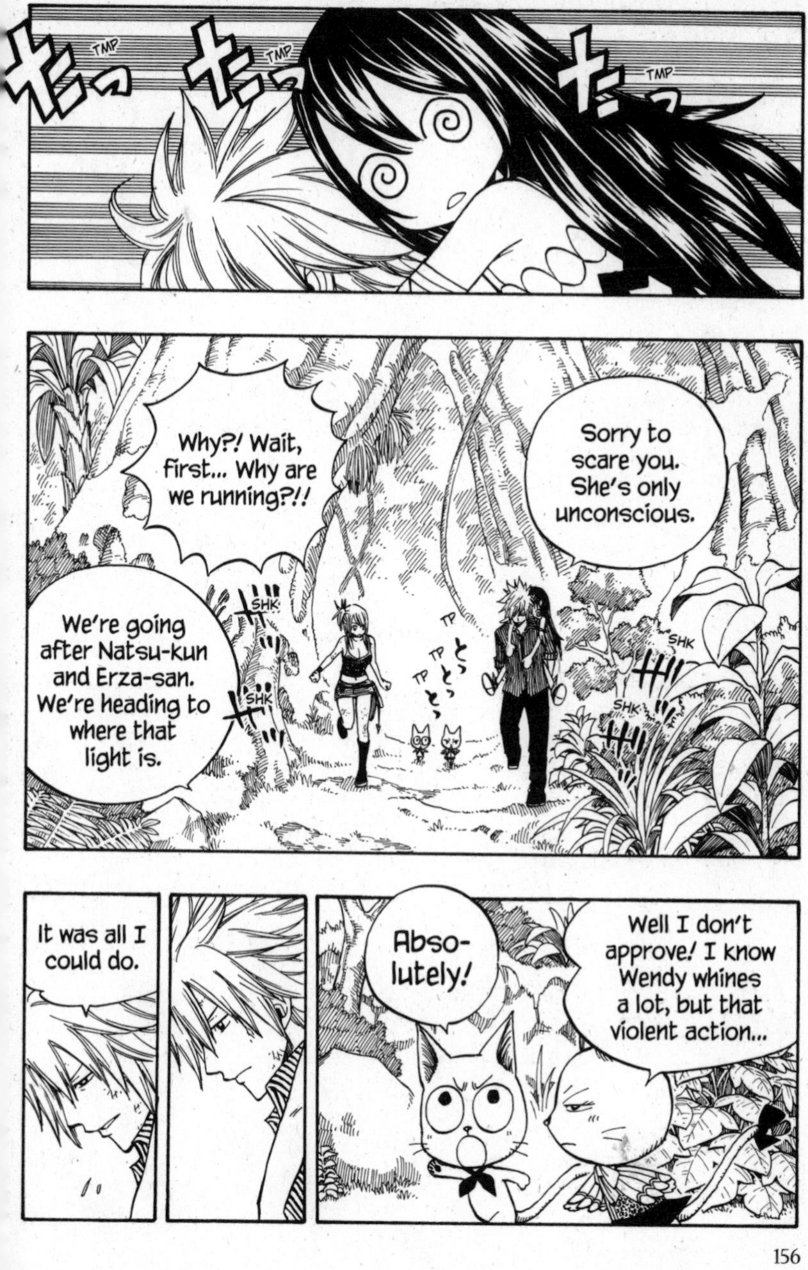
TMP
TMP
TMP
Sorry to scare you. She's only unconscious.
Why?! Wait, first... Why are we running?!!
SHK
TP
TP
TP
SHK
SHK
We're going after Natsu-kun and Erza-san. We're heading to where that light is.
SHK
Well I don't approve! I know Wendy whines a lot, but that violent action...
Abso-lutely!
It was all I could do.

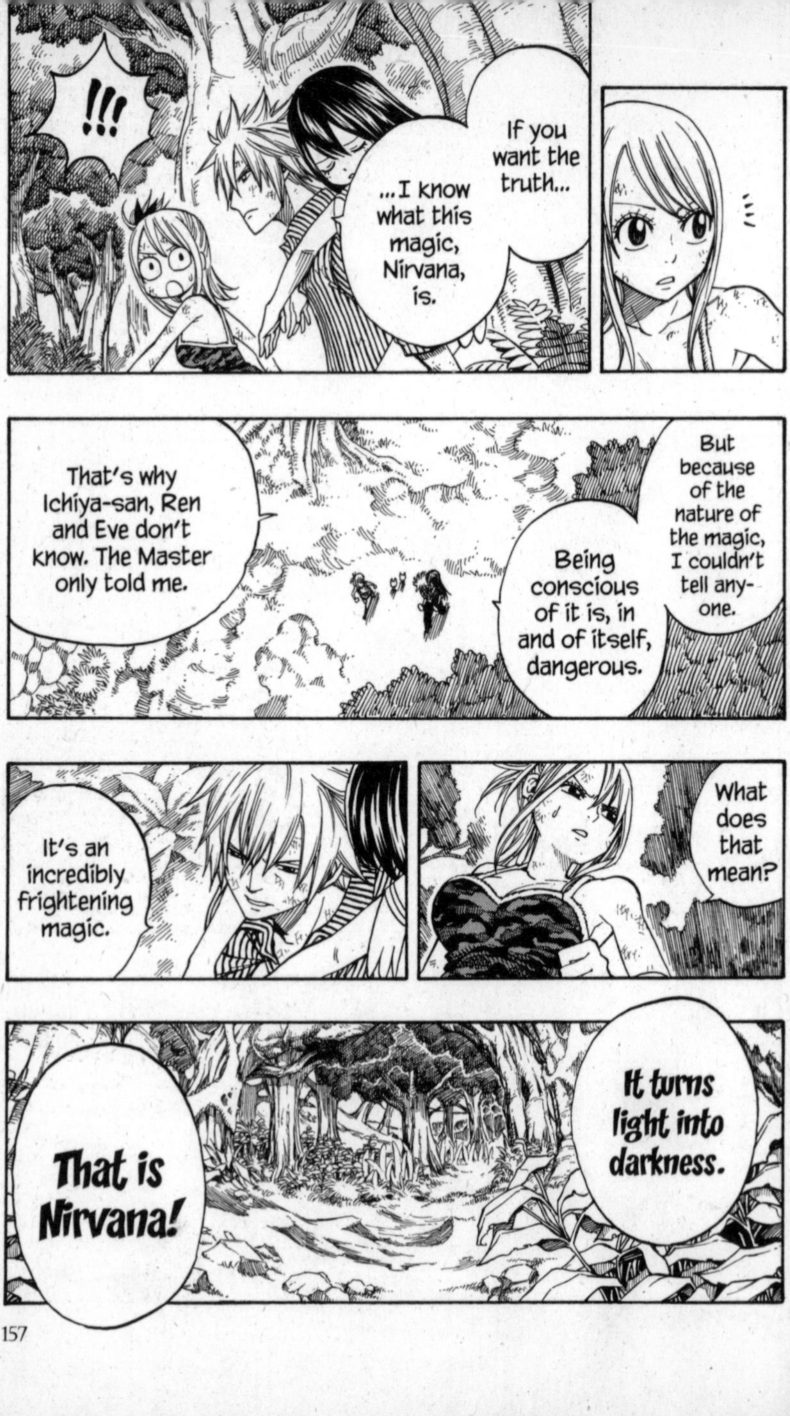
!!!
If you want the truth...
...I know what this magic, Nirvana, is.
But because of the nature of the magic, I couldn't tell any-one.
Being conscious of it is, in and of itself, dangerous.
That's why Ichiya-san, Ren and Eve don't know. The Master only told me.
What does that mean?
It's an incredibly frightening magic.
It turns light into darkness.
That is Nirvana!

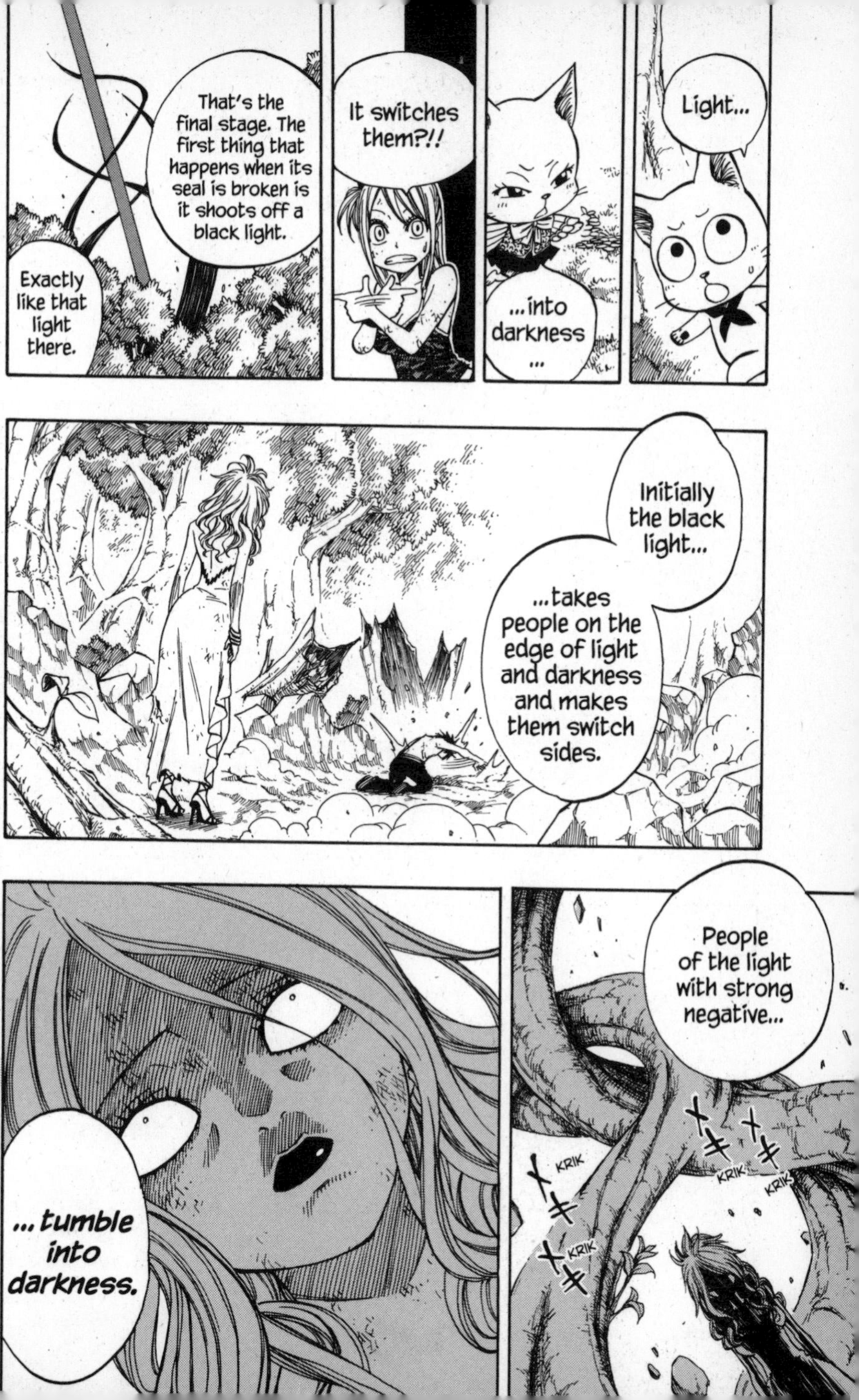
Light...
...into darkness ...
It switches them?!!
That's the final stage. The first thing that happens when its seal is broken is it shoots off a black light.
Exactly like that light there.
Initially the black light...
...takes people on the edge of light and darkness and makes them switch sides.
People of the light with strong negative...
KRIK
KRIK
KRIK
KRIK
...tumble into darkness.

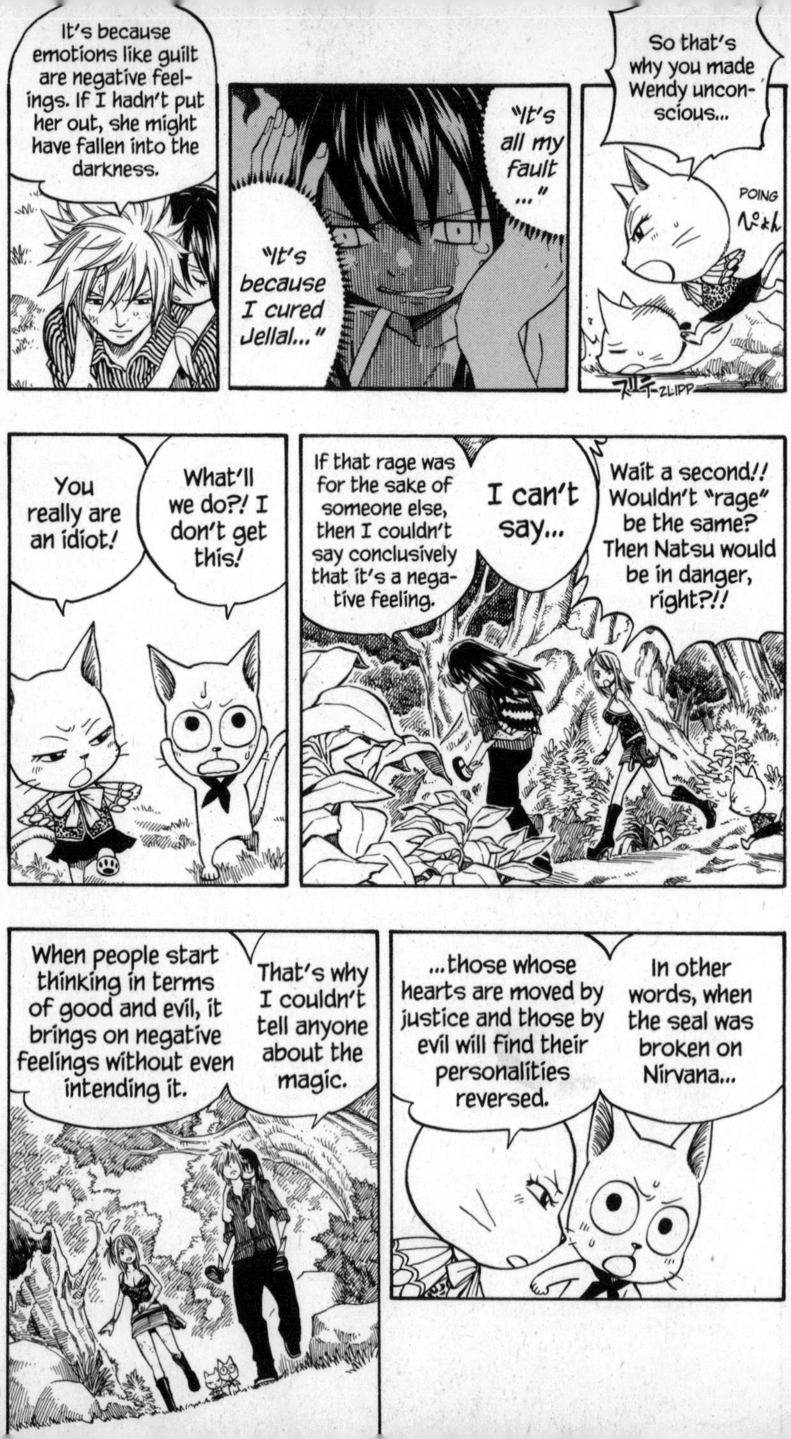
So that's why you made Wendy unconscious...
POING
ぺよん
ZLIPP
"It's all my fault..."
"It's because I cured Jellal..."
It's because emotions like guilt are negative feelings. If I hadn't put her out, she might have fallen into the darkness.
Wait a second!! Wouldn't "rage" be the same? Then Natsu would be in danger, right?!!
I can't say...
If that rage was for the sake of someone else, then I couldn't say conclusively that it's a negative feeling.
What'll we do?! I don't get this!
You really are an idiot!
In other words, when the seal was broken on Nirvana...
...those whose hearts are moved by justice and those by evil will find their personalities reversed.
That's why I couldn't tell anyone about the magic.
When people start thinking in terms of good and evil, it brings on negative feelings without even intending it.

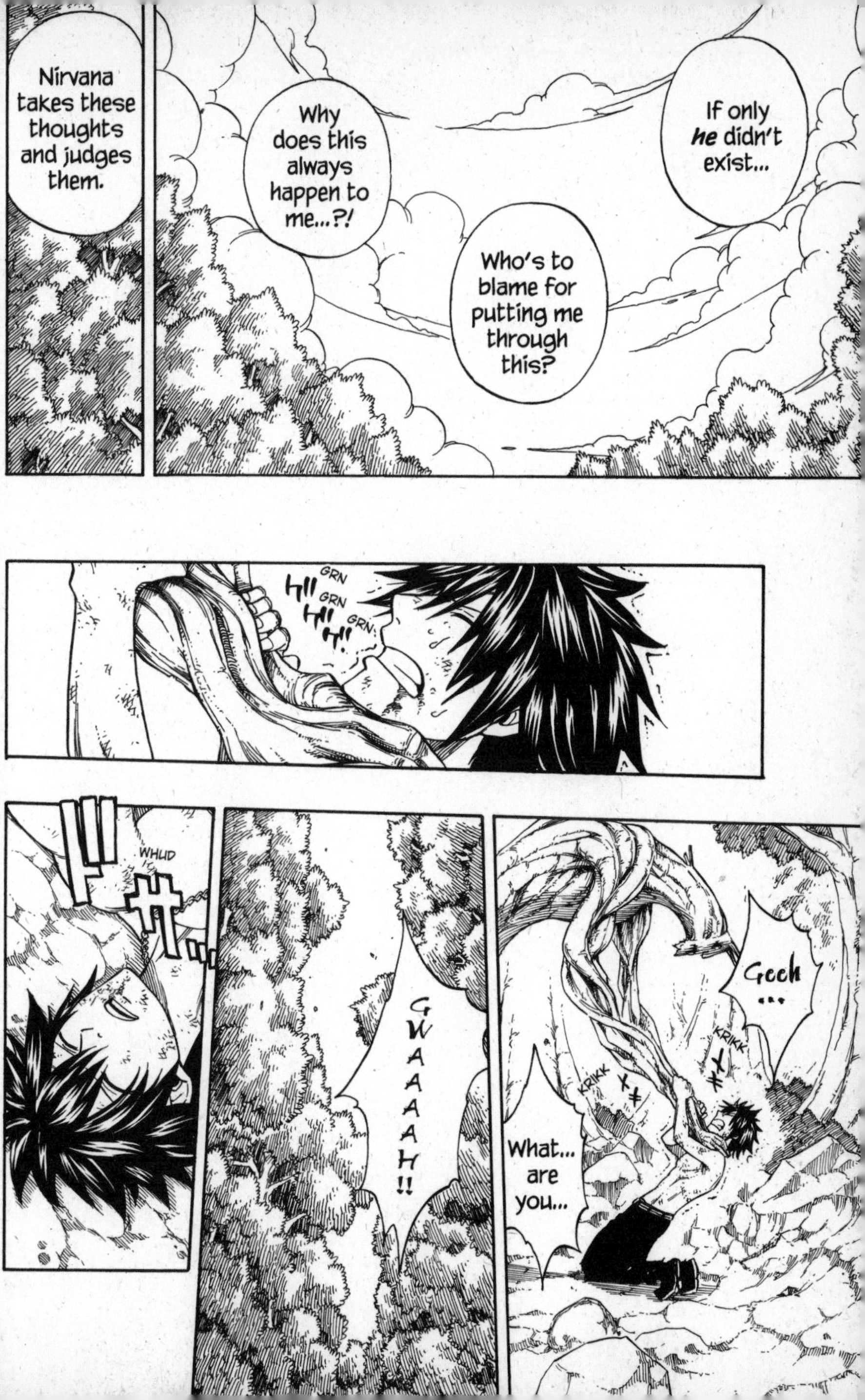
If only *he* didn't exist...
Who's to blame for putting me through this?
Why does this always happen to me...?!
Nirvana takes these thoughts and judges them.
GRN GRN GRN
Geeh...
KRIKK
KRIKK
What... are you...
GWAAAAAH!!
WHUD

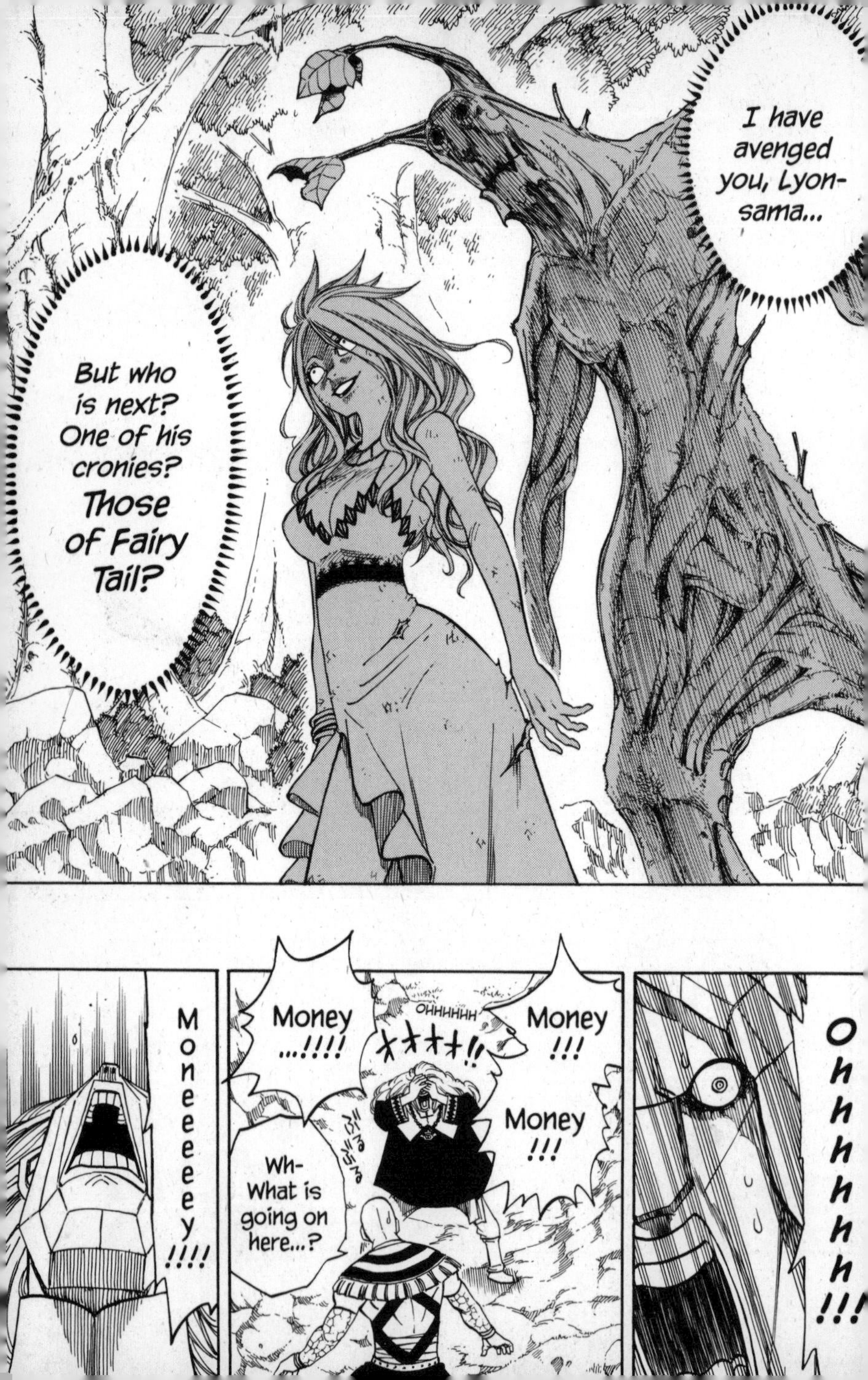
I have avenged you, Lyon-sama...
But who is next? One of his cronies? Those of Fairy Tail?
Ohhhhhhh!!!
Money !!!
Money !!!
OHHHHHH
Money ...!!!!
Wh- What is going on here...?
Moneeeeeey!!!!

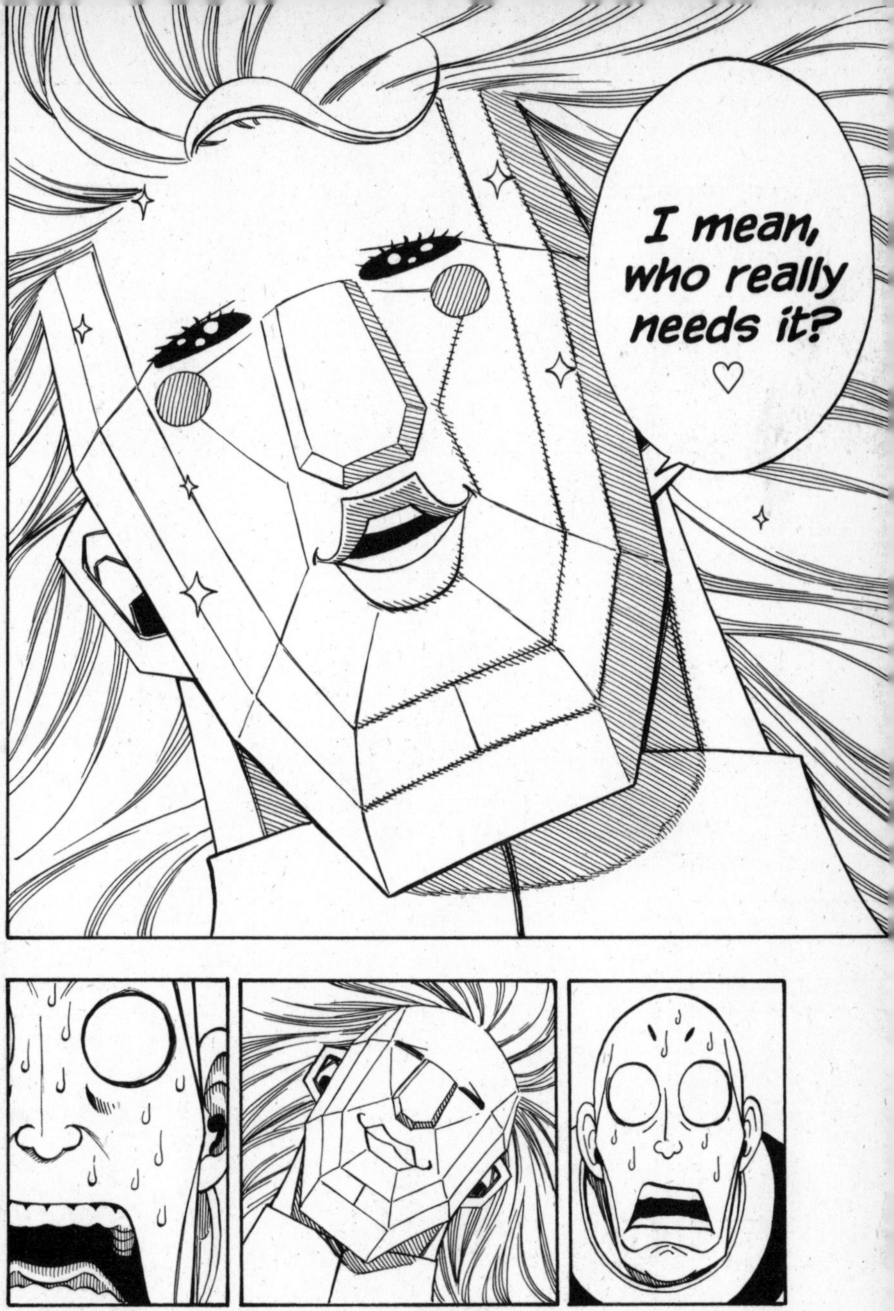
I mean, who really needs it? ♡

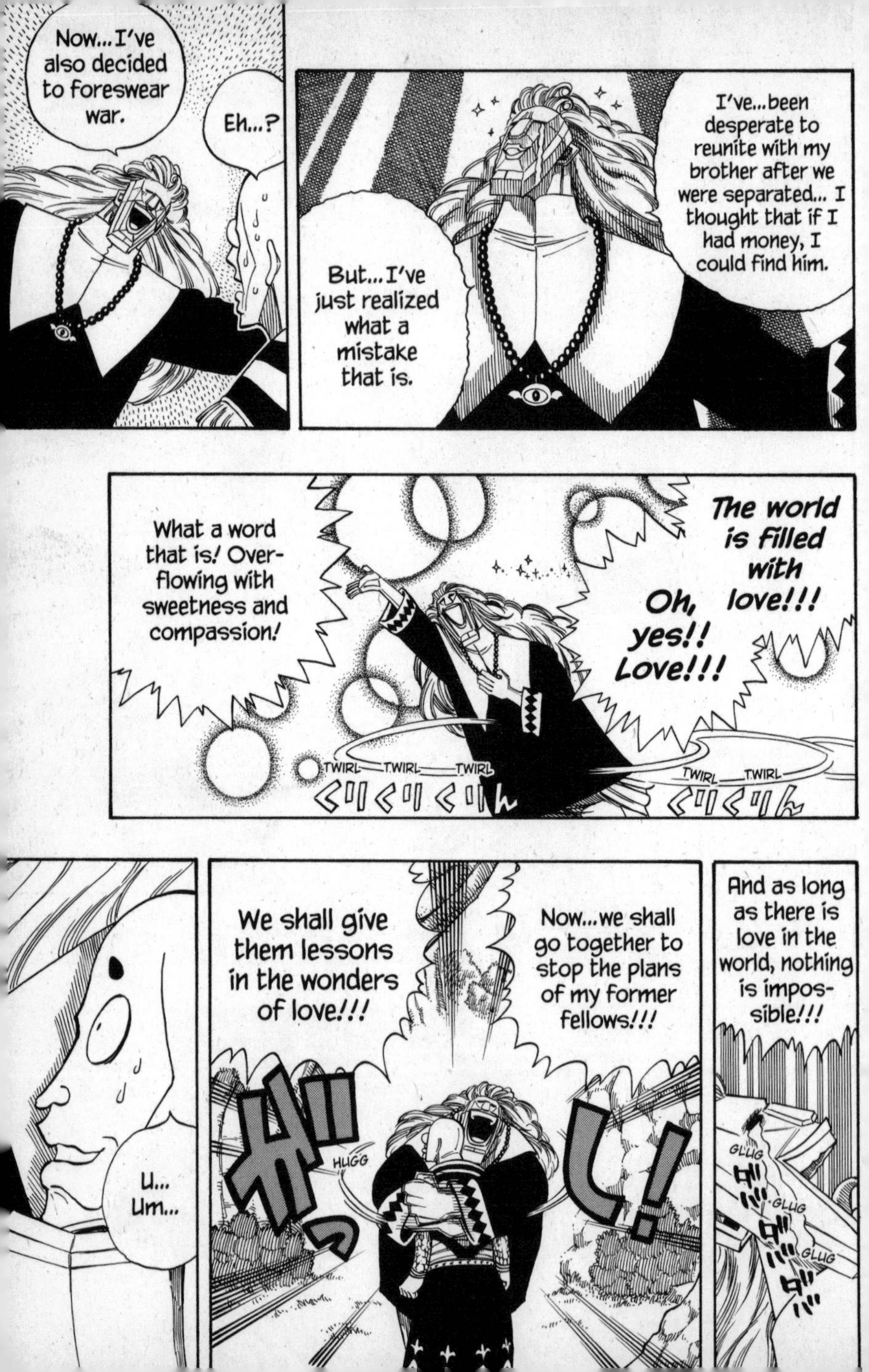
I've...been desperate to reunite with my brother after we were separated... I thought that if I had money, I could find him.
But...I've just realized what a mistake that is.
Now...I've also decided to foreswear war.
Eh...?
The world is filled with love!!!
Oh, yes!! Love!!!
What a word that is! Over-flowing with sweetness and compassion!
TWIRL TWIRL TWIRL
TWIRL TWIRL
And as long as there is love in the world, nothing is impos-sible!!!
GLUG
GLUG
GLUG
Now...we shall go together to stop the plans of my former fellows!!!
We shall give them lessons in the wonders of love!!!
HUGG
U... Um...

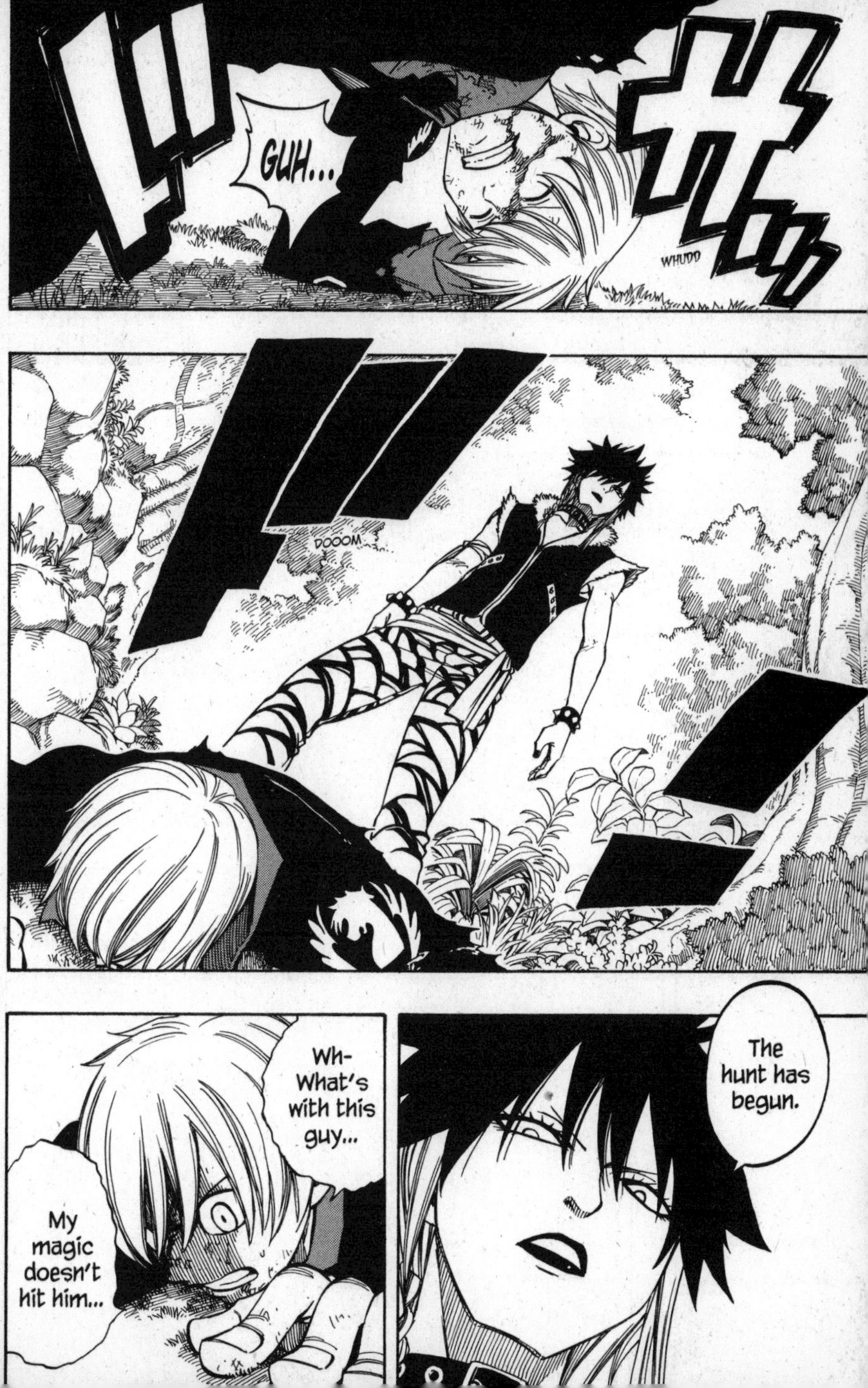
GUH...
WHUDD
DOOOM
The hunt has begun.
Wh- What's with this guy...
My magic doesn't hit him...

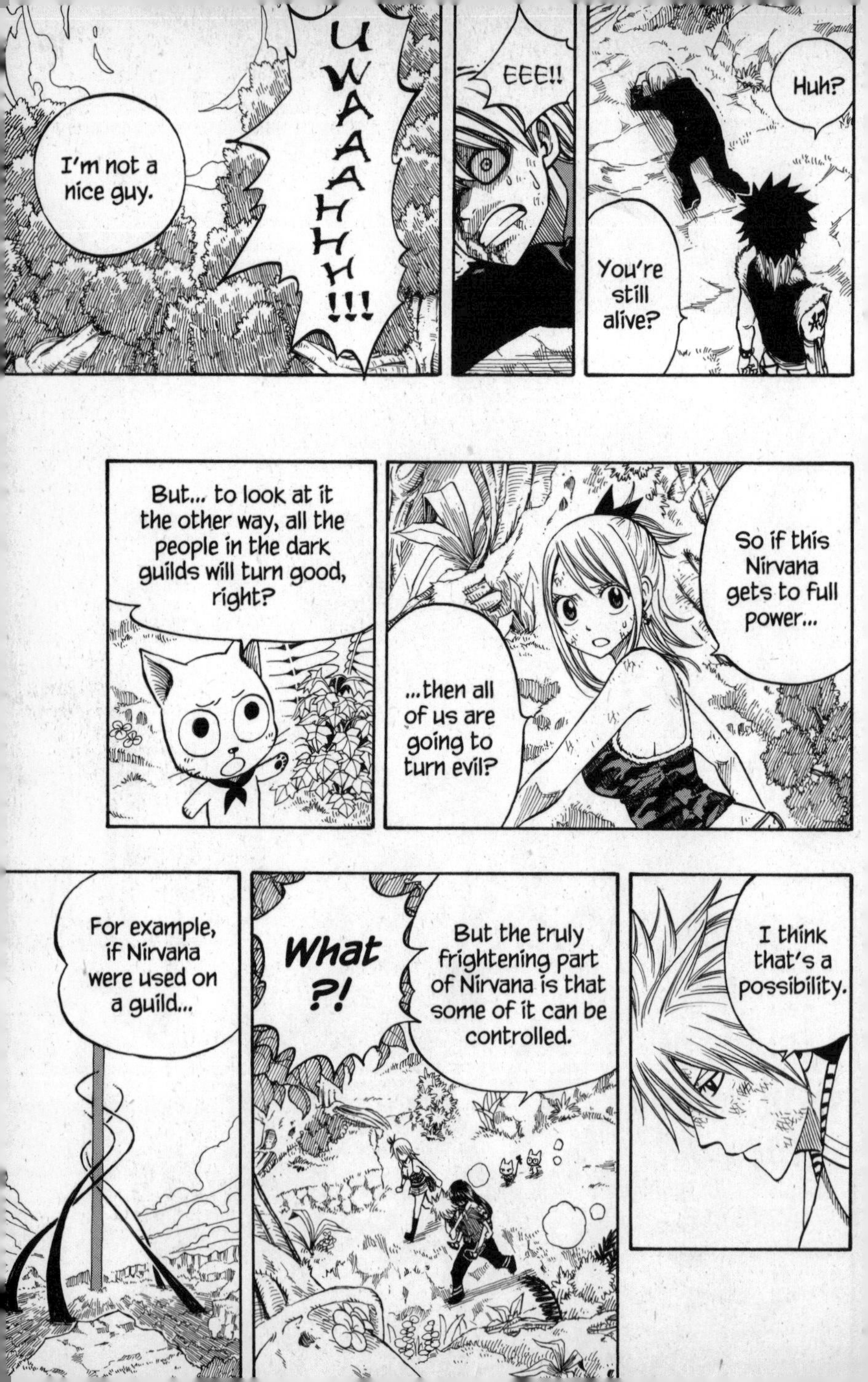
Huh?
You're still alive?
EEE!!
UWAAAHHH!!!
I'm not a nice guy.
So if this Nirvana gets to full power...
...then all of us are going to turn evil?
But... to look at it the other way, all the people in the dark guilds will turn good, right?
I think that's a possibility.
But the truly frightening part of Nirvana is that some of it can be controlled.
What ?!
For example, if Nirvana were used on a guild...

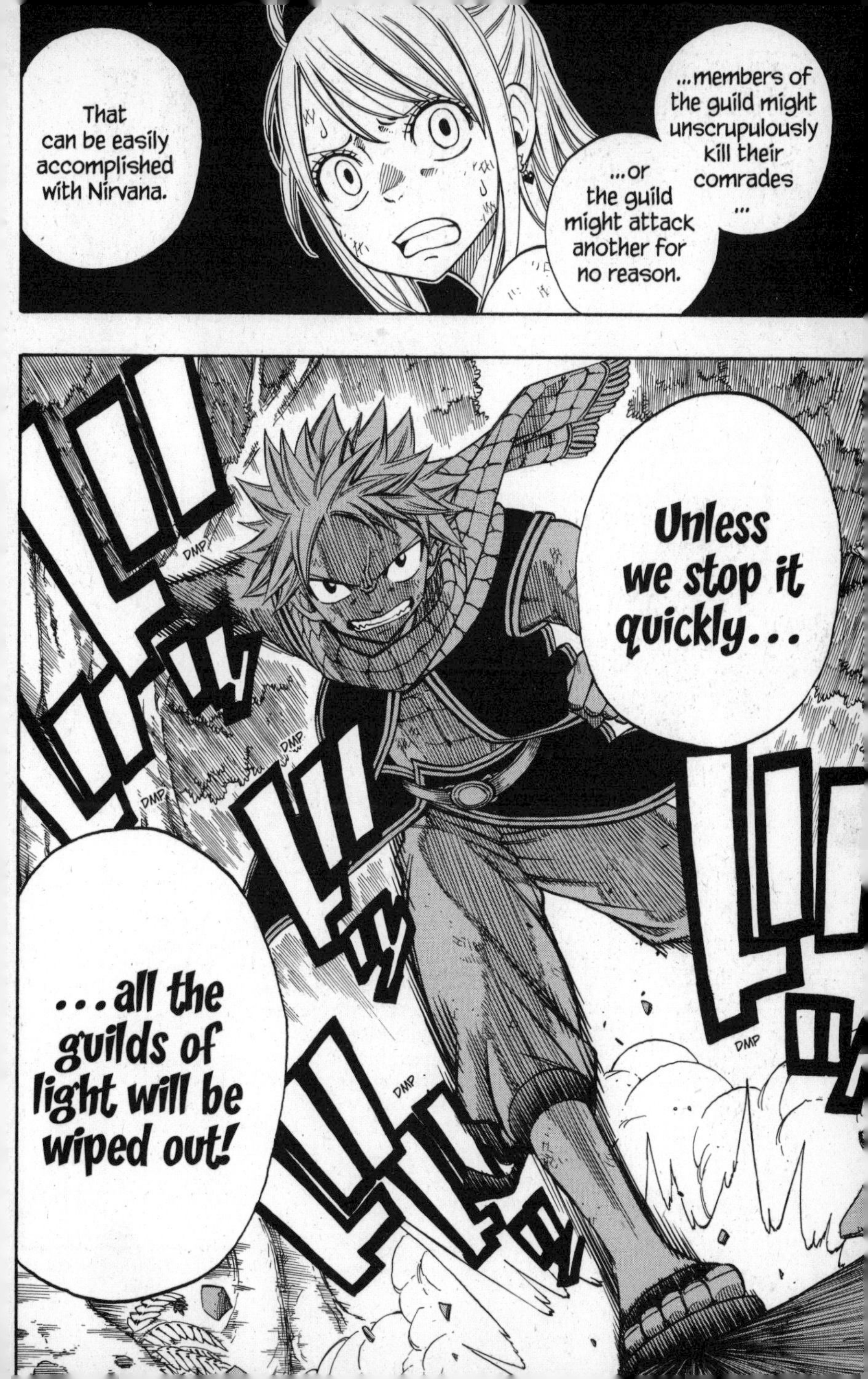
...members of the guild might unscrupulously kill their comrades ...
...or the guild might attack another for no reason.
That can be easily accomplished with Nirvana.
Unless we stop it quickly...
...all the guilds of light will be wiped out!
DMP
DMP
DMP
DMP
DMP

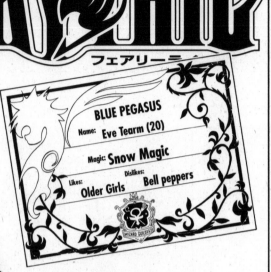

FAIRY TAIL

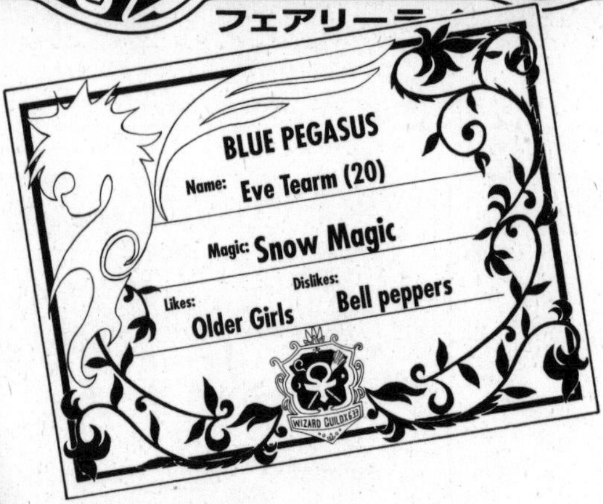
BLUE PEGASUS
Name: Eve Tearm (20)
Magic: Snow Magic
Likes: Older Girls
Dislikes: Bell peppers
WIZARD GUILD

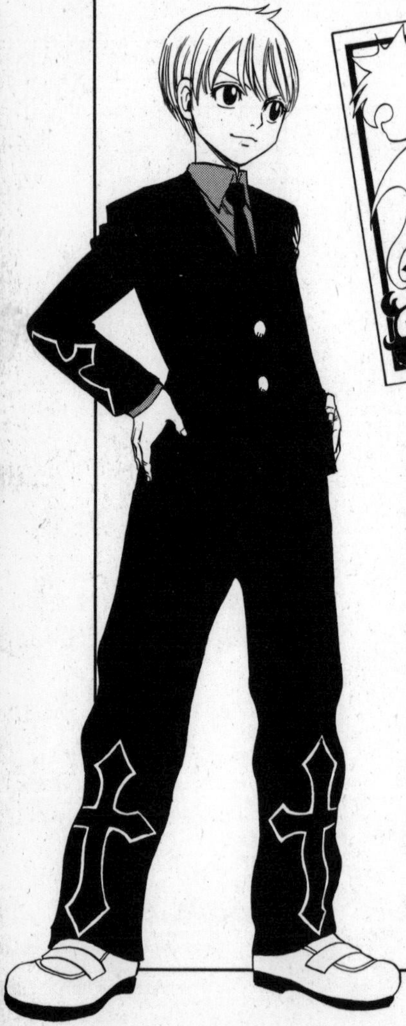

Chapter 143, Celestial Spirit Brawl

Remarks

The magic of this recent arrival to the Blue Pegasus guild is powerful enough to turn everything visible into a winter wonderland in an instant. His attacks use "snow rocks" and cause avalanches. Before joining the guild, he interned with the Magic Council's enforcement and investigation squad, the Rune Knights. But when the council was disbanded in disgrace, Eve realized that he needed a new future and decided to enter a guild.

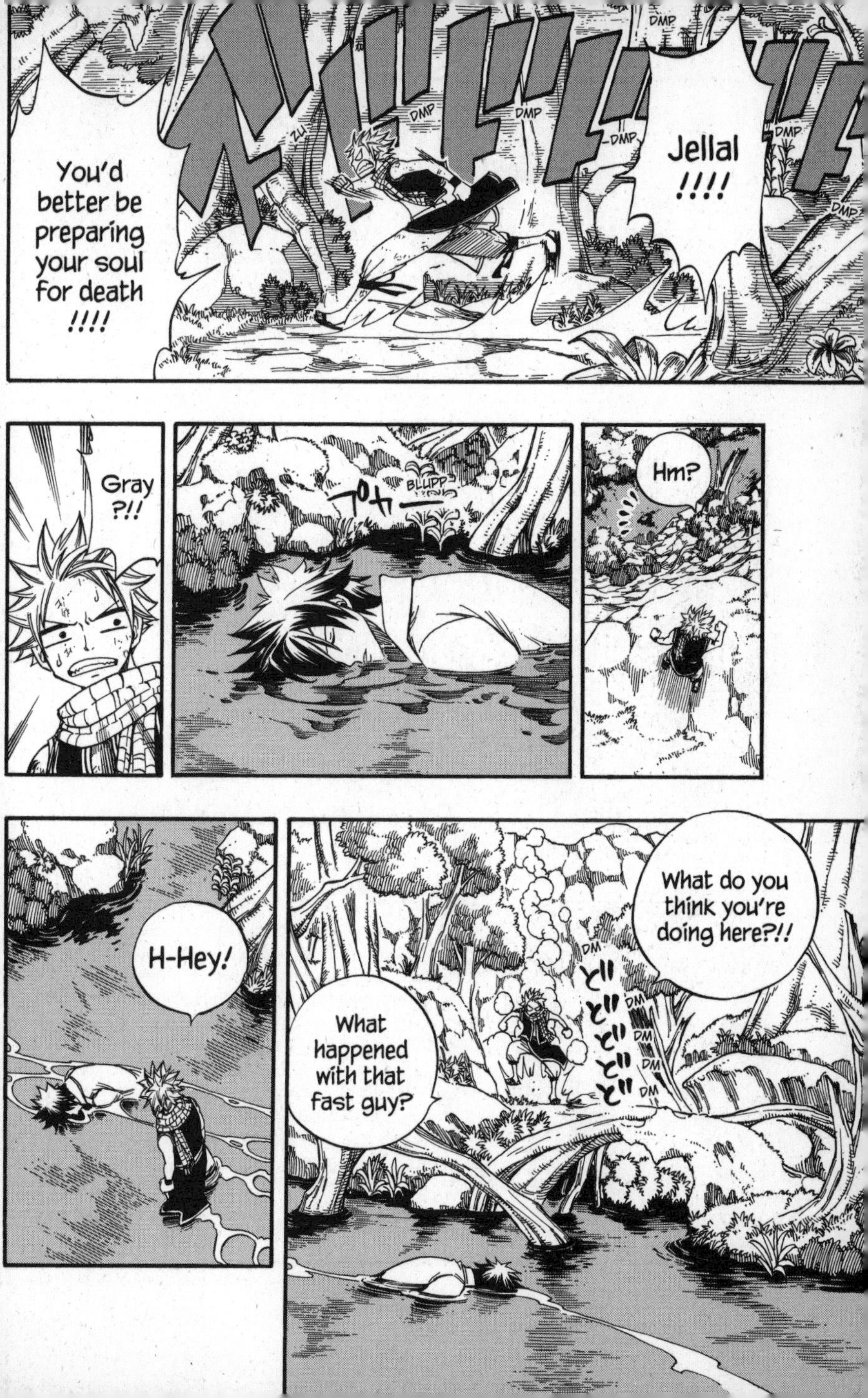
DMP
Jellal !!!!
DMP
DMP
DMP
DMP
ZU
You'd better be preparing your soul for death !!!!
Hm?
BLUPP
Gray ?!!
What do you think you're doing here?!!
DM
DM
DM
DM
What happened with that fast guy?
H-Hey!

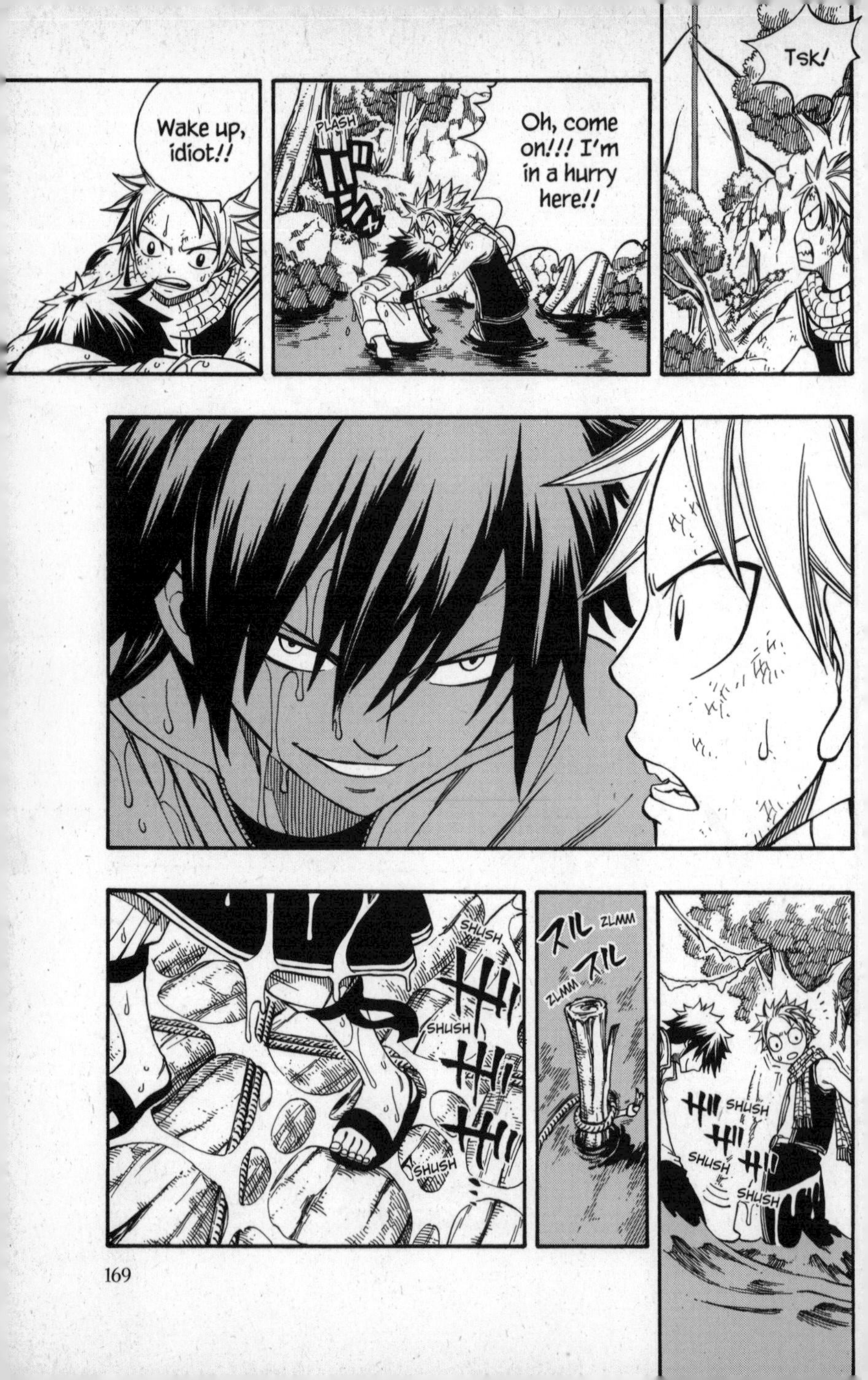
Tsk!
PLASH
Oh, come on!!! I'm in a hurry here!!
Wake up, idiot!!
SHUSH
SHUSH
SHUSH
スル
ZLMM
スル
ZLMM
SHUSH
SHUSH
SHUSH

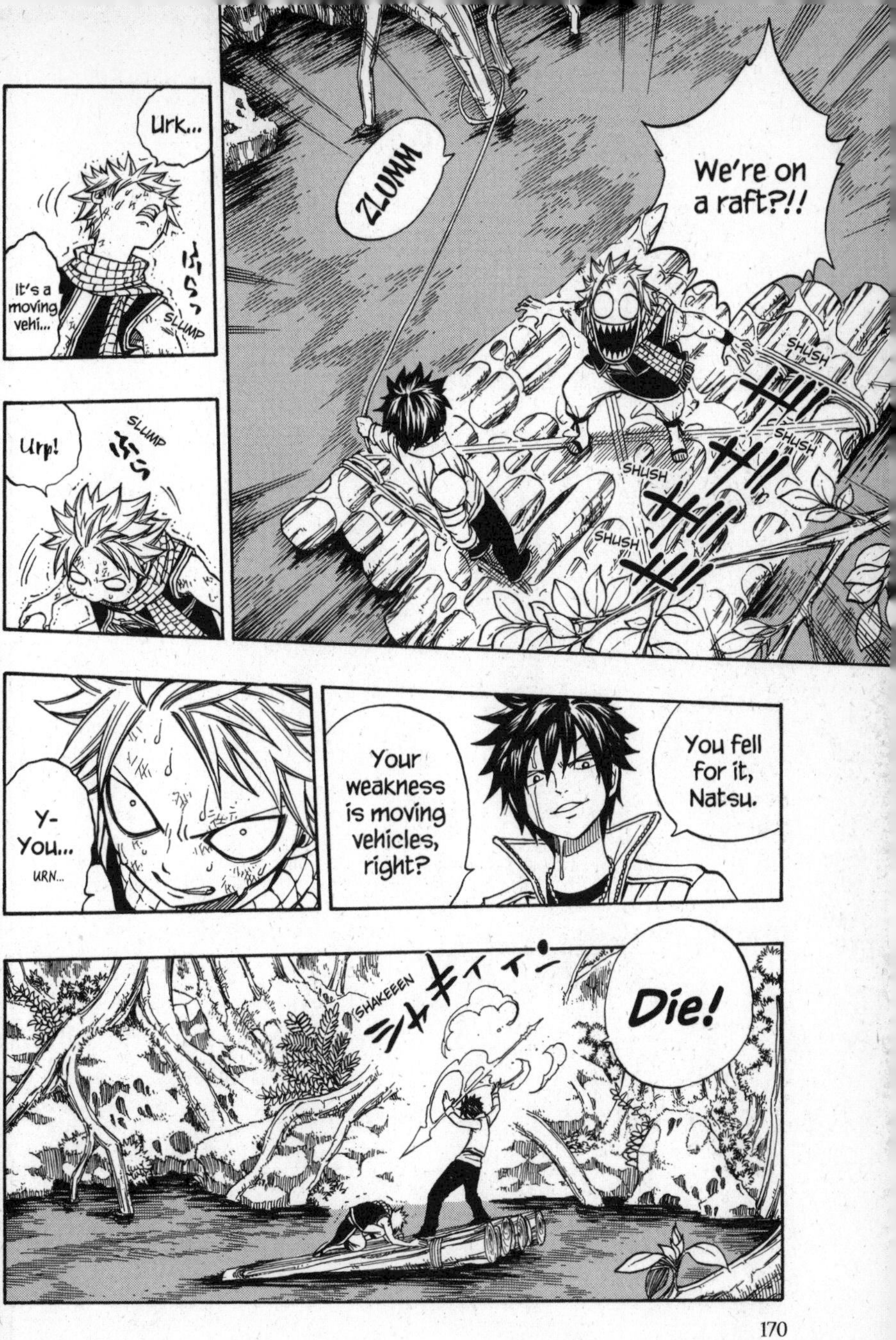
We're on a raft?!!
ZLUMM
SHUSH
SHUSH
SHUSH
SHUSH
Urk...
It's a moving vehi...
SLUMP
Urp!
SLUMP
You fell for it, Natsu.
Your weakness is moving vehicles, right?
Y- You...
URN...
Die!
SHAKEEEN

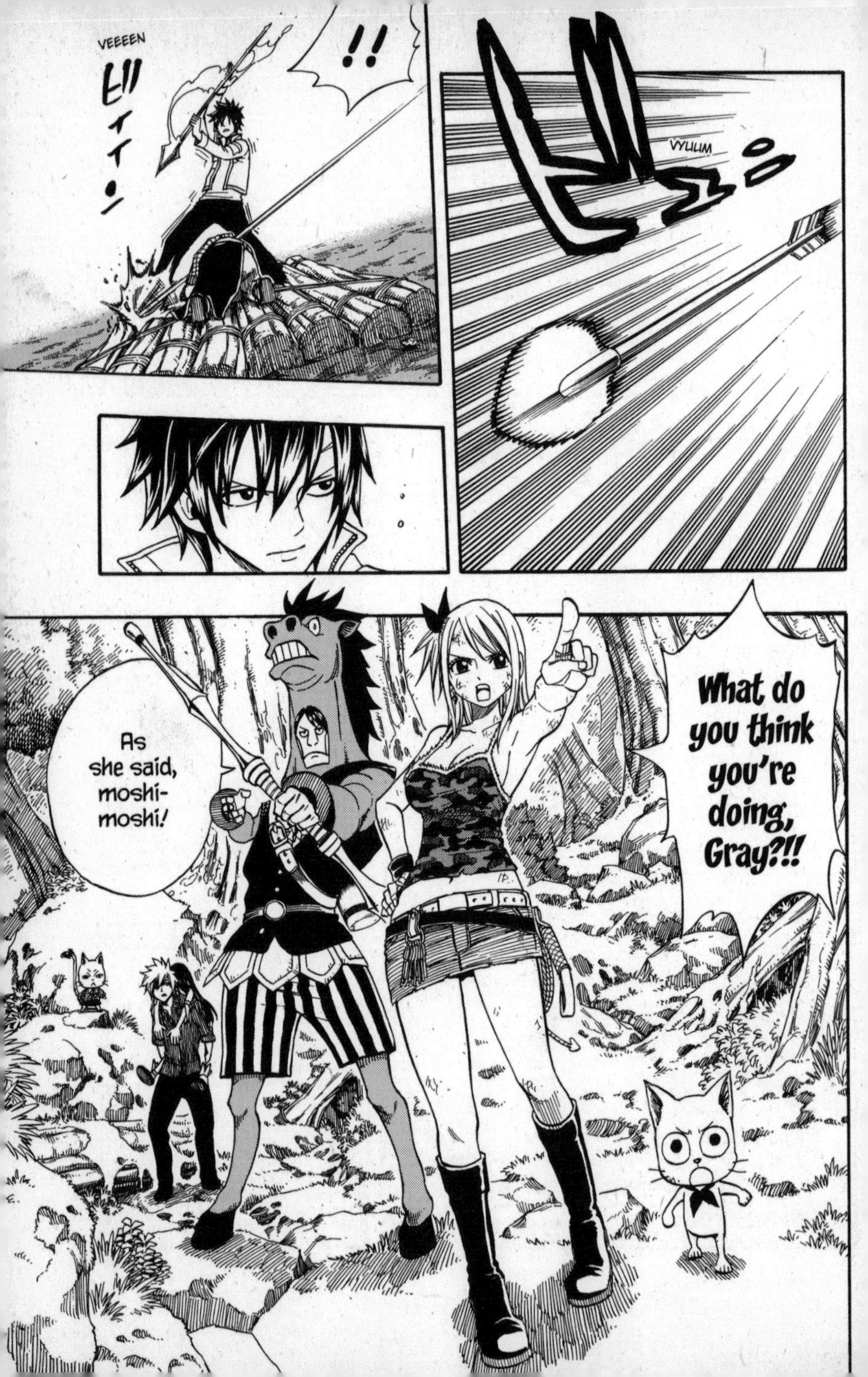
VYUUM
!!
VEEEEN
ビィイイ～ン
What do you think you're doing, Gray?!!
As she said, moshi-moshi!

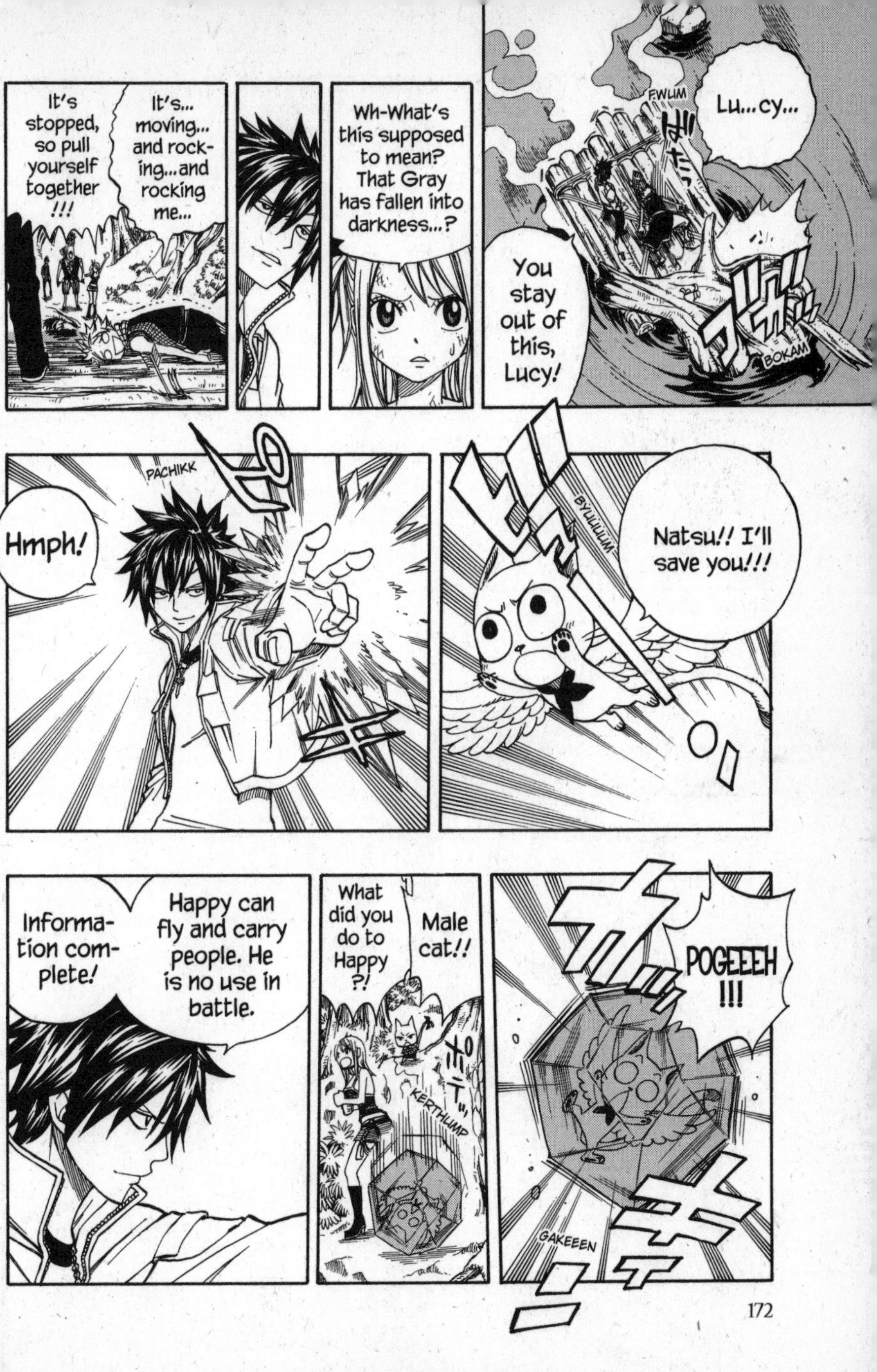
Lu...cy...
FWUM
You stay out of this, Lucy!
BOKAM
Wh-What's this supposed to mean? That Gray has fallen into darkness...?
It's... moving... and rocking...and rocking me...
It's stopped, so pull yourself together!!!
BYUUUUN
Natsu!! I'll save you!!!
PACHIKK
Hmph!
POGEEEH!!!
GAKEEEN
Male cat!!
What did you do to Happy?!
KERTHUMP
Happy can fly and carry people. He is no use in battle.
Information complete!

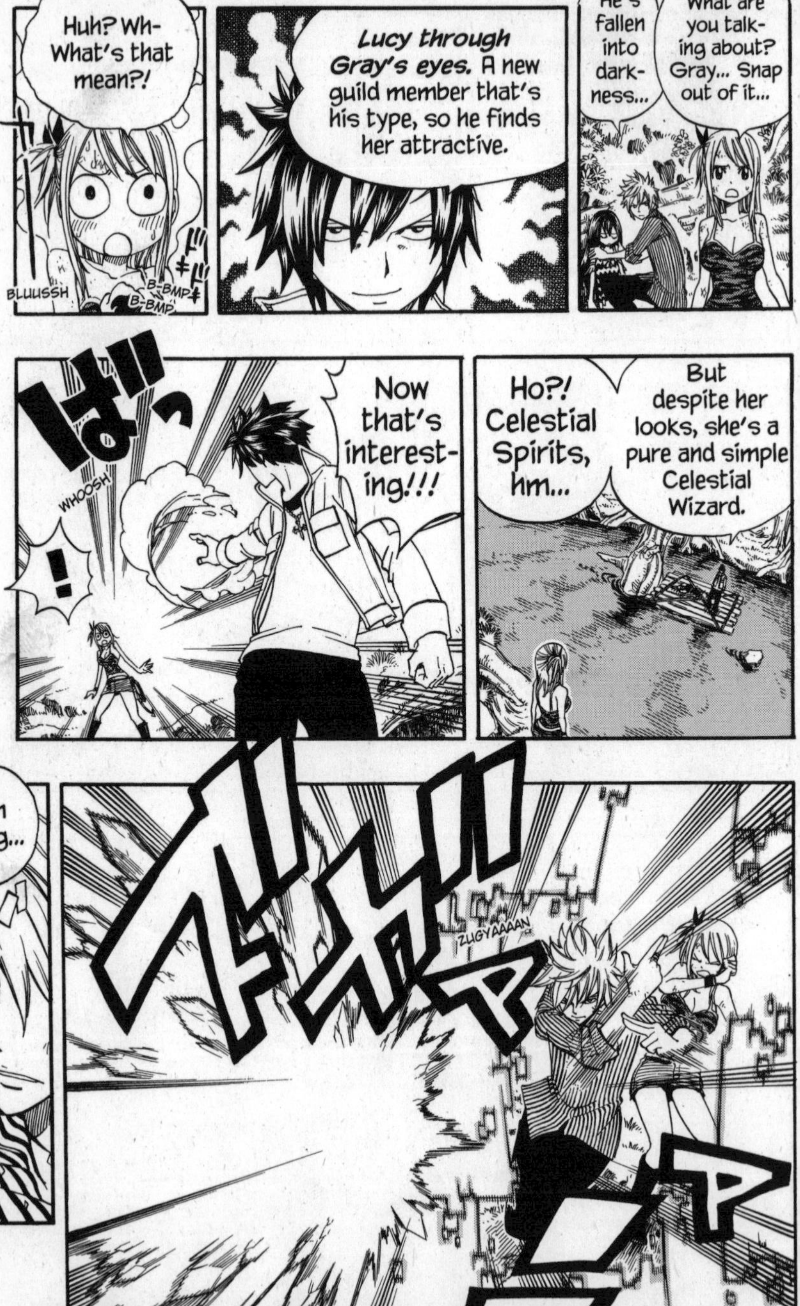
What are you talk-ing about? Gray... Snap out of it...
He's fallen into dark-ness...
Lucy through Gray's eyes. A new guild member that's his type, so he finds her attractive.
Huh? Wh- What's that mean?!
BLUUSSH
B-BMP
B-BMP
But despite her looks, she's a pure and simple Celestial Wizard.
Ho?! Celestial Spirits, hm...
Now that's interest-ing!!!
WHOOSH
!
ZUGYAAAAN
I'm wrong...
TCH!

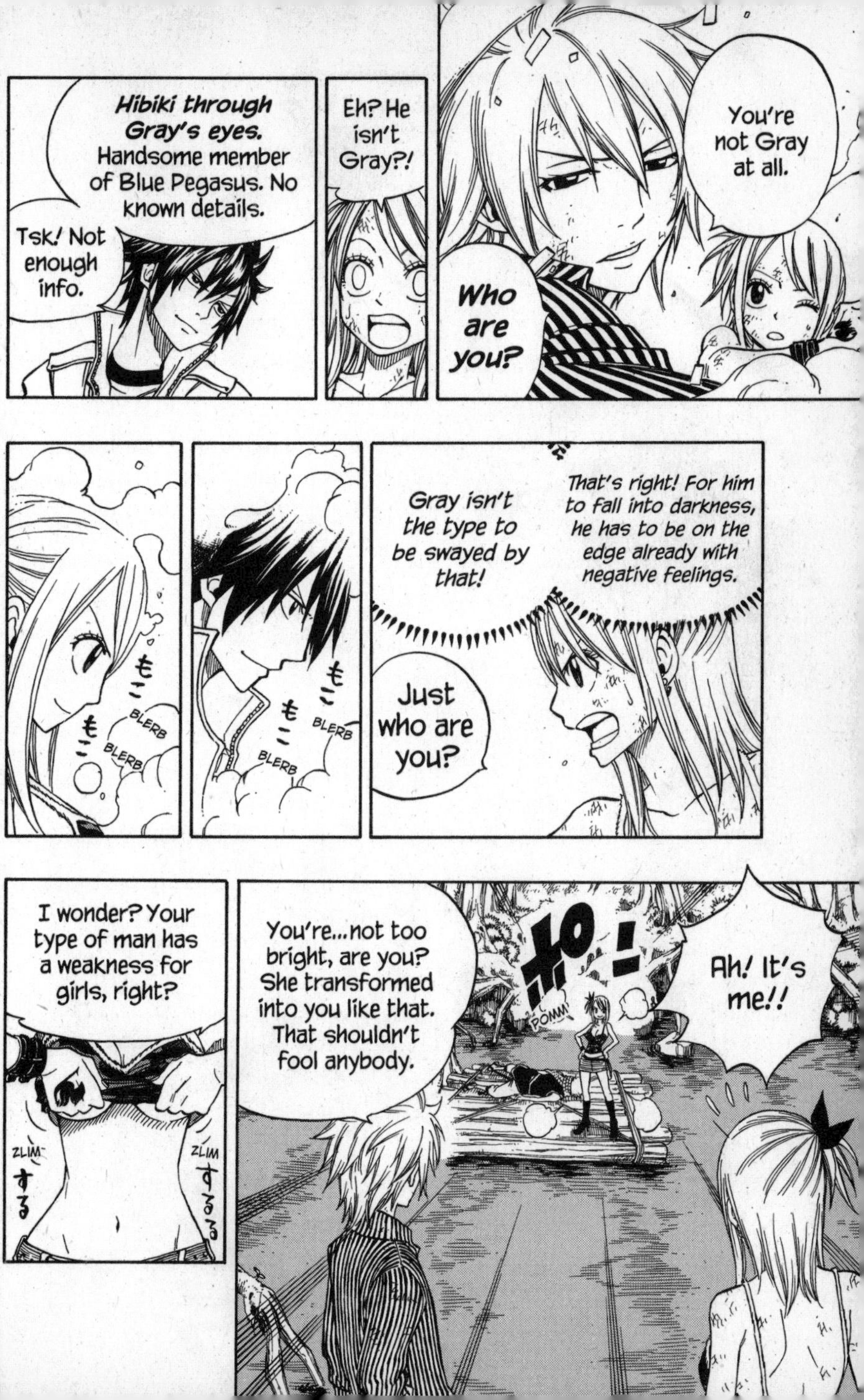
You're not Gray at all.
Who are you?
Eh? He isn't Gray?!
Hibiki through Gray's eyes. Handsome member of Blue Pegasus. No known details.
Tsk! Not enough info.
That's right! For him to fall into darkness, he has to be on the edge already with negative feelings.
Gray isn't the type to be swayed by that!
Just who are you?
もこ もこ
BLERB BLERB
もこ
BLERB BLERB
Ah! It's me!!
POMM
You're...not too bright, are you? She transformed into you like that. That shouldn't fool anybody.
I wonder? Your type of man has a weakness for girls, right?
ZLIM するる
ZLIM する

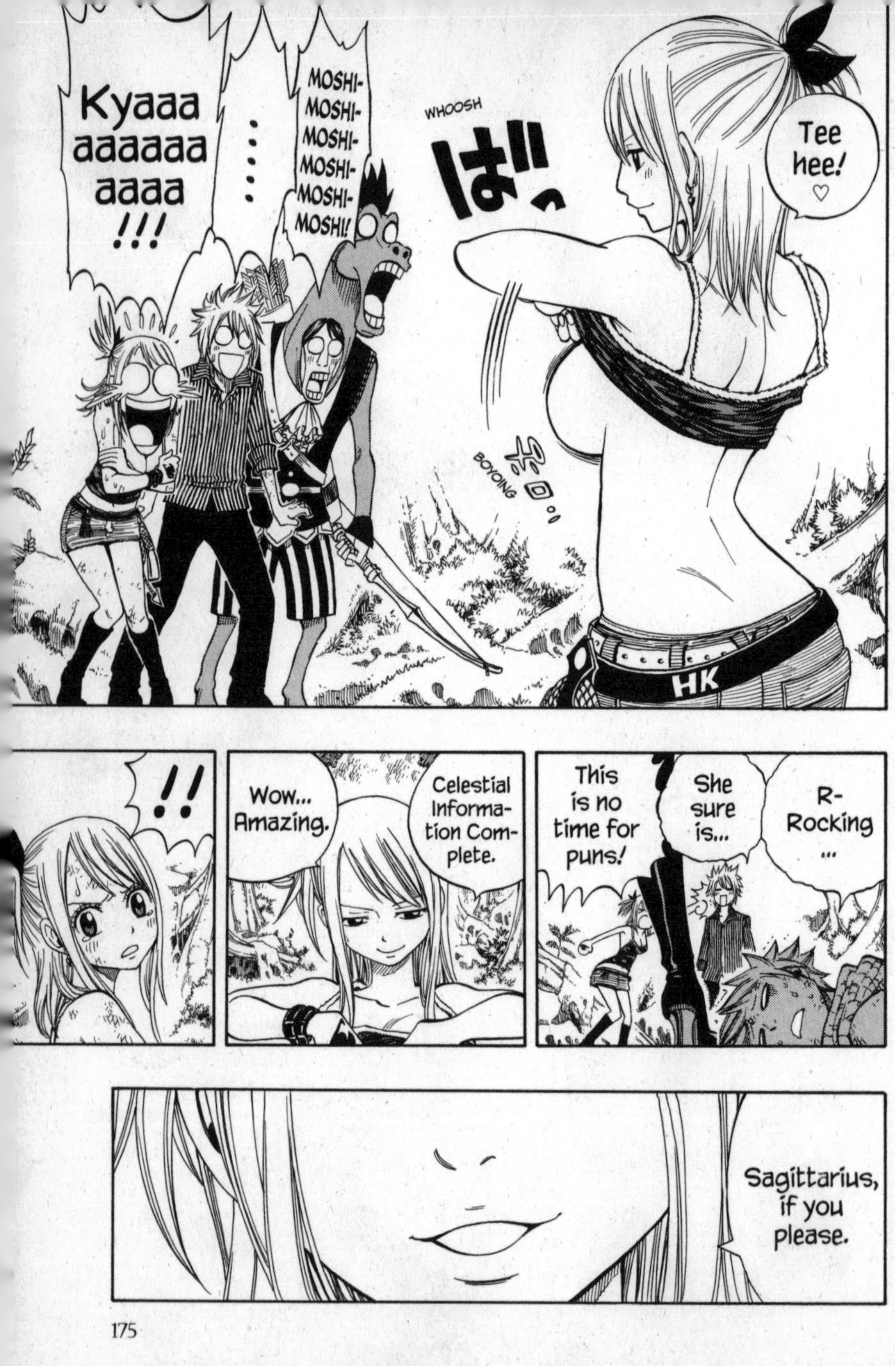
Tee hee! ♡
WHOOSH
ばっ
BOYOING
MOSHI-MOSHI-MOSHI-MOSHI-MOSHI-MOSHI!
...
Kyaaa aaaaaa aaaa !!!
R-Rocking ...
She sure is...
This is no time for puns!
Celestial Information Complete.
Wow... Amazing.
!!
Sagittarius, if you please.

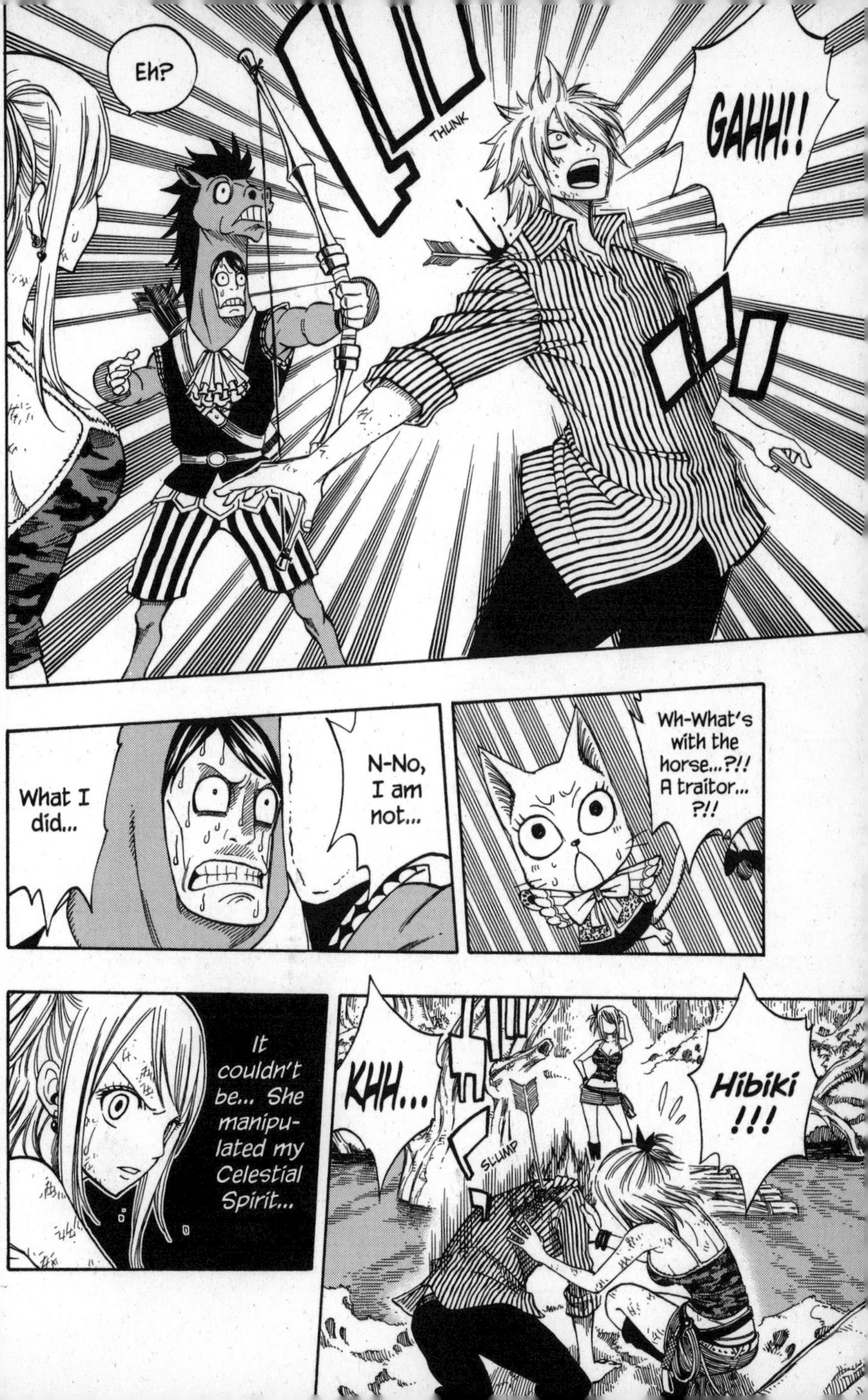
GAHH!!
THUNK
Eh?
Wh-What's with the horse...?!! A traitor...?!!
N-No, I am not...
What I did...
Hibiki!!!
KHH...
SLUMP
It couldn't be... She manipulated my Celestial Spirit...

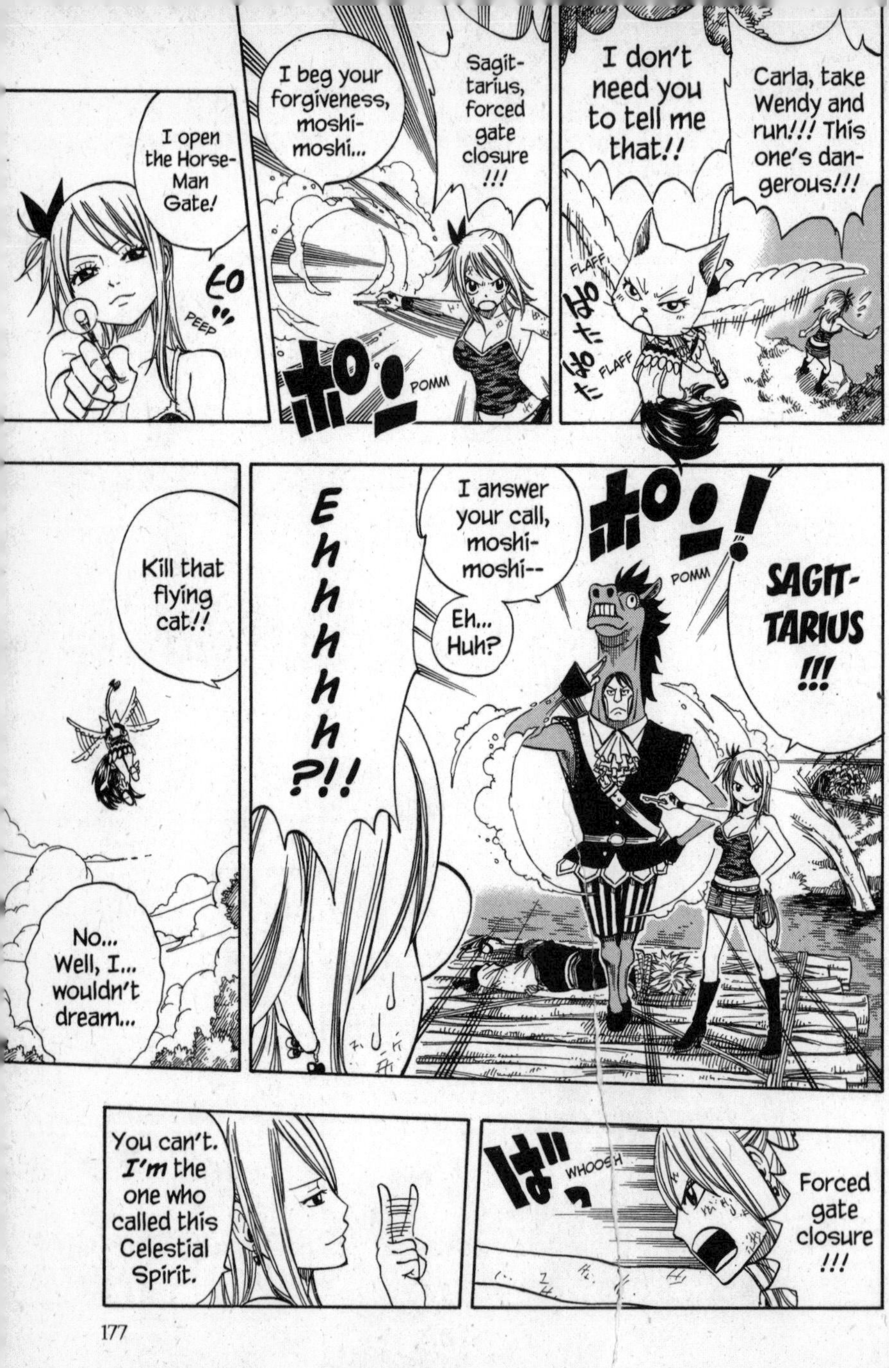
Carla, take Wendy and run!!! This one's dangerous!!!
I don't need you to tell me that!!
FLAFF
FLAFF
Sagittarius, forced gate closure!!!
I beg your forgiveness, moshi-moshi...
POMM
I open the Horse-Man Gate!
PEEP
SAGITTARIUS!!!
POMM
I answer your call, moshi-moshi--
Eh... Huh?
Ehhhhhh?!!
Kill that flying cat!!
No... Well, I... wouldn't dream...
WHOOSH
Forced gate closure!!!
You can't. *I'm* the one who called this Celestial Spirit.

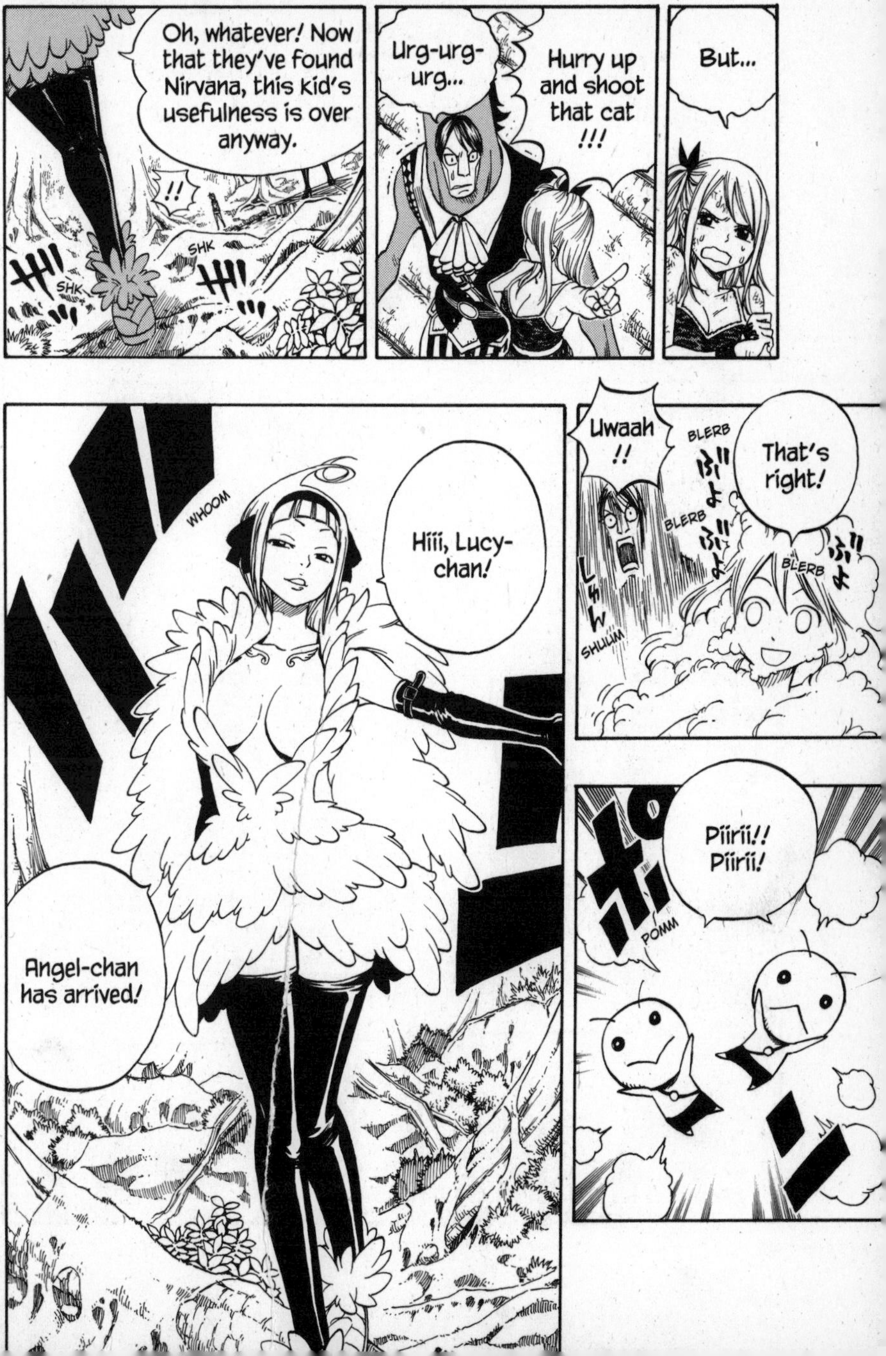
But...
Hurry up and shoot that cat!!!
Urg-urg-urg...
Oh, whatever! Now that they've found Nirvana, this kid's usefulness is over anyway.
!!
SHK
SHK
That's right!
BLERB
BLERB
BLERB
Uwaah!!
SHUUM
Piirii!! Piirii!
POMM
Hiii, Lucy-chan!
WHOOM
Angel-chan has arrived!

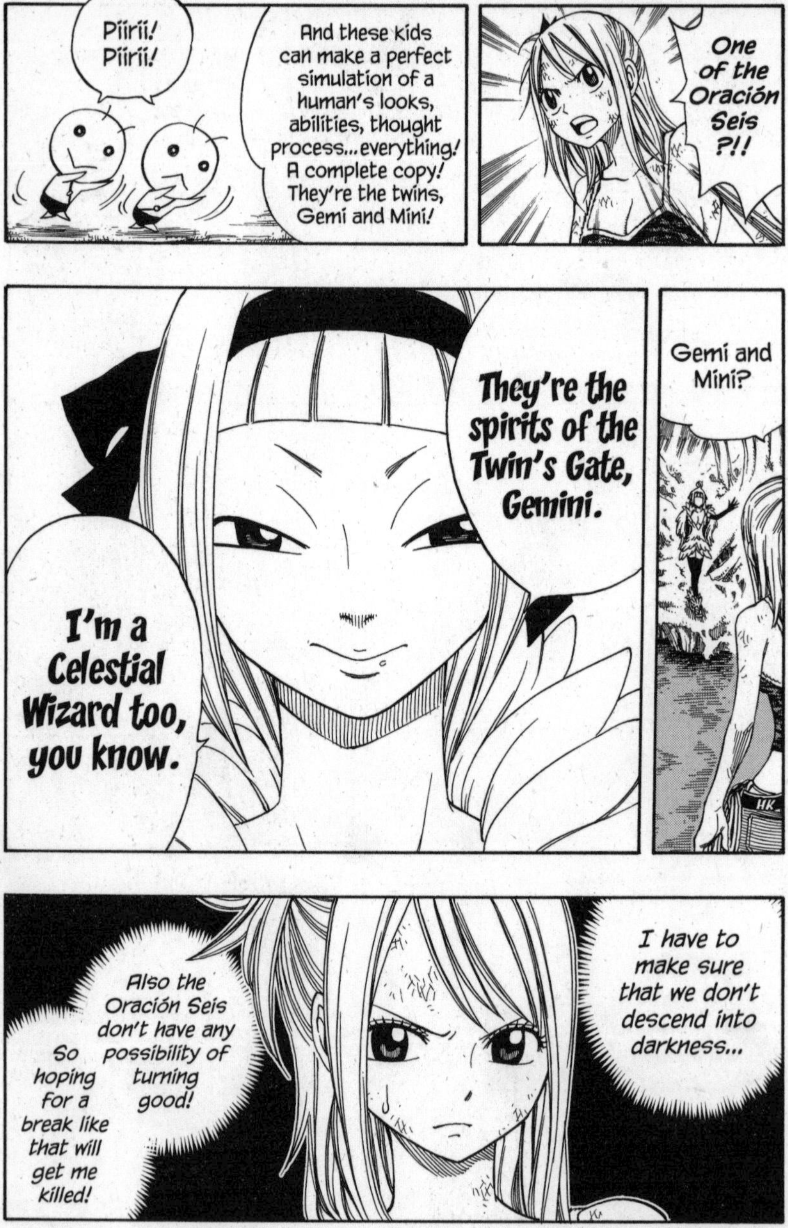
One of the Oración Seis ?!!
And these kids can make a perfect simulation of a human's looks, abilities, thought process...everything! A complete copy! They're the twins, Gemi and Mini!
Piirii! Piirii!
Gemi and Mini?
They're the spirits of the Twin's Gate, Gemini.
I'm a Celestial Wizard too, you know.
I have to make sure that we don't descend into darkness...
Also the Oración Seis don't have any possibility of turning good!
So hoping for a break like that will get me killed!

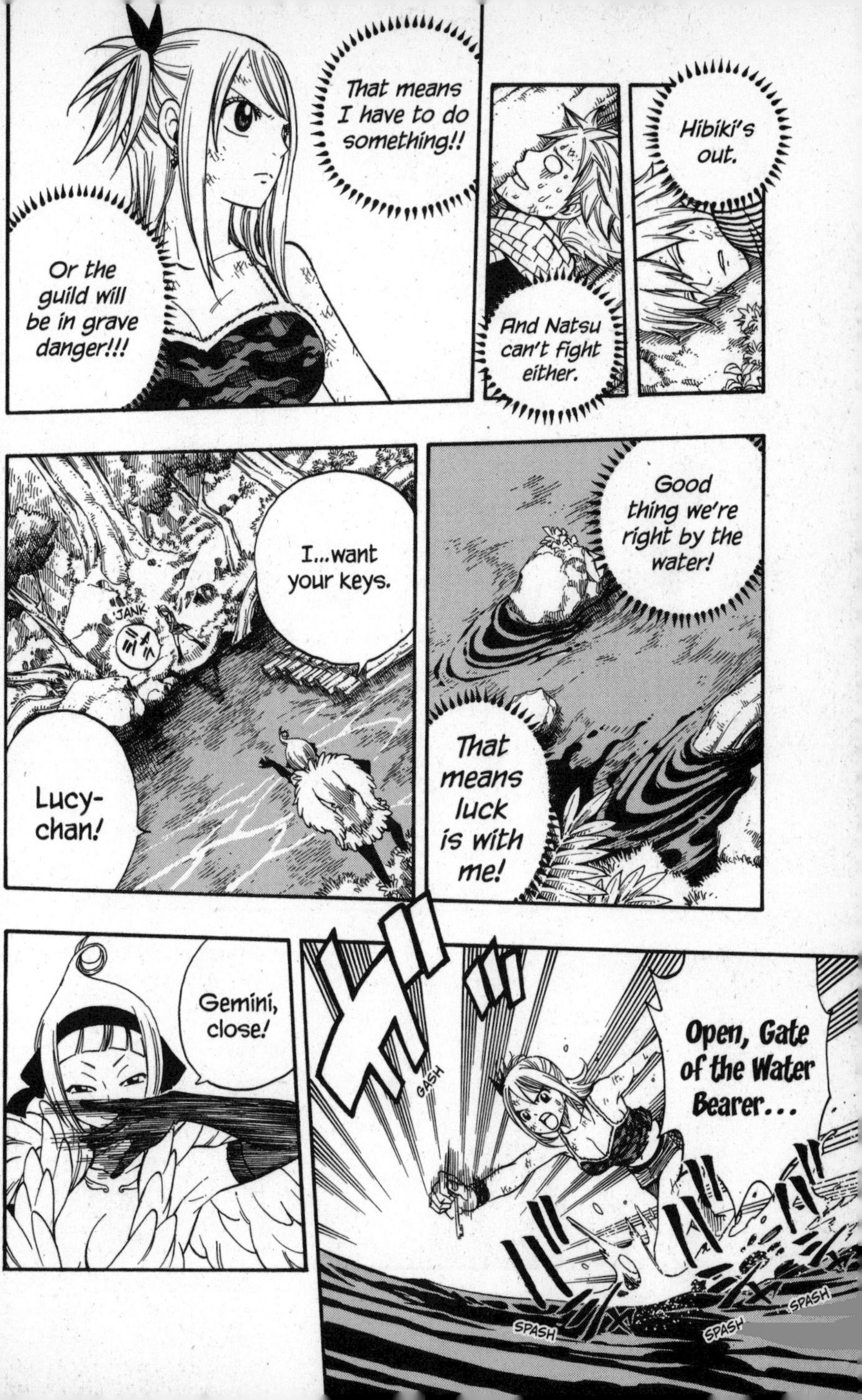
Hibiki's out.
And Natsu can't fight either.
That means I have to do something!!
Or the guild will be in grave danger!!!
Good thing we're right by the water!
That means luck is with me!
I...want your keys.
JANK
Lucy-chan!
GASH
Open, Gate of the Water Bearer...
SPASH
SPASH
SPASH
Gemini, close!

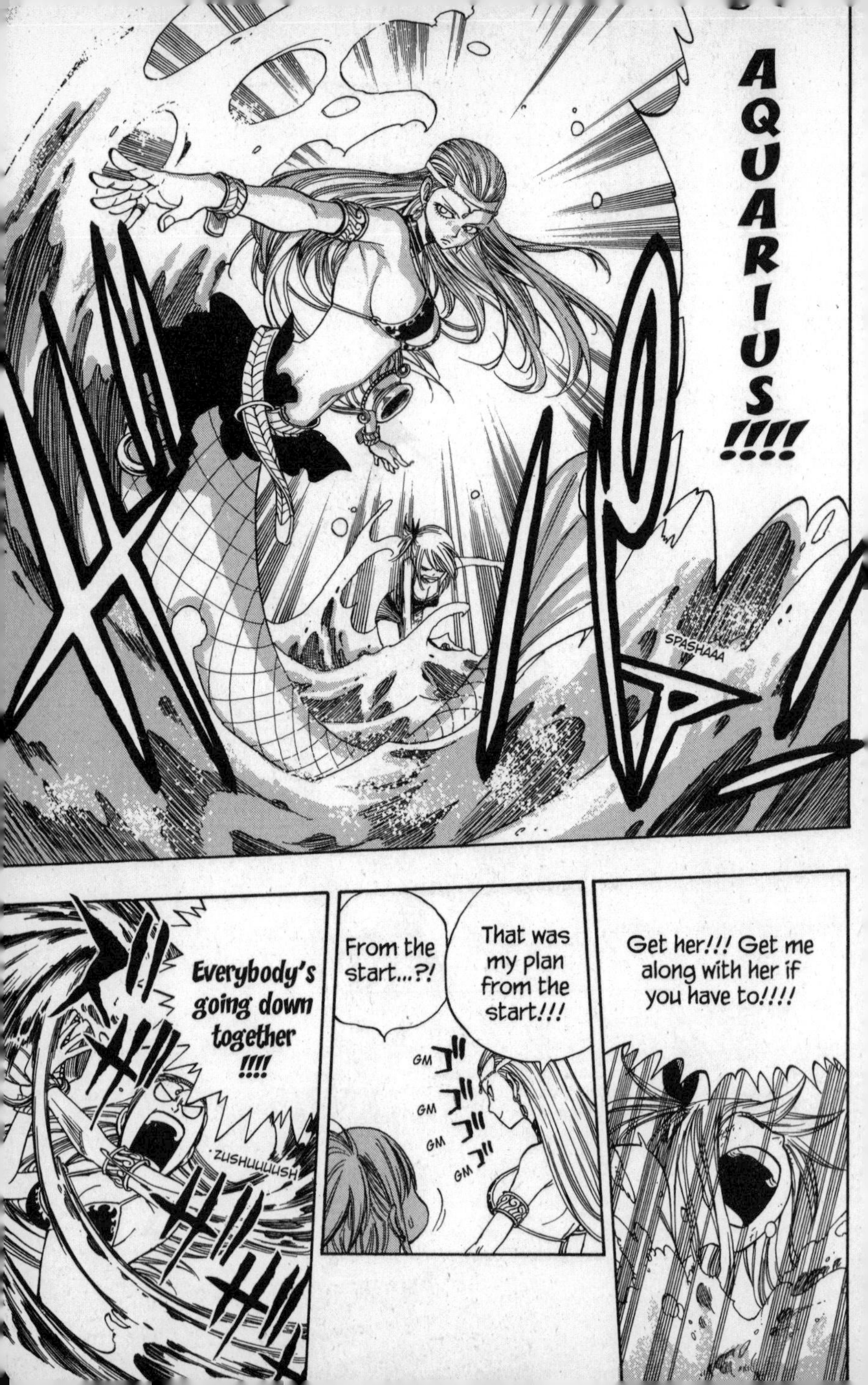
AQUARIUS!!!!
SPASHAA
Get her!!! Get me along with her if you have to!!!!
That was my plan from the start!!!
From the start...?!
GM
GM
GM
GM
Everybody's going down together!!!!
ZUSHUUUUUSH

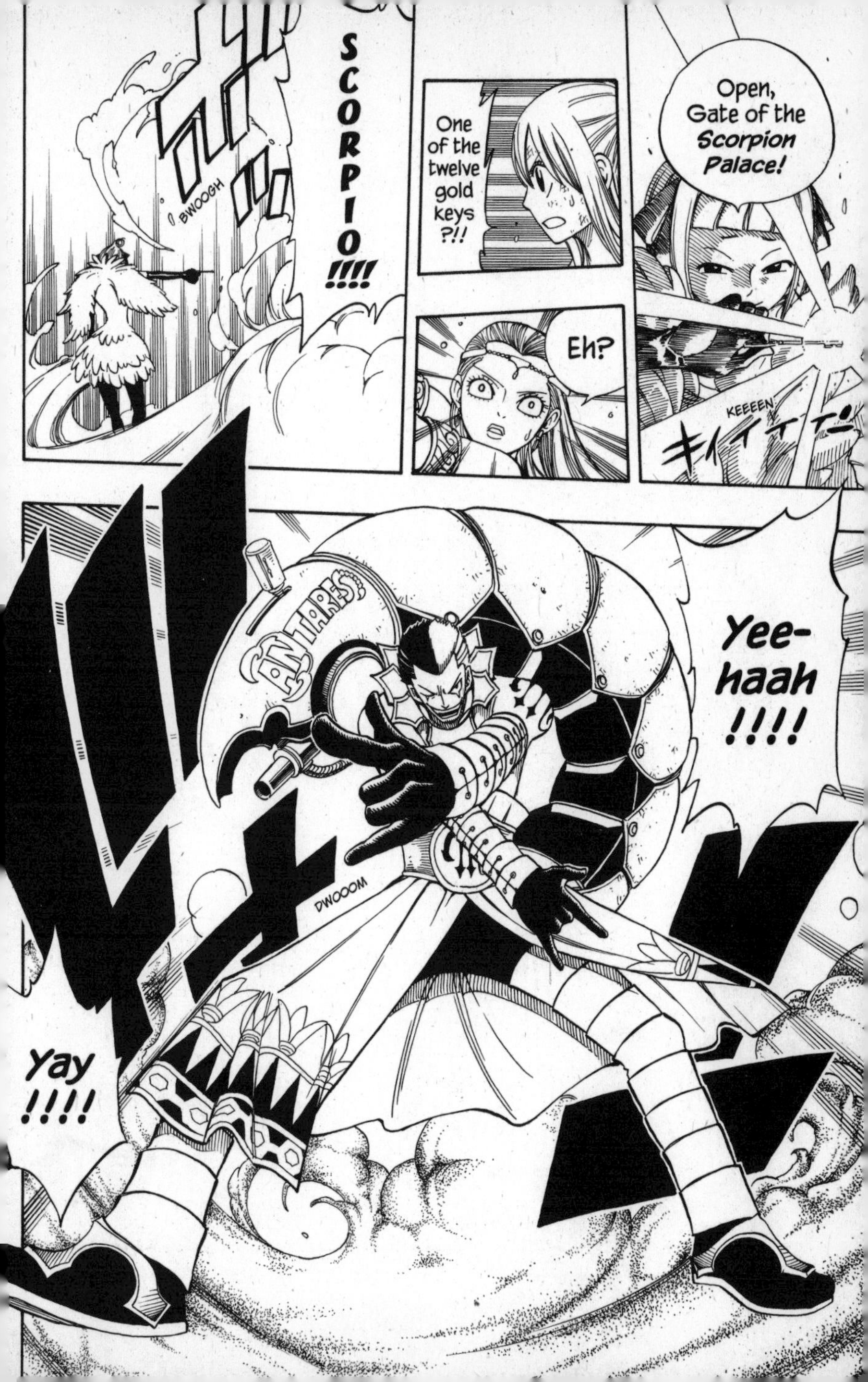
Open, Gate of the Scorpion Palace!
KEEEEN
One of the twelve gold keys ?!!
Eh?
BWOOGH
SCORPIO!!!!
Yee-haah!!!!
DWOOOM
Yay!!!!

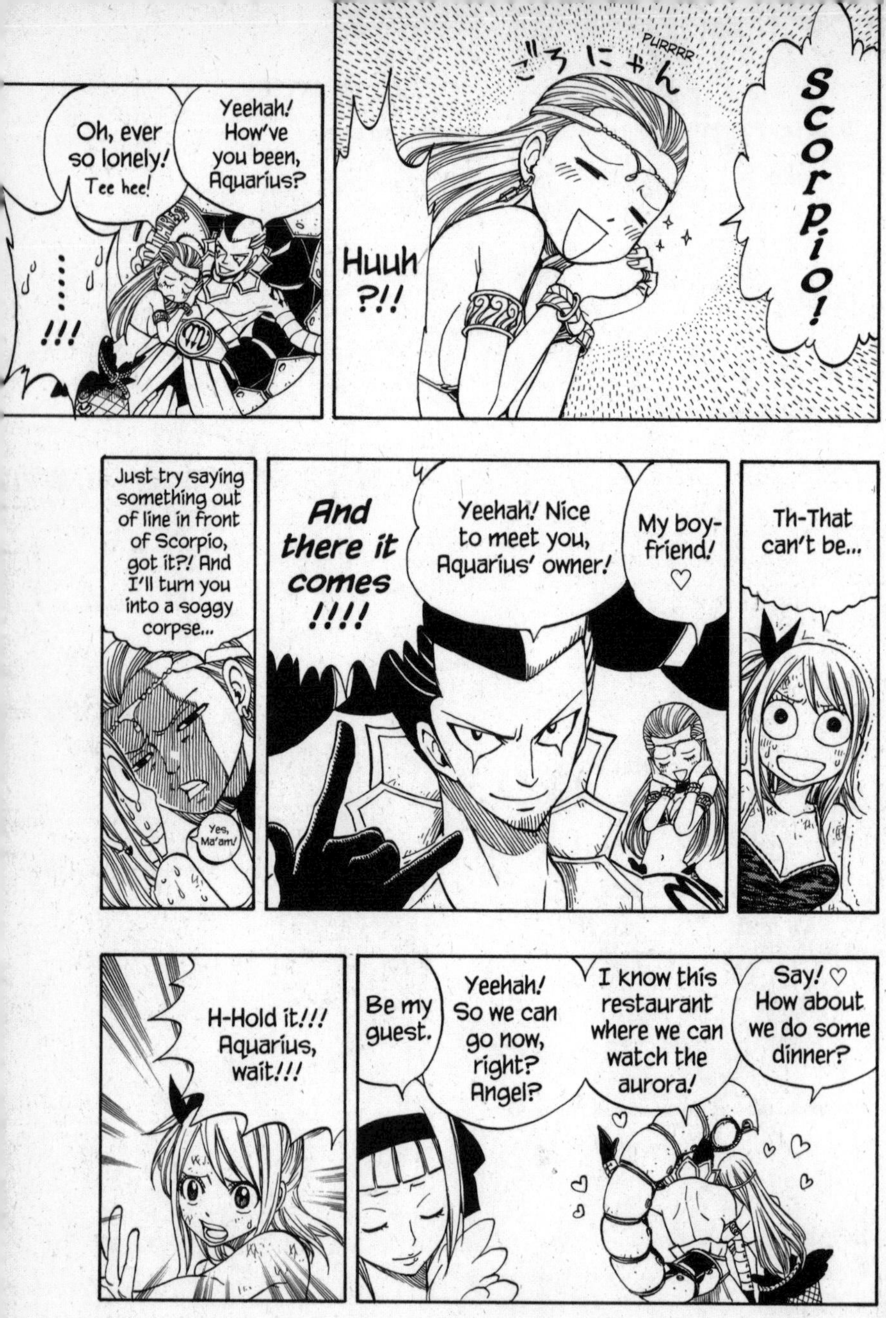
PURRRR
ごろにゃん
Scorpio!
Huuh?!!
Yeehah! How've you been, Aquarius?
Oh, ever so lonely! Tee hee!
......!!!
Th-That can't be...
My boy-friend! ♡
Yeehah! Nice to meet you, Aquarius' owner!
And there it comes!!!!
Just try saying something out of line in front of Scorpio, got it?! And I'll turn you into a soggy corpse...
Yes, Ma'am!
Say! ♡ How about we do some dinner?
I know this restaurant where we can watch the aurora!
Yeehah! So we can go now, right? Angel?
Be my guest.
H-Hold it!!! Aquarius, wait!!!

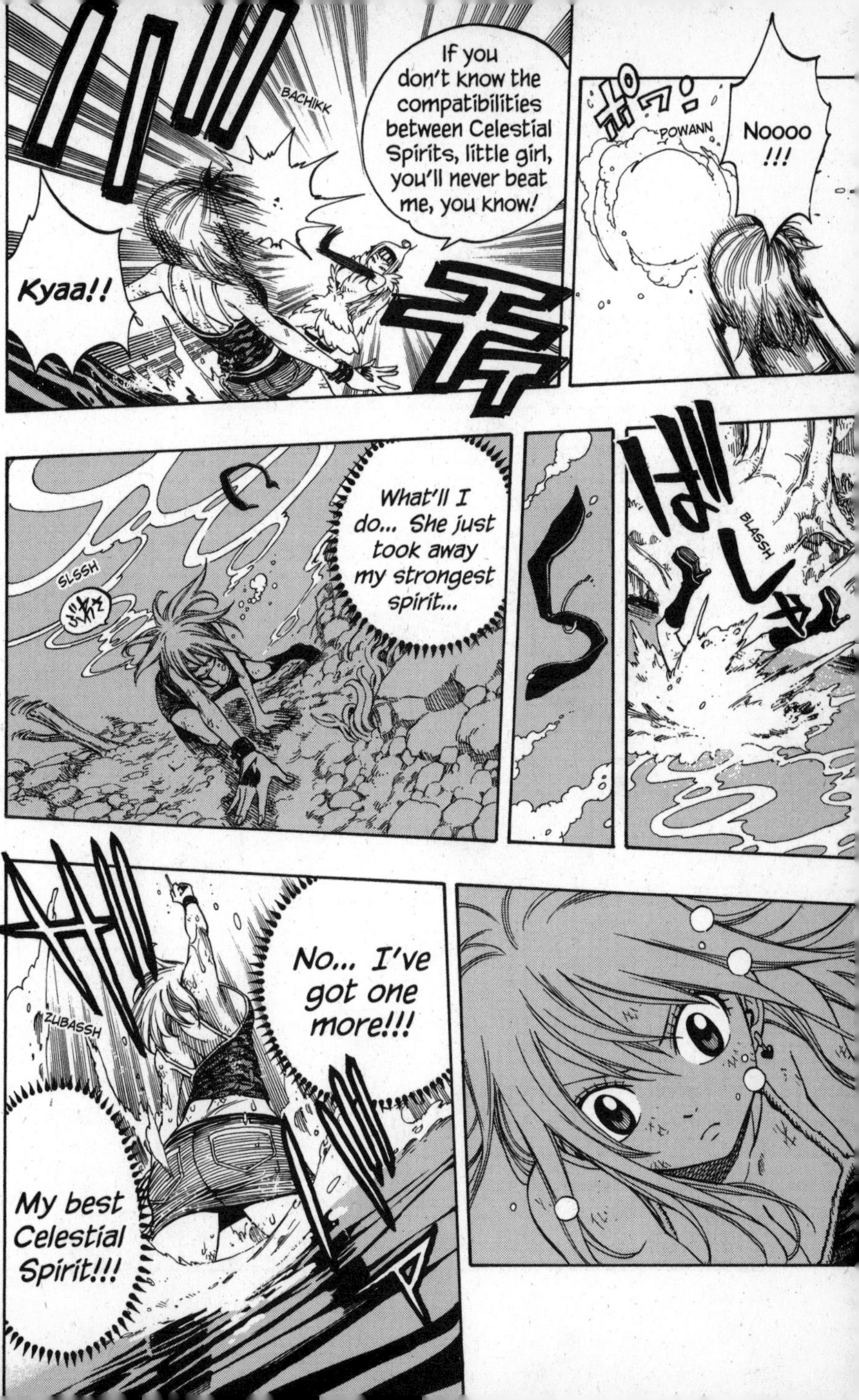
POWANN
Noooo!!!
BACHIKK
If you don't know the compatibilities between Celestial Spirits, little girl, you'll never beat me, you know!
Kyaa!!
BLASSH
SLSSH
What'll I do... She just took away my strongest spirit...
ZUBASSH
No... I've got one more!!!
My best Celestial Spirit!!!

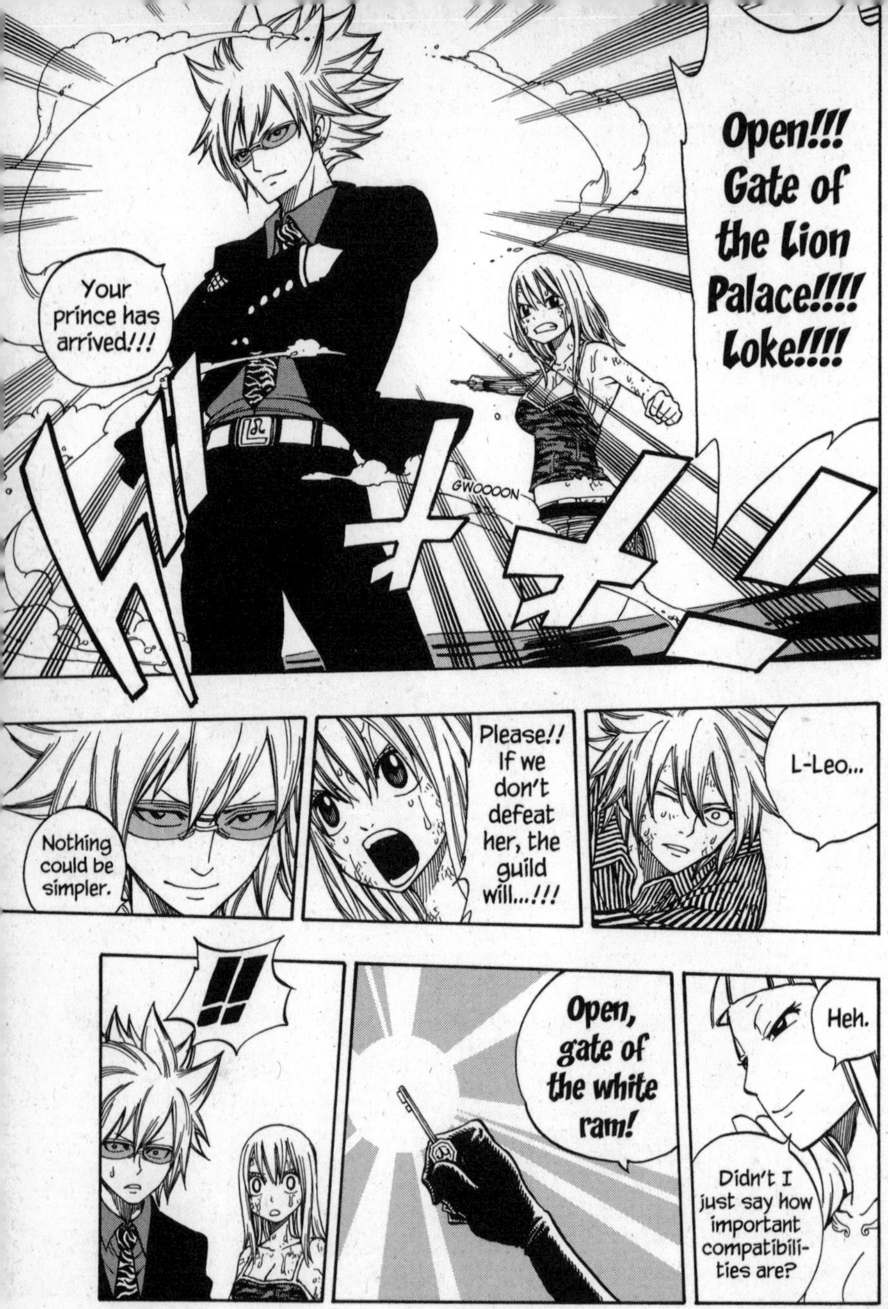
Open!!! Gate of the Lion Palace!!!! Loke!!!!
Your prince has arrived!!!
GWOOOON
L-Leo...
Please!! If we don't defeat her, the guild will...!!!
Nothing could be simpler.
Heh.
Didn't I just say how important compatibilities are?
Open, gate of the white ram!
!!

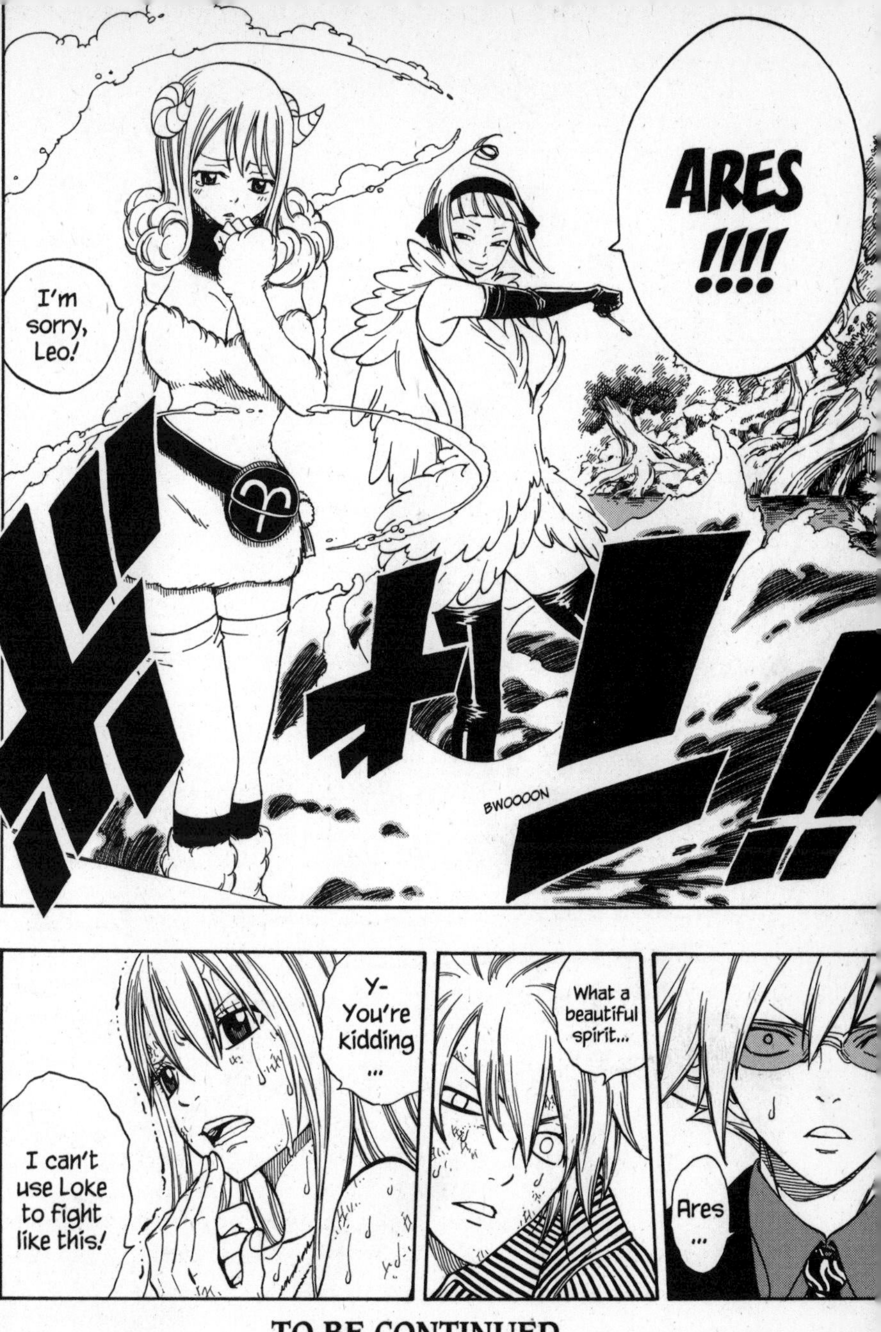
ARES !!!!
I'm sorry, Leo!
BWOOOON
Ares ...
What a beautiful spirit...
Y- You're kidding ...
I can't use Loke to fight like this!

TO BE CONTINUED

Afterword

"You look like a criminal in your picture for Volume 16!!" is how everyone around me criticized the picture. So this time, you get my regular face... or so I thought, but I can't seem to get a good picture! For some reason, I seem to be in the habit of scowling whenever a picture is taken. Since what seems like forever, people have said that I've got an evil look in my eyes, and when a picture is being taken, it only seems to get worse. So how does a person come up with a natural-looking smile? It's hard!

On a different subject, here in Volume 17, I did it again. An earth-shaking twist!! Jellal's back...!! Yeah, sorry about that. I just wasn't thinking ahead. (laughs) ..... but when I say things like, "I just wasn't thinking ahead," I get letters from fans telling me that when I say such things, it makes them uneasy. I guess so... I guess any fan would feel uneasy when the author of a work they love is an airheaded idiot. I know I say, "I wasn't thinking ahead," or, "I don't know myself what's coming up in the future," but to be a stickler with words, what I really mean is, **"I haven't quite decided which future to choose."** That would be closer to the reality of the situation. With every new plot twist, it presents a number of different possibilities for the story to run. For example, with Jellal back in the picture, I have come up with three different ways that the big picture can play out. I also have come up with quite a few different ways the story will flow until it gets to those three conclusions. This is how I usually work, imagining a wide variety of possibilities. So please don't worry. I'm busy every day worrying over the best way to create a fun, engaging manga that will meet everybody's expectations. Well... There are still times when my mind is a complete blank, but you know how it is.

Continued from the left-hand page.

: We've explained a mystery! Ding, ding!

: And we have her signature, "ignoring Lucy's question!"

Mira : Time for the next question.

Most of the names of guilds so far have used the names of mythical beasts, but what's the meaning of Oración Seis?

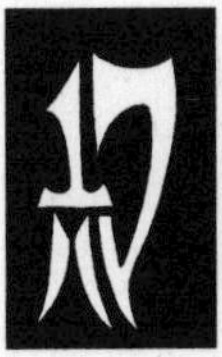

Lucy : If you want a literal translation:
Oración = Prayer
Seis = Six
That's what the words mean.

Mira : So the meaning of the name is, "Six Prayers"?

Lucy : There's no mythical beast name in that guild though, huh?

Mira : Oh? ..... Sure there is!

Like Cobra, for example.

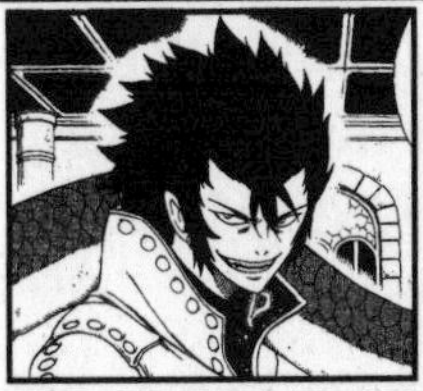

: That isn't the name of a guild! And it isn't a mythical beast either!!!

: We've explained a mystery! Ding, ding!

Lucy : A-And...the final question.

Please tell me who Lucy is in love with.

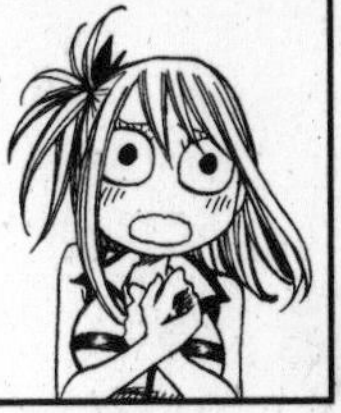

Mira : I'd like to know myself.

Lucy : There's nobody with that distinction.

: We've explained a mystery! Ding, ding!

: What? There's that little interest?! But, wait! What's that "Ding, ding" thing you do every time?!

Mira : Ah? Whatever are you talking about?

: I can't understand why you'd play dumb about that...

Mira : Eh heh heh! Well for example, even if it's something of a dubious answer, if I say that at the end, it sounds like the mystery's been explained, right?

Lucy : Just some psychological trick?

: We've [illegible]ained a myste[illegible]rinnng!

: Suddenly it changes!!!

We are looking for questions about Fairy Tail! Send yours to:

Kodansha Comics
451 Park Ave. South, 7th Floor
New York, NY 10016

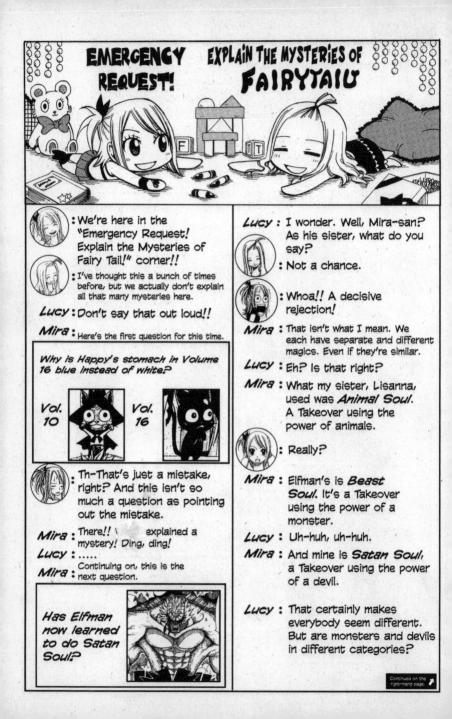

EMERGENCY REQUEST!
EXPLAIN THE MYSTERIES OF FAIRYTAIL

: We're here in the "Emergency Request! Explain the Mysteries of Fairy Tail!" corner!!

: I've thought this a bunch of times before, but we actually don't explain all that many mysteries here.

Lucy : Don't say that out loud!!

Mira : Here's the first question for this time.

Why is Happy's stomach in Volume 16 blue instead of white?

Vol. 10

Vol. 16

: Th-That's just a mistake, right? And this isn't so much a question as pointing out the mistake.

Mira : There!! \ explained a mystery! Ding, ding!

Lucy : ......

Mira : Continuing on, this is the next question.

Has Elfman now learned to do Satan Soul?

Lucy : I wonder. Well, Mira-san? As his sister, what do you say?

: Not a chance.

: Whoa!! A decisive rejection!

Mira : That isn't what I mean. We each have separate and different magics. Even if they're similar.

Lucy : Eh? Is that right?

Mira : What my sister, Lisanna, used was *Animal Soul*. A Takeover using the power of animals.

: Really?

Mira : Elfman's is *Beast Soul*. It's a Takeover using the power of a monster.

Lucy : Uh-huh, uh-huh.

Mira : And mine is *Satan Soul*, a Takeover using the power of a devil.

Lucy : That certainly makes everybody seem different. But are monsters and devils in different categories?

Continued on the right-hand page.

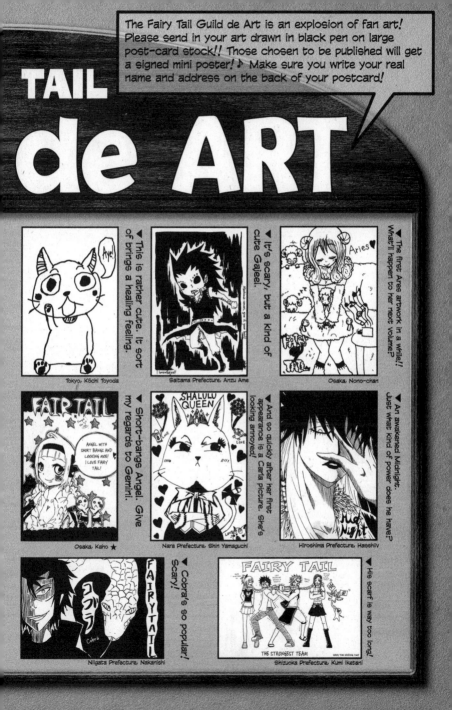

TAIL de ART

The Fairy Tail Guild de Art is an explosion of fan art! Please send in your art drawn in black pen on large post-card stock!! Those chosen to be published will get a signed mini poster!♪ Make sure you write your real name and address on the back of your postcard!

Aries♥

Osaka, Nono-chan

▼The first Ares artwork in a while!! What'll happen to her next volume?

Saitama Prefecture, Anzu Ame

▼It's scary, but a kind of cute Gajeel.

Aye!

Tokyo, Kôchi Toyoda

▼This is rather cute. It sort of brings a healing feeling.

Mid Night

Hiroshima Prefecture, Hasshiiv

▼An awakened Midnight. Just what kind of power does he have?

SHALULU QUEEN
LOVE
LOVE
LOVE

Nara Prefecture, Shin Yamaguchi

▼And so quickly after her first appearance is a Carla picture. She's looking annoyed!

FAIR TAIL
ANGEL WITH SHORT BANGS AND LOOKING MOE! I LOVE FAIRY TAIL!

Osaka, Kaho ★

▼Short-bangs Angel. Give my regards to Gemini.

FAIRY TAIL
THE STRONGEST TEAM

Shizuoka Prefecture, Kumi Iketani

▼His scarf is way too long!

FAIRYTAIL
コブラ
Cobra

Niigata Prefecture, Nakanishi

▼Cobra's so popular! Scary!

Send to Hiro Mashima, Kodansha Comics
451 Park Ave. South, 7th Floor New York, NY 10016

FAIRY GUILD

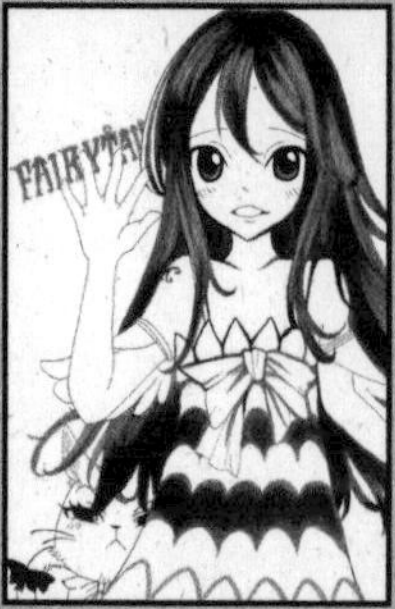

▼ I've gotten lots of Wendy illustrations!!

Tokyo, Lio

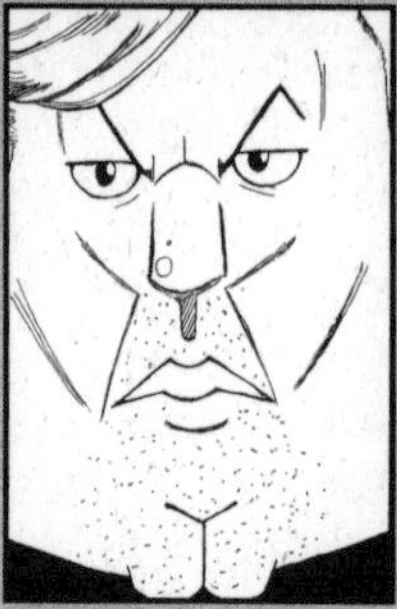

▼ His face is so big, it's busting out of the card!

Tokyo, Reiō

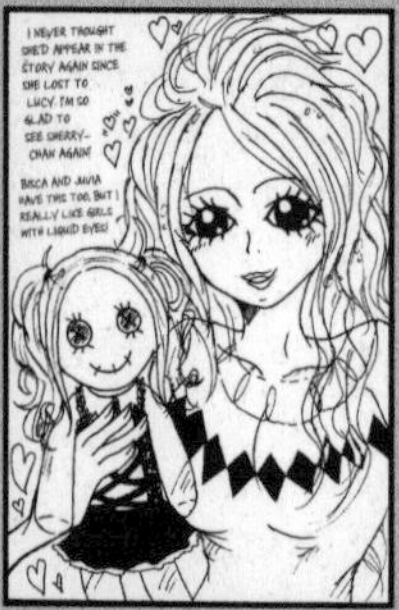
I NEVER THOUGHT SHE'D APPEAR IN THE STORY AGAIN SINCE SHE LOST TO LUCY. I'M SO GLAD TO SEE SHERRY-CHAN AGAIN!
BISCA AND JUVIA HAVE THIS TOO, BUT I REALLY LIKE GIRLS WITH LIQUID EYES!

▼ Sherry with a makeover. I wonder if she'll show up a lot?

Shizuoka Prefecture, Haruka Hirayama

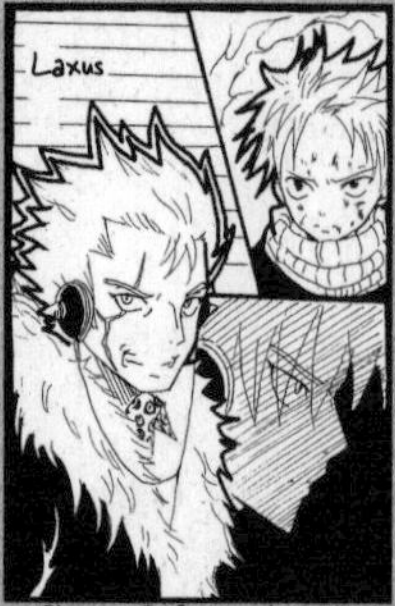
Laxus

▼ Laxus and Natsu. I wonder if they're going to fight again.

Okayama Prefecture, Ayaka Ikeda

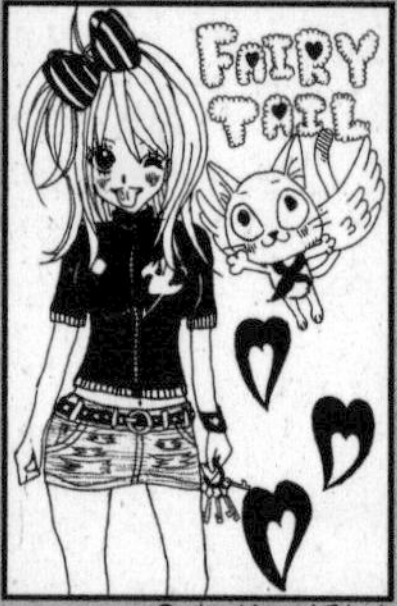
FAIRY TAIL

▼ This one's so cute, I have to put it in here!

Osaka, Manami Takeda

REJECTION CORNER

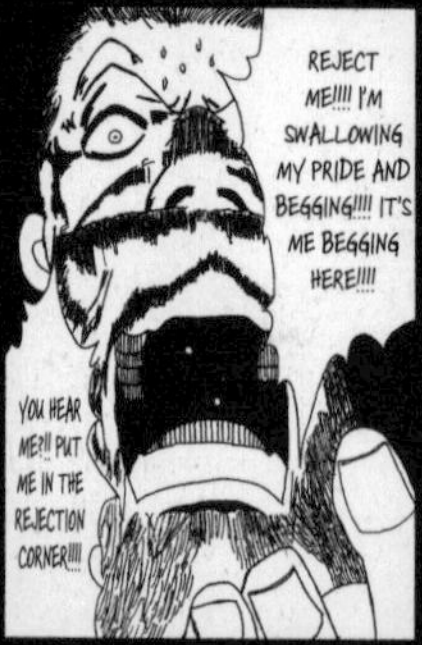
REJECT ME!!!! I'M SWALLOWING MY PRIDE AND BEGGING!!!! IT'S ME BEGGING HERE!!!!
YOU HEAR ME?!! PUT ME IN THE REJECTION CORNER!!!!

Nara Prefecture, Yama-san

▲ Yeah, I didn't mean to, but I laughed. D-Dammit... Ha ha ha...

Any letters and post cards you send means that your personal information such as your name, address, postal code, and other information you include will be handed over, as is, to the author. When you send mail, please keep that in mind.

Translation Notes:

Page 6, All's fair in money and war

Hoteye has an obsession with money, and as such, he tend to confuse classic proverbs by adding the word money in place of the original word. In Japanese, he took the proverb, *Koi ni jouge no hetate-nashi* ("Love doesn't recognize any higher or lower ranks") and changed the word for love, *koi*, to money, *okane*, to make his new proverb. This translation took an English proverb that also involved love (and the general idea) and substituted in "money."

Page 24, Priestess receiving the words of the Gods

In Japanese they were referring to the *miko* of ancient Japan who, unlike their modern counterparts, were the main priestesses of the Shinto religion. The first *miko* recorded is the Empress Himiko of the third-century Japanese country of Yamatai described in a small section of the Chinese epic, Romance of the Three Kingdoms.

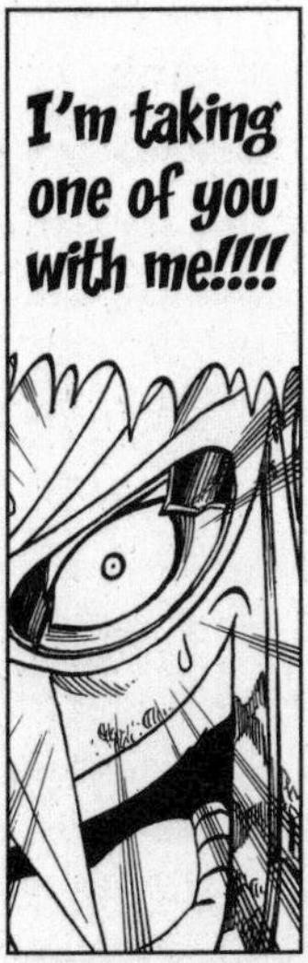
I'm taking one of you with me!!!!

Page 119, I'm taking you with me!

What he said in Japanese was a phrase (*ichinin-issatsu* or "One Man, One Kill") that is one of the slogans for the radical, ultra-nationalist right-wing extreme of Japanese politics. The movement espouses some violent ideals such as dying in order to kill someone else *(ichinin-issatsu)*, and killing one for the good of many, *(issatsu-tashô)*. On a lighter note, Japanese baseball has taken this same term of *ichinin-issatsu* to describe a relief pitcher who is called in to face one and only one batter before the next relief pitcher is brought in.

Page 183, There it comes

In Japanese, Lucy used the now-famous Japanese phrase *Kitaaaaa!* to describe the scene with Scorpio. The phrase which literally means "He/She/It is here!" was popularized by the novel-cum-entertainment phenomenon Densha Otoko (Trainman). Although the Trainman fad has come and gone, the phrase still survives. I can't say I'm exactly sure just what Lucy is referring to. It could be the hand gestures which resemble the hand gestures of some good-looking Japanese male pop idols and celebrities. Or it could be the "boyfriend" himself.

Preview of Fairy Tail, volume 18

We're pleased to present you an unlettered preview from Fairy Tail, volume 18. Please check our website (www.kodanshacomics.com) to see when this volume will be available.

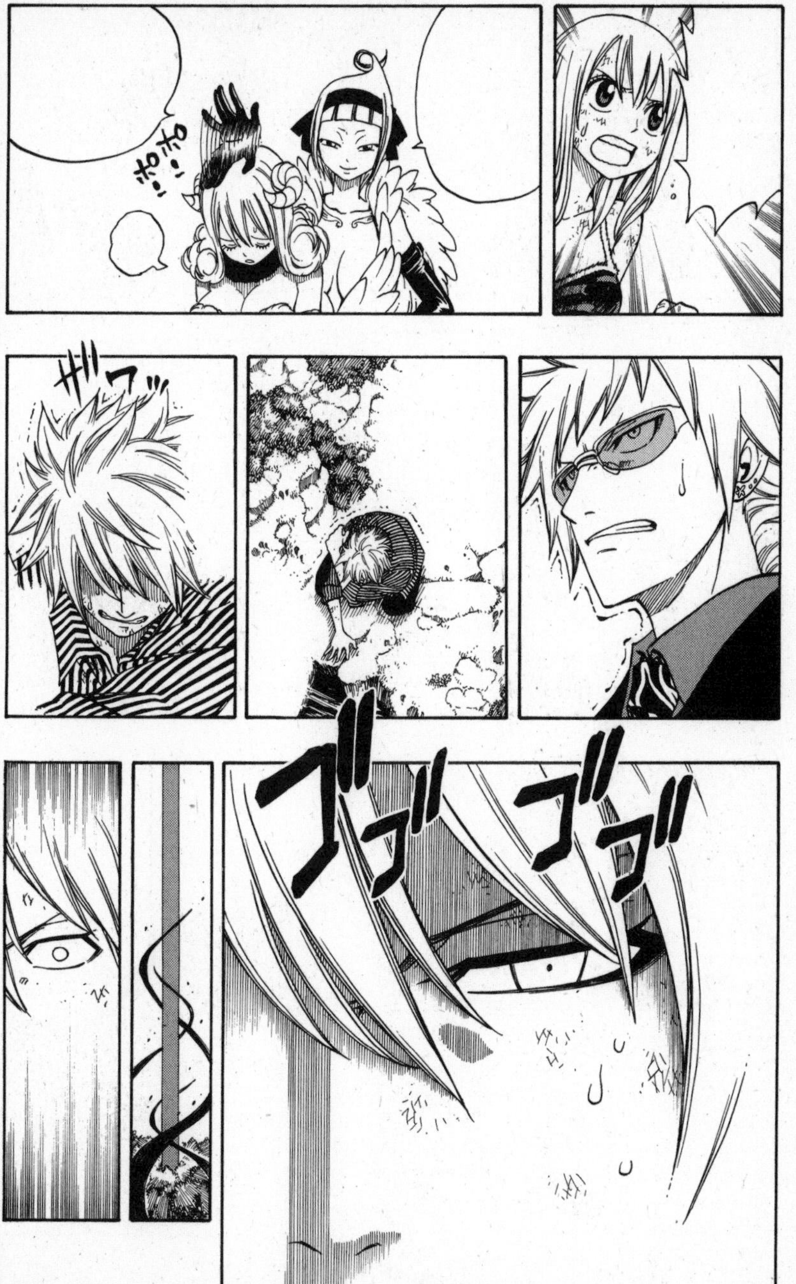
ポ！ポ！
ザワッ
ゴゴ ゴゴ

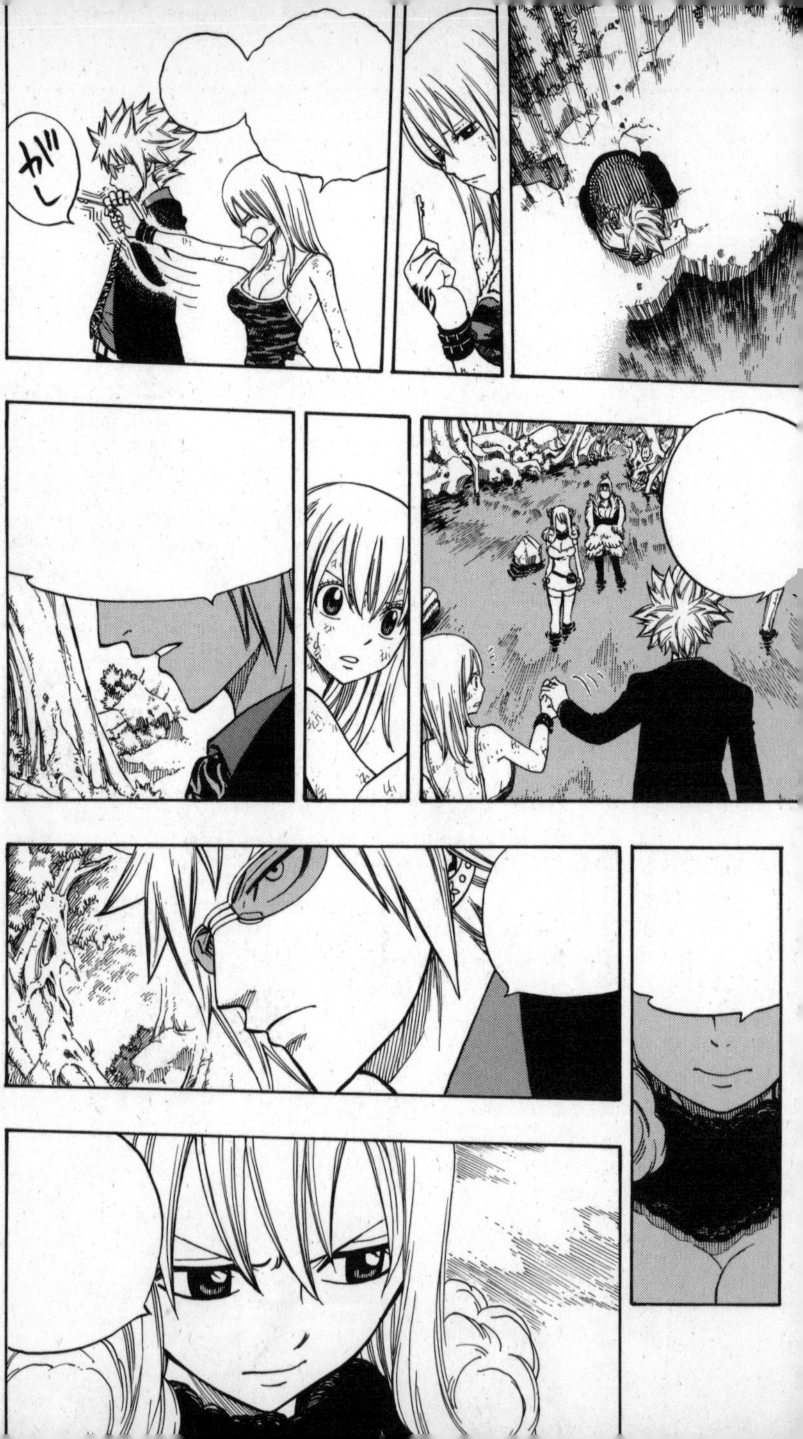
がし

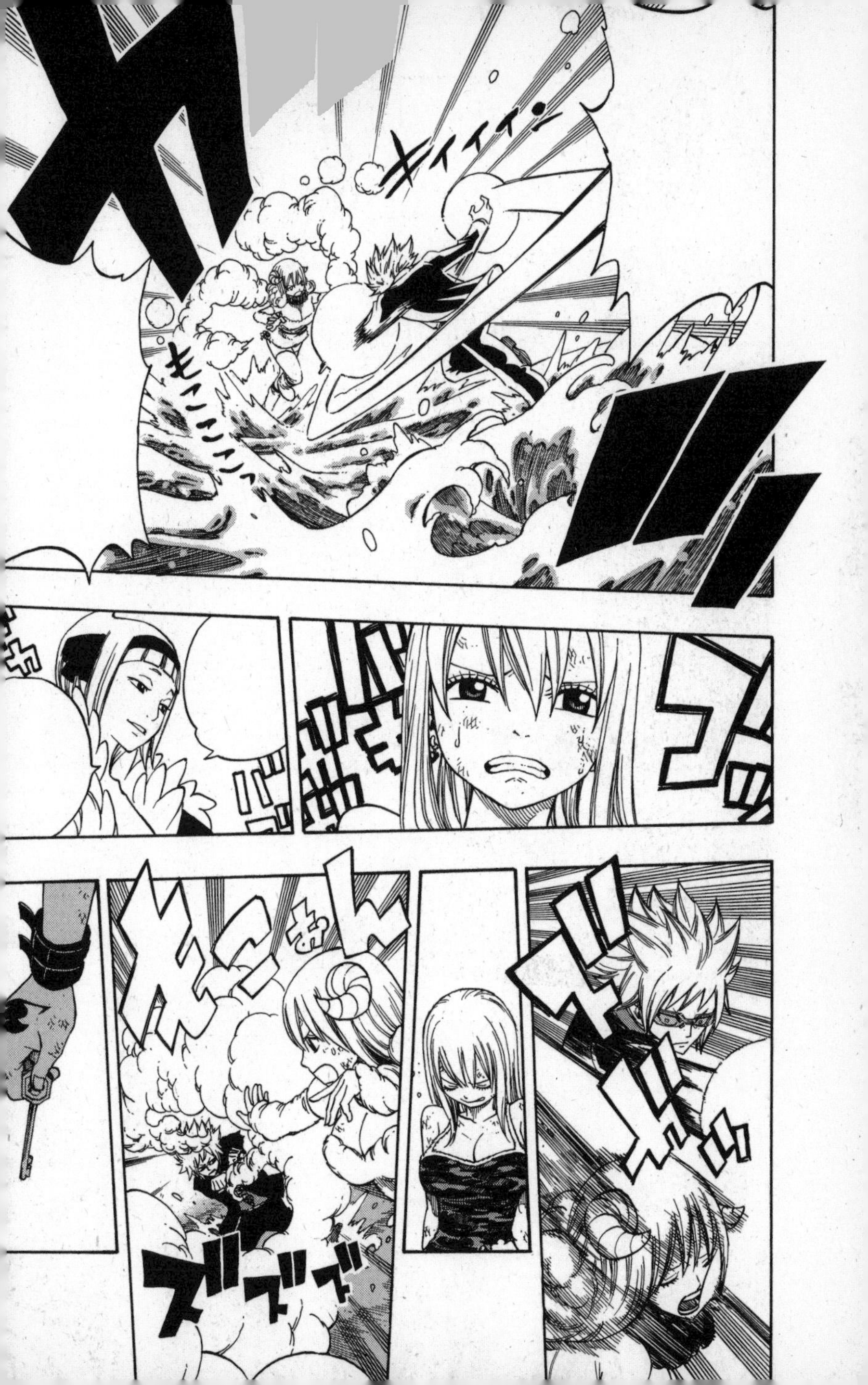
キイイイン

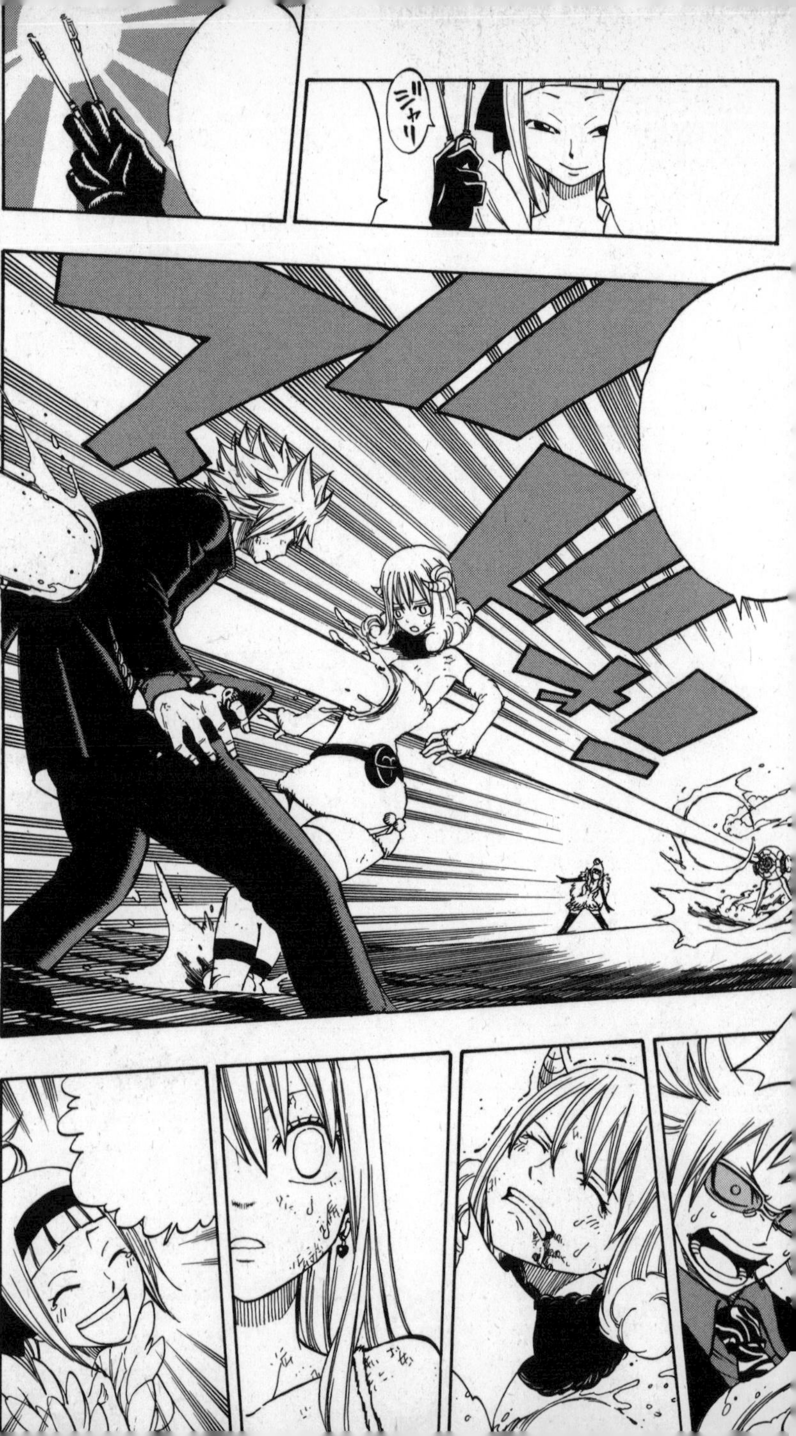
ジャリ

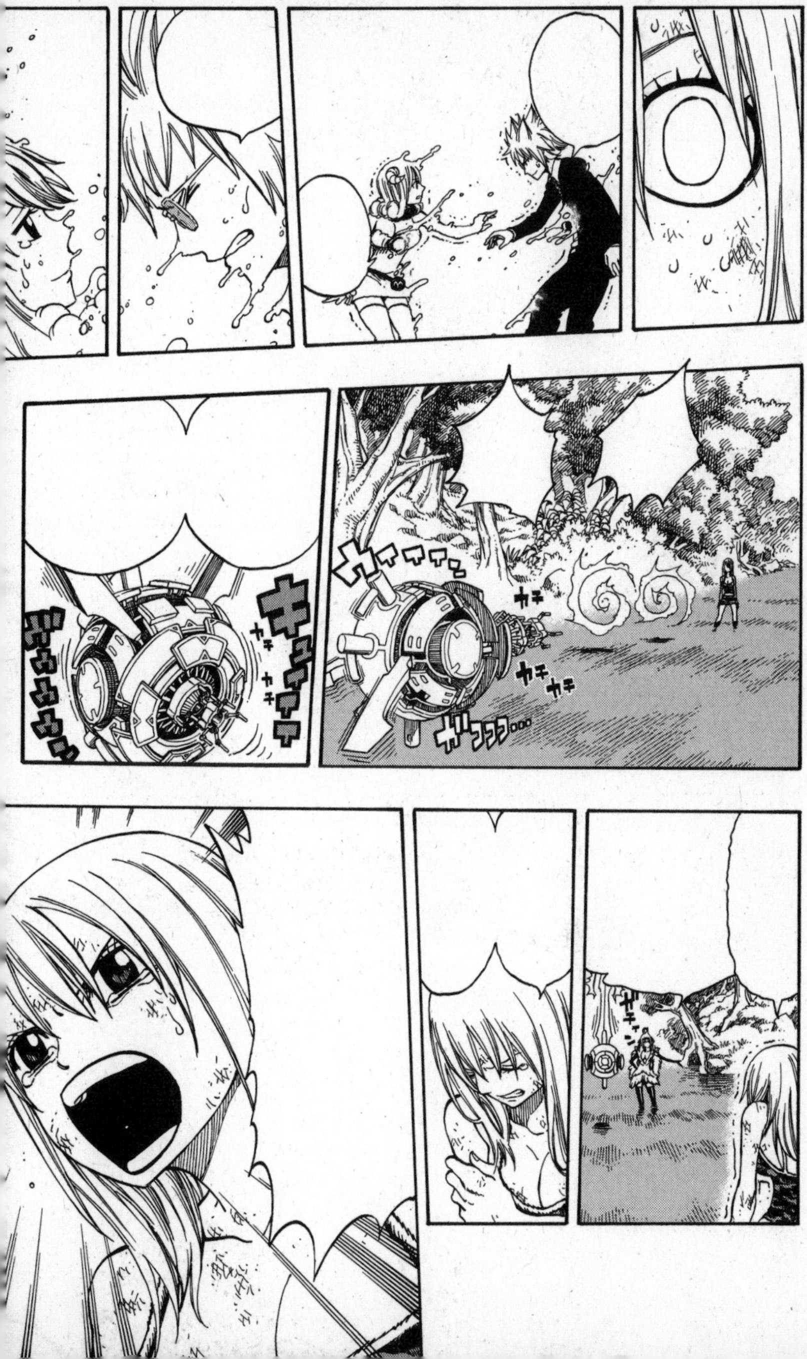
ウィィィン
カチ
カチ カチ
キュイイイ
カチ
カチ

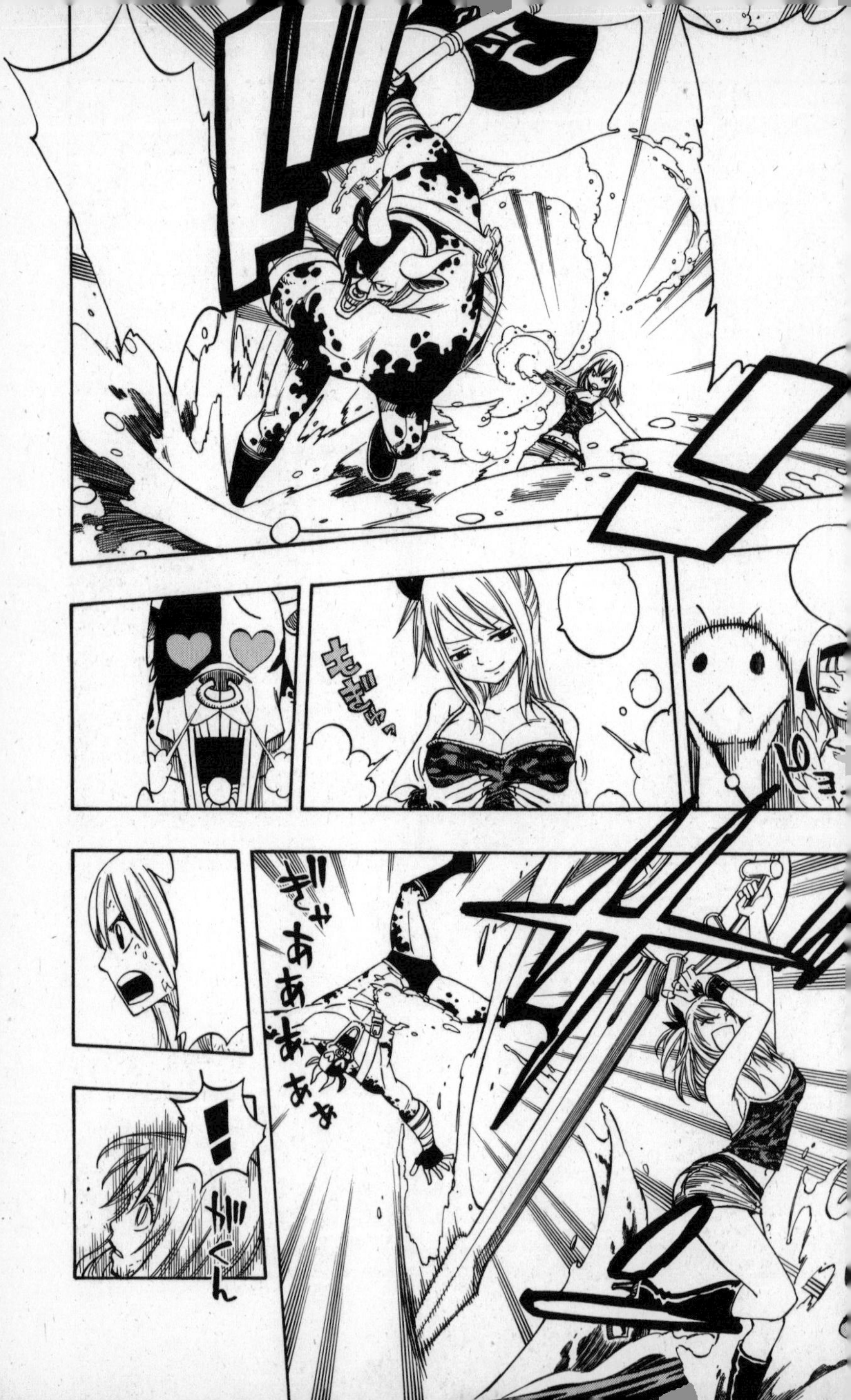
もぎゃっ
ぎゃあああああ
!
がくん

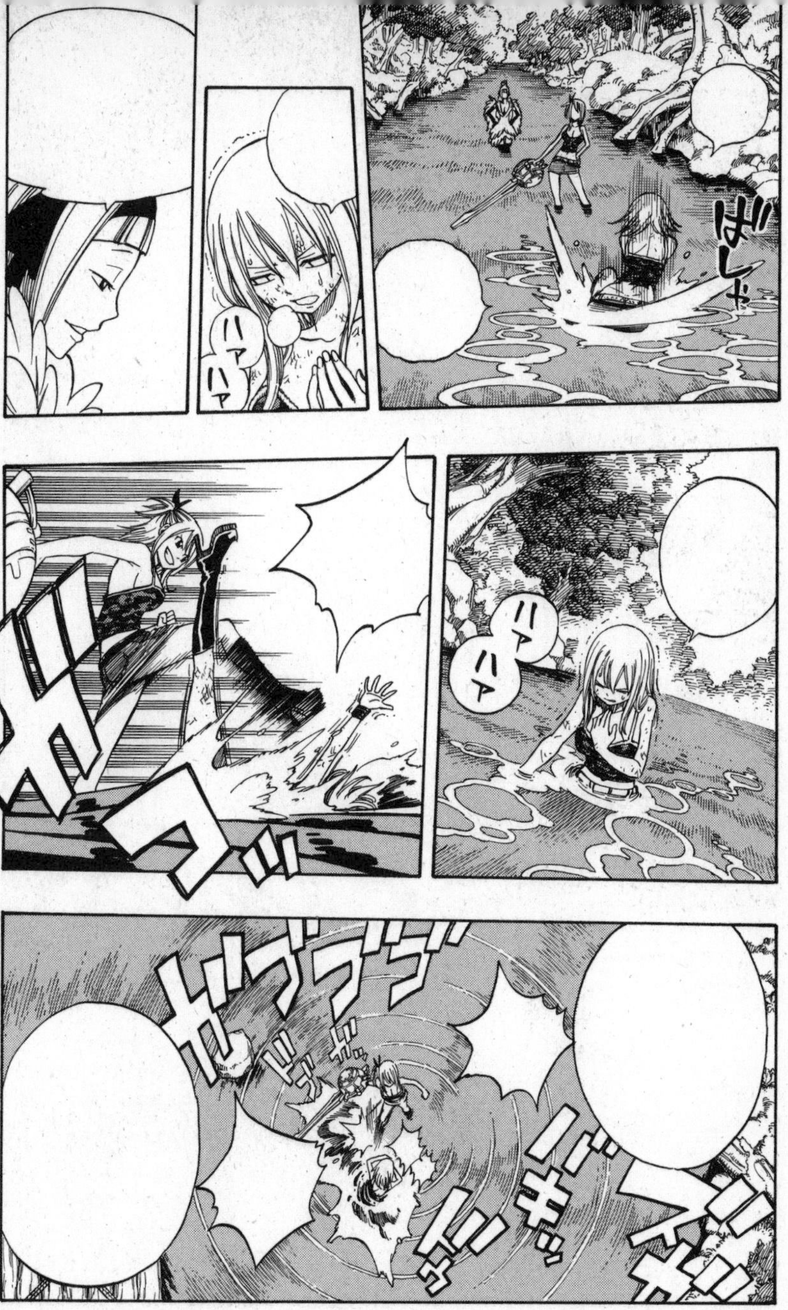
ばしゃ
ハァ ハァ
ハァ ハァ

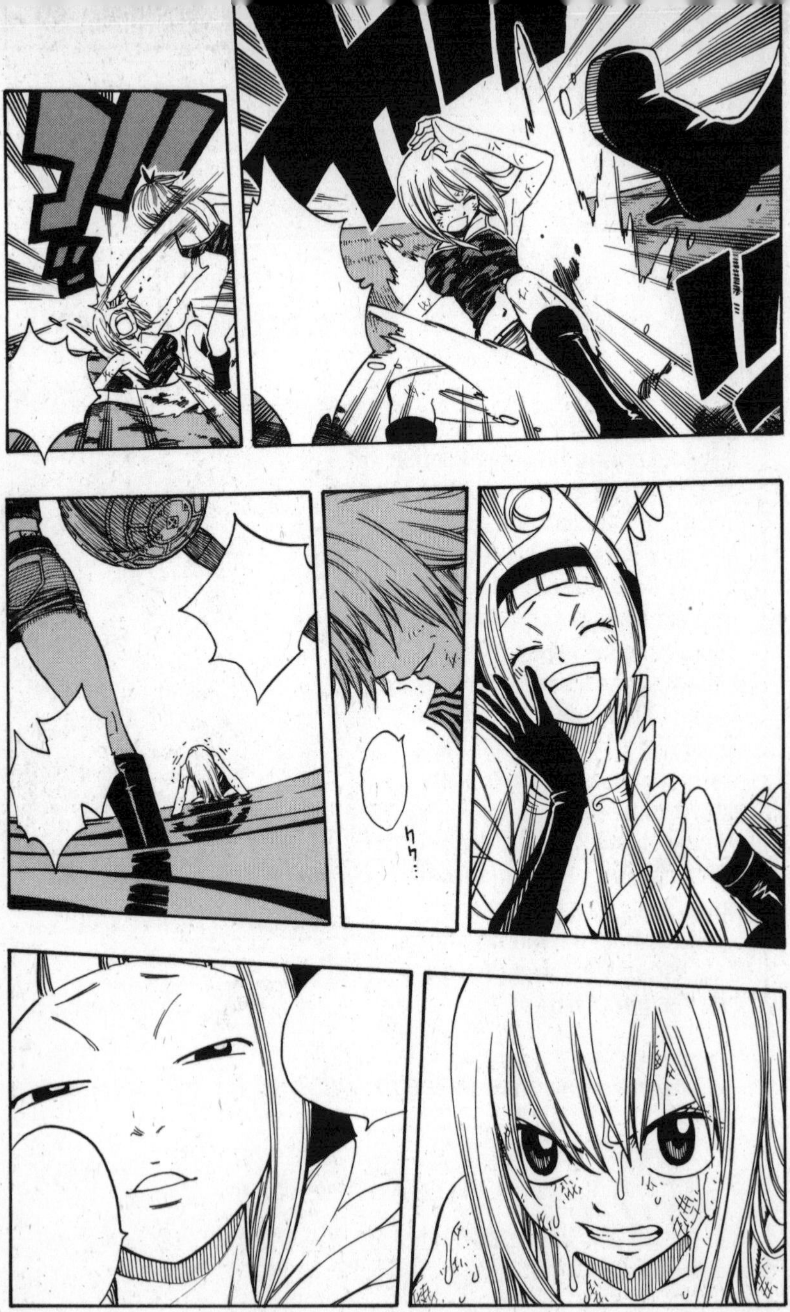
クク…

NEGIMA!™
MAGISTER NEGI MAGI

BY KEN AKAMATSU

Negi Springfield is a ten-year-old wizard teaching English at an all-girls Japanese school. He dreams of becoming a master wizard like his legendary father, the Thousand Master. At first his biggest concern was concealing his magic powers, because if he's ever caught using them publicly, he thinks he'll be turned into an ermine! But in a world that gets stranger every day, it turns out that the strangest people of all are Negi's students! From a librarian with a magic book to a centuries-old vampire, from a robot to a ninja, Negi will risk his own life to protect the girls in his care!

NEGIMA!
MAGISTER NEGI MAGI

by
KEN AKAMATSU
CREATOR OF *LOVE HINA!*

FOR MATURE AUDIENCES AGES 16+

Ages: 16 +

Special extras in each volume! Read them all!

BY OH!GREAT

Itsuki Minami needs no introduction—everybody's heard of the "Babyface" of the Eastside. He's the strongest kid at Higashi Junior High School, easy on the eyes but dangerously tough when he needs to be. Plus, Itsuki lives with the mysterious and sexy Noyamano sisters. Life's never dull, but it becomes downright dangerous when Itsuki leads his school to victory over vindictive Westside punks with gangster connections. Now he stands to lose his school, his friends, and everything he cares about. But in his darkest hour, the Noyamano girls give him an amazing gift, one that just might help him save his school: a pair of Air Trecks. These high-tech skates are more than just supercool. They'll enable Itsuki to execute the wildest, most aggressive moves ever seen—and introduce him to a thrilling and terrifying new world.

Ages: 16 +

Special extras in each volume! Read them all!

Fairy Tail volume 17 s a work of fiction. Names, characters, places, and incidents are the products of the author's imagination or are used fictitiously. Any resemblance to actual events, locales, or persons, living or dead, is entirely coincidental.

A Kodansha Comics Trade Paperback Original

Published in the United States by Kodansha Comics, an imprint of Kodansha USA Publishing, LLC., New York.

Publication rights for this English edition arranged through Kodansha Ltd., Tokyo.

First published in Japan in 2009 by Kodansha Ltd., Tokyo.

ISBN 978-1-612-62054-1

Printed in the United States of America.

www.kodanshacomics.com

9 8 7 6 5 4 3 2 1

Translator/Adapter: William Flanagan
Lettering: AndWorld Design

TOMARE!

[STOP!]

You're going the wrong way!

Manga is a completely different type of reading experience.

To start at the *beginning*, go to the *end!*

at's right! Authentic manga is read the traditional Japanese way—
m right to left, exactly the *opposite* of how American books are
d. It's easy to follow: Just go to the other end of the book and read
:h page—and each panel—from right side to left side, starting at
top right. Now you're experiencing manga as it was meant to be!